A STUDENT'S GUIDE TO
FIRST-YEAR WRITING

32nd Edition

2011–2012

HAYDEN
HM
McNEIL

Printed in the United States of America

10 9 8 7 6 5 4 3 2 1

ISBN 978-0-7380-4460-6

Hayden-McNeil Publishing
14903 Pilot Drive
Plymouth, MI 48170
www.hmpublishing.com

HallA 4460-6 F11

Printed on 100%
Recycled Paper

Acknowledgements

The completion of the *Student's Guide* requires the coordination and dedication of many different people. Although we are the editors of the *Guide*, we don't make the revisions alone. First and foremost, we'd like to thank both of last year's acting Writing Program Directors, Dr. Anne-Marie Hall and Dr. Amy Kimme Hea, for their tireless advice on our chapter revisions, their administrative guidance and support, and their constant protection of this text's publication and the continued distribution of the funds it generates to support the UA Writing Program. This year's *Student's Guide* is a particularly special edition, as it is the first *Student's Guide* to include full-color printing and 100% recycled paper. Dr. Hall and Dr. Kimme Hea were instrumental in helping us develop the groundwork and the design for a full-color, more environmentally-conscious textbook.

We also owe many thanks to our publisher, Hayden-McNeil, and especially to our outstanding editor Lisa Wess and our layout designer Christine Victor—thanks for your support and enthusiasm. It has truly been a pleasure working with both of you on this version of the *Guide*. Hayden-McNeil also generously supports the annual essay contest by providing cash prizes, journals, and pens to the winners, a cash prize for the Hayden-McNeil Difference and Inequality Student Essay Award, and a cash prize for the Cover Art Contest.

The UA Writing program is one of the best in the nation, which allows us to work with excellent faculty, staff, and graduate students in the process of revising the *Guide*. We are grateful to the course directors, Patrick Baliani, Amy Kimme Hea, Carol Nowotny-Young, D.R. Ransdell, and Erec Toso, for their invaluable input on the *Guide*. In addition, we'd like to thank Chris Minnix, Penny Gates, Monica Vega, Sara Vickery, and Lourdes Canto for their continued support throughout the publication process.

As a 32nd edition, this book is the result of over three decades of contributions, help, and advice from innumerable people whose influence can still be seen in these pages. Without all of you, this book would not be where it is now—a reflection of a collaborative Writing Program comprised of dedicated and caring instructors. We would like to extend our thanks to our predecessors and colleagues throughout the years.

A Student's Guide to First-Year Writing editors,
Jennifer Haley-Brown
Jerry W. Lee
Caitlin Rodriguez

Table of Contents

Craft Boxes

PART I Introduction to First-Year Writing

PART II Strategies and Concepts

PART III Assignments

PART I
INTRODUCTION TO FIRST-YEAR WRITING

Introduction to First-Year Writing

1.1 Writing at the University of Arizona: An Overview

Welcome to the University of Arizona! During your stay here, you'll do a lot of writing, and you'll begin the journey toward becoming a stronger, more confident writer in your first-year writing classes.

What does it mean to be a "writer," anyway? Being a "writer" means different things to different people. The kind of writing you do depends on several factors. One of these factors is your **purpose**. In other words, why are you writing and what do you hope to accomplish with your writing? Another factor is your **audience**. You might ask yourself, "Who is going to read my writing?" You will make choices that correspond to the answers of these questions. That's why a reporter who works at the *Arizona Daily Star*, for example, writes an article for the newspaper using a journalistic style. If that reporter were asked to write a formal report for her boss, she would use a different writing style, and still a

> The red terms you'll find throughout this book are glossary terms. See the Glossary near the end of the book for a definition.

different one if she were writing a letter to her grandmother or an e-mail to a friend. Even if the reporter sought to put the same story into an article, a report, a letter, and an e-mail, these texts would look quite different depending on her purpose for relaying the information and the particular audience that she had in mind when writing.

What type(s) of writing do you do? Why do you write certain things (e-mails, diaries, essays, and so on)? It might be helpful for understanding audience and purpose to think of the kinds of writing you'll do here at the university, as well as in your community and in your career (reports, blogs, e-mails, memos, letters to the editor, and so on). Your first-year writing courses are designed to guide you to *evaluate* writing situations and respond accordingly. As a result, you'll be better prepared for the challenges in both your university and professional careers, as well as in your pursuit of social and political interests. In addition to providing the tools to succeed in academic writing, the University of Arizona's first-year writing curriculum stresses **critical analysis**, a skill that allows you to adapt your writing **style** and **tone** to whatever type of writing you need or want to pursue outside of the classroom.

In order to help you achieve your own writing goals and to ensure that your first-year composition courses prepare you well for university expectations, the Writing Program has developed the following outcomes for first-year writing classes.

By the end of the first-year composition sequence, you will be able to demonstrate the ability to:

- Assess the strategies writers use to achieve their purposes.

- Write persuasive documents that provide appropriate and effective evidence for various audiences, situations, and purposes.

- Develop critical analyses of personal, public, and scholarly issues based on research, observations, and reflections from your own experiences.

- Revise your drafts in response to feedback from readers and offer useful feedback to other writers on how to revise their writing.

- Produce research and writing using appropriate academic conventions.

- Reflect critically on your own writing processes.

Our program brings together students and teachers from a variety of cultures, languages, and academic disciplines. Writing courses are designed to challenge you to explore such diversity. Instructors in the program come from various programs in English, including creative writing, literature, applied linguistics, and rhetoric and composition. In addition, your peers represent the many possible majors across the curriculum. Both teachers and students come from across the country and from around the world. All of these sources of difference lead to an exciting variety of materials, class activities, discussions, and assignments. Instructors may encourage you to explore issues or topics that are challenging or even troublesome in order to push you to examine your ideas in writing. You might find that some texts or class discussions make you uncomfortable. Sometimes you might struggle with the material because it conflicts with your personal belief system, but working with controversial issues can help you define and articulate your own position in relation to the complex **context** surrounding those issues.

First-year writing classes, also known as composition classes, are usually much smaller than your other general education classes, which means that you will have the opportunity to get to know your instructor and classmates on a more personal level. Many instructors make use of full-class and small-group discussion. In this setting, your responsibilities as an individual student will be more clearly defined. We find student Ray Hum's advice especially pertinent here:

> The true value of an English composition class is largely dependent on the student. If the student approaches the class with high motivation, then the class will certainly be enjoyable and valuable to him or her. If, on the other hand, the student approaches the class with a disinterested attitude, then the class will inevitably be a waste of time to him or her.

While the small size of your first-year writing class may mean that your instructor has high expectations for your participation and work, there are many benefits to the smaller group, including the opportunity to receive feedback and assistance from your instructor and your peers. Chris Clark provides the following advice to fellow students:

> The most important thing all freshmen should know in order to succeed is that you have to go to class. English is probably the most common course at UA, and success later starts in the beginning. You will find that the majority of students taking English 101 and 102 are freshmen just like yourself, and going through the same things you are. It's a good chance for you to make friends while starting college out on the right foot. English 101 and 102 teachers are also well aware that you are going through a big adjustment and are sensitive to that. Not only have I found that the English teachers go out of their way to help accommodate new students, but they also act as advisors if you need help.

In addition to helping your transition to college go smoothly, these classes teach you a variety of techniques in writing and composition that will help you immensely in other classes up until the time you graduate. These techniques will aid you in your NATS classes, your TRAD classes, and even upper-division classes. By attending class, doing the work, and applying it elsewhere, you are setting yourself up for a successful career at the UA. Good luck!

1.2 A Guide to the *Guide*

The *Student's Guide* offers useful information specific to the University of Arizona's first-year writing program.

Part I of the *Guide* gives an overview of first-year writing. This first chapter is a general introduction and examines some assumptions that underlie college writing. It also discusses grades and gives an overview of each course in the first-year writing sequence, including its goals and major assignments.

Part II introduces you to several strategies and concepts in writing. It guides you through various components of the writing process you'll need to know to write a successful essay. Here you will learn what to do even before you begin writing, how to engage in the process of research at the university, how to get started writing, and how to use feedback to improve your writing.

Part III explains how to apply the strategies discussed in Part II to the specific assignments you will encounter in first-year writing. Each chapter has subsections that outline different ways to think about an assignment or paper, as well as different strategies that you may choose to employ.

Part IV provides a collection of sample essays written by students and instructors in the Writing Program over the last few years. We hope these student sample essays will serve as a springboard for discussion in your classroom. They are meant to give you an idea about what an academic essay might look like and also to give you the opportunity to critique strengths and weaknesses of the content, organization, evidence, language, or style of different essays. We believe our selections will show you different kinds of writing, help you brainstorm about your own projects, and make your experience in first-year writing more manageable and rewarding.

Appendix A describes the many tutoring resources available at the University of Arizona to help you with your writing. It tells you what to expect from their services. Some are open to all students and are free of charge, whereas others are restricted or charge a fee.

Appendix B lists various campus resources and their contact information.

Appendix C lists the computing centers and resources on campus.

Appendix D provides information specifically for students whose first language is not English. It includes tips from instructors and other ESL students, as well as a list of resources that may be of help.

Appendix E describes the *Student's Guide* Essay Contest, the Jan Lipartito Historical Remembrance Essay Contest, the Hayden-McNeil Difference and Equality Essay Contest, and the annual *Guide* Cover Design Contest. It also lists the winners and judges for 2011.

In short, this book will introduce you to the world of college writing. We hope that, like us, you'll find that you enjoy writing and believe that writing well is a vital way to learn and communicate effectively.

1.3 High School vs. College Writing

By Faith Kurtyka

> "I like the writing in college better than high school because it's not just you read a book, you write about it, you read a book, you write about it. It's actually like you can think and apply it more. It's more relevant. Creative. More interesting. "
>
> —A First-Year Student at UA

Although the course you're in is called "English," it will likely be very different from the English courses you took in high school. This section encourages you to think about ways your high school English classes might be similar to or different from your college English classes. The section also presents recommendations from interviews with several groups of first-year students. The students were asked about their high school and college experiences, and what advice they would offer to incoming first-year students.

Using the following chart, consider some of the similarities and differences you've noticed between the expectations of college-level writing and high school-level writing. Discuss topics listed in the left column of the chart with your teacher and classmates, noting what you learned about each topic in your high school English classes and filling in the "High School" column as you do. In the third column, you'll find some ways of making the adjustments between high school and college English courses.

	High School	The University of Arizona	UA Resources and Advice for Adjusting
Revision		You will turn in at least two submissions of every paper. You will receive feedback on your writing from your instructor and your peers, which you will be expected to incorporate into your final submission.	See your instructor in office hours to make sure you understand his or her feedback, or go visit a writing tutor at the Think Tank or at the Writing Skills Improvement Program (see Appendix A).
Grammar and Mechanics		In college, it is assumed that you know the basic rules of standard written English.	Check out a style manual like *Rules for Writers* for specific rules. Proofread your own work carefully, or ask a friend to proofread for you. Also try reading your paper out loud to catch awkward sentences.
Grading		80% or more of your grade will be based on the papers you write. Less than 20% of your grade is determined by quizzes and smaller writing assignments. You will typically receive few, if any, extra credit opportunities.	Examine the sample rubrics in Chapter 1 (see pg. 11), and ask your instructor about his or her grading style. Read the assignment sheet carefully to make sure you're meeting the assignment requirements.
Content		You may read short stories and articles, or analyze photographs, movies, or TV shows.	Read carefully. You can use many of the close reading skills you learned in high school in college.
Time for Writing		Your writing needs to get done outside of class. You are responsible for making time for writing.	Start your work *early*. If your teacher assigns outlines or drafts, take them seriously and you'll have less work to do later on.
Effort Required		You will need to start early and work through a writing process to get good grades.	See Chapter 4 on writing as a process.

Peer Review		Your classmates will be depending on you to give them feedback on their papers to help their grades.	Remember that if you can evaluate someone else's work, it helps you evaluate your own. Make your peer reviews thorough and honest.
Getting Help		You will need to decide for yourself if you need help, and if you do, you will need to make time to go to office hours to work with your instructor.	You can find your instructor's e-mail, phone number, office location, and office hours on the syllabus. Ask for help early on—not at the last minute.
Technology		You are responsible for getting access to technology and you are responsible for technological problems —this includes lost work, printing, and figuring out a new computer or computer program.	Use the computer labs available on campus (see Appendix C). Get your paper printed well in advance of the class period when it's due.

The students interviewed had the following suggestions for first-year students who wanted to do well in their writing classes:

- **On Time Management:** "Start writing early. Don't procrastinate. Even if it's a month away. You can wait a week, but make sure [you get started], even if it's like a simple step. Like you just write an outline really quick."

- **On "Rough Drafts":** "Writing good first drafts helps a lot. For like the first essay in our class, my rough draft was terrible. I didn't try on it at all. It was like 'Whatever, I just want to get this done.' And then when I had to write my final, I had to work so hard and it was so annoying. So for this second essay, I tried a lot harder on my outline, so writing the final wasn't as stressful."

- **On Effort:** "One paper can make or break your grade. So you want to do your best on every assignment, because you can't just make it up just like that."

- **On Preparing to Write:** "In high school, I would turn in papers and show up for tests, it's just the preparation in the meantime I never did. I would always just wing papers the night before and get high C's or B's on them. And so I settled on those grades, but here I can't settle on that. So I just do like an outline just to get thoughts going, and then a few days later like expand on it, three points for each major point. Just simple stuff—it really helps."

While in high school the bulk of your effort on a paper may have been the night before it was due, in college it helps to spread out your effort, beginning with the day the paper is assigned. Your teacher may assign "invention" activities that prompt you to "invent" ideas for your paper—an outline, for instance—and though it's tempting to not spend time on these because they're not the "real" paper, they can help a lot with getting your ideas on paper, relieving some tension about writing the paper, and making less work for yourself later on.

To clarify some of your expectations in this class, discuss the following with your classmates and your teacher.

- Describe some of the writing assignments you did in high school. What were the requirements? What was your writing process?

- What did you learn about writing in high school?

- What do you expect to learn about writing in college?

- How did your high school experience differ from the descriptions above?

- What kind of student were you in high school and what kind of student do you want to be in college?

- Ask your teacher to elaborate on how he or she feels the writing in your class will be different from the high school writing experiences you've described.

1.4 Grading and Rubrics in First-Year Composition

In order to understand how grading functions in your first-year composition classes, keep the previous section in mind. Grades are meant to help your writing improve over the process of a course, not to punish you for mistakes you make while writing. In deciding upon a grade, your instructor evaluates how well all the various elements of your essay work together to achieve that assignment's specific goals.

A rubric is a tool that your instructor may use to grade your essays. It often resembles a chart with rows for categories of writing criteria and columns that describe achievement levels. These columns usually progress from the highest level of achievement on the left to the lowest level on the right. On the following page, we have included part of a sample rubric that indicates the standards of the Writing Program. The four broadly defined areas of an essay according to the Writing Program are: **content**, **organization**, **expression**, and **mechanics**.

The areas of achievement are defined as follows:

- **Content:** This usually includes a strong thesis, developed arguments, and a clear understanding of the assignment.

- **Organization/Form:** Your instructor will be looking for a well-ordered essay with clearly organized paragraphs as well as clear transitions between different thoughts.

- **Expression/Style:** This category focuses on a formal and academic tone as well as fluent and precise diction with a minimum of awkward moments in the overall essay. It also takes into account a polished, professional-sounding writing persona.

- **Mechanics/Conventions:** While this category includes Standard Written English (SWE) grammatical conventions, it also focuses on proper MLA formatting and proper citation techniques.

When your instructors create the rubric for your assignments, they will fill in rows with their own descriptions of each area of achievement. For example, they will use your **assignment sheet** to determine the specific required form or the necessary content for that specific essay. When you first receive your assignment sheet, read carefully and try to find and highlight these requirements. When you receive your graded essay with the rubric attached, you will see these requirements emphasized in the rubric's categories. The filled-out section that is included here focuses on the **mechanics** row and shows the shifting level of achievement in each progressive column. Keep in mind that the rubric your instructor uses may differ from this sample rubric.

Sample Grading Rubric—Mechanics Category

	Superior	Strong	Competent	Weak	Unacceptable
Mechanics	No errors in standard grammar, spelling, or punctuation to distract readers. Flawless use of MLA formatting.	Very few errors in standard grammar, spelling, or punctuation to distract readers. One or two minor errors in formatting.	Occasional errors in standard grammar, spelling, or punctuation that may distract readers. Three or more errors in formatting.	Frequent errors in standard grammar, spelling, or punctuation that distract readers. Frequent minor errors or one to two major errors in formatting.	Serious problems with grammar, spelling, or punctuation. Not formatted according to MLA guidelines.

After your instructor has graded your essay, you will probably see something similar to the circle on the sample rubric. This shows where your essay scored in that category. Notice that the "Mechanics" category in this rubric has **similar language** in each box. It is clear in these descriptions that the column furthest to the right indicates the most difficulty in that category with improvements seen in each shift to the left. This is how the rubric functions in each row. Each time your score moves one column to the left, this shows that you've improved in that category. Remember that the middle column indicates **competence**. This column is used when a student shows adequate achievement in that category. Every move to the left of that column shows *significant* achievements above a competent performance.

Finally, your instructor may offer additional written comments alongside your rubric. You should read the final comments with an eye to how they'll help you with your future writing. Remember that writing is a **process**, just as your progress through first-year composition is a process. Your writing will improve progressively if you use these rubrics as a tool to assist your learning instead of concentrating on one or two errors that you believe lowered your grade. Look at the categories where you scored lowest overall and focus there for your next assignment. For more information on your class's grading criteria, speak to your instructor directly about the specific requirements for your essay.

Remember that this is just one possible approach to grading. Each instructor will devise and use specific sets of grading criteria for a given essay assignment based on those and other standards. They may also enlist the class to assist with determining grading criteria. However, while the rubric that you receive in class or the names for these categories may vary, the emphasis on these four areas of expertise exists throughout the Writing Program.

Building a Rubric from an Assignment Sheet

The assignment sheet and your in-class lessons work together to tell you exactly what your instructor is looking for when he or she is grading your essay for each assignment. When you read an assignment sheet, you should highlight or underline everything your instructor requires or suggests. Then remember that the middle column on a standard rubric indicates "competence." This means that you have **adequately** completed all of the requirements of the assignment but there may be some elements that could be improved.

Use one of your assignment sheets to practice filling in the blank rubric on the following page.

1. Write down elements from the assignment sheet or in-class lectures that describe what the essay's purpose, or **thesis**, should be in the "competent" column of the "thesis/content" row.

2. Do the same for elements concerning clear organization, style, and mechanics.

3. Now, ask yourself how to alter those descriptions so that they belong in the "strong" column. What makes the difference between a "competent" thesis and a "strong" thesis?

4. Fill in the "strong" column completely before beginning on the "superior" column. Remember that "superior" represents the highest possible level of achievement. How do you change your descriptions from "strong" to "superior" to reflect that?

5. Now, go backward. If "competent" represents the minimum requirements being met, then "weak" would represent that these requirements were *almost* met. "Unacceptable" is the lowest level of achievement and often indicates that very few if any requirements in that category were met.

Understanding the relationship between your assignment sheets and rubrics will help you to both identify what your instructor is looking for in an assignment and recognize how to achieve the highest grade possible.

	Superior	Strong	Competent	Weak	Unacceptable
Thesis/Content					
Organization					
Style					
Mechanics					

1.4

Additional Information Regarding Grades and Policies

Incomplete Grades

You may be awarded the grade of I (Incomplete) *only* at the end of a semester and *only if you have completed at least 70 percent of the coursework*. Your instructor will fill out the required form, which specifies the work to be completed and the due dates. You and your instructor must sign the form, stating agreement to the terms.

Grade Appeals

The Writing Program is committed to providing you with fair, clear, and useful responses to your writing, and we will process grade appeals in an efficient and objective fashion. A grade appeal is based on the quality of the writing and the grades awarded to that writing. If you disagree with a specific grade or with the grading policy outlined in the course syllabus, speak immediately with your instructor. You may also speak with your instructor's faculty supervisor or the Course Director, but they will not become involved in considering changes in grades until after the semester when you file a grade appeal.

If you believe your *final course grade* in a writing course was unfairly or incorrectly given, you should first meet with the instructor of the class and then with the Course Director. Go to Modern Languages 380 for complete instructions.

1.5 Manifesto on Written Feedback

Recently, several writing instructors at the University of Arizona developed the following "Manifesto on Written Feedback":

From The University of Arizona Writing Instructors to Our Students

In collaboration with Professor Nancy Sommers, during her recent visit to UA, the following UA writing instructors thoughtfully and respectfully submit the following objectives and opinions on how to read and use comments on written assignments: Rosanne Carlo, Anne-Marie Hall, Faith Kurtyka, Rachel Lewis, Jessica Shumake, and Cassie Wright.

1. We would like you to understand that our comments are part of the teaching and learning process. We write comments not just to evaluate your essay, but to help you see how the lessons about writing from class emerge in your writing. One way to better understand the purpose of our comments is to actively participate in class and carefully read the rubric and the assignment sheet. These are the ways we communicate with you ahead of time about what we are looking for in your writing.

2. We would like you to know that we intend our comments to be constructive. We value your ideas and want to learn from you and hope that you will use our comments to learn from us as well.

3. We would like you to approach each essay not as an independent unit, but as a brief moment in your overall development as a writer. Our comments are meant to be useful to you in this assignment and your future writing.

4. We would like you to accept responsibility for using our comments in the revision process. We also expect you to share your strengths as a writer in commenting on your peers' papers.

5. We would like you to understand that comments are both descriptive and evaluative. Writing a letter grade is perhaps the least interesting thing we do as writing instructors. Take the time to re-read the entire essay alongside our comments to understand the grade in context. We invite you to use our comments as an opportunity to talk further about your writing.

This manifesto should give you a better understanding of how instructors generate written responses to your writing and how they hope you will use these responses. The manifesto also reflects the fact that there is a relationship between the instructor's comments and the letter grade you will ultimately receive in the class, but it encourages you to use both the grades and the comments as tools for improving your writing throughout the semester.

1.6 Overview of English 101/107

Goals

In English 101/107, you should learn how to:

- Analyze texts through close reading.

- Develop strategies for analyzing texts for particular purposes, audiences, and situations.

- Analyze the ways in which authors use textual conventions to achieve their purposes in specific contexts.

- Write essays that develop analyses with evidence drawn from the texts you read.

- Incorporate other writers' interpretations into the analyses you write.

- Practice research, reading, writing, and revision strategies that can be applied to work in other courses and in different professions.

- Create multiple, meaningful revisions of your writing and suggest useful revisions to other writers.

- Analyze and reflect on your progress as an academic writer.

Overview of the Course

You probably learned a lot about writing in high school English, and this course will build on what you learned, asking you to think about writing and reading in ways that you may not have experienced before. This semester you'll read a variety of texts closely and carefully, and you'll write essays that analyze those texts. Your instructor will ask you to design clear, complex thesis statements for your essays and to support them with specific details and evidence from the text(s) you're working with. You'll also work on expressing your own ideas and opinions in writing.

One thing you'll often hear is that reading and writing never take place in a vacuum but always occur within a specific **context** or situation. In other words, the way you read and interpret a text will be influenced by your personal beliefs and values, your upbringing, your social, cultural, and economic background, and so on. The students in your class will "see" a text from their own unique perspectives, opening up the possibility for numerous interpretations of the text. Likewise, the texts you will read in English 101/107 are informed by the authors who write them, as well as the social, historical, and political contexts in which they are created.

This course will also help you learn how to integrate sources correctly into your paper to support your arguments. You need to follow bibliographic conventions to be able to write as a member of the academic community. To this end, you'll follow the guidelines of one commonly used style of documentation, the format used by the Modern Language Association (MLA). Other professional organizations may require different formats for references, but the MLA guidelines, widely used in English and related disciplines, will give you a model to work from. Another step in writing for academic audiences is learning how to share your own ideas about texts and effectively use feedback from other students and from instructors. This course will give you the chance to practice these things. Gradually, you'll become more skilled at constructing focused and compelling pieces of writing. In the midst of this work, you will refine your writing style by paying more attention to mechanics, grammar, and usage.

You'll have the opportunity to analyze a variety of texts, which will help you develop an even broader perspective on how authors use language and images to communicate their ideas. In analyzing this array of texts, you'll gain proficiency in writing and reading that will help you in your other courses and outside college.

Essential Terms

- **Text**: A text in this course may refer to written, visual, spatial, or auditory **pieces**. A text can mean a piece of writing, a photograph or film, an event or place, or even sounds that can be analyzed.

- **Context:** By context, we mean the circumstances surrounding the creation and reception of a text. In this course you'll examine texts in various contexts—for example, the personal associations of readers, the biographical backgrounds of writers, related historical events, and political purposes. The best contexts to study are those that illuminate the meanings and uses of the text.

- **Audience:** Just as all texts are written in a particular situation for a specific audience, you should keep your own audience in mind as you write essays for this course. Unless your instructor specifies otherwise, you should write for a general academic audience. This means that your readers are likely to have read the text you are discussing (or texts similar to it) and will require only a brief summary of the text and only the most pertinent details on its context or the writer. Your audience will appreciate a clear focus, a complex argument grounded in specific supporting details, a careful reading of the text, and a thesis that includes qualifications that anticipate opposing arguments.

- **Thesis:** As you construct your essays, you'll define your thesis to meet the needs of a particular audience, academic and otherwise. Your thesis will be expected to briefly summarize the basic argument of your essay. A thesis usually becomes apparent to a reader in the introduction to the essay, although it may be stated in a later part of an essay or even remain unstated or implied.

The Assignments

In this course, you'll practice three types of analysis by writing three major essays, each with two or more drafts. Short in- and out-of-class writing assignments will help you prepare for these essays. You will also prepare a Final Exam Portfolio.

Note that your instructor might vary the specific nature and order of the essay assignments. Sample essays appear in Part IV of the *Guide*. All essays require analysis, argument, and revision. Some essays require research.

- **Analysis Essays** focus closely on the text itself in a limited context. For instance, you might analyze the writer's **rhetorical** strategies or the literary, textual, or cultural features that shape your response to the text. You might also compare the strategies or features evident in two different texts or explore your personal reactions to the text(s). Some of your instructors may assign literacy narratives as a form of analysis. In all cases, however, your analysis will depend on a **close reading** of the text(s).

- **Text-in-Context Essays or Contextual Essays** focus on a text and its relationship to a larger context, such as the author's biography, the historical or cultural situation surrounding the text, a particular theoretical approach such as feminism or psychoanalysis, the literary tradition to which the work belongs, or a related set of texts. Contextual analysis depends on close reading, research, argument, revision, and synthesis. Research for this paper will be limited in focus; your instructor may even provide a few sources for you to use. These essays emphasize your ability to evaluate and incorporate sources effectively.

- **Journal Responses** focus on your responses to what you read, see, write, and hear over the entire semester, in and out of class. They can include spontaneous entries and responses to formal prompts. These short texts will help you synthesize and reflect on your reading and writing experiences and prepare you for writing your essays.

- **Reflection and Revision** focus on specific aspects of writing you have learned or practiced over the course of the semester. Your portfolio will consist of a revised essay and an essay that explains your revisions and reflects on your writing process.

The series of assignments you will work through in this course builds from close reading to analyses of broader contexts, to an expanded analysis that takes your own context into account, culminating in a portfolio that showcases your work throughout the semester. In summary, English 101/107 will give you the skills to analyze texts in a specific context, build arguments about texts, conduct detailed and relevant research on texts and their contexts, and revise your work and reflect on your revisions. Student Adrian Sotomayor offers the following testament to the emphasis and importance of analysis:

> Get ready for a year full of analysis! Whether you like it or hate it, you will have to analyze everything you read. The first essay, textual analysis, was both the easiest and the hardest to write. It was easy because I had the option of choosing a story that interested me from several that were presented; thus, it helped me form a relatively strong argument about the text. On the other hand, I had previously taken English 100 but had taken a semester break from English. This created my initial struggle in which I was lost and forgot most, if not all, of what I had learned. To get by, I started to read the *Student's Guide* to see what other students had to say (yep, the same thing you are reading now). It helped me see that I wasn't alone and actually helped with the tips that some students gave.
>
> For the text-in-context essay, research proved to be more tedious than it could have been. Since I live so far from the U of A and I had no gaps between classes, I found it hard to actually set apart some time to go to the library and research a topic. So my tip to you is, do your research early! You will find that sometimes you will have to change your thesis or you will not have enough evidence. Finding this out early gives you more time to go back and look up information. If you write this paper the night before, you will find yourself struggling to find information due to the large amount of time that research requires. Good luck, and don't procrastinate!

Developing different methods or styles of reading will help you deal with the large amount of reading you'll be asked to do in college and in the workplace. For more on close reading strategies, see Chapter 3.

You can find sample essays for each of these assignments in Part IV of the *Student's Guide*. As you browse through the sample essays, keep in mind that the specific essays you produce will vary depending on your instructor's emphasis and on whether you are enrolled in 101 or 107.

Essential Readings for English 101/107

Part II: Strategies and Concepts

- Chapter 2: Academic Writing: Writing for Specific Audiences and Purposes

- Chapter 3: Close Reading and Interacting with the Text

- Chapter 4: Writing as a Process

- Chapter 5: Re-Visioning Your Work

- Chapter 7: Research as Part of the Writing Process

Part III: Assignments

- Chapter 8: Analysis

- Chapter 9: Text-in-Context (Contextual Analysis)

- Chapter 13: Personal and Reflective Writing

Part IV: Sample Essays

1.7 Overview of English 101/197B with a Writing Studio Component

Goals

In addition to the goals indicated in Section 1.6, you will learn how to:

- Identify concepts and functions of "story" and how they relate to literacy and critical awareness in writing, reading, language, and education.

- Analyze literacy practices as artifacts that are inseparable from culture, economy, and social politics.

- Engage in weekly writing workshops where you will practice writing and revising your work.

Overview of the Course

English 101 with a writing studio focuses on the same goals and skills as English 101, only it carries an additional one credit "studio" course. This fourth credit, English 197B, is a required part of the course and is intended to help you improve your writing by giving you extra practice working on and revising your assignments in class.

Like English 101/107, English 101 with a studio component focuses on close reading and analysis. Thus you might also want to read the Overview of English 101/107, located in Section 1.6 for more information about how close reading and analysis inform the course. Given the diverse makeup of sections, instructors may emphasize different areas of craft and content in the writing studio, and the course content may vary slightly across sections.

Aside from the studio component of 101/197B, this course differs a bit in terms of the types of texts you'll be reading and the assignments you'll be writing. For example, English 101/197B focuses on the concept of **literacy** and the ways it is practiced, so you will primarily be reading texts that deal with such subjects as writing, reading, language, and education. As you read these texts, you will work to locate the ways in which literacy practices become embedded with cultural, historical, economic, and socio-political meanings. You will also consider the ways in which access to education is affected by race, gender, social class, and other factors.

For instance, before the abolition of slavery, African Americans were prevented from learning to read and write because those in power, white men of higher class standing, felt that such access to education would empower African Americans to challenge their social positions. During this historical period, a man named Frederick Douglass wrote about his experiences as a slave who was learning to read and to write, and he describes his acquisition of literacy in ways that illustrate the social inequalities he faced in doing so. Because he did not have access to the same resources as those in power—pen, paper, and books, for example—Douglass had to use what he had available to him. He learned to write by marking on wooden logs and fences; he read newspapers he found on the street. In short, the ways in which he achieved literacy were shaped by the social, political, and historical climate of that time.

In examining the ways in which literacy practices are informed by contextual factors, as in the example above, you will begin to develop a critical understanding of writing, reading, language, and education. You will also be able to consider your own literacy practices and how they are shaped by your individual experiences and the social context in which you live.

Essential Terms

Narrative: Any story that describes events or experiences, whether fictional or factual, can be considered narrative. Thus newspaper articles that describe recent events or novels that describe a character's journey follow a narrative structure. When you are telling a group of friends about your most recent camping trip, you are telling a narrative as well.

Literacy Narrative: A personal narrative that focuses on an event or events in the author's acquisition of literacy. Literacy narratives can explore a specific, significant experience with writing, reading, and/or language, or they can discuss how writing, reading, and/or language have played a role in the author's past experience.

1.8 Overview of English 109H—Honors English Composition

Goals

In Honors English Composition, you should strengthen your ability to:

- Analyze texts through close reading and critical thinking.

- Develop strategies for analyzing texts for particular purposes, audiences, and contexts.

- Write essays that develop analyses with evidence drawn from the texts you read.

- Practice research, reading, writing, and revision strategies that can be applied to work in other courses and in different professions.

- Use the conventions of scholarly research, analysis, and documentation; practice research as a *process*.

- Create multiple, meaningful revisions of your writing and suggest useful revisions to other writers.

- Analyze and reflect on your progress as an academic writer.

This course will build upon the skills you developed in your high school English classes. Honors English Composition has as its emphases close reading, critical thinking, analytical writing, and researched writing. The course will help you to achieve and effectively use the recursive processes of active reading, writing, researching, providing feedback to other writers, and doing all steps of revision. You will learn the process of doing research, which will include finding your own sources and learning how to incorporate them into a complex and well-developed argument. In Honors English Composition you may be asked to write either a text-in-context essay or a rhetorical analysis essay, since both types of essays place texts in context. You will read a variety of texts. For example, you may be assigned to read literary texts (of fiction, poetry, or nonfiction), films, visual arts, or a combination of these genres. In this course you should attain all of the goals of first-year composition listed in Section 1.6. Below are some examples of recent assignments for English 109H.

Assignments

- **Poetics Essay:** In this paper you will perform a literary analysis or a close reading of a text. You will engage in a variety of reading and writing related exercises culminating in an essay demonstrating superior critical reading, thinking, and writing skills. You will be prompted to deepen and refine your given strengths as a critical thinker and writer.

- **Rhetorical Concerns Essay:** In this assignment you will address rhetorical concerns through the construction of a text-in-context essay, a rhetorical analysis essay, *or* a cultural analysis essay. You will again perform individual scrutiny of texts, but this time you will be considering your ideas in broader contexts. Your instructor may choose to emphasize historical, sociological, cultural, aesthetic, and interdisciplinary issues when guiding you to write this essay.

- **Research Process Assignment:** This assignment may take many forms but is designed around the idea of research as a *process*. This assignment focuses on accessing and incorporating library and Internet resources as well as incorporating other forms of research (like interviews or case studies) into an analytical essay. You may be asked to work in groups while developing projects and to share available campus resources. In some classes, you will have the opportunity to present your findings to the class.

- **The Final Exam:** You will write a reflective essay that synthesizes the concerns of the course. A theoretical text may function as a lens to help you make connections to themes and concepts. Your teacher will choose the best final exam format for your particular class. You may have an in-class essay, a take-home exam, an in-class presentation to other students, or even a reflective introduction to your research project.

Essential Readings for Honors English Composition
Part II: Strategies and Concepts

- Chapter 2: Academic Writing: Writing for Specific Audiences and Purposes

- Chapter 3: Close Reading and Interacting with the Text

- Chapter 4: Writing as a Process

- Chapter 5: Re-Visioning Your Work

- Chapter 7: Research as Part of the Writing Process

Part III: Assignments

- Chapter 8: Analysis

- Chapter 9: Text-in-Context (Contextual Analysis)

- Chapter 10: Rhetorical Analysis

- Chapter 11: Exploring a Controversy

- Chapter 12: Writing Public Arguments

Part IV: Sample Essays

1.9 Overview of English 102/108

Goals

In English 102/108, you should learn how to:

- Read texts to assess how writers achieve their purposes with their intended audiences.

- Devise writing strategies suited to various rhetorical situations.

- Develop an argument with persuasive appeals to your audience.

- Locate and analyze evidence to develop an argument.

- Develop ideas with observations and reflections on your experience.

- Revise in response to feedback from readers to improve drafts.

- Use the conventions of scholarly research, analysis, and documentation.

- Use the conventions of academic writing, including how to write clear, convincing prose.

Overview of the Course

In your second semester of first-year writing, you will learn how to make informed arguments about issues and texts in order to contribute to existing knowledge. You will learn that all writing has some element of *persuasion*, even if it's subtle. For example, creative writing is persuasive because even novelists have to keep their readers interested in the story and make characters and their actions believable. Academic writing is particularly persuasive because scholars have to put forth arguments that build on previous arguments to develop new knowledge. The job of scholarly and professional writing is to persuade readers to accept the new argument and the new knowledge. However, in academic and professional communities, an argument is not typically a "fight" that the participants strive to win by overpowering their opponents. Instead, an argument arises from a difference in views and, as such, is an opportunity for further investigation.

An interesting argument in your major or on the news may provide you with the opportunity to investigate what the **controversy** is about. Why do people disagree? What underlying values and assumptions underlie their various viewpoints? By investigating various positions on an issue, you'll come to understand more fully where you stand and why you feel as you do.

English 102/108, then, centers on argument and persuasion. You will learn to identify and analyze the **rhetorical strategies** people use to persuade others, and how they use language, evidence, and their surrounding situations to make their arguments convincing.

You will also learn to conduct in-depth **research** into a given controversy to understand the arguments surrounding it and why certain people involved believe the way they do. This will require you to investigate more than simply the "pro" and "con" sides of the issue and to think about the complex arguments in-between these extremes. You will learn to examine these various opinions and to analyze the strategies of persuasion that inform them. In short, your goal will be to understand the many complex arguments that comprise a controversy.

Only when you understand the arguments surrounding a controversy will you be able to make your own **public argument**—something else you will learn in this course. Your instructor may give you opportunities to create public arguments in media forms other than written essays, including videos, speeches, Web pages, posters, PowerPoint presentations, or other forms. The goals of the public argument you create will be to take a stance on the issue and to present your points in a way that would be effective for your target audience. Further, your goal will be to add to the existing body of knowledge that surrounds the issue.

Essential Terms and Concepts

Rhetoric: You may have heard this term used in a negative sense, for example, to describe a manipulative political speech as simply "empty rhetoric." However, in first-year writing we use this term in its classical sense as **the art of persuasion**. This sense of rhetoric includes the various strategies an author or speaker uses to accomplish his or her purpose for a specific audience. A rhetorical analysis is concerned with how writers and speakers use words in particular situations to achieve definite goals.

Inquiry: You might have first heard this term in the sense of "investigation," as in a police inquiry. At the university this definition still applies. An inquiry is a line of investigation into an issue, topic, or problem. Focusing on a particular line of inquiry helps academics and professionals narrow the scope of their efforts, and in this class, it can help you carry your work forward from one assignment to the next.

Rhetorical Situation: The production of texts takes place within **contexts**— the circumstances surrounding and influencing the creation and reception of a text. Context is one of the elements of a rhetorical situation; the others are the intended audience and the author's purpose. When analyzing the rhetoric of a text, you should take into account these elements of the rhetorical situation.

Rhetorical Strategies: These are the methods an author chooses to construct the text, develop ideas, and write persuasively. They can include the types of evidence used to support the argument, the author's voice, even the format of the text. When you analyze the rhetoric of a text, you will look at these choices in terms of the rhetorical situation and determine how well they work in that situation.

The Assignments

- **Rhetorical Analysis:** You will begin the semester by critiquing the arguments of others. This type of analysis goes beyond the work you did in English 101/107 by focusing on and evaluating arguments. Rhetorical analysis comes in many different forms, which are communicated in Chapter 10, *Writing Public Lives*, and your instructor's lessons.

- **Controversy Analysis:** The next assignment still emphasizes argument, but your task is to research a controversy and present an analysis of the emerging arguments surrounding the controversy. This assignment also challenges you to perform academic research to support your claims about the controversy you are analyzing.

- **Public Argument:** Following your research assignment, you'll be asked to take a side on the issue you've researched and present a public argument. Public arguments can come in various forms (speeches, editorials, Web pages, posters, etc.), but all use the rhetorical devices you learned during the first assignment to persuade an audience in some way.

- **Reflection and Revision:** You'll reflect on your writing over the course of the term and write a critical assessment of it. This reflection seeks to track the improvements you've made over the course of the semester or your entire first-year writing course.

Essential Readings for English 102/108

Part II: Strategies and Concepts

- Chapter 2: Academic Writing: Writing for Specific Audiences and Purposes

- Chapter 3: Close Reading and Interacting with the Text

- Chapter 4: Writing as a Process

- Chapter 5: Re-Visioning Your Work

- Chapter 6: Working with Sources: Summary, Paraphrase, and Quotation

- Chapter 7: Research as Part of the Writing Process

Part III: Assignments

- Chapter 10: Rhetorical Analysis

- Chapter 11: Exploring a Controversy

- Chapter 12: Writing Public Arguments

- Chapter 13: Personal and Reflective Writing

Part IV: Sample Essays

1.10 Using *Rules for Writers* to Improve Your Writing

Rules for Writers by Diana Hacker is a text that, along with your *Student's Guide*, will help you to achieve the goals of your first-year writing courses. A good writing handbook can help you to become a better writer. It's a quick reference to the **rules and strategies** currently valued in academic and professional writing. It's not really a textbook to use in one class and then discard at the end of the semester. Rather, a writing handbook is a continuing guide for most of the writing questions you'll have during your entire college career and beyond in your personal and professional life.

Take a quick tour of *Rules for Writers* to see all that it has to offer you.

- Glance at the "Brief Menu" inside the front cover or the "Detailed Menu" inside the back cover.

- Fan through the pages to see how the book is organized and how easy it is to find what you're looking for.

- Read the "How to Use This Book and Its Web Site" section starting on page xv.

- Try one or more of the book's tutorials starting on page xix.

- Try a few exercises to get your feet wet.

- If you're an ESL writer, turn to the "ESL Menu" on page 618 for specific ESL hints throughout the book and separate sections on the most common ESL transfer errors.

Turn to the handbook whenever you have any questions about writing. Your writing instructors might assign pages for you to read and digest, especially sections about the writing or research processes, or guidelines for writing a successful academic argument. Your instructors might also assign a few exercises to help you with grammar (*Should I say "The number of children is" or "The number of children are"?*), style (*Can I use "lots of" in my research paper?*), or punctuation skills (*Should I use a comma before this "and"?*). Your handbook can answer all these questions.

Your handbook will also help you understand and respond to your instructors' feedback. Your instructors might mark your texts with a simple symbol or refer to a specific page or section in the handbook. For example, if you're having problems expressing *parallel ideas*, your instructors might mark your text with the parallel symbol //, with a reference to the handbook page number or section that discusses parallelism. The list of revision symbols on page 619 shows a shorthand system that your instructor may use—with handy references to sections in the handbook. So, think of *Rules for Writers* as a friend to turn to for good advice, for all those writing questions you'll face not only in first-year writing, but also throughout your undergraduate studies and perhaps in your professional career.

PART II
STRATEGIES AND CONCEPTS

Academic Writing: Writing for Specific Audiences and Purposes

2.1 Academic Writing: An Overview

You probably write daily, from e-mailing friends to making out grocery lists to taking notes in a class, but in your first-year writing classes, you will be asked to consider what it means to be a "writer" in an academic context. **Academic writing** generally involves:

- Writing for specific purposes and for specific audiences.

- Following discipline-specific style guidelines and genre conventions.

- Incorporating credible research to support arguments and/or observations.

However, even the term "academic writing" is often too general because different disciplines in the university value different conventions and different types of academic writing. Think about the different forms of writing you have been asked to do in the past. For example, imagine a lab report you would write in your chemistry lab:

- Your **target audience** would be your chemistry lab instructor and other students in your lab.

- Your **purpose** would be to detail what you discovered from the experiment.

- You would follow the **genre conventions** of a lab report, including:

  o writing in an objective (non-biased) tone.

  o including sections like an introduction or overview of the experiment, materials, methods, observations, and conclusions.

  o providing concrete, specific details about the observations made during the experiment.

  o using those details to support your conclusions (your analysis of what you observed).

  o avoiding the use of "I" in the narrative of your report.

These conventions are common in the sciences, but they are quite different from the kind of writing you would do in a literature class, where you might be asked to write an analytic essay about a character in a novel. Your observations in this case would not come from watching an experiment in action, but rather from what you notice as you read. In this case,

- Your **target audience** would be your literature instructor and others interested in literature scholarship.

- Your **purpose** would be to present a relatively unique and sophisticated interpretation of the novel.

- You would follow the **genre conventions** of a literature analysis, including:

  o presenting a thesis statement of your argument early on.

  o supporting your thesis with concrete, specific details and passages from the novel, properly cited.

  o presenting this evidence through logically divided paragraphs.

  o citing interpretations of the novel and other ideas that are not your own.

  o using "I" purposefully, and usually sparingly.

Being an effective academic writer thus requires that you always consider the purpose of your writing, your target audience, and the context in which you are writing.

Considering your audience, purpose, and other contextual factors is a crucial part of becoming an effective writer because, as the above examples (the chemistry lab report and the literature analysis essay) illustrate, each academic discipline has its own way of writing and communicating with people inside the discipline. You can think of groups of people who share a unique way of communicating as **discourse communities**. A discourse community shares a discipline-specific set of writing and speaking practices, as well as specialized vocabulary that is understood by members of the group. As a college student, you likely belong to several different discourse communities, from your major field of study to each extracurricular group to which you belong. For example, if you're a chemistry major, then you have a specific way of talking and communicating with others who study and teach chemistry: you all share a set of common vocabulary and communication practices unique to the field of chemistry. The same would be true if you belong to a student organization like Animal AdvoCATS, where members of the group also have communication practices that are unique to them.

Genre Conventions in Writing

By Rosanne Carlo

It is worthwhile to consider different types of writing as belonging to different "genres" of writing. By understanding rhetorical elements that shape different genres, including audience, purpose, tone, and writing conventions, you will begin to see how different genres are defined and distinguished. In your composition class, you will be asked to think critically about texts in several genres. The questions and analysis about genre can serve as a starting point into a conversation about your own writing. Use the following chart to consider some genres. Discuss these genres with your classmates, and try to come up with at least three writing conventions for each of the genres listed.

2.1

Genre of Writing	Possible Target Audience(s)	Purpose(s)	Tone	Genre Conventions
Chemistry Lab Report				
Business Letter				
Eulogy (a speech to be given at a funeral)				
Textual Analysis Essay for English 101				
Literacy Narrative				

Take a moment to jot down the various discourse communities to which you belong. Ask yourself these questions:

- What are the communication practices of each group?

- How do these practices differ across groups?

- What are some of the group- or field-specific terms used by the group?

- How does your writing and speech change from one group to the next?

Thinking about these questions will enable you to understand the concept of discourse community and to recognize the ways in which academic writing is shaped by different situations.

The most important aspect to note about academic writing, then, is that it changes from one discipline to the next. While all academic writing shares some common features—formality in tone, for example—there are major differences as well. Your job as a writer will be to note the writing conventions within the academic disciplines you encounter and to apply them in your own writing. You may sometimes find that writing "academically" is a challenge, since it often demands that you learn to step back from your usual writing process and reflect on the attitudes and habits that have shaped who you are. Success in college, however, requires that you learn to master the conventions of academic discourse across disciplines and in your major course of study.

2.2 Academic Writing Conventions at the Word Level

Research in the field of linguistics highlights a number of important differences between formal and informal English. One of these differences involves verbs. In many situations, English has two or more options to express an action or event. The choice is often between a multiple-word verb and a single verb. Often in spoken English, a multiple-word verb is used; however, for academic written English, generally a single verb is preferred. Here's an example:

1. According to some government scientists, **coming up with** clear proof of global warming has been difficult.

2. According to some government scientists, **providing** clear proof of global warming has been difficult.

An important goal for academic writing is to be concise. However, that is not always the case in spoken English. The following is a comparison of academic verbs versus verbs you would encounter in everyday speech. Notice that the verbs in the second column are comprised of two or three words.

Verb in Academic Writing	vs.	Verb in Informal English
accelerate		speed up
investigate		look into
accompany		go with
eliminate		get rid of
endure		put up with
explore		think about
research		find out about

Certain verbs, because of their ability to convey meaning concisely, appear more frequently in academic writing than others. The following list of verbs has been shown to be among the most important in academic style. You may not want to use some of these words while talking among friends, but consider adopting them as you write to an academic audience.

abandon	accelerate	access	accompany
accomplish	accumulate	achieve	address
advocate	assert	assume	aid
cause	characterize	comply	conclude
connect	construct	constitute	contrast
decrease	define	denote	develop
determine	dramatize	eliminate	emphasize
enable	enact	establish	evaluate
formulate	guarantee	identify	illustrate
imply	interpret	investigate	juxtapose
maintain	posit	portray	presume
present	prevail	process	reach
require	restrict	specify	suggest

2.2

Choosing Specific Words

By Angel Miller

One of the best ways to be specific is to choose words that carry the exact meaning you are trying to convey—and those probably aren't the words that you use every day while talking to your family and friends. That's because the best words for writing are different from the best words for speaking. When we are speaking, we commonly use words that don't carry much meaning because we are able to fill in the missing meanings through body language, eye contact, and even the tone of our voice. But when we write, we can only create meaning through word choice.

Choosing Specific Verbs

A **verb** is a word that conveys action. When we talk, we use verbs to show that some kind of action is taking place. When writing, try to avoid words such as *be*, *do*, *make*, *have*, *go*, *get*, *say*, *walk*, or *show*. A good way to make your verbs stronger is to pay attention to the action itself. What is the *manner* of the action? If you're describing movement, how is the motion taking place? The manner of action can affect the entire meaning of the sentence. Look at this sentence:

Julie was surprised to see John **walk** toward her.

How would the meaning of the sentence change if we used a more specific verb than "walk"? See the following three examples:

Julie was surprised to see John **sprint** toward her.

Julie was surprised to see John **shuffle** toward her.

Julie was surprised to see John **tiptoe** toward her.

Choosing Specific Nouns

A **noun** is a person, place, or thing. It can be a concrete thing, like a pencil, or an abstract thing, like philosophy. When writing, avoid imprecise nouns like *thing*, *stuff*, and *person* or *people*. Those words just don't include enough information for your reader to follow along with your explanation. Use nouns as a way to paint a picture of the scene for the reader—the more specific they are, the more understandable and engaging your writing will be. Look at the following sentence:

John left a lot of **stuff** on the floor of his room.

How would the meaning of the sentence change if we used a more specific noun than "stuff"? See the following three examples:

John left a lot of **clothes** on the floor of his room.

John left a lot of **books** on the floor of his room.

John left a lot of **garbage** on the floor of his room.

Choosing Specific Adjectives

An **adjective** is a word that describes a noun. Adjectives include words like studious, critical, helpful, thoughtful, and academic. Because adjectives are supposed to add description to a sentence, take extra care that the adjectives you use provide the kind of description you want. Vague adjectives, such as *good*, *little*, *nice*, *strange*, or *old*, can cause confusion for the reader because they tend to be ambiguous and are based on opinion. What is "strange" to one person might seem boring and average to another person, and what you might consider "old" your grandparents might think of as being recent. This ambiguity means that the words we use need to convey as much information as possible.

When you use an adjective, you're describing something, so why not take your description all the way? The more specific your description is, the more you are able to pinpoint the exact attributes of your subject—which means your reader will have a more precise understanding of what you're trying to explain.

Pretend that you want to describe a place that you feel is sad. What is sad about it? Close your eyes

2.2

and imagine that you are actually there. What does it look like? Smell like? Who else is there with you? Pick out as many specifics as you can that convey the meaning that you are trying to express and work them into your description.

Adverbs: Avoid When Possible

An **adverb** is a word that describes a verb. For example, carefully, critically, frantically, and meticulously are all adverbs. When we speak, we place much of our meaning in adverbs, especially adverbs that are used to emphasize, such as *very* or *really*. Adverbs such as very or really, although they may be useful in conversation as a way of adding emphasis to an adjective or verb, add much less meaning, if any, in writing. As a rule, you should avoid relying on adverbs to convey meaning in your writing. For example, look at the following sentence:

He **walked angrily** out of the room.

One could instead use a more precise verb, thereby rendering the adverb unneccessary:

He **stalked** out of the room.

The majority of your meaning should be portrayed in your verbs, nouns, and adjectives. If you use strong adjectives and verbs, you'll find that you won't need to rely heavily on adverbs. If you find yourself searching for an adverb to make your point, find one that adds information. For example, imagine that you were to write:

He whispered quietly.

In the above sentence, **quietly** doesn't add much meaning to the sentence, because unless you're trying to be ironic, one can't really whisper **loudly**. However, the *occasional* adverb might be helpful. One could write:

The villain smiled.

But compare that to:

The villain smiled menacingly.

The adverb **menacingly** conveys a completely different type of smile, and there's no verb that captures a similar enough meaning.

Using Clear and Specific Description

Stating exactly what you mean can be difficult because you already know what you're talking about, so you don't have the same questions about the topic as your reader does. If you find yourself struggling to figure out whether or not you are describing or explaining your subject clearly enough, look through your essay, and in every paragraph, ask yourself *who, what, when, where, why,* and *how.*

For example, imagine one of the sentences in your essay looks something like this:

The photo's use of contrast between dark and light things shows danger.

You might ask yourself:

- What are the elements in the photograph that the sentence is discussing?

- How do they show danger?

- What kind of danger do they show?

After answering those questions, your sentence might look more like this:

The photo's use of contrast between the darkness of the alleyways and the light of the storefronts emphasizes the dangers hidden just out of sight.

Note that the second sentence is much clearer and more descriptive in its meaning; even without seeing the photograph that is being discussed, you can understand the point of the sentence. Could someone who had never encountered your text (in this case a photograph) understand your meaning? Answering this question is necessary for academic writing, since it requires writers to be specific—to choose specific verbs, nouns, adjectives, and adverbs.

2.2

Using Gender-Neutral Language

In addition to specific language, you also want to be aware of the kinds of nouns you use in your writing, especially those nouns that are used broadly to refer to a group of people. For example, in the past, "man" and "mankind" were terms that were used to refer broadly to humans—both male and female. However, some people, including feminist scholars and activists, have worked to bring attention to the ways in which language can exclude certain groups and privilege others. Nowadays people realize that many of the terms used in the past—like "man" and "mankind"—no longer work effectively, especially considering we live in a time period when women have garnered a greater sense of equality than in the past. Believe it or not, many of the first writing manuals and grammars—texts that provide guidelines for language use—were written when women could not attend school, so using words like "man" *were* in fact meant to refer to men only! Gender-neutral terms are conscientious choices for writing because these terms help to ensure inclusivity, not exclusivity.

For example, look at the following sentences. Which of these sentences are the most inclusive of diverse readers? Why?

1. Men have long debated over whether or not drilling in the Arctic should be allowed.

    Men and women have long debated over whether or not drilling in the Arctic should be allowed.

    People have long debated over whether or not drilling in the Arctic should be allowed.

2. A student who does not do his homework will probably not pass the course.

    A student who does not do her or his homework will probably not pass the course.

Here are some examples of gender-neutral words and phrases:

one	**s/he**	**people**
humankind	**women and men**	**person**
humanity	**human beings**	**she or he**

Using gender-neutral language also means being aware of job or position titles that exclude. For instance, most of you probably grew up using words like "policeman" or "fireman" to refer to these professionals. With more women entering into these fields, the titles "police officer" and "firefighter" are now preferred. Similarly, job titles like "stewardess" and "waitress" have been replaced with titles like "flight attendant" and "server," respectively, since they can refer to both women and men.

In addition, you also want to avoid using words or phrases that rely on racial, ethnic, gender, class-based, national, religious, political, or other group-based stereotypes. When writing about certain groups of people, you should rely on information about these groups that comes from credible sources—not common assumptions, or worse, misconceptions. Oftentimes, stereotypical representations of specific groups of people are inaccurate and offensive, and using them can undermine your **credibility** as a writer.

2.3 Style Conventions in Academic Writing

Another writing convention you'll learn in first-year writing deals with your ability to craft arguments that are supported with concrete details. When you make an academic argument, for example, your audience expects you to have carefully considered all the facts before coming to a conclusion. If you make an argument that relies on generalizations or makes sweeping assertions, your audience may find it difficult to agree with your points. This is why **hedging** is often used in academic writing. Hedging is sometimes also called "qualifying" your argument. Hedging means avoiding unequivocal statements of opinion, or making such statements as if they were fact. Instead, hedging requires that you try to use more open-ended phrasing that acknowledges the existence of different viewpoints.

For more on rhetorical conventions in academic writing, refer to the Academic English boxes on pages 2, 23, and 359 in *Rules for Writers*.

There are two main functions of hedging: 1) giving the writer more credibility by appearing more balanced and 2) creating a more appropriate stance for the writer in terms of audience reactions.

After reading the following sample sentences, discuss these two functions of hedging. What are the differences in meaning for these sentences? Which sentence sounds the most informed and credible? Why?

1. People are absolutely opposed to genetic engineering, but it provides benefits for humanity.

2. Some people are absolutely opposed to genetic engineering, but it may provide benefits for humanity.

3. Some people are opposed to genetic engineering, but it may eventually provide many benefits for humanity.

Some useful hedging words:

usually	**essentially**	**perhaps**	**may**
actually	**apparently**	**often**	**some**
likely	**broadly**	**somewhat**	**somehow**
potentially	**normally**	**theoretically**	**maybe**

Some students may avoid hedging because they fear it might make them appear to be less credible, but judicious hedging lets your reader know that you understand the limitations of your claims, and that you're not trying to deceive anyone. This, on the contrary, boosts your credibility as a writer.

Active vs. Passive Voice

Another stylistic convention you'll learn about in first-year writing is use of verb tenses. Recall earlier in the chapter when you read about the conventions you might follow if you were writing a chemistry lab report—the use of the personal "I" in the report, in particular. Many scientific disciplines avoid using the personal "I" because they want to emphasize the action being performed, not the person responsible for the action. This is the main difference between the active and the passive voice: passive constructions focus on the action performed while active constructions give emphasis to the agent, or performer, of the action.

Passive Voice

Many academic genres (particularly experimental science) make use of the passive voice. Experimental scientists deem the actions performed—the details of the experiment—most important, not necessarily the scientists who perform the experiment. Whereas English typically follows the Subject-Verb-Object (or SVO) order, passive constructions follow an Object-Verb-Subject (or OVS) order. Essentially, a **passive construction** moves the object of a sentence to the subject position.

For more on the passive voice, see *Rules for Writers*, pages 80–83.

For example:

Subject-Verb-Object Order (Active voice)			Object-Verb-Subject Order (Passive voice)		
John	threw	the ball	The ball	was thrown	by John
Subject	**V**erb	**O**bject	**O**bject	**V**erb	**S**ubject

Some say that you should always avoid the passive voice, but it's not *always* the best idea. One thing to consider is what you want to emphasize in your sentence—what you want your readers to recognize as the primary focus. Is it important to know who is doing what? Is it obvious? Does it matter who is doing the action? Put those characters in the subject position even if you must use a passive verb.

You can use passive voice to:

- Call attention to the receiver of the action rather than the performer:

  The audience was insulted by the movie's jokes.

- Point out the receiver of the action when the performer is unknown:

  A wallet was stolen from the library.

- Make a statement if the performer is not significant:

  The votes were counted and Samantha was elected president of the student body.

- Point out the receiver of the action when you want to avoid calling attention to the performer. There can be good reasons why a writer might want to do this! Consider:

  The factory workers were fired yesterday and the factory was closed.

  Nike fired the factory workers yesterday and then the multinational firm closed the factory.

What are the political implications of these statements? Who might prefer to use each one in such an announcement?

Active Voice

The active voice generally provides more clarity for the reader and should therefore be used when it's especially important to know exactly who did what to whom.

One easy way to maintain active voice in your writing is to watch out for the "to be" verbs that are preceded by other verbs. In other words, be careful if you see any of the following words immediately before another verb:

- is
- was
- are
- were
- be
- been

As a rule, a verb in the passive voice *must* include a "to be," so whenever you see one of these "to be" verbs, there's a chance you're writing in the passive voice. Spend several minutes examining the chart on the following page. In the left column are sentences in the passive voice. Phrases in parentheses are optional— all sentences in the passive voice include "by," but it is often implied or omitted (see above for an explanation as to why sometimes the subject is irrelevant and therefore omitted). In the right column are corresponding active constructions. Try to imagine why a passive sentence might be preferred to an active one, or vice versa, depending on what you're trying to communicate.

2.3

Passive Voice	Active Voice
The fundraiser **is organized** by Ms. Ponikarovsky each year	Ms. Ponikarovsky **organizes** a fundraiser each year.
	Ms. Ponikarovsky **is organizing** a fundraiser each year.
The fundraiser for sick children **was sponsored** by the KHL.	The KHL **sponsored** the fundraiser for sick children.
	The KHL **was sponsoring** the fundraiser for sick children.
The fundraisers **are hosted** each year by Mr. and Mrs. Yuskevich.	Mr. and Mrs. Yuskevich **host** the fundraiser each year.
	Mr. and Mrs. Yuskevich **are hosting** the fundraiser each year.
Ideas for expanding it **were thought** of (by Mr. and Mrs. Afinogenov).	Mr. and Mrs. Afinogenov **thought** of expanding it for next year.
	Mr. and Mrs. Afinogenov **were thinking** of expanding it for next year.
Mr. Fedotenko **will be honored** (by the board) for his generosity.	The board **will honor** Mr. Fedotenko for his generosity.
	The board **will be honoring** Mr. Fedotenko for his generosity.
The fundraiser **has been attended** by Mr. Fedotenko each year.	Mr. Fedotenko **has attended** the fundraiser each year.
	Mr. Fedotenko **has been attending** the fundraiser each year.
$1 million **will have been donated** by Ms. Irbe by the end of the year.	Ms. Irbe **will have donated** $1 million by the end of the year.
	Ms. Irbe **will donate** $1 million by the end of the year.

You'll notice that the active voice gives you more options and therefore allows you to be more precise in your writing. If the passive sentence doesn't serve a specific purpose, the active voice is generally the better option. However, using active voice does not come naturally to most people. You can start by looking for passive "to be" verbs when you revise your paper drafts. Go through and circle every "to be" verb that you see, and then decide whether it's more important to hide or show the subject performing the action. Most of the time, you'll find that active voice makes for stronger, clearer writing.

For more advice on using active voice, see *Rules for Writers*, pages 80–83.

While the above examples do not cover every stylistic convention of writing in academic contexts, they will help you get started. Whether to write in active or passive voice, whether to use "endure" instead of "put up with," or whether to use "usually" versus "always"—these are all choices you will make as a writer. More than anything, the examples of style conventions in this chapter should encourage you to think about the stylistic choices you make, since these choices should be informed by the audience to whom you are writing and your purpose for writing.

2.4 You Know It When You See It: A Practical Approach to Style

By Gina Szabady

Sentence Variety Show: Style at the Sentence Level

There's more to style than just choosing different words to say the same thing. When you revise your essays to improve style, you should also pay close attention to sentences. For one thing, having lots of similar sentences in a row can make even an interesting topic boring. To keep your reader interested, **make your writing livelier by using a variety of sentence types**. For example, examine these sentences:

1. One in four first-year college students drops out before the end of his or her first year. Many students are unprepared for college schoolwork. Others don't seek out the help they need to be successful.[1]

2. Many students are unprepared for college schoolwork while others don't ask for the help they need to be successful. One in four first-year college students drops out before the end of his or her first year.

Although these sentences have similar wording, the first set of short, choppy phrases fails to generate interest and momentum for the reader. The first set of sentences also leaves the reader to figure out how the information in each of the phrases is related. However, the second sentence goes further in explaining the relationship among the three pieces of information by combining two of them into one sentence and leaving the third in its own phrase, placing additional emphasis on it. If you wanted to show a different kind of relationship between the three ideas, you could put the information into a sentence with different emphasis, like this:

3. One in four first-year college students will drop out before the end of his or her first year because many students are unprepared for college schoolwork, although others don't seek out the help they need.

When you revise sentences, **think about what information you want to emphasize**. Place those ideas near the beginning of a combined sentence or in a separate sentence. If two ideas are of equal importance, put them in a sentence that treats them equally. In sentence number two, the combination puts equal emphasis on students being unprepared for college schoolwork and students not seeking out the help they need. However, sentence three places more emphasis on the unprepared students by putting "others don't seek out the help they need" after a comma at the end of the sentence.

---

[1] Whitbourne, Jonathon. "The Dropout Dilemma: One in Four College Freshmen Drop Out. What Is Going On Here? What Does It Take to Stay In?" *College and Careers*, Mar. 2002: n.p. Print.

Have I Got a Sentence for You!: Strategic Style Choices

Just like you might choose different words to describe a website to your grand-mother than you would use to tell a friend about it, you will **choose different types of sentences to accomplish different results in your writing**. For example, writers often need to describe the relationship between two ideas when making an argument or transitioning from one idea to another in adjoining paragraphs. Consider the following sentences:

1. Students devote a great deal of time to the admissions process. They forget to prepare for the academic and personal challenges that lie ahead.[2]

2. Because students devote so much time to the admissions process, they forget to prepare for the academic and personal challenges that lie ahead.

In the first sentence, the reader is given all the information to figure out the writer's argument, but the reader must put it all together him or herself. In sentence two, the writer embeds the cause and effect argument in the structure of the sentence using the word "because." The reader is more easily able to understand that devoting so much time to the admissions process *causes* students to forget to prepare for challenges ahead. Other words, like *although*, *since*, *when*, *after*, *before*, *while*, and *unless*, can also be used to create this kind of sentence. Note that "because" can be moved but the relationship between ideas remains clear:

3. Students forget to prepare for the academic and personal challenges that lie ahead because they devote a great deal of time to the admissions process.

Even though this kind of sentence works well for particular tasks, it's not the best tool for every job. For example, when you are explaining something complicated or giving several perspectives on the same issue, simpler sentences are often better. Consider how the following sentences deal with data:

1. Although 18 percent of students study only once or twice a week, students who study daily are 40 percent more likely to earn an "A" than students who do not study daily; only 41 percent of students study every day.[2]

2. "Students who study daily are 40 percent more likely to earn an 'A' than students who do not study daily. Only 41 percent of students study every day, and 18 percent study only once or twice a week."

Sentence one attempts to show relationships among the different bits of information, but just ends up being confusing. In sentence two, the writer focuses on presenting the data clearly and leaves making connections with other ideas to different sentences. Explaining the connections among ideas in every sentence can become confusing. Introduce new ideas or information from an outside source in a clear, simple way. You can explain context and offer analysis in sentences that follow. When you write your essays, **practice combining sentences in lots of different ways** to make sure you have a variety of sentences that is both interesting to your reader and strategic in explaining your ideas.

---

[2]Hildebrand, Bruce. "Female College Students Study More, Make Higher Grades and Graduate In Less Time." *The Association of American Publishers*, 23 Aug. 2005. Web. 30 Sep. 2010.

Stay Tuned: Making Good Style a Habit

Good writing is not formulaic, and thus, the best recommendation is to consider both the situation in which you are writing and what you are trying to accomplish. Here are a few style tips from this section:

1. **Make the reader's job as easy as possible.** In most cases, saying something to the readers is your very reason for writing. Choose words they can understand and put them into sentences that make your purpose as clear as possible. Careful proofreading and editing are also needed to avoid typographical errors that make deciphering your intended meaning more difficult.

2. **Say what you mean and know what you are saying.** It can be tempting to use unfamiliar words or phrases from a thesaurus to eliminate redundancy or to make you sound smarter. However, you run the risk of saying something you don't mean when you choose a word you don't know. Always look up words before you use them, make sure to read all the definitions carefully, and be sure you understand how the word is used in context. When in doubt, go with a word you know for sure over one you don't.

3. **Consider the relationships between your ideas.** Before you can write sentences that make clear how your ideas connect to one another, you need to know what those connections are. For some people, this means writing outlines or idea maps; for others, it means writing lots of experimental drafts. Whatever drafting strategies you choose, take the time to work out your ideas fully so that you can explain them clearly to your audience in the final draft.

4. **Practice, Practice, Practice. Revise, Revise, Revise.** Like playing guitar or juggling, the best way to improve your writing is to practice, by writing a lot. Keeping a journal or taking notes on your reading material for classes is one way to practice, but so is writing e-mails or updating Facebook. Whenever you write, make thoughtful choices about style. Whenever you read, look carefully at the choices other writers are making. You can even try copying down sentences you like and practice writing your own sentences with a similar structure. Practice by rewriting confusing or overly complex sentences from your textbooks or elsewhere so that they are simple and clear.

2.4

2.4

Close Reading and Interacting with the Text

3.1 Close Reading: An Overview

We often read texts just once or scan them for relevant or important information. For example, you might skim the "Arts & Leisure" section of the newspaper to find film times, or you might read an encyclopedia entry about the *Mona Lisa* quickly for the information you are most interested in. You might also scan a chapter in a biology textbook, looking for important terms that will be on your next exam. But such one-time reading for information is insufficient for the tasks you'll perform in your first-year writing courses. In addition to reading a text for information, you'll need to read texts with a particular **purpose**. You should plan to read any text, especially those you write about, at least twice because you will need to get a feel for how language is being used in the piece and to review specific elements of the text in order to develop your analysis.

For more on close reading, see *Rules for Writers*, pages 346–47.

When you practice **close reading**, you focus your attention on the aspects of the text that seem most important. One common way to think about the strategies you use when you read is to divide the process into three phases: before reading closely, active reading, and reviewing. To read more effectively, you should first **scan** a text to get a basic sense of the text and its purpose. Then, in the second phase of the process, you should **read more closely for content and meaning**, considering how the text is constructed. In addition, you should consider your reactions to the text. How does it affect you emotionally and intellectually? During your second reading, engage your text in a dialogue by asking questions on the page and picking out the most important points. In the third phase of the process, you should **review the text and your responses** to form some general conclusions. If you take a moment to review your reading, you will remember it more effectively; you will be better prepared to write and talk about it because you will have reduced the reading to some main ideas, rather than leaving yourself with a confusing jumble of details.

Phase One: Before Reading Closely

Before you start reading, consider some basic questions about the text. Reflecting on broad elements such as the title, subject matter, and organization will help you to understand the text faster as you're reading and will save you time in the long run. Some questions you might want to ask at this stage include:

- What assumptions do you have about the text after reading the title? What does it suggest to you?

- What do you think the subject of the text is going to be?

- Look at the opening to the article, essay, or story—just the first paragraph or even just the first few sentences. What does it suggest to you?

- What are the headings of chapters and major sections? What can you learn from these?

- Scan the conclusion of the text. What does the author consider most important for the audience to remember, and why is it important?

Examining these larger elements does not take long, but doing this will prepare you to understand the material in the body of the text. By studying the structural features before reading the main text, you'll better understand the organization and will therefore read more effectively.

Phase Two: Active Reading

Now that you have scanned the text, you're ready to begin reading it in detail. When you practice close reading, you should think of yourself as an active participant engaging the material; you want to make the text your own. Reading actively will make it easier for you to remember what you have read and will enable you to use it effectively in your writing. While you are reading, you should *always* raise questions about **what** is happening and **how** it is significant. If you're reading a short story, for instance, talk back to that story by ***annotating*** and/or writing in your journal, noting your thoughts about the narrative, the characters, and the plot. Ask yourself questions like:

- How do you feel about what is happening in the text?

- Where is the text headed? Why is it headed in that direction?

- How do certain word choices or images make you feel?

- What does the text remind you of?

- Note what you think the author's overall purpose is at different points in the text—does it seem to change at any point?

After reading, you may want to return to your notes on specific events in the text to see what in the story caused you to feel as you do.

Phase Three: Reviewing for Analysis

Once you have read a text carefully, made annotations, and taken notes, you need to think of how you will use what you read in your writing. You can often read more effectively by thinking as specifically as you can about how you are going to use the reading in your assignments. For example, if you have annotated a text that will serve as your **primary source** for **textual analysis** or **rhetorical analysis**, you will probably use the annotations to help you clarify the claim you are making about the text, to identify the passages you think are most relevant to your argument, and to define the main points that you will discuss and analyze in your essay. On the other hand, if you are reading an article as a **secondary source** to provide background on a topic you're researching, but the ideas are difficult to grasp because the article is written for scholars and uses a complicated structure and technical vocabulary, you'll probably first want to look carefully over the text and then make frequent annotations as you read to help you understand the author's main ideas.

Your annotations will help to guide your analysis in your own writing, so take the time to read your notes while considering what the author of the text wanted to convey as well as how he or she tried to convey it. This will develop a helpful overall understanding of the text regardless of whether you intend to use it as a **primary** or a **secondary** source. Sections 3.5 and 3.6 offer specific ways you can review and reorganize your annotated notes after reading and use them to form a complete analysis of a text.

> For help with annotation and determining what to look for, see section 3.2. You can also find samples of annotation in sections 3.3 and 3.4. For help with annotating for research essays, see Chapter 7.

3.2 Annotation and Close Reading

By Annie Holub

When you read more complex texts, you need to interact with the text so that you don't miss things that might be hard to see. By interacting with the text, we mean one simple thing: write on it. Annotation is the process of writing notes and comments about a text. Back in high school, you were more than likely told specifically NOT to write in your textbooks, but in college, they're yours—you paid for them—so feel free to make as much use of them as you'd like. Write in the margins. Underline things. Take notes on the pages. You can also annotate texts by having a piece of paper handy for notes if you're borrowing books or planning on selling them back in a more pristine condition—just remember to keep track of the page numbers and/or lines from the text you're annotating so you can find things again later.

What Am I Supposed to Look for or Write Down?

Here are some steps that will help you annotate any text that you're reading:

1. **Underline** words or phrases that confuse you or seem important.

2. **Circle** words you don't know or words that pop up more than once. Look up the words you don't know, and write the definition next to them.

3. Write ideas and comments in the **margin** that come to you as you read. If something in a text reminds you of something, write down what that line reminds you of and why.

4. If something surprises you or seems funny, put an **exclamation point** by it.

5. If something completely confuses you or doesn't make sense, put a **question mark** there so you know where to go back and re-read more closely.

6. What kind of feeling or tone are you getting from the text as you read? Try to **jot down a couple of words** that describe the tone. If the tone changes, mark where it happens.

7. Who is talking? What do you know about the speaker/narrator?

8. Who is the speaker/narrator talking to? What do you know about the audience?

9. What is the speaker/narrator trying to tell the audience?

10. Are there certain images that stand out, or that seem to reoccur? Keep track of these somehow (I use **stars in the margin** for this).

We may all be brilliant, but often we don't remember everything we thought of five minutes after reading a text, so it helps to have notes. And that's all annotation is, your notes about the text you're reading.

The following is an annotation of Stephen Crane's short story "The Snake."

Wended = winding?

Oppressive heat, cicadas, like a summer day in the Sonoran desert. Not a very picturesque scene?

The brook is fighting with the rocks—maybe more things will fight with each other?

Where the path wended across the ridge, the bushes of huckleberry and sweet fern swarmed at it in two curling waves until it was a mere winding line traced through a tangle. There was no interference by clouds, and as the rays of the sun fell full upon the ridge, they called into voice innumerable insects which chanted the heat of the summer day in steady, throbbing, unending chorus.

A man and a dog came from the laurel thickets of the valley where the white brook brawled with the rocks. They followed the deep line of the path across the ridges. The dog—a large lemon and white setter—walked, tranquilly meditative, at his master's heels.

Suddenly from some unknown and yet near place in advance there came a dry, shrill whistling rattle that smote motion instantly from the limbs of the man and the dog. Like the fingers of a sudden death, this sound seemed to touch the man at the nape of the neck, at the top of the spine, and change him, as swift as thought, to a statue of listening horror, surprise, rage. The dog, too—the same icy hand was laid upon him, and he stood crouched and quivering, his jaw dropping, the froth of terror upon his lips, the light of hatred in his eyes.

Slowly the man moved his hands toward the bushes, but his glance did not turn from the place made sinister by the warning rattle. His fingers, unguided, sought for a stick of weight and strength. Presently they closed about one that seemed adequate, and holding this weapon poised before him the man moved slowly forward, glaring. The dog with his nervous nostrils fairly fluttering moved warily, one foot at a time, after his master.

But when the man came upon the snake, his body underwent a shock as if from a revelation, as if after all he had been ambushed. With a blanched face, he sprang forward and his breath came in strained gasps, his chest heaving as if he were in the performance of an extraordinary muscular trial. His arm with the stick made a spasmodic, defensive gesture.

The snake had apparently been crossing the path in some mystic travel when to his sense there came the knowledge of the coming of his foes. The dull vibration perhaps informed him, and he flung his body to face the danger. He had no knowledge of paths; he had no wit to tell him to slink noiselessly into the bushes. He knew that his implacable enemies were approaching; no doubt they were seeking him, hunting him. And so he cried his cry, an incredibly swift jangle of tiny bells, as burdened with pathos as the hammering upon quaint cymbals by the Chinese at war—for, indeed, it was usually his death-music.

"Beware! Beware! Beware!"

The man and the snake confronted each other. In the man's eyes were hatred and fear. In the snake's eyes were hatred and fear. These enemies maneuvered, each preparing to kill. It was to be a battle without mercy. Neither knew of mercy for such a situation. In the man was all the wild strength of the terror of his ancestors, of his race, of his kind. A deadly repulsion had been handed from man to man through long dim centuries. This was another detail of a war that had begun evidently when first there were men and snakes. Individuals who do not participate in this strife incur the investigations of scientists. Once there was a man and a snake who were friends, and at the end, the man lay dead with the marks of the snake's caress just over his East Indian heart. In the formation of

---

Margin annotations:

- Ridge is also sort of like "rift."
- Why this specific detail about the dog?
- Tranquilly meditative = really, really calm—why both words?
- Assonance makes this sound ominous.
- Also ominous.
- Ominous.
- Even the dog is scared.
- Seems instinctual—he's in hunting mode.
- The snake's body or the man's? Could be both? Why call attention to what his body does as opposed to what his mind does?
- Snakes also muscular.
- Also instinctual—snake-like, even?
- Snake is mystical, otherworldly
- This sounds like what happens to the man in the previous paragraph—snake and man have similar instincts?
- Instinct
- Lots of emotion in the snake's rattle—why liken to Chinese at war? Makes the snake more exotic?
- Man and snake share same emotions.
- Instinctual again!
- What's with this parable? Why an East Indian? Exotic, strange—the snake caresses with his body, he has no hands, the caress = death.

3.2

What is the narrator saying about Nature here if the snake is the "supreme point"? Snakes are hellish, worse than fire...

devices, hideous and horrible, Nature reached her supreme point in the making of the snake, so that priests who really paint hell well fill it with snakes instead of fire. The curving forms, these scintillant coloring create at once, upon sight, more relentless animosities than do shake barbaric tribes. To be born a snake is to be thrust into a place a-swarm with formidable foes. To gain an appreciation of it, view hell as pictured by priests who are really skilful.

Tone Biblical, but then "really skilful" seems out of place.

Death-fingers again—see third paragraph.

As for this snake in the pathway, there was a double curve some inches back of its head, which, merely by the potency of its lines, made the man feel with tenfold eloquence the touch of the death-fingers at the nape of his neck. The reptile's head was waving slowly from side to side and its hot eyes flashed like little murder-lights. Always in the air was the dry, shrill whistling of the rattles.

Repeated again—the snake's rattle is like someone talking.

"Beware! Beware! Beware!"

Perspective seems distant— where is the narrator? Who's seeing this? Who's telling us this story?

The man made a preliminary feint with his stick. Instantly the snake's heavy head and neck were bended back on the double curve and instantly the snake's body shot forward in a low, strait, hard spring. The man jumped with a convulsive chatter and swung his stick. The blind, sweeping blow fell upon the snake's head and hurled him so that steel-colored plates were for a moment uppermost. But he rallied swiftly, agilely, and again the head and neck bended back to the double curve, and the steaming, wide-open mouth made its desperate effort to reach its enemy. This attack, it could be seen, was despairing, but it was nevertheless impetuous, gallant, ferocious, of the same quality as the charge of the lone chief when the walls of white faces close upon him in the mountains. The stick swung unerringly again, and the snake, mutilated, torn, whirled himself into the last coil.

???

Time moving very very slowly.

The lone chief loses.

Instinct makes you crazy—how can he feel the emotions of his forefathers?

And now the man went sheer raving mad from the emotions of his forefathers and from his own. He came to close quarters. He gripped the stick with his two hands and made it speed like a flail. The snake, tumbling in the anguish of final despair, fought, bit, flung itself upon this stick which was taking his life.

It's the stick doing the killing, not the man—the man is only wielding the stick.

Like the Chinese-war thing; man is superior to the snake here but the snake is also hell and worse than fire?

At the end, the man clutched his stick and stood watching in silence. The dog came slowly and with infinite caution stretched his nose forward, sniffing. The hair upon his neck and back moved and ruffled as if a sharp wind was blowing, the last muscular quivers of the snake were causing the rattles to still sound their treble cry, the shrill, ringing war chant and hymn of the grave of the thing that faces foes at once countless, implacable, and superior.

Rover? C'mon!

"Mr. Snake" = condescending. Something cute to show the girls.

"Well, Rover," said the man, turning to the dog with a grin of victory, "we'll carry Mr. Snake home to show the girls."

Why didn't the dog do anything? Just a battle between man and snake?

His hands still trembled from the strain of the encounter, but he pried with his stick under the body of the snake and hoisted the limp thing upon it. He resumed his march along the path, and the dog walked tranquilly meditative, at his master's heels.

3.2

After annotating this story, already I can see some patterns. I can identify the tone and perhaps begin to make an argument about what this story is about on a deeper level. Based on the annotations above, I know I need to explore themes and ideas like the struggle between man and nature and what the snake represents about nature. There's definitely something here about instinct as well.

Try it for yourself:

- Read and annotate a story of your choice from *Writing as Revision*—try something short but challenging, like Kate Chopin's "Story of An Hour," or Karen Brennan's "Floating."

- Read and annotate whatever your instructor assigned you to read for the next class.

- Read and annotate something you were assigned to read for another course.

Why Annotate?

Once you've read through something for the first time and marked up the text with your notes, then you can go back and try to find **patterns** and think more about things that confused you. Student Brittney Martinez makes a good point about the time-saving benefits of annotation:

> ❝My suggestion for the Text-in-Context essay for future English 101 students is to read the primary text, which was a novel for my class, very carefully and put annotations in the margins of the book, so you won't have to read the whole novel over again to find a specific quote. ❞

Instead of reading the whole book or story again, you just need to reread the parts you already pulled out and your notes about those parts. Annotation makes thinking deeply about the text you're reading much easier: Maybe you realize that you circled a certain word more than once—why? Maybe something that confused you at the beginning makes more sense now that you've read the whole thing. Maybe you noticed certain kinds of images popping up more than once, or a certain feel to the text. Maybe you noticed that the audience doesn't really seem to be listening to the speaker. Start asking yourself why these things you noticed might be happening. What effect do these things have on you as a reader?

Annotating a text is the first, and in many ways, most important step toward analyzing that text. If you are actively reading and processing the text as you go, writing down ideas as they pop up and marking things to go back to and ponder, you are already starting to take apart the text to see how it works, which is the basic definition of analysis. The things you underline or highlight may very well end up being the things you cite and quote in your textual analysis essay. The things that confused you may lead you to the meaning and significance of the text, which in turn may lead you to your argument about the text. Mortimer Adler wrote in his essay, "How to Mark a Book" that "mark-

For more advice on reading arguments closely, see *Rules for Writers*, pages 371–79.

3.2

ing up a book is not an act of mutilation but of love. You shouldn't mark up a book which isn't yours." And you make a book you already own more yours by **annotating** it—you haven't made that book a part of your educational experience until you've thoroughly interacted with it through annotation. It might as well just continue sitting on the shelf, its spine uncracked. And what's the point of spending time reading something if you can't incorporate it in some way into your own educational life and work?

3.3 Reading Like a Detective: Force and Form in Poetry

By Tom Nurmi

Imagine: your high school English teacher gives you a difficult and archaic poem. You understand a few lines. The next day, he rattles off the "deeper meaning" as if he has the magical answer key. You write it down. You spit it back on the test, learning nothing. You hate poetry.

If this sounds familiar, you're not alone. And yet poetry, along with visual art, is among the oldest forms of human expression and storytelling. If it is so entwined with human experience, then understanding human history requires understanding something about poetic language and metaphor. How can we approach poetry in a more relevant and productive way?

The first problem is that poems are often taught (and written) but rarely really *read*. In this section, we're going to ask a certain set of questions about a poem based on how it forces you to read it. The idea of **force** is important to poetry. Poetry tries to say familiar things in new ways by forcing language out of its usual patterns and into strange new designs. Our questions will allow you to draw specific conclusions about these designs, making writing about them easier.

A major theme of this book is the idea that all texts are in context, situated between writers and readers who shape their production and reception in a fluid, reciprocal relationship. Poetry is no different. It is both a bunch of words on a page and **an event**. It requires a reader at a specific moment in time and space, in a particular cultural context. So what makes poetry, poetry? Is poetry different from prose? If so, why does that matter?

There are many different ways of answering these questions—and you should think beyond what is given in this chapter—but any answer you give wrestles with the issue of **form**, a concept closely related to **genre**. Poetry is difficult to read because it is patterned in specific ways that force you to read it on its own terms. In this way, poetry fundamentally differs from a newspaper article or a novel. For example, poetic patterns might include rhythm, rhyme, meter, repeated words, repeated images, line breaks, stanza breaks, spatial organization on the page, etc. This patterning is the form of the poem. Sometimes the form of a thought matters more than the expression itself. For example, we can say, "Standing up for your beliefs is courageous." But this statement doesn't strike us as particularly profound. However, when we read e.e. cummings' poem "i sing of Olaf glad and big" (1931), we have a different, more forceful experience of that statement. When we read a poem, we are more aware of how language is charged with emotion, texture, and violence.

Think about how genre works in film. You watch a horror movie with certain expectations about how the film will play out (don't get naked in the lake alone!). You generally know the story arc of a Kate Hudson romantic comedy. Hate turns to love; Matthew McConaughey takes his shirt off. In both cases, you have generic assumptions that shape your viewing of the film. When those assumptions are challenged, and things don't go according to "form," you're surprised and more interested. The exact same idea is at work in poetry. In order to see it, we need a set of questions to ask the poem as we read.

We ask these questions the same way a detective asks questions about a crime scene. Detectives are excellent close-readers, and shows like *CSI* are popular because they magnify reading skills to ridiculous degrees. Detectives have sharp powers of induction. They read a scene for specific details (axe in the wall, wallet on the counter) that can help them create a larger narrative about what happened. So let's read a poem with a few questions in mind, detective style:

1. What are the patterns, and what doesn't make sense or seem to fit?

2. What techniques were used to make the patterns?

3. What is the context?

4. What conclusions can we draw based on the evidence?

5. What is our argument?

i sing of Olaf glad and big

—*e.e. cummings (1931)*

i sing of Olaf glad and big
whose warmest heart recoiled at war:
a conscientious object-or

his wellbelovéd colonel(trig
westpointer most succinctly bred)
took erring Olaf soon in hand;
but—though an host of overjoyed
noncoms(first knocking on the head
him)do through icy waters roll
that helplessness which others stroke
with brushes recently employed
anent this muddy toiletbowl,

while kindred intellects evoke
allegiance per blunt instruments—
Olaf(being to all intents
a corpse and wanting any rag
upon what God unto him gave)
responds,without getting annoyed
"I will not kiss your fucking flag"

straightway the silver bird looked grave
(departing hurriedly to shave)

but—though all kinds of officers
(a yearning nation's blueeyed pride)
their passive prey did kick and curse
until for wear their clarion
voices and boots were much the worse,
and egged the firstclassprivates on
his rectum wickedly to tease
by means of skillfully applied
bayonets roasted hot with heat—
Olaf(upon what were once knees)
does almost ceaselessly repeat
"there is some shit I will not eat"

our president,being of which
assertions duly notified
threw the yellowsonofabitch
into a dungeon,where he died

Christ(of His mercy infinite)
i pray to see;and Olaf,too

preponderatingly because
unless statistics lie he was
more brave than me:more blond than you.

As you can see, certain spots are already highlighted. These are the kinds of annotations that make reading poems easier. They mark your reading experience. When you return to the poem, you already have a map to guide your analysis. And remember that these are just one set of annotations. Your own close reading might be very different but valid nonetheless. The key is using specific details to work inductively. Now let's try to answer the questions.

1. *What are the patterns? What do you notice as you read? What doesn't make sense or seem to fit?*

Examples:

• Inconsistent use of capital letters	["i" vs. "Olaf," line 1]
• Words run together	["responds,without," line 19]
• Words separated	["object-or," line 3]
• Use of parentheses	["(a yearning nation's blueeyed pride)," line 23]
• No periods	[except the final line, 42]
• Repetition of religious imagery	["God," line 17, and "Christ," line 38]
• References to nationalism	[lines 19, 23]
• Quotations using profanity	[lines 19, 33]
• Violent actions	[lines 8, 24, 28–30]

2. *What techniques were used to make the patterns?*

Examples:

• Line breaks	["head / him," lines 8–9]
• Stanza breaks	["…your fucking flag / straightaway…" lines 19–20]
• Internal rhyme	["war" and "or," lines 2–3]
• Ambiguous or double-meaning	["object-or," line 3]
• Speaker addresses "you"	[line 42]

3. *What is the context? Who is speaking in the poem? To whom? What ideas are being communicated? What is the author's context? What is your context as a reader?*

Examples:

- Speaker "sing[s]" (line 1) to the addressee, "you" (line 42).

- Speaker both celebrates Olaf's commitment to his beliefs and dramatizes the violence done to him by referring to him as an "objector" to war who is thus treated as an "object" by others (line 3).

- After he was drafted into the Army in 1918, Cummings went to Camp Devens, Massachusetts for training. His poems written after World War I often celebrate nonconformist characters and attack depersonalized mass culture.

- Olaf's stance on war and subsequent treatment resonates with today's geopolitical climate in a number of interesting ways.

4. *What conclusions can we draw based on the evidence? What is the effect of patterns in the poem? Why are they used? What larger claim is the speaker making?*

Examples:

- Cummings uses broken syntax, discontinuous rhythm, and unusual spacing to force the reader into an emotional state similar to Olaf's. For Cummings, modern life is in continuous flux. The poem's beginnings, endings, and fragments reflect that view. Only Olaf has a proper name; he stands out.

- The speaker ends the poem with the statement, "he was / more brave than me:more blond than you" (line 43), implicating the contemporary reader in Olaf's fate.

5. *What is our argument? What are we trying to say about the poem? What details are we using?*

Example:

- The poem's speaker ironically "sings" in an older elegiac form to celebrate Olaf's modern resistance to accepted norms like nationalism, mythic narratives of war, and masculine heroism that are embodied in specific visual stereotypes such as "a yearning nation's blueeyed pride" (line 23).

Notice how we answer the questions, moving from details in Questions 1 and 2 to longer sentences in Questions 3 and 4 to a single sentence in Question 5. We've worked inductively like a detective to create a narrative that draws on specific patterns noted earlier. The final step is constructing an argument, a process that will be described in detail in later chapters. But whatever you argue, remember that attention to patterning—how the poem forces you to read it—is the key aspect for any interpretation you make.

3.4 Annotation for Context

Whenever you consider the time period in which a text was written or the relationship of the author to the text, you are thinking about the text in a certain context. There are several possible contexts for any text, and when you close read and annotate a text you might be thinking about these contexts. In this section you will see a reader's annotations of *The Declaration of Sentiments*, primarily written by Lucretia Mott and Elizabeth Cady Stanton. Mott and Stanton met for the first time in 1840 at the World Anti-Slavery Convention in London, England. It was at this convention that they determined the need for a convention on the rights of women. In July 1848, the Seneca Falls Convention met in Seneca Falls, New York. This document was debated and refined at this convention and then released to the public. It draws heavily on the language and form of the United States *Declaration of Independence*. Therefore, you might read the *Declaration of Sentiments* from two different contexts: its historical context in relation to the Declaration of Independence or its current context in relation to the present day.

When you annotate a text, you can make comments that will help you identify the outside factors that influence the way you read it. Sometimes your annotations help you to realize that you have been reading the text in a certain context. You may not have realized this until you started commenting on these aspects of the text. While reading the annotated excerpt, try to identify some of the outside factors that seem to be a part of this reader's or listener's experience of the speech. Is this reader thinking about history? Religion? Current cultural factors? The genre of a signed document? The political atmosphere in the 1840s? What other outside factors affect your own reading of this text?

For more on context see Chapter 9.

The Declaration of Sentiments

Created by Lucretia Mott and Elizabeth Cady Stanton

Signed by 100 men and women at the Seneca Falls Convention, July 19–20, 1848

> When, in the course of human events, it becomes necessary for one portion of the family of man to assume among the people of the earth a position different from that which they have hitherto occupied, but one to which the laws of nature and of nature's God entitle them, a decent respect to the opinions of mankind requires that they should declare the causes that impel them to such a course.

> We hold these truths to be self-evident: that all men and women are created equal; that they are endowed by their Creator with certain inalienable rights; that among these are life, liberty, and the pursuit of happiness; that to secure these rights governments are instituted, deriving their just powers from the consent of the governed. Whenever any form of government becomes destructive of these ends, it is the right of those who suffer from it to refuse allegiance to it, and to insist upon the institution of a new government, laying its foundation on such principles, and organizing its powers in such form, as to them shall seem most likely to effect their safety and happiness.

> Prudence, indeed, will dictate that governments long established should not be changed for light and transient causes; and accordingly all experience hath shown that mankind are more disposed to suffer, while evils are sufferable, than to right themselves by abolishing the forms to which they are accustomed. But when a long train of abuses and usurpations, pursuing invariably the same object, evinces a design to reduce them under absolute despotism, it is their duty to throw off such government, and to provide new guards for their future security. Such has been the patient sufferance of the women under this government, and such is now the necessity which constrains them to demand the equal station to which they are entitled.

Margin annotations:

What is the importance of adding "sentiments" to the title? What did this word mean in 1848?

Begins just like the *Declaration of Independence*, makes you think about the founding of a new kind of nation.

What do they mean by this phrase? The *Declaration of Independence* spoke for all humans as one family, but this purposefully separates humans into different portions.

Mott and Stanton retain the religious tone of the original document.

I think what they're saying here is that this document explains the reasons they're calling for a change, just like the *Declaration of Independence*. Who is the tyrant being rebelled against in this document?

Another deletion: "among men". The implies that women ought to be as welcome in government as men are. Women can create declarations and make policies as well as men can. Is this Declaration a testament to that?

Basically, they're saying that it's easier to let bad conditions continue as long as they're bearable. What bad but bearable conditions do we have in today's world that might be worthy of a Declaration?

This addition is emphasized by beginning the sentence in a familiar way.

"Suffer"—appealing to the reader's sense of guilt? Women the reader cares for are suffering.

Patient suffering. This shifts the emotional appeal from guilt to pity or empathy.

"Constrains" also evokes pity—they are forced to make a stand. Does this make women seem weak or strong?

They're calling for a change because they feel morally obligated to do so, not just because they want to. What other evidence does their language show that they feel a moral imperative to make this call for a change?

3.4

Repetition emphasizes that these are similar injuries. If we do not blame the founding fathers for their actions, can we blame these women?

The authors claim that man has a specific goal in mind: to establish an "absolute tyranny" over her. How is this claim effective and how is it not? What other tyrannies could they be silently alluding to? Is this less or more personal than the *Declaration of Independence*, which addresses the King of England as the tyrant?

The right to vote emphasizes a woman's position in government decisions.

Also the right to vote. How is this different from the above complaint? Does it strike a different tone?

The history of mankind is a history of repeated injuries and usurpations on the part of man toward woman, having in direct object the establishment of an absolute tyranny over her. To prove this, let facts be submitted to a candid world.

- He has never permitted her to exercise her inalienable right to the elective franchise.

- He has compelled her to submit to laws, in the formation of which she had no voice....

"He" must stand for all men here, or maybe just for men in government.

Initial Observations

Already, clear themes begin to emerge from the text. Notice that Mott and Stanton use the text of the *Declaration of Independence* as a base while changing strategic words. Why do you think they did this? They also emphasize the *suffering* of women several times and focus on the role of women in government decisions. What is their purpose?

Noticing themes or trends can be starting points toward making claims about a text. Here, Mott and Stanton's central task is to announce their ambitions and make clear their discontent (in order to hopefully encourage a change in policy). What specifically are they unhappy with? We know that Mott and Stanton were trying to encourage both women *and men* of their time to acknowledge these injustices, but some men would likely have dismissed their words. What methods were employed to capture the attention of this type of audience? Look back at the text and consider the ways that the language draws on women's suffering, safety, and happiness. This should help in developing your interpretation.

Once a clear picture begins to form about the purpose of a text, it may be useful to go back and reread the text to test and reaffirm the observations you've made and find additional strategies the author used to convey his/her purpose.

3.5 Moving from Notes to Prewriting

There are many different ways you can turn your notes and initial observations into an overall interpretation of a text. These are some options your instructor may ask you to try in the process of preparing to write.

Make an Inventory of Textual Strategies

See section 8.1 for specific strategies used in textual analysis. See Chapter 10 for examples of rhetorical strategies.

After annotating your text, consider taking an inventory. The annotation process involves putting down your thoughts as you read. When you take inventory you actually begin to sift through that information. Make a list of items that seem especially important to what the text is doing overall and group them into categories. In an inventory of your reading, you look for **patterns** in your responses to see what they add up to, and you review the text itself to strengthen your overall impression. More specifically, you may:

- Scrutinize the text for patterns and repetitions of words, images, phrases, argument structure, examples, and writing **strategies**.

- Decide how these patterns affect the **message** conveyed by the text. Remember that there are multiple possible messages. Make sure that the strategies you are focusing on all seem to directly relate to the message you want to discuss.

- Consider how these patterns are similar to or different from those you have noticed in other texts on the same topic, and thus how the text you are examining is **unique** or worth discussing.

In Stephen Crane's story, for example, you might notice that he begins by describing the landscape and the day, alludes to the Bible, repeats terms such as *instinct* and *war*, and uses assonance. You might also look at repetition, types of images, or word choices in order to help you define an argument or claim about your reading of the text. In the *Declaration of Sentiments*, you might think about the allusions to other civil rights endeavors or the appeals to various emotions in the audience. These are all examples of writing **strategies** that contribute to an author's process of communicating a **message**. By noticing these details and categorizing them, you can see which details were important to the author/speaker and make decisions about your own writing on the topic.

Section Summaries

Summaries can help you map the development of a text you read so you can see where it's going and how it gets there. For example, if you're writing an analysis of a journal article and your entire paper depends on your understanding of it, you'll want to create thorough summaries of each section or paragraph that highlight the author's main points, and the ways in which those points are supported and analyzed. This would also be important when reading a short story or novel because understanding narrative structure is a crucial step to writing about literature.

A **section summary** can be as simple as a short description of each paragraph. The main advantage of section summaries is that they are quick to construct, especially if you've already annotated the text. When creating a section summary, you should accurately describe the main ideas in a portion of the text. Focus on larger themes rather than specific textual strategies and try to paraphrase the author in your own words. Practice on the next page by creating section summaries of the first three paragraphs of the *Declaration of Sentiments*.

3.5

Section Summary Practice: *Declaration of Sentiments*
Paragraph 1:
Paragraph 2:
Paragraph 3 :

Remember that a section summary should focus on the key idea of each paragraph or section, providing you with a quick reference to the different parts of the arguments in the text.

Idea Mapping

While summary outlines work well for many students, some writers prefer a more visual approach, such as mapping out the ideas of a text. Idea mapping, also called **webbing** or **clustering**, visually represents how the ideas in a text are related to both the main point(s) and each other. While the summaries emphasize linear structure, an idea map emphasizes the interconnectedness of ideas.

For more information on summarizing, see Chapter 7 and *Rules for Writers*, pages 417–18 and 424.

3.5

Mapping would work better than section summaries for texts that are less linear. As demonstrated by the partial map of Crane's story that follows, an idea map can reveal different information than an outline. Notice that the map shows how different parts of the story relate to each other—something you can't see in the summaries.

Idea Map of Stephen Crane's "The Snake"

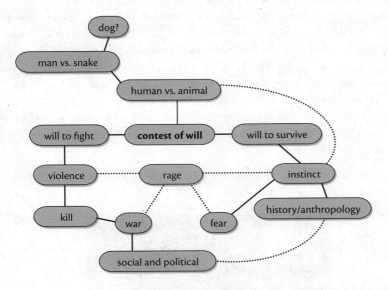

You can use the web or cluster as the starting point in creating a linear outline or journal. This can be done by following various paths represented in the map. Based on the diagram above, for example, you could create an outline or a prose-format inventory by filling in the connections between the circled ideas. The words that are highlighted in the paragraph below are the same words that are circled in the cluster above, showing one way you might incorporate these ideas into a more linear prose format:

"The Snake" is about a **contest of will**. The story examines the **will to fight** and the **will to survive**. The story shows how the contest of will is motivated or complicated by **instinct** and emotions like **rage** and **fear**, and how this contest of will is tied to human history. It also has more **social** or **political** connections like **war**. There is clearly a contest between **humans and animals** in the story, but where does the **dog** fit in? Rover seems more aligned with the **man** than the **snake**. What does this say about **history** and evolution? Everything is brought together in an act of **violence**, when the man kills the snake.

Visual mapping can help you articulate what you see a text doing, saying, and interrogating overall. When drafting a textual analysis essay, you would want to explore in more detail the "how" and "why" claims and questions articulated in such an inventory, using and discussing specific examples from the text to make your own statements about how the text works.

For more tips on close reading and organizing your ideas, see *Rules for Writers*, pages 11–16.

See Chapter 8 for more on writing a textual analysis essay.

3.5

3.6 Taking Analytical Notes

By Carie Schneider

The Observations/Inferences Chart

When taking notes on texts, I like to organize my thoughts into charts. The **Observations/Inferences** chart is one of the simplest, and can help me create a draft **thesis** for a **textual analysis**. First, I look at the text (either reading through it or, for a visual text, looking at it closely) and take note of **techniques** or **features** that I immediately notice. These should be actual observations that are physically present in the text, which no reasonable person would disagree with—things like "he uses repetition," "lots of metaphors," "there are two chairs in the picture" etc. Then I'll go back through my observations, and try to figure out what each of these features could **mean**, **signify**, **symbolize**, or **represent**. These can be whatever comes to mind; they don't have to be provable, they're just whatever I *infer* from the features I noticed. I'll list these under the "Inferences" column.

Here's an example Observations/Inferences chart for a visual analysis of a photograph, *No Swimming* by T.C. Reed:

Photo courtesy of T.C. Reed

Observations	Inferences
Color = greenish tint, sort of yellow-green	It's a sickly color, reminds me of disease, something is wrong
Looks like abandoned swimming pool, no water	It used to be nice but now it's trashy, abandoned. Lack of water = lifeless?
Two chairs	People used to be sitting there, maybe very recently? But they left.
Open door by the chairs, light comes in	Maybe the people who were in the chairs left through the door. Light shining through door seems welcoming, beckoning to better place?
Magazine on one of the chairs	Person in chair was reading magazine before leaving—maybe something they read in the magazine made them want to leave?
Trash on the ground	Trash shows people used to be here. Also that nobody cares about this place anymore.
Edge of pool says "SHALLOW!" with exclamation mark	It's probably just a warning not to dive in the pool, but maybe it could mean that society is shallow? The exclamation mark is like a warning, emphasis.

In order to write a **thesis** about the photograph as a whole, I'll need to organize my thoughts even further, grouping the techniques or features ("observations") into categories, and trying to decide what I think the overall message or meaning of the photograph is.

Looking back at my chart, it seems that some of the main categories of features could be "color," "composition" or "placement of objects," "lighting," and maybe "symbolism" or "objects used as symbols." These categories are going to be my body paragraph topics—I can change them around as I write and revise my drafts, but for my first outline and draft, I think I'll stick with these.

Now I have to figure out what I think the image means; I need to interpret the overall **message** for my reader. The image could be telling a sort of "story"— maybe there were people there once who may have left. I think maybe the photograph could symbolize or represent how people are leaving urban areas in

3.6

America. Maybe it's saying something about the decline of our cities, how buildings are being abandoned and people are leaving for the suburbs and gated communities. That might seem like an "out-there" interpretation, but as long as I can back it up with observations of the photograph, the claim is totally plausible.

Another Kind of Note Taking: "Three Columns"

The "**Three Columns**" chart is similar to the "**Observations/Inferences**" chart, but it incorporates my own reactions to the text, which makes it useful for reader-response assignments. It also doesn't necessarily associate meanings with individual elements, like the "Observations / Inferences" chart does. In the "Three Columns" chart, I begin with my reactions and responses to the text, listing any emotions or feelings it brings up. Then I go through it again and catalog the techniques or features used in the text (this is just like the "observations" column). The last step is to brainstorm some possible meanings or messages of the text—either as a whole, or just the meanings of individual parts. Here's an example of the "Three Columns" chart, based on the same photograph:

Reactions/Responses/ Emotions	Techniques/Features/ Elements ("observations")	Meaning/Messages/ Interpretations
creepy	Empty swimming pool	Abandonment?
Dirty and icky	Trash all around	How people don't care about their world, pollution?
The color is really weird	Greenish color	So much of our city is empty or abandoned—the economy is bad
mysterious	Abandoned—no people	Maybe about people leaving cities for suburbia? Wanting better life?
	Chairs, one w/ a magazine	
	Open door with light coming through	
	Word "shallow" on ground	

3.6

These two kinds of charts help to focus your note taking so that you can begin to form supportable thesis statements. They practice determining **messages** that texts convey as well as discovering the **strategies** authors use to communicate with their audiences. For one way to turn these notes into thesis statements, see the thesis statement craft boxes in Chapters 8 and 9.

Works Cited

Adler, Mortimer. "How to Mark a Book." *Center for Applied Philosophy: The Radical Academy*. Center for Applied Philosophy, n.d. Web. 2 May 2006.

Crane, Stephen. "The Snake." *The Literature Network*. Jalic, n.d. Web. 16 Mar. 2008.

Mott, Lucretia and Elizabeth Cady Stanton. "The Declaration of Sentiments." *U.S. Constitution Online*. Steve Mount, 1995. Web. 2 Feb. 2011.

Reed, T.C. *No Swimming*. n.d. Photograph.

3.6

Writing as a Process **4**

4.1   Writing as a Process: An Overview

4.2   Discovering Your Writing Process

4.3   Understanding the Rhetorical Situation

4.4   Invention Strategies

4.5   Drafting

4.6   Revising

4.1 Writing as a Process: An Overview

Writing can be a wonderfully (and sometimes painfully) messy process. Sometimes you feel in control and know what you want to say and how to put it down on paper. Other times you might feel as if your essay has somehow gotten away from you and you don't know how to get it back. More often than not, the writing process is a combination of both of these feelings.

It can be overwhelming to try and think about everything from developing ideas to spelling words correctly at the same time. But breaking down the writing process into stages can help you to avoid feeling overwhelmed. In this chapter, you will:

- Discover what type of writer you are.

- Encounter some strategies to discover what to write about.

- Find ways to assess the rhetorical situation before you write.

- Learn how to focus your ideas by creating an outline.

- Learn about the drafting process, including strategies for writing introductions, thesis statements, and paragraphs.

- Discover the basics of the revision process (which will be covered in more detail in Chapter 5).

If you approach writing as a process, you can hone your writing skills in a more focused way and improve the effectiveness of what you write. If you spend some time familiarizing yourself with the writing process, you will be better able to improve your writing and leave your composition courses feeling more confident in your ability to compose different types of documents, such as analysis papers, lab reports, timed exams for history class, or letters to potential employers.

This chapter guides you through the process of composing an essay, showing you different ways to approach assignments. Keep in mind that everyone writes differently; some people quickly write a whole first draft and then begin revising, while others revise after writing each sentence or phrase. It could be that some strategies are more effective than others. You have to discover what works best for you, which will become the basis for your own writing process.

For more information about the writing process, see *Rules for Writers*, pages 1–39.

4.2 Discovering Your Writing Process

Different writers often have distinct writing habits that dictate how they write. Lisa Ede, an English professor, has identified four basic types of writers:

- **Heavy Planners.** These writers "generally consider their ideas and plan their writing so carefully in their heads that their first drafts are often more like other writers' second or third drafts. As a consequence they often revise less intensively and frequently than other [writers]. Many [heavy planners] have disciplined themselves so that they can think about their writing in all sorts of places—on the subway, at work, in the garden pulling weeds, or in the car driving to and from school" (32).

- **Heavy Revisers.** These writers "need to find out what they want to say through the act of writing itself. [. . .] Heavy revisers often state that writing their ideas out in a sustained spurt of activity reassures them that they have something to say and helps them avoid frustration. These writers may not seem to plan because they begin drafting so early. Actually, however, their planning occurs as they draft and especially as they revise. Heavy revisers typically spend a great deal of their writing time revising their initial drafts. To do so effectively, they must be able to read their work critically and be able [. . .] to discard substantial portions of the first draft" (32–33).

- **Sequential Composers.** These writers "devote roughly equal amounts of time to planning, drafting, and revising. [. . .] [S]equential composers typically rely on written notes and plans to give shape and force to their ideas. And unlike heavy revisers, sequential composers need to have greater control over form and subject matter as they draft" (33). These writers often slowly squeeze out paragraph after paragraph, rereading and revising as they draft, working from outlines, planning ahead.

- **Procrastinators.** Although we all occasionally procrastinate, the group Ede labels as "procrastinators" are people who habitually delay writing anything until they can only write a final draft. They might wait until the night before the paper is due to begin; therefore, they only have time to scribble out one draft and maybe, if they are lucky, to proofread it before handing it in (36). Procrastinators may justify their process by claiming that they work well under a deadline, but they have rarely explored alternative approaches. If you are a procrastinator, you might be surprised at how much your writing improves through multiple drafts.

Do any of these sound familiar? You might find that you exhibit a combination of the above approaches or even undergo a different process depending on whether you're writing an essay for a history class or a summary of a lab experiment. Ask yourself the following questions:

- What type(s) of writer do you consider yourself to be?

- Does your writing process include several of the above approaches? If so, which ones?

- Does your writing process seem to be successful? What are your strengths and weaknesses?

- Do you think it might be beneficial for you to try a different approach? Why or why not?

The important thing here is not to pinpoint exactly what kind of writer you are but to recognize your general tendencies and consider the advantages and disadvantages of your approach. For example, if you know you're mostly a heavy planner or a heavy reviser, you can look more carefully at the specific writing strategies suggested in those areas to expand your ways of planning or revising. In addition, you can deliberately work to develop new writing strategies. That way, if your usual method ever fails you, you'll have another option for how to proceed.

Regardless of what type or types of writer you consider yourself to be, you should note that writers go through various stages as they move through the writing process: **inventing**, **focusing**, **drafting**, and **revising**. Writing would be much easier if the writing process were a simple matter of moving through these stages in a step-by-step way. However, writing is sometimes more messy and less orderly. The writing process is **recursive**, meaning we move forward by looking backward at what we have already written to re-evaluate what we have said, make changes, and often think of new ideas as we look back at what we wrote. Thus, not all your ideas will come to you in the invention stage. Even experienced writers do not arrive at all their ideas before they write. Writers often read or write to brainstorm, then they read some more, talk to other people, begin drafting, decide to refocus the essay, read some more, freewrite, write a new thesis statement, throw out huge sections of a paper and import new material, revise the new draft heavily, and finally proofread and edit.

If you accept that the writing process is often messy and unclear, you may be more open to new ideas as you write and revise. Also, continue to keep in mind that writing is a multifaceted process that doesn't just magically happen when you sit down in front of your computer. It can start when you're walking across campus or shopping in the UA Bookstore. You might see something outside or engage in a conversation with an acquaintance that leads to an idea for your writing. You go home and write this down, but then later, as you're riding the CatTran or walking down 4th Avenue, you rethink what you wrote and decide to revise it again. Writing is a layered process and, as mentioned before, can be messy. Just don't get overwhelmed at the mess—relish it and continue to play with and revise your ideas as they come. Above all, don't think your ideas have to be perfectly worked out during the drafting stages. Writers who make the mistake of expecting a "perfect" draft often have trouble writing down any of their thoughts and may end up forgetting many early insights that could have proven valuable.

4.3 Understanding the Rhetorical Situation

One of the first steps in the writing process is learning how to carefully evaluate your **rhetorical situation**, which includes the **purpose**, **audience**, and **context** for which you are writing. This is something you should do every time you write. The rhetorical situation will affect the language, evidence, and tone that you develop, increasing the effectiveness of your writing because you can tailor it to each particular situation.

Considering your rhetorical situation means that you ask yourself these questions:

- What topic do I want to share with my readers?

- Who will be my readers and why?

- What do they already know or believe about the topic?

- What do I want them to understand about the topic?

- How am I going to organize and develop my ideas to make them convincing to these readers?

For more information on considering your audience, refer to Chapter 12.

As you move through the writing process, you will often make differing choices based on your audience, your purpose, and the context. After you leave your writing class, you will be writing for varied purposes and audiences. To help you transfer what you learn in your writing classes to these writing situations, you should consider how different rhetorical situations affect how and what you write. Reflecting on how your assumptions differ from your readers' can also help you better understand your own views and assumptions, analyze and critique others' views, and learn to communicate with others—no matter what you end up doing when you're out of school. Improving these skills will help you handle various academic tasks in your undergraduate studies and write more confidently and effectively in your future career or work in the community.

For more ideas on how to assess your writing/rhetorical situation, see *Rules for Writers*, pages 2–11 and Chapter 10.

Defining Your Purpose for Writing

Discovering your purpose for writing is essential because it largely determines other decisions you make in your writing process: what to include, how to include it, and what not to include. For example, for a persuasive essay, you might choose to argue that medical doctors should become more open-minded about treating the common cold using alternative medicines, like herbs (Echinacea), vitamins (Vitamin C), and minerals (Zinc lozenges). If you decide your purpose is to influence Western doctors, you might write your essay as an editorial to doctors in *The New England Journal of Medicine*, structuring your argument in a way that a medical audience would find most convincing and using scientific studies and medical language. On the other hand, your purpose may be to refute an opinion cited in a *New York Times* article that criticized the "guru" of alternative medicine, Dr. Andrew Weil, and his treatments of the common cold. In this case, you might choose other persuasive strategies to make your point, perhaps telling a personal story of how Weil's treatments helped you. Each of these purposes dictates that you emphasize different aspects of the issue—each suggests a particular focus, audience, language, tone, and organization.

For more ideas about how to define your purposes for writing, see *Rules for Writers*, pages 6–8.

Identifying Your Audience

Audience plays complex roles in the writing process. You might think that writing for your first-year composition class is a simple matter of telling your instructor what you think she or he wants to hear. However, you will discover that even in essays you write for specific college classes, your audience is usually more complex than just catering to your instructor. Often, your instructor will tell you a specific audience he or she wants you to consider, or your instructor may ask you to identify your audience. You may find that writing effectively requires you to begin by writing with yourself as the only audience so that you can establish a personal stake in what you are writing. In writing classes, you will be collaborating with others on your writing, and you should find that these discussions of drafts give you a much more concrete sense of writing for real readers. Student Julie Espy's thoughts below reveal how her awareness of multiple audiences has changed since high school:

> Over the past year, I've stopped just writing what I think my teacher wants to see in my paper like I usually did in high school. I concentrate more on what I really want to say, how I want to say it, and doing it in a way that gets my point across. Keeping an open mind, and coming up with new ideas has allowed me to write some great papers. Having lots of other people read your paper is one of the best things you can do. It gives you different perspectives on your work, many of which you may not have thought of. You can incorporate other people's strengths to make your paper better, and strengthen your own writing skills in the process. This also allows you to see how your paper really does affect the audience you are presenting it to, not just how you think it will affect them.

For more ideas on how to think about audience, see *Rules for Writers*, pages 8–10 and 360–61.

Look at how the following sentence would be altered based on your assessment of the audience:

For an American audience: Canadian Prime Minister Stephen Harper met with Mexican President Felipe Calderón last week.

For a Canadian audience: Stephen Harper met with Mexican President Felipe Calderón last week.

For a Mexican audience: Canadian Prime Minister Stephen Harper met with Felipe Calderón last week.

For more on analyzing your audience, see the craft box on page 242.

When you write, it is critical to try to know your readers and to be aware of their assumptions and expectations. Try to see your readers (your audience) by asking yourself questions like these:

- What are their beliefs and assumptions?

- What kind of language is appropriate for them?

- What are their sociopolitical and economic backgrounds?

- What position might they take on the issue you're addressing?

- What will they want to know from you?

- In general, how can you best persuade them?

Imagining your reader's response can actually help you through the writing process. For example, when you come to what seems like a dead end and you feel blocked, you may want to stop writing and take a minute to imagine that you were talking to your readers. What would you tell them? What would they find most interesting or unclear in your topic, and how would you make the topic clearer or more interesting?

Understanding the Context

Imagine you want to ask your supervisor at work for extra hours to help pay for college. Now put yourself in the following two contexts:

- You've never been late to work, and you were recently selected as employee of the month.

- You've shown up to work late for your last three shifts (for various reasons), and you missed a shift last week because you "forgot" you had to work.

In both cases, you'd have to be able to explain clearly why you deserve a raise, beyond simply saying "I want more money." In both cases, you'd consider the history of your relationship with your supervisor. However, because the two contexts are very different, the same audience (your supervisor) basically becomes two different people in the different situations (a pleased supervisor vs. an extremely irritated supervisor). The way you'd approach it would be based on your assessment of the rhetorical situation.

When writing for class, you should also consider the context and how it will shape and guide your writing. Let's say you've chosen to analyze Jonathan Swift's "A Modest Proposal." In the class discussion of the essay, you got the sense that your classmates generally found the humor and sarcasm to be entertaining. This is the context you have, and it will help you to determine how receptive your audience would be to certain statements you make. Compare the following two sentences:

- "The humor and sarcasm are not only entertaining for the reader, but also crucial to the persuasiveness of Swift's essay."

- "Although the humor and sarcasm in Swift's essay are entertaining, such tactics may undermine the significance of the overall argument being made."

Two different arguments are being made, but both are being shaped by the same context—in this case, the awareness that most readers generally appreciate the humor and sarcasm in Swift's essay.

4.4 Invention Strategies

The process of writing begins even before writing starts. Perhaps you have heard the term "**prewriting**." This is the stage that generally involves thinking about your writing situation, exploring possible topics to write about, choosing a topic, generating ideas about the topic, researching the topic, and outlining the essay. Depending on the type of essay you are assigned to write, or depending on the kind of writer you are, one or more of these steps might not be part of your prewriting process. For example, if your instructor gives you a topic to write about, you don't need to choose the topic, or if you're writing a personal, reflective essay, you probably won't need to do research. Invention can happen anywhere—not just when you're at your desk and in the mindset to write. A lot of this might go on in your head, so pay attention to your ongoing thoughts about your topic so that you can remember them later on when you are drafting.

> For more discussion on choosing a topic for a research paper, see Chapter 7 and pages 382–85 in *Rules for Writers*.

Generating Ideas about Your Topic

After a preliminary assessment of your rhetorical situation, you need to start generating ideas for your topic and testing your assumptions or preconceived notions about your topic, purpose, audience, and organization. Listed below are some of the strategies many experienced writers use to generate ideas.

Journal responses are great for jotting down ideas. Your instructor might assign specific journal entries to help you find a topic or a focus for an essay. You might also use your journal for other purposes:

- To **record your responses to the assigned readings**. For this purpose you would pick passages from the readings that spark your interest, quote them, and discuss why they struck you as important.

- To **write down memories, observations, and passing thoughts** that are relevant to your writing assignments. Many writers find that jotting down their random thoughts on a topic helps them get through the most intimidating phase of the writing process: sitting down and beginning to write when your mind is as blank as the page in front of you.

If you write your thoughts in your journal throughout the semester, you can leaf through it as you search for a point of entry into an analysis of a text or use it to help you define the issues you find compelling enough to explore further in an essay.

Freewriting is designed to trick your unconscious into shaking loose some ideas by turning off the critical editor in your head that often causes writer's block. It works like this: Set yourself an amount of time—say five or fifteen minutes—and write nonstop for that period.

The Imagination in the Writing Process

By Ben Ristow

Writing is an act of the imagination and perhaps one of the best ways for us humans to interact with real and invented worlds. The act of writing always begins in nowhere, in the void of the blank page, and arrives (hopefully) at somewhere, and what is made visible on the page becomes a small testament to our experience as creatures of a special gift. You have heard about various techniques in evaluating your rhetorical situation, invention strategies, and sage advice from fellow students about coming to speak on the page, but the imagination is valued ground we have yet to speak of, and perhaps one of the most indispensable gifts you must cultivate as writers.

Do you remember how when you were five years old and you told your parents there was a black bear in the front yard who was flinging herself about on your favorite tire swing? It was a June morning, and your parents had not yet had their coffee, and inevitably, they told you to quit being

so silly and to finish your Cheerios. If you were luckier though, one of your parents asked you how big this particular bear was, where it strolled in from, or if you really wanted to ask the bear to dance with you after breakfast. Bears are dangerous, and presumably characters for youngsters to avoid, but what is more hazardous is to stifle the engine of the imagination once it starts to hum. We might think that the imagination is what leaks out of our ears as we age or that it is the particular mental turf of one kind of writer or another. Is it only the poets who imagine? Only fourth graders in Miss Duncan's class? The imagination, if I may speak candidly on its behalf, does not always like to be told what-how-where-when-why to do something, but it also must be a crucial faculty to nourish (or itch) as your writing process develops.

During the process of invention and drafting, my students often get stopped before they begin. The classic student question goes something like "How do we know what to write about?" The question is honest to be sure, but it assumes the instructor has something for you to write about that will please them, and whether your instruc-

- Don't go back and fix your spelling or grammar.

- Don't pause—barely lift your pen from the paper or your fingers from the keyboard.

- Don't reread until you have finished.

Try freewriting not only at the beginning of the brainstorming process, but any time you can't figure out what comes next as you write your first draft or anytime you need to clarify an explanation or illustration you're having trouble getting just right. If this is the case, try freewriting on a separate piece of paper or on a new screen so that you won't feel like you need to keep what you've written. You'll find new words and new ideas, and you'll likely be refreshed.

Looping is a variation of freewriting: You review what you've produced in a freewriting exercise, circle some phrases or words that interest you, and use them as the starting point for another round of freewriting. You can continue looping until you've focused on an idea you want to pursue.

tor gives you less or more room to come up with a writing topic, you will find it better and more gratifying to generate your own imaginative questions. What has begun to interest you as a Planetary Sciences major? How do Martin Luther King Jr. and Malcolm X's rhetoric differ? Why would Shakespeare include all those fools in his plays? Imagining questions that seem irresistible to you and your imagination will give you the momentum to write further and with greater devotion.

As you begin writing and drafting, it is often instinctual to write once through and leave that essay well enough alone, but if you keep the imagination on board, you know that the introductory paragraph (for instance) can always be re-imagined with different detail, voice, audience, or purpose. Allowing the imagination to function fully is to realize that it is not often satisfied with the first or second way of saying something. More often the imagination likes to move fluidly through your essay, and by focusing your imagination on particular tasks, such as honing a new introductory paragraph or finding

a better voice to reach your audience, you will avoid the sporadic or superficial cosmetic revisions that tend to bog down the early stages of the writing process.

Rewriting and rearranging your words around the new ideas your imagination discovers in the process of writing requires the mental flexibility and fluidity of an ocean fish. It is easy to keep the first word or the first sentence as it darts through your mind, but it often helps to pause to entertain the larger movements and sheen of larger fish as they jet across your brain or try to hover toward the bottom and just out of sight. Pausing to hunt can become procrastination, so it is important to swim while you look for words and concepts you wish to communicate. Writing creates imagination in the process of production and revision, and it acts as the stimulation that triggers the waterfall of words or the prickle that forms on your neck when you see a profound work of art. Imagination requires no particular training; it can be flexed like a muscle, it can be hummed like a poem, or it can be bent like a tool to your latest writing task.

Brainstorming is where you list any idea that comes to mind. As with freewriting and looping, you need to find a way to turn off your critical voice as you create a list of possible topics. The main rule here is not to criticize your ideas while you construct your list. Rather, push yourself to write as many ideas as possible. As you get closer to writing, you may find that ideas you had previously discarded seem more interesting or doable, or you may find a way to combine aspects of two or more ideas.

Talking is a very useful invention strategy. It is especially effective in helping you deal with a blank screen. Often you think of an idea in your head over and over again, but you just don't know how to put it on paper. When this happens, you might want to talk about it with imagined readers or your instructor, classmates, or any friend who is willing to listen.

Clustering is also called **mapping** or **webbing**. It is a visual invention technique that involves the following steps:

- Place a significant word at the center of a piece of paper.

- Brainstorm by adding words or phrases that relate to the original word.

- Draw lines among them and circle these. (As you draw visual links among related ideas, consider what idea or fact links those ideas, and write down terms or details that form those links.)

- Continue attaching words and phrases to any of the circles on the diagram.

When you're done, your page will look like a web filled with bubbles. Your webbing will represent a mapping of the concepts and relations that are important in your topic. This conceptual mapping can be very useful if you are a visual learner who sometimes gets lost in trying to find the right word for an idea. After clustering, you'll have some important ideas written down in words; now your job is to articulate the connections among those ideas.

Web that Explores Online College Classes

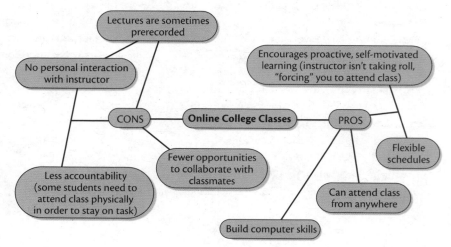

Asking key questions is a common technique that a reporter might use when investigating a story. These questions include the five W's that enable a journalist to get the crucial details for a story: *who*, *what*, *where*, *when*, and *why*. A reporter may then ask a sixth question to deepen his or her sense of what happened: *how* did the event occur? Using these questions will help you consider a topic from various angles. For example, consider how the following basic questions might apply to a novel such as *Harry Potter*:

1.   **Who** is the author? Who are the main characters? Who are the primary and secondary audiences? Who might have influenced J.K. Rowling's writing of this novel?

2.   **What** are the important plot points? What happens to the main character? What happened to the author before, during, and after writing the novel?

3.   **Where** does the novel take place and what do we learn by comparing and contrasting the different settings?

4.   **When** did Rowling write the novel? When does it take place? Are there contemporary connections with events and themes in today's world?

5.   **Why** does Harry take such risks against his powerful enemies? Why do some people identify with his character while others find him annoying?

6.   **How** did Rowling come up with these characters and this storyline? How does the novel reflect the cultural characteristics of the time in which it was written? How does the novel invite us to reflect on social issues such as inequalities of race, class, and gender?

As you can see, these questions move from description to analysis, allowing you to consider multiple aspects of a text or topic. You could use the same technique with topics such as stem-cell research or restrictions on streetlights in Tucson. After being assigned an essay, what steps will you take to begin generating some idea of what you will write about? You may want to try several approaches in order to determine which will be most successful. Consider which techniques you want to try first.

> For more examples of prewriting strategies, see *Rules for Writers*, pages 11–16.

Outlining is another strategy many writers use when writing an essay—*after* generating ideas but *before* writing a first draft. An outline does not have to be divided up into elaborate divisions to be a useful writing tool. Outlines can be helpful at those points when you have many ideas that can go in multiple directions or if you're having a hard time focusing on one aspect of a single issue. An outline will help you organize all your relevant thoughts. This will allow you to reconsider some of your points or examples and dismiss irrelevant or insignificant points even before you create a rough draft. Traditionally, an outline looks like the table of contents of a book and includes brief points that represent each part of an essay. The main parts of an outline are generally the same, but the contents will change depending on the type of essay you're writing. On the following page, you'll find a sample outline template for a text-in-context essay.

> For more information about outlining, see *Rules for Writers*, pages 17–20.

4.4

However, it is not the only one way to outline an essay. Depending on the assignment your instructor requires, you might need to change its structure. Also, you may find that outlining can be useful as a revision strategy, when you're trying to figure out whether you've chosen the best organization for what you've already written. Try outlining your work at different stages in the writing process to see what works best for you.

ESSAY OUTLINE TEMPLATE

Introduction

- Draw readers into the essay. (See "Tips on Writing Introductions" craft box in this chapter for some ideas.)

- Introduce the text—**summarize** and explain its significance.

- Introduce the context.

- State your **thesis** and **forecast** (what your essay will prove and how you will prove it).

Body Paragraphs

- **Point** → Give your first argument about how the text informs a certain context.

- **Illustration** → Give examples from the text that show how you reached your point.

- **Explanation** → Give examples from outside sources that show the accuracy of the point you made; support your illustrations with research.

Repeat as Needed

Conclusion

- **Paraphrase** your thesis and main points.

- Connect to the larger world.

- Leave your readers thinking about your topic.

- See "Tips for Writing Conclusions" craft box in this chapter for more ideas on concluding your essay.

Keep in mind that, as mentioned above, the points you have in the outline, the organizational structure of your essay, and the content of the paper depend on the expectations of each type of essay and on your instructor's assignment requirements. Writing instructors might have different perspectives on how you should approach the writing assignment and might emphasize different elements of an essay such as content, organization, and voice. Therefore, be sure to find out what your instructor expects you to do with the assignment.

4.5 Drafting

Drafting is likely the most time-consuming stage of the writing process. Most experienced writers know that their writing will go through multiple drafts before they can consider a work to be "finished." Still, drafting can also feel like the most productive part of the writing process, because it's the stage in which you're actually taking the ideas in your head and transforming them to words on paper.

Beginning is often the toughest part. Some writers might feel daunted by the blank page or screen and experience writer's block, even if they have a detailed outline. If you find yourself struggling with these writing challenges, you might start by writing your opinion or key ideas, keeping in mind that you can always go back and revise to meet the needs of your readers. This approach is like freewriting. Don't worry about getting it right! Once you've begun, your ideas might come faster. Then go back and get rid of the first few sentences, revising toward a better introduction. You can always hit delete, so don't worry if you're not completely satisfied with the words on the page while you're drafting. You can also save multiple drafts of your essay, trying out different organizational patterns, key points, or tones. Some writers find it helpful to print out a draft and read it on paper to see what works best. You may even decide to integrate a few of your drafts to complete your final essay. Also, if you need some direction about where to go with your essay, don't forget that your instructor welcomes you in office hours.

Regardless of your writing habits, remain flexible as you write, because your ideas will often evolve as you write. Be wary of locking yourself into a set outline—unless you're short on time. Instead, give yourself permission to go back and rework earlier sections if, halfway through your writing, you discover a new angle or a better approach.

> For more information about drafting your essay, see *Rules for Writers*, pages 20–27.

Drafting a Thesis Statement

The **thesis statement** is a statement that dictates what the writer believes is the central idea of the essay. Some writers like to think of the thesis statement as a sort of "contract" with the reader; as a writer, you're making a promise to readers that the paper they're about to read is about what the thesis says the paper is about. The writer presents readers with the basic argument through the thesis, which usually appears in the introductory paragraph and is usually one (and occasionally two) sentences.

Although a thesis statement usually occurs in the introduction, it's not always written, at least not clearly, in the first draft of the introduction. Some writers need to start drafting with a clear argument, or thesis, in mind. Others might have a vague notion of their argument and should just start writing. They may end up writing the thesis after they have completed a draft and then they will use the thesis to help them focus paragraphs on points that are related to their

> For more ideas on how to draft a thesis statement, see *Rules for Writers*, pages 21–24 and 411–12, and the craft boxes on pages 156 and 176 of the *Guide*.

thesis. Regardless, by the time you've reached the end of your first or second draft, you'll likely have a much clearer idea of what your essay is trying to accomplish. The key is to be aware of this part of the writing process and to be ready to rewrite what you thought was your thesis. Then make sure your thesis matches what you actually argue in the body of the essay.

Be open to the idea that as you write and revise, you might change your mind about an issue. You might need to narrow your thesis because you have too much information to include in one short essay, or you might change your focus altogether. Modifying your thesis is a normal part of writing, but you might need to discuss the change with your instructor, depending on how close you are to the final deadline. Keep in mind that if you cannot identify the main idea of your essay, your readers will have the same difficulty. Be sure to think through your thesis carefully before submitting your essay.

It is important to make sure that your thesis statement is appropriate for the type of essay you're writing. For example, in a researched essay intended to persuade an academic audience, you generally need an argumentative thesis that clearly states your point of view on the issue. For a reflective essay, on the other hand, you might not need such an explicit kind of thesis; you might develop your ideas so that they work toward a unified theme throughout your essay, or you might choose to state your thesis in a less explicit way until you have laid out your evidence. The reason for this may be that you believe that your readers will not accept your viewpoint until you have provided evidence for it since they have a different perspective on the issue. However, remember that readers may misunderstand your point unless you state your thesis statement clearly. Your instructor will clarify what to expect in each writing situation. But for many academic essays, readers expect a clear, direct thesis statement by the end of the introduction to help guide them through your essay.

To check the effectiveness of your thesis statement, English professors Toby Fulwiler and Alan R. Hayakawa suggest that you think about the following questions:

- **Is it interesting?** A thesis should answer a question that is worth asking. For example, you might ask:

  What tricks do advertisers use to mislead the public? or

  In Amy Tan's short story "Mother Tongue," what does the relationship between the narrator and her mother reveal about those characters' society and environment?

An argumentative thesis should take a position on a debatable issue and should include a proposal for change: *Mountain bikes should be allowed on wilderness trails.* The thesis for a reflective essay might provide an especially thoughtful way of approaching a topic without stating a definite conclusion on the issue; for example, *I have never understood why my parents got divorced, but I have come to understand that it was not my fault.*

- **Is it precise and specific about what is at issue?** You can sharpen your understanding of the thesis by stating what the issue is exactly as you see it. For instance, consider how much more effective it might be to argue that mountain bikes should have more access to specific wilderness trails rather than to argue that they should have more access to the wilderness in general. Often you can make a thesis more specific by introducing qualifications that acknowledge your readers' concerns: *Nobody wants to be run down by a wilderness bike on a narrow trail, but if mountain bikers were given access to designated trails, hikers would know when to look out for mountain bikers.*

- **Is it manageable?** You probably collected more information than you can actually write about during prewriting. Take this opportunity to narrow both the thesis and the paper you expect to write, often by making it more precise or by adding qualifiers that specify what sorts of cases you are considering.

- **Does it adequately reflect my research and the expected shape of my paper?** Your thesis should relate to all of the examples and evidence that you researched. Instead of ignoring facts or examples that complicate your claim, you should revise it to better explain that information.

Paragraph Development

Paragraph breaks are important because they signal to readers where one idea ends and another begins. A single body paragraph should have a single main idea. You have likely been taught that each body paragraph needs a **topic sentence**—that is, one sentence that states the main point of the paragraph. Some instructors may ask that the topic sentence be the first sentence of your paragraph and some may not. However, every paragraph should include a topic sentence and every other sentence in the paragraph should develop, illustrate, or define the idea in that topic sentence.

> For more information on developing effective paragraphs, see *Rules for Writers*, pages 39–57.

Recognizing a Strong Thesis vs. a Weak Thesis

Read the following thesis statements. Consider which ones seem to be the strongest and weakest. Try reworking the samples below to better match the criteria outlined above.

1. Hemingway's story "A Clean, Well-Lighted Place" serves as a metaphor for loneliness and old age.

2. Television news presents an exaggerated view of violence in today's society.

3. "The Yellow Wallpaper," by Charlotte Perkins Gilman, challenges patriarchy.

4. Many advertisements for alcoholic beverages employ images that are degrading toward women.

5. Colleges and universities should eliminate letter grades and instead evaluate each student on a pass/fail basis.

PIE (Point, Illustration, Explanation) Structure: A Useful Way to Develop Paragraphs

PIE is an acronym for Point, Illustration, and Explanation. PIE is a helpful way to think about paragraph development, especially for analysis essays and persuasive arguments. Remember, however, that PIE is just one of several ways to develop a paragraph. The following section created by Dr. Anne-Marie Hall, a professor in the UA English department, discusses the important features of a PIE paragraph:

PIE refers to the structure of well-written paragraphs that provide full coverage of the single topic each individual paragraph should address. In academic writing, in particular, each paragraph should address *one* point.

Readers should be able to identify the separate points that you are making, but they should also realize that the points are cohesive—they cannot be teased apart or else the whole purpose of the paper is weakened. That is, readers should be able to notice the **point**, the **illustration**, and the **explanation** for themselves, but they should also be able to understand what it all means by seeing how each works together to make and express a single, coherent idea.

Point

This is the **topic sentence of the paragraph**. It is one of the claims you've identified as supporting your essay's primary argument, or thesis. Your essay should consist of a number of such supporting claims. Each topic sentence should be one of the first two or three sentences in any paragraph. It should cover the whole paragraph—everything the paragraph does will relate to this point. Any information that doesn't go under this point belongs in a different paragraph. Remember: one paragraph, one point!

Illustration

This is **the best textual evidence** you have to support your paragraph's point. It's the part of the PIE that consists of needed evidence such as another author's ideas and language, your own personal experiences and ideas, or a combination of the two. You can provide such evidence in the form of direct quotations, paraphrases, summaries, personal narratives, or a combination of these. You need to give your readers as much textual or personal evidence as appropriate to *show* your point. Remember the saying, "Don't merely *tell* me, *show* me what you mean." Also, remember to be consistent; stick to making *one* point.

Explanation

This is **your reasoning of the connection between the point and the illustration(s)**, and it is how you connect your purpose in the paragraph to the goal of the paper as a whole. Without it, your point can easily be misunderstood or received ambiguously. Therefore, make sure you take ample time to give readers your detailed insight into the text you are dealing with by explaining the point and illustration(s) you make. Don't leave your reader guessing what you might mean. You must convince readers that you understand your own point, how your illustration(s) support it, and how both relate to your essay's thesis.

Note that you can alternate between illustration and explanation several times within the same paragraph, as long as every illustration is explained.

The following are examples of paragraphs using the PIE structure:

> For the most part, the examples of writing by younger students are provided by Twain simply to make us laugh. Twain reports that one student wrote "The three departments of the government is the Present rules the world, the governor rules the State, and the mayor rules the city" (45). Another student wrote that "The first conscientious Congress met in Philadelphia" (Twain 45). The first passage is humorous not only because it is a run-on sentence, but also because we know that the student meant to say that the president "rules" the United States, not the "world." The second passage is also worth a laugh, because of a very obvious misunderstanding; the student used the word "conscientious" when he intended to use "Continental." In both cases, they are innocent errors, and Twain doesn't offer us much commentary.
>
> A few lines down, however, Twain suggests that a mistake in a student's writing reveals some greater truth about American society. One student writes that "The Constitution of the United States is that part of the book at the end which nobody reads" (Twain 45). We can assume that the student was thinking of the word "index" or "appendix," but Twain writes in response to this passage that "Truth crushed to earth will rise again" (45). Twain is suggesting that we might as well not read the Constitution because the rights granted by it are in name only, and not always a material reality. When he says that the truth will "rise again," he is perhaps arguing that society can only deceive itself for so long, that truth will eventually surface, even if it is in the most unlikely places, such as in the pages of a young student's notebook.

For more samples of PIE paragraphs, see Chapters 8 and 9.

Part of creating a PIE paragraph is integrating sources correctly. Remember, for MLA in-text citation you normally need, in parentheses, the *author's last name* and the *page number* the cited material came from—unless you mention the author in your signal phrase. **You *must* use in-text citation for direct quotations, paraphrases, and summaries.** Basically, if you're using information that isn't your own original idea and isn't general and well-known public information, you must both cite it in the text and list it on your works cited page.

For more information about paraphrasing, summarizing, quoting, and integrating and documenting sources, see Chapter 6 and *Rules for Writers*, pages 415–63.

Once you have mastered the PIE paragraph, which is an excellent paragraph model in any academic argument, your instructor may encourage you to experiment with other types of paragraphs.

Tips on Writing Introductions for Essays

By Adam Meehan

When a reader picks up your essay for the first time, your introduction is the first thing that he or she will read. It is very important, then, for your introduction to make a good first impression. Of course, this can be challenging, as an introduction requires you to grab your reader's attention, provide necessary context, and introduce your argument in a relatively small amount of space. As a result, your introduction needs to be intriguing, articulate, and precise. While this is easier said than done, there are certain strategies that can help you get started.

Given that there are many different types of essays—analytical, argumentative, narrative, reflective, etc.—each introduction will be unique. Generally speaking, however, the introductions that you will write in your First-Year Composition courses should follow these guidelines:

1. Every introduction should **grab the reader's attention**, which can be done several ways:

   - Begin your essay with a quotation that relates to your topic. A famous quote—or a quote from a famous person—may earn an important recognition from your reader and make him or her want to read further.

   - Begin with an interesting/surprising fact or statistic. This strategy is used often in journalistic pieces; giving your readers a heavy dose of "reality" is a great way to get them interested.

   - Relate a compelling anecdote. As a rule, people are drawn toward narratives. Just as a novelist or short story writer seeks to get you involved in a story, you can draw your readers into your essay by starting with an anecdote that piques their interest.

   - Start with a rhetorical question. Opening with a question is a great way to get your readers interested in your topic. For example, asking your readers "Would you feel more or less safe if the person sitting next to you in class was carrying a concealed weapon?" is likely to make them ponder their feelings on the subject, which will in turn make them want to keep reading your essay.

2. Your introduction should also **forecast what direction your essay will take**. While some writers choose to be more explicit with this information than others, you generally want your readers to get a sense for what your topic is, why it's important, and how you will go about discussing it. Below is an example of an implicit forecast:

   - With the popularity of recent films like *Food, Inc.*, there is now an abundance of widely-recognized evidence that the food industry in America should be re-examined. The problems that exist in the meat, agriculture, and food distribution industries suggest that, while the cost may be higher, eating organic food is ultimately better for the environment and for personal health.

Here is an example of an explicit forecast:

   - The popularity of recent films like *Food, Inc.* is evidence that many Americans are ready for major changes in the food industry. This paper will explore the problems that exist in the meat, agriculture, and food distribution industries. It will argue that, despite higher costs for consumers, eating organic food is better for the environment and for personal health.

As you can see, each example contains the same information and each provides a sort of "road map" for the reader, which highlights the path that the essay will follow. The second example, however, is more explicit and uses metadiscourse—words or phrases used by the writer that comment on the writing itself—to present the writer's plan for the essay.

3. Every introduction should include a thesis statement that lays out your main argument. If your introduction consists of more than one paragraph, the thesis doesn't always have to appear in the first paragraph, but be sure it is somewhere in one of the introductory paragraphs. Consult Section 4.5 for more on strategies for creating successful thesis statements.

4. Be careful, however, to avoid certain "traps" with your introduction. These "traps" may include—but are not limited to—the following:

    - *The Vast Generalization.* Bold, sweeping claims like "Since the beginning of time, humans have been searching for their place in the world" cannot be proven, and do not contribute directly to your argument. While these assertions may appear to add a certain degree of importance or an "epic" quality to your paper, they in fact are unoriginal and unsophisticated, causing readers to call into question your credibility as a writer.

    - *Introducing Evidence.* While it may sometimes be necessary—when road-mapping your argument, for example—to mention some component(s) of your argument, you do not want to start getting too far into the content of your argument within the body of your intro-duction. One, the reader might not have the proper context to understand the evidence. Two, you'll need to provide the evidence later anyway, so there's no need to repeat the same ideas in your essay.

    - *The Book Report.* Book reports tend to follow a certain formula: They introduce the writer and the text; they give a brief summary of the text; they list other interesting facts about the writer and/or text. Many students fall into the trap of using this formula in academic papers. Remember that your readers (your instructor and your classmates) have read the text in question, so an introduction that merely introduces and/or summarizes the main text or texts at hand shows a lack of audience awareness.

    - *Too Much Information.* Perhaps the most common trap is providing *too much* information. Often the anxiety over "what to say" in the introduction, along with the fear of not being able to meet the required page length or word count, causes students to add "fluff," or information that is not serving an important purpose. Be sure that each sentence in your introduction is *doing* something to convey a necessary piece of information. One way to determine what information is "necessary" is to go through each sentence in your introduction and ask yourself, "Do my readers really *need* this sentence?" and "Does this sentence actually make my essay stronger?" If the answer is "no," then consider cutting it.

4.6 Revising

Revising is the last stage in the process that we'll cover in this chapter. It's not last because it is the least important phase in writing but because you have to have something written to revise. In fact, it's so important that we devote an entire chapter (Chapter 5) to discussing revision, so we'll be brief here and just introduce this stage in the process. Revisions can be divided into **global revisions**—changes in the overall organization and development—and **local revisions** such as editing a particular sentence. We'll discuss this distinction in the following

Tips for Writing Conclusions

One of the most important parts of your paper is the conclusion, for it will contribute to the reader's final impression of your essay. You may have been taught to use the conclusion as a place to restate your thesis and introduction as a way of reminding readers of your main points. This may be appropriate in some contexts, but it also may suggest that the reader didn't read the whole essay or understand the argument, which is generally not the case for the relatively short essays written in a first-year course. A conclusion that simply repeats what the writer has already stated in the rest of the essay is not pulling its weight, so to speak, because it does little to contribute to the overall meaning of the essay. Following are some different ways to approach a conclusion:

- **Answer the "So What?"**

  The conclusion can provide the "so what" of your whole essay, placing it in a wider context and showing how and why your argument matters in a larger sense. Some students have been cautioned against introducing new information in the conclusion, and this is certainly an important consideration. Nevertheless, it is possible to "open up" your essay at the end without including material unrelated to the rest of the essay, as long as you provide your reader with the connections between your essay's main argument and those larger issues.

- **Circle Back**

  The conclusion can return to an interesting example or story you've introduced in the essay, such as an anecdote from the introduction, and rethink/reframe that story through the new knowledge you've offered in your essay. This brings the entire essay together.

- **Look Forward**

  Again, you generally shouldn't start an entirely new argument in a conclusion, but it can be helpful to tell your readers what still needs to be done. For example, what new research is necessary to advance the issue you're discussing? What ideas do you have for resolving a controversy between sources? Where might the controversy be headed?

- **Paint a Picture**

  The conclusion can end with a forceful example or image that really drives the message you have been conveying home. Just as compelling examples can provide interesting starting points for essays, they can make for memorable conclusions that engrain in your readers' minds the point of your essay.

- **Summarize Claims**

  The conclusion of an essay can simply restate your major arguments, although if you choose this method, you will want to rephrase your main claims, rather than simply repeat them.

chapter, but you need to understand that revision is about more than just "fixing" your paper after it's written—it goes much further than such local revisions as correcting spelling mistakes or comma errors. Revising is something that you'll want to do throughout the writing process—you can revise your ideas, your focus, and your writing again and again. As student Greta Bauer learned, multiple revisions of a particular essay can be particularly helpful:

> The Writing Center guided me through my first semester. I went there for every paper, more than once, which is the key. When you think your paper is perfect go again, because there is always going to be something that you missed. Correcting your paper as many times as possible is the golden key to getting the grade that you want.

> For more information about revising your essay, see *Rules for Writers*, pages 27–39 and Chapter 5 of the *Guide*.

Revision means to "see again," to re-envision your work-in-progress in order to assess how well it conveys your purpose for your audience. Revision is probably the most critical but most underrated part of the writing process. To revise your essay is to ask yourself questions like these:

- "What is my essay really saying?"

- "What do my readers really need to understand to accept my thesis?"

- "Have I supported my points with enough details?"

- "Are there any sections where I have lost my focus on the thesis? If so, do I need to freewrite more or conduct more research to link those paragraphs to my thesis?"

A crucial step in revising is to establish enough distance from your work to enable you to distinguish what you intended to say from what you actually wrote. This ability is basic to being able to re-envision your essay, and it's a difficult skill even for experienced writers. One technique is to read your essay out loud to yourself, rather than just reading silently on the computer screen or the printed page. Another technique is to put the essay aside for a period of time—a few days or at least several hours—so you can return to it with fresh eyes. Unfortunately, however, given the time constraints in most college classes, finding this kind of time is difficult. Fortunately, you can rely on people other than yourself and your instructor—your peers. The next chapter about using feedback will give you guidelines for how to give feedback to peers and how to use the feedback you receive. In addition to peer feedback, you should also strengthen your own ability to re-envision your writing. We continue this discussion about revision in the next chapter.

Works Cited

Ede, Lisa. *Work in Progress: A Guide to Writing and Revising*. New York: St. Martin's, 1992. Print.

Fulwiler, Toby and Alan R. Hayakawa. *The Blair Handbook*. Upper Saddle River: Prentice Hall, 1997. Print.

Rosenwasser, David, and Jill Stephen. *Writing Analytically*. Fort Worth: Harcourt Brace, 1997. Print.

Twain, Mark. "English as She Is Taught." *The Complete Essays of Mark Twain*. Ed. Charles Neider. Cambridge: Da Capo, 1991. 36–47. Print.

Re-Visioning Your Work

5.1   Feedback, Peer Review, and Revision: An Overview

5.2   Practicing Global and Local Revision

5.3   Tips for Successful Workshopping *by Laura Gronewold*

5.4   Receiving and Making Sense of Comments

5.5   Feedback Leads to Revision *by Jen Heckler and Kristen Haven*

5.6   Revising Multimedia Projects

5.1 Feedback, Peer Review, and Revision: An Overview

As you read in Chapter 4, writing is a process that includes invention, drafting, and revising. Revision is a crucial part of the writing process, but revision isn't easy: when you've been working hard on an essay, it can be difficult to step back from what you've written and see it from the perspective of another reader. Therefore, seeking feedback from your peers and instructor will help you to identify areas that could be improved by revisions. Keep in mind that your first draft won't be your final draft. Neither will your second or "final" drafts be truly final. It's also important to remember that revision is an *ongoing* process. It's tempting to want to leave a "final" draft as-is because you've done the work and want to be finished, but your success in first-year writing as well as in future writing will depend, in part, on your willingness to revisit your writing multiple times and consider angles that need to be rewritten to get your point across to your readers. Throughout the revision process, the feedback you receive from instructors and peers will help you develop your ideas, improve your evaluation of the writing situation, and organize your text to fit your purpose and audience. You will not only *receive* feedback in various ways from your instructor, peers, tutors, and other readers, but you'll also *give* feedback to your classmates. Giving and receiving feedback is important for many reasons:

- **The feedback that you give and receive can offer a fresh perspective to a draft.** Often, writers are too close to their own work to imagine it taking any other shape. Because they already understand what they are trying to say, they have trouble locating areas that need more clarification. Outside readers can tell the writer what does and does not make sense to them.

- **The process of giving and receiving feedback helps you to understand the complexities of composition,** particularly the qualities that make a piece of writing effective for a given audience and situation.

- Through the process of reviewing your own drafts, providing feedback on your peers' drafts, and reading the feedback you receive from other readers, **you will develop your skills as a writer.** For example, you will develop the assessment skills necessary to evaluate the peer feedback that you receive. This will help you learn how to make critical choices about the revisions you need to incorporate in order to best serve the purpose of your essay.

- This process of **reconsidering, assessing, and revising will aid you in the recursive practices of writing** and will guide you toward informed choices about audience responses and needs.

Because every writer has a unique writing process, part of the challenge of writing is finding a revision process that works for you. Small group work helps most writers revise their writing because peer feedback is an excellent way to get a new look at your paper. You will also receive feedback from your instructor, either in the form of written comments or in group or individual conferences.

You will also be responsible for providing feedback for your peers on their work. There are many ways to provide feedback—some of them described below—and your instructor will have his or her variation on these activities. The ways you'll receive feedback include **written or oral comments** from your instructor, small-group **peer review sessions, conferences** with peers and your instructor, and whole-class reviewing or **workshopping.** We also strongly encourage you to seek additional feedback from the Writing Center, which is part of the Think Tank, and the Writing Skills Improvement Program. Below, we have included experiential advice from former first-year writing students:

> You can find the contact information for the Think Tank, WSIP, and other resources in Appendix A.

- **Don't Procrastinate:** "I think the main reason I was successful in English 101 was that I always finished drafting my papers a few days before they were due. This helped lift all the stress off my heart. Then, I would re-read my papers over and over again. Every time I reread my paper, I made changes in the text. I was not a great writer by any means, but being ahead of time helped me succeed." —*Nick Vaughn*

- **Reading aloud to Revise:** "I find it very useful to read each draft of my essay out loud before turning in the final draft. That way I can listen to certain phrases that might not make sense and paragraphs that don't flow." —*Bethany Bell*

- **Recognize that Writing is a Process:** "I always thought writing draft after draft of a paper, and the whole revising process, was a huge waste of my time. I have a good foundation in composition, and I thought my first draft would be just as good as a final draft. I never wrote first drafts, second drafts, or final drafts. It was always just a one-time thing. I would sit down at a computer and write. Whatever came out, that would be what I would turn in. This year, I was forced to go through the whole drafting process. We were required to not only turn in our first draft, second draft, and final draft; we had to do assignments that showed the research we were doing and what we thought of it. To an experienced procrastinator such as myself, this was hell. This class forced me to go through the entire process, which my teachers have been trying to get me to follow for years. What resulted from this process really impressed me. All the papers I have ever written could have been so much better. This shows that revising and rewriting are not pointless efforts of teachers to make their students work hard to no end. They actually help. That is probably the most valuable lesson I have learned about writing this year." —*Katherine Byrnes*

- **Be Prepared for Peer Review:** "Peer review is an excellent tool for improving essays. However, if an adequate rough draft is not presented to reviewers, then useful feedback cannot be expected." —*Britt Burridge*

- **Give Constructive Criticism during Peer Review:** "When doing a peer response, be honest. The student won't benefit from your opinion if it's glossed over with fluffy language. And don't ditch the peer response. It is very helpful to have someone else's opinions and/or ideas during the revising stage, especially if you are all writing on the same topic but their argument opposes yours." —*Christina Stephens*

  "When writing peer edits, really dig deep into their paper. Don't just look for the obvious, because they are writing a peer edit for you as well. Think what would be useful for you." —*Rebecca Peterson*

- **Be Prepared for Instructor Conferences:** "It is very important when you go into your conference with your teacher that you have a strong thesis and a good sense of direction for your paper. It helped me very much to receive advice from my teacher because I had a good start and knew what I wanted to do, thus my teacher was able to give me good advice to refine my ideas. I know that you can fall into the trap of knowing that it's still a couple of weeks from being due, so why start it early? It really makes a difference in getting strong feedback." —*Richard Karasch*

As the previous advice demonstrates, revision takes many forms. This chapter is intended to provide a foundation for writing and revision strategies, but you can find additional writing and revision techniques that address the following:

- **Tips on Writing Introductions and Conclusions for Essays** in Chapter 4: Writing as a Process

- **Thesis Statement Recipes** in Chapters 8 and 9: Analysis and Text-in-Context

- **Vivid Description** in Chapter 13: Personal and Reflective Writing

These craft boxes are separated into blue shaded boxes so that you can find them easily.

5.2 Practicing Global and Local Revision

> For more advice about and examples of global and local revision, see *Rules for Writers*, pages 27–39.

You might consider the revision process in terms of large and small revisions, or **global revisions** and **local revisions**. **Global** revisions are the large-level changes you make to an essay's argument, organization, or style. These changes will have a greater impact on your essay as a whole. Since global revisions may require you to move paragraphs around, eliminate sections of writing, or change the focus or audience, it will reduce your overall workload if you do these revisions first, before starting the local revisions. Otherwise you might change the tense or sentence structure of an entire paragraph only to realize you will not even be using that paragraph in the final section of the essay!

Local revisions, on the other hand, are smaller changes that occur at the sentence and paragraph level. When you read carefully over your work to check for grammar mistakes, typos, misspelled words, and awkward sentences, you are revising your paper locally. Another way to think about this basic type of revision is to see it as revising the surface of your paper. If you haven't read your textual analysis essay in a few weeks and then pick it up again, you'll probably see it through fresh eyes and find sentences to rearrange, vague adjectives to enliven, weak verbs to strengthen, grammar mistakes to address, and so forth. At the very least, you should perform multiple surface revisions of any paper you turn in for a grade, as even small errors can affect the overall presentation of your work. Such local changes are necessary and important, but they are only one part of the revision process.

Suggestions for Global Revisions

Every draft and every revision is an important part of the writing process. In the early drafting stages, you might not feel confident about your ideas. This is completely normal. In fact, you may not even know what you think about a text or a topic until you start writing. When you plan to write multiple drafts and make use of revision in your writing process, you will see drafting and revising as important parts of developing a successful essay. Don't let yourself feel discouraged; instead, just keep writing.

Why are You Writing? Revising for Purpose, Argument, and Thesis

When you write an academic essay, you write with a specific purpose in mind. Once you have written a draft, you are ready to assess your purpose. The following questions will be helpful when you do this. You can use your answers to these questions to help you with your first set of global revisions.

- What do I hope to achieve with this essay?

- What are the requirements of the assignment?

- Am I making an argument? If so, what is the argument? How do I support the argument?

- Does my essay have a thesis? How does the thesis relate to my purpose?

- In what ways does my essay achieve my purpose? In what ways does it fail to achieve my purpose?

> For more on thesis statements, see Chapter 4.

Who is the Reader? Revising for Audience

Sometimes students confidently assert, "I write for myself," and, of course, it is always good to write for yourself. At the same time, in college writing you must write not only for yourself but also for the academic community. When you write in college you are writing as a scholar *for other scholars*. Your audience is important because your writing is designed to reach and affect your audience. So when you perform global revisions, remember to consider how your audience might understand your essay. You might consider the following questions when revising for audience:

- Who, specifically, is going to be reading this essay? (My instructor, my classmates, members of my academic community, members of the local community, etc.)

- Is there more than one intended audience?

- What biases might my readers have? What are their values and expectations?

- What strategies might be particularly effective or ineffective with these readers?

- How much information do I need to give my audience?

- What kind of language is suitable for this audience?

- What tone should I use with my audience? Do I use this tone consistently throughout my draft?

> For more on audience, see Chapters 2, 10, and 12.

As you examine the role of audience in your essay, you might realize that you need to define certain terms or explain certain concepts because if you don't, your audience will not understand the point you are trying to make. On the other hand, you may realize that you have provided *too much* explanation of ideas that your audience will already understand. You should remove anything that might bore or insult your audience. If you are writing for an academic audience, remember that a fairly formal academic tone is generally appropriate. Being aware of your readers and trying to anticipate their critiques and their expectations will make your writing much more effective.

Suggestions for Local Revisions

After you have globally revised your essay, you are ready to start local revisions. Revising at the local level allows you to demonstrate the general proficiency of your writing. Start by correcting any errors. Run a spell-check, check for grammar, and make sure that your paper is formatted according to your instructor's specifications, but local revisions are not just about correcting mistakes. In fact, this can be a fun part of revision because you can work to perfect your *style*. Once you have created a strong essay and checked it for mistakes, you can fine-tune the way you express your ideas. The following list includes stylistic elements you might consider when performing local revisions:

Wordiness: Too many words take all the energy out of a sentence. Practice expressing your ideas concisely. See how many unnecessary words you can eliminate from your writing. For example:

> **Instead of:** In light of recent discoveries in English Composition Studies, it has come to be known that students have trouble connecting ideas in texts they read to historical events in the time the texts were written.

> **Try:** Students have trouble making connections between the texts they read and their historical contexts.

For more on word choice, see Chapter 2.

Active and Passive Voice: Do you fall into the habit of overusing the passive voice? Passive voice can obscure the meaning of a sentence by hiding the sentence's action or actor. This can lead to vague, unclear, and even boring writing. Try to use strong (active) verbs like *perform*, *interrogate*, *organize*, and *persuade*, rather than passive "to be" verbs like *am*, *is*, *are*, *was*, and *were*.

> **Instead of:** The idea was considered by Mrs. Mallard.

> **Try:** Mrs. Mallard embraced the idea.

For more information about active and passive voice, refer to Chapter 2 in the *Student's Guide* and pages 80–83 of *Rules for Writers*.

Remember that using academic verbs like "maintain," "constitute," "decrease," and "suggest" can help your writing sound more scholarly and professional.

Tense Usage: Be consistent with your verb tenses. While you do not need to write your entire essay in a single tense, make sure that if you do change between the present and the past or future tense, there is a logical reason to do so.

Pronoun Usage: Pay attention to the pronouns (I, you, we, he, she, they) you use in your essay. Pronouns are little words, but they carry a lot of power. For example, Jamaica Kincaid's use of the pronoun "you" in *A Small Place* often makes readers feel as if they are under attack. What effect do your pronouns have?

Variety: One of the best marks of good writing is variety. By varying the types of sentence structures, paragraph structures, vocabulary, and punctuation that you use, you can help your reader to stay focused and engaged. Look for repeated sentence structures, words, punctuation, and phrases, and experiment until you have included more variety and fluidity in your writing.

5.3 Tips for Successful Workshopping

By Laura Gronewold

The most important thing to bring to your workshop is an open mind. As a former editor at a book publishing company, I can tell you that everyone needs an editor. Even the very best writer sends her/his writing through at least four different drafts, and along the way the writer collaborates with other editors and writers so that a number of people contribute to the final, polished product. (That is the reason authors thank so many people in the acknowledgments at the beginning of books.) So think of your peer group as a group of editors working together to produce the best essay possible—a clear, coherent argument; a focused thesis statement; supporting examples; and careful textual analysis. Only after several pairs of eyes have seen your work will it truly be finished.

To achieve the most success in your workshops, you can do a few things ahead of time. First, **get to know your classmates**. You are more likely to give *and* receive valuable feedback if you know your workshop partners' names and feel comfortable with them. Second, **pay attention in class** when your instructor talks about writing. Although your instructor will likely give lectures on writing technique and style, some of the best "aha!" moments happen in class discussions about your assigned texts. Third, **carefully read the texts** assigned for your class and think about how you can emulate an author's style, tone, or argumentation. If you like the way a particular author uses personal experience or builds credibility through her/his writing voice, then strive in your own writing to model your argumentation or tone after the original author's work. When you get to workshop, you can also refer to the texts you've read for class. For example, in your feedback on another student's paper, you might suggest that she/he write her/his introduction in imitation of an introduction written by an author such as Malcolm Gladwell (who wrote *The Tipping Point*). Finally, **begin drafting early**! This will allow you to participate in your workshop with a *full* draft. (Believe me, published authors do *not* begin their writing at the last minute!) Your understanding of the assignment will allow you to read your workshop partners' work thoroughly so that you can give them detailed feedback to improve their essay.

Advice for the Writer

Come to the workshop prepared to receive a critique of your work. Even if you feel that your draft is well-written with a clear argument, remember that your classmates will give you constructive criticism that will help make it even better.

Remember to bring an attitude of open-mindedness to your workshops so that you can *really* listen to what ideas your classmates offer to improve your essay.

- Listen to the criticism you receive with a non-judgmental attitude.

- Listen quietly to the discussion of your work when it is happening.

- Take notes! You should have a page of *specific* notes that you can refer to when you revise your paper.

- Ask questions throughout the process so that you are clear on the feedback being offered by your classmates. At the end of the discussion, voice any additional concerns or questions about your essay.

After workshop, you will have a number of drafts with comments from your classmates, as well as your notes from the class period during which your essay was critiqued. Once you have that feedback, take a day off. This will give you some distance from your writing and will help you consider the comments from your workshop partners from a more objective angle. Getting some distance from your writing *and* from the critiques offered by your peers will allow you to begin your revisions with a fresh start. As you revise, think about the different comments from your readers. Do they all say that you need a more focused thesis statement? Then you should be mindful of the consistency of the comments. However, if only one student comments about your paragraph breaks, then you will need to assess whether or not you want to change that. Remember, this is your essay, so you will need to consider your intentions and the effect you want to achieve, and how you will incorporate your readers' comments to help sharpen your argument and tone in your paper.

Advice for the Reader

Your job as a reader is to carefully assess your classmates' drafts so that you can give them detailed feedback about their essay. You should be able to tell the writers **what** needs to be fixed in their essays, but you should also provide advice about **why** the writers need to rewrite their essays, as well as suggestions for **how** the writers can improve their essays. Giving written (and verbal) feedback is another genre within which you will work in this class, and it requires practice and skill, just like any other form of written or verbal communication. Even if you feel like you are not the best writer in class, your feedback during workshop is very important! If you are not clear about why a paragraph is in another student's essay, it is not because you don't "get it." It is because the paragraph does not have smooth enough transitions or a clear link to the thesis statement. Sometimes the most powerful feedback points out the thing we might think is "obvious."

As you read through your peers' drafts, consider the following:

- Read the writing as closely and carefully as possible.

- Consider the writer's intentions and provide *specific* feedback.

- *Read the essay at least twice.*

- Write specific suggestions for revision on each page as you are reading.

- At the end of the essay, give your overall reflections about the argument, the organization, the tone, and the style.

Giving Written Feedback

Your goal when you critique your workshop partners' drafts should be to write specific comments and questions that the writer can understand later, even if you are not there to explain them. Marginal comments such as "good!" or "???" are vague and will not help when the writer revises. Instead, strive for comments such as "Your close reading and analysis of this quote helps explain your argument," or "This sentence is confusing. How does it relate to the rest of your paragraph?" Make sure you give your classmates feedback about the argument and not only the grammar and style—after all, it is much easier to correct a poorly phrased sentence than it is to fix a flawed argument. Your workshop partners need your help, and you need theirs. Learning to give and receive useful feedback on your drafts is one of the most productive things that you will learn in your writing class. When you can lean on each other, you will benefit from both the writing *and* reading process of the workshop.

Questions to Consider When Giving Feedback

- *Introduction:* Does the introductory paragraph establish the **theme or idea** of the essay? If the introduction jumps around or is not specific, then it will confuse your reader. If the introduction does not give the basic facts about the topic (summary of a text, overview of a political issue), then the reader will be confused. As the reader, your job is to make suggestions for how the writer can make her/his introductory paragraph specific and interesting.

- *Thesis Statement:* Does the author have a precise **thesis statement** (or central claim) that includes a **specific opinion** that the reader can agree or disagree with? If you cannot agree or disagree with the thesis statement, then it is not a strong argument. Your job is to provide suggestions to the writer so that she/he can make her/his topic more focused and include an opinion. Oftentimes, the opinion can come from answering a question, such as, "What do we conclude or learn as a result of looking more closely at these particular aspects of the novel/issue/essay?"

- *Summary and Analysis:* Does the author have too much summary of the text's plot, or too much vague information about a research topic? How can the writer add quotations from the text? How can the writer incorporate her/his own opinion, and not just offer a summary of experts' opinions? Your job is to make suggestions for places in the essay where the writer can add analysis. Mark places where the writer can do more close reading of a quotation by underlining words or phrases, or mark the margins where the writer could offer her/his own opinionated analysis of a research topic.

- *Use of Quotations:* Does the writer use **direct quotes or statistics** from the primary texts to introduce points and support her/his argument? Does the writer then explain why the quotations are important? Are the quotations introduced with a signal phrase? Your job is to make suggestions for how the writer can introduce her/his quotations clearly with signal phrases.

- *Use of Secondary Sources:* Does the writer integrate her/his secondary sources appropriately in the essay? Does the writer make it clear to the reader when another text is being quoted? Do you ever have any questions about the original source for a quotation or an idea (especially if it is an idea that is paraphrased)? Your job is to help the writer establish credibility and ensure that all of her/his sources are utilized effectively.

- *Organization:* Does the organization of the essay make sense? Should any paragraphs be moved around?

Getting the Most out of Your Workshop Experience

In order to really benefit from a writing workshop, you will need to do several things. First, come to the workshop prepared. This means that you need to submit the very best draft you can write to your peers for their feedback, and you also want to spend plenty of time reading your peers' papers in order to give them quality feedback. Second, come to the workshop with an open mind. Instead of trying to defend your essay, listen carefully and thoughtfully to your peers when they give you feedback. Ask questions about their suggestions. Take some time to think through your options. Remember, you don't have to make all the changes your peers or instructor suggest, but you do want to give careful consideration to their feedback. Third, give helpful, specific, constructive feedback to your peers. Although it is nice to tell your peers what you like about their essays, this is only helpful if you explain your opinion in detail and let them know why you like it. Here you will see some examples of *not very helpful*, *somewhat helpful*, and *very helpful* workshop comments.

Not Very Helpful

"I really like this paper!"

This is friendly, but provides no concrete suggestions for the writer.

"Well, I'm just not that into poetry, so I couldn't get into your paper."

This comment is about the reader, not the paper. It does not provide any suggestions for revision.

"You use way too many commas."

Even if this critique is correct, it is often more productive to offer global advice rather than local suggestions.

Somewhat Helpful

"I really like your first body paragraph, but after that you kind of lose me."

This comment identifies strong and weak areas but does not tell the writer what makes them strong or weak.

"You assume that I already know what this poem is about and that I think it's a great poem. Since I don't know anything about the poem, I feel alienated when I read this paper."

- *Transitions:* Does the author have smooth transition phrases between her/ his paragraphs and sentences?

- *Conclusion:* Does the conclusion leave you with one new thing to consider? Does it do more than simply restate what has already been argued?

Discussing Your Peer's Essay during the In-Class Workshop

When you come to class, you will need to be ready to discuss your classmates' writing. Think about the ways you have talked as a class about the essays, fiction, poetry, and/or film texts you have read. When you talk as a class, you are not making judgments about the *writer*, but you are making assessments of the *writing*. The same goes for workshop. You want to keep your comments constructive and *always specific to the writing*, so that the author of the essay will have concrete suggestions for improving and reorganizing her/his draft.

This honest reaction identifies the assumptions made in the draft. It might also identify an opportunity for global revision, if the assignment requires the writer to assume that the reader is unfamiliar with the poem.

"In this sentence, the commas actually make it harder to understand. Maybe you should take them out."

This local editing comment might be appropriate at a later stage of workshopping. It effectively identifies a problem sentence, it connects the idea (or the content) to the form, and it provides a specific suggestion.

Very Helpful

"I really like this paragraph because you choose an interesting example from the text and in the last sentence you show how this paragraph supports the thesis. Maybe you could do this more in your other body paragraphs."

This comment identifies what makes the paragraph strong and gives the writer specific suggestions for improving the weaker paragraphs.

"If you gave a little bit of summary and background at the beginning of the paper, it would really help me to understand what's going on, because I've never read the poem before. You could also connect your argument about racism in this poem to a recent event, which would help people who don't know much about poetry to be more interested in your overall argument."

This comment expands the Somewhat Helpful comment, by providing specific suggestions for revision.

"In this sentence, the commas actually make it harder to understand. You could take them out. In the next sentence, you have an unnecessary comma again, but the sentence is also a run-on. Try making this into two separate sentences, which would make it easier to understand and would give the paragraph more variety."

Again, this is a local revision suggestion, but it identifies specific problems, provides specific suggestions, and addresses both clarity and style.

During your workshop, your instructor will be in the classroom, listening and participating with the group. Your instructor will help guide the workshop with questions, comments, and ideas to help you focus on giving constructive criticism to your classmates, but the heart of any workshop's success is you and your classmates. Remember: The goal of the workshop is not just to give your classmates feedback, but to train yourself to make these same assessments of your own writing in the future.

5.4 Receiving and Making Sense of Comments

As you read above, your peers can be a valuable source of comments and suggestions for your writing. Another valuable source is, of course, your instructor. Writing instructors are experienced academic writers themselves, which means that they're familiar with the conventions and expectations of academic writing. Therefore, they can help you locate the strengths and weaknesses in your essay. However, don't underestimate your peers' commentary; they are in the process of writing an essay just as you are and thus will have valuable insights and questions for you that might push you in a clearer direction.

Throughout the course, your instructor will play various roles. She or he will support you as you plan, draft, and revise your essay. Your instructor will ask questions to help you understand the rhetorical situation of each writing assignment, to teach you ways to interact with your audience, and to offer pointers about how better to reach that audience. Your instructor will also evaluate your essay by assigning a grade to your final draft.

J.D. Salinger's Multiple Revisions of "A Perfect Day for Bananafish"

All authors usually go through multiple revisions of their writing before they find the right "final" draft.

In 1951, J.D. Salinger's *The Catcher in the Rye* was published. The book's popularity was unexpected and so overwhelming that Salinger became a recluse and retreated to the small town of Cornish, New Hampshire, where he would remain until his death in 2010. Salinger wasn't exactly the most social person, but it's hard to imagine being so successful that you need to resort to hiding from everyone. However, success didn't always come easy for Salinger.

A decade before *The Catcher in the Rye* was published, Salinger was determined to have one of his short stories appear in *The New Yorker*. It was his favorite magazine and he was convinced it was his ultimate goal as a writer. So in 1941, at age 22, Salinger submitted seven stories. The magazine rejected all seven. They finally accepted one the next year, a story called "Slight Rebellion off Madison." (Imagine submitting eight essays to your instructor and passing only one of them.)

He still wasn't satisfied, however. So in the meantime, he kept trying. He submitted more stories, dozens of them, but was rejected every time over the next four years. He even tried poetry in 1945 but was rejected for that too. In 1947, he submitted a story called "Bananafish," and the editors at

It's easy to focus just on the grade your final draft earns, but you should remember that your instructor's comments on your paper are just as—possibly even more—important than the grade she or he assigns. These comments can help you think about how to approach new drafts of this essay or even how to approach later writing assignments in this class or in other classes. Many instructors respond to your work by noting areas that are strong or interesting while, at the same time, noting areas that could use more attention. Additionally, instructors often use questions as a way to converse with you, to show their interest in your work, or to give suggestions for future revisions. If you are ever confused by your instructor's comments, then you should ask your instructor to clarify them. This is the perfect time to visit with your instructor during office hours.

Once you receive written and oral comments from your peers and instructor, how do you decide what to use? What do you pay attention to first? What if there's too much for you to take in all at once? This can sometimes happen if you're doing a whole-class workshop. Here's some advice:

See "A Manifesto on Written Feedback" in Chapter 1 to learn more about how instructors understand the role their comments play in your drafting process.

- **Read through all the comments** from all the reviewers before making revisions.

- **Watch for patterns** in the responses you receive. If three out of four readers suggest you expand a certain point, chances are good that future readers would want you to say more about it, too.

- **Look for global issues** such as content, focus, and organization that need attention before you attend to local problems such as grammar and word

The New Yorker said they liked *parts* of it but felt that there was no "point" to the story. They asked him to revise, and the rest goes like this:

1. He added a new scene, which made the new version about *twice* as long as the original.

2. The second draft was again rejected.

3. He made more revisions to the story.

4. He changed the title to "A Fine Day for Bananafish."

5. The third draft was finally accepted, but not before changing the title to "A Perfect Day for Bananafish."

Afterwards, Salinger became something of a sensation. Even so, he was rejected three more times in 1948 and seven more times in 1949 (Yagoda 233–34). But when he published *The Catcher in the Rye* in 1951, it solidified his place in American literary history.

This is a true story, and the point of it is this: **even for the greatest authors of our time, they didn't get it right the first time**. If people were perfect, we wouldn't need to revise our writing. But we're not. There's a reason why pencils have erasers and why keyboards have backspace keys. Writing takes a lot of patience, and most of the time, a *lot* of revising. So if you ever need a reminder of how important revising your work is, or if you think it's something that you don't or shouldn't need to do, just think about how much revising it took to make it "A *Perfect* Day for Bananafish."

choice. You will waste your time if you fix sentences that you decide to delete later on because they were tangential.

- Always **keep an open mind** as you read comments. Try to see it from the reviewer's point of view. Did you leave out important information or explanation that would solve the problem?

- If you really think a comment is questionable, **ask other readers what they think**. Sometimes you will decide not to take action on a suggestion or comment.

- Think critically about all comments and then make the revisions you think are most important for the purpose and scope of your work. **You are the writer and you make the final decisions.** Just try to make well-informed decisions.

5.5 Feedback Leads to Revision

By Jen Heckler and Kristen Haven

In the following sample rough draft, a student explores her interpretation of Raymond Carver's "So Much Water So Close to Home." As conscientious writers, we as instructors try to provide students with the feedback we'd like to receive. As you read,

- Reflect on these comments—can you break them down into local and global?

- How would you rewrite your paper based on these responses? (Remember that it makes sense to consider global feedback first.)

- Which comments would you take into consideration?

A Draft with Instructor Comments

Give your paper an original title as you continue revising.

Draft of essay one

"So Much Water so Close to Home"

You have a broad introduction, which successfully eases readers into your discussion; however, there are a few places where being more specific will help readers understand your purpose. For example, what is "over done violence"?; "dangerous and unfortunate situations"?; "shady"? These are interesting descriptive words, but they are broad and general; consequently, readers will not know what you are talking about. How does all of this relate to the story?

Suspicious behavior and over done violence are all scary tell tale signs of a criminal. People that are often involved in dangerous and unfortunate situations usually have obvious characteristics that seem to comply with their behavior. In the short story, "So Much Water So Close to Home" a housewife Claire is terrified of her shady husband. Claire hears about a murdered girl close by to the place her husband and his friends were fishing and camping. Claire is immediately very aware of his actions and is investing him and facts about the murder for fear that it was in fact of her husband. Whether or not Claire's husband is really guilty, he gives many signs that could cause someone to believe, in this situation Claire, that he did murder the young girl.

Author name?

This sentence sounds like it contradicts itself. First you mention that she is "aware of his actions" (what actions? Fishing?), and then I hear mention of murder. What's the connection?

Use first or third person instead of second.

Many people would expect that when something traumatic and mysterious happens to you on a trip, one of the first things you would do when you got home was to tell your family about it so that would understand the severity of the situation and be sure their family members had nothing to do with such a bad situation. The exact opposite happens to Claire and her husband. Claire's husband sees a girl dead in the water when he is camping, but he and his friends decide to just leave her there overnight and deal with it in the morning. Claire's husband comes home and goes to sleep and doesn't say anything to Claire about it until later the next day. "'Why didn't you tell me last night?' I asked. 'I just…didn't. What do you mean?' he said" (280). Rightly so Claire found it wierd that she woke up to hear her husband screaming cusses in to a telephone and then he saying to her "I have to tell you something" (280). The situation is awkward, one would think that if you dragged a body to police in the morning and were wanted for murder you might want to first tell your wife about it. This is one of the many odd behaviors that Claire's husband displayed.

Slang—"curses" or "obscenities" would be better.

Comma splice.

Stay in present tense.

Clarify what you mean by this phrase.

Another sign that there might be a problem is a person's violence and overall behavioral tone. Throughout the short story, Claire's husband is increasingly moody and violent. At different points, Claire's husband snaps out at her and even acts in a violent manner. "Suit yourself then. I could give a fuck less what you do" (285).

Dropped quotation. Integrate.

Stuart, Claire's husband, starts to really scare Claire with his overzealous behavior and temper. Claire does not understand why Stuart needs to really act like this, and this causes her to question his behavior and the murder situation. If Stuart had been normal and not lashed out at her in specific situations, she would less likely want to question, but since he acted in such a harsh way it caused her to question his motives.

A common characteristic of a criminal can often be substance abuse. Many criminals have problems that root from an alcohol addiction or other drug problem. Yet because one decides to partake in these activities does not necessarily mean they are out to kill someone. In the short story, Stuart is constantly drinking and smoking, even around his child. When Claire mentions she wants to go to the store, alcohol is the first thing Stuart asks to get. When Stuart seems upset or wanting to do something, smoking or alcohol is seemingly the first thing he turns to.

Redundant—"situation" used twice. This is broad for a topic sentence. Perhaps letting readers know what you are trying to prove will help guide them. Your thesis seems to say that her husband (What is his name?) killed someone. Is that what you are trying to show in this paragraph?

Use more precise vocabulary here—how is it bad?

I thought you said he killed the girl in your thesis…

Run-on—needs punctuation.

Great quotation, but it's dropped into the text without integration. Introduce it, and explain how it illustrates your point.

Sp. weird. Actually, "strange" or "startling" might work better here.

Is this your topic sentence? It seems like all of your topic sentences are at the end of paragraphs. Perhaps you should move them to the beginning, so that readers will know what you are trying to prove. Check for this throughout.

Wordy. Try using "is." "Common" already tells us says the same thing as "can often be."

Use a quotation from the story to back up these claims.

Again, a general topic sentence. Think about making a claim about the text here.

He was harsh, so she suspected him of murder? I think this is making a huge leap here. What else made Claire suspect Stuart? Was it his reaction to the subject of the discussion?

How does this paragraph relate to your thesis? It seems like it is contradicting what you are trying to prove.

"struggles" would read more smoothly.

Okay, I'm hearing that it doesn't matter if he's guilty or not guilty; his actions prove he is guilty. Doesn't this seem rather repetitive? This is also a rather general final sentence. Keep the story in mind.

Throughout the short story, "So Much Water So Close to Home" Claire is afraid that her husband is involved in the murder of a young girl. Stuart's actions start to become very mysterious and shady to Claire, and she is struggling with believing her husband. There are many different things Stuart does that would make many people believe he is guilty. The point is that whether or not he is guilty his actions prove otherwise. A person's actions can have a great impact on the people around them and cause them to be more and more questionable.

Just a few questions: 1. Are you trying to illustrate that Stuart is capable of killing someone or are you trying to prove that there is a "problem"? Or are you trying to prove something else that I missed? I'm not exactly sure. Your thesis sounds like you are trying to prove that Stuart's behavior indicates that he has the potential to kill someone, but that is not what your topic sentence says here... Perhaps you should mention Stuart's name before this paragraph. 2. Does Claire suspect Stuart of murdering the girl? 3. What is the overzealous behavior like?

Revisions in Action

After receiving her instructor's feedback, the student reworked her draft. Compare the two versions. Then consider:

- Would you have integrated the instructor's feedback in ways other than this student did?

- What additional changes would you have made?

- Do you see more local or global revisions at work here?

- How does the student define the writing situation? How can you tell?

- Considering that this is still a rough draft, how would you revise this paper again both globally and locally? List three suggestions for each.

Revised Draft

A Criminal Mind in Carver's "So Much Water So Close to Home"

Suspicious behavior and violence are all seemingly obvious telltale signs of a criminal. People that are often involved in dangerous situations usually have obvious characteristics that seem to comply with their behavior. What things do many consider traits of a criminal? Does one have to be shady or over violent? What about if a person is just displaying suspicious behavior or acting in a dangerous manner? In Raymond Carver's short story, "So Much Water So Close to Home" a housewife Claire becomes terrified of her shady husband, Stuart. Claire hears about a murdered girl close by to the place her husband and his friends were fishing and camping. Claire begins to become more and more nervous that her husband was involved with the death of the girl, and starts to analyze her husband Stuart's actions. Whether or not Stuart is really guilty, he gives many signs that would cause any person to believe that he is guilty.

A person's actions are key in determining a crime situation and Stuart does not seem to be innocent.

Carver's portrait of guilty behavior hinges on Stuart's lack of communication with Claire surrounding the discovery of the dead girl. Truth and honesty, two devices that hold a relationship together, are two devices that Stuart fails to uphold. His initial silence regarding the discovery of the dead girl in the water near a campsite he is vacationing at with friends, and his ensuing reticence and verbal abuse lead the reader (and Claire) to suspect his capacity for serious, even murderous, violence.

One of the actions that causes Claire to question her husband is his late mentioning of the dead body he encountered on the trip. Many people would expect that when something traumatic and mysterious happens to them on a trip, one of the first things they would do when they got home was tell their family about it so they would understand the severity of the situation and be sure their family members had nothing to do with such an awful situation. The exact opposite happens to Claire and her husband. Claire's husband sees the body in the water, but he and his friends decide to just leave her there over night and deal with it in the morning. Claire's husband comes home and goes to sleep and doesn't say anything to Claire about it until later the next day. Claire is deeply troubled by this lack of communication. "Why didn't you tell me last night? I asked. "I just...didn't. What do you mean? he said" (280).

Rightly so Claire finds it unsettling that she wakes up to hear her husband screaming obscenities into a telephone and *then* saying to her "I have to tell you something" (280). Claire questions her husband because she finds it odd that he would not tell her when he got home that he saw a dead body on his camping trip. If Stuart helped get the body to authorities in the morning he would have to know the police are going to call and question him about it. What did he think his wife would feel if we were getting police calls? It doesn't make sense that he did not tell her quickly that there had been some problems on his fishing trip. The situation is awkward; one would think that if you dragged a body to police in the morning and were wanted for murder you might want to first tell your wife about it. This is one of the many odd behaviors that Claire's husband displayed.

Stuart's violence and overall behavioral tone are indicative of his dangerous potential. Throughout the short story, Claire's husband is increasingly moody and violent. At different points Claire's husband verbally lashes out at her and eventually abuses her physically. When Claire tells him she wants to spend the night alone, he snaps, "Suit yourself then. I could give a fuck less what you do" (285). Stuart starts to really scare Claire with his overzealous behavior and temper, and particularly with the way he responds to her confusion and questions with sexual advances rather than answers. Claire does not understand why Stuart acts like this; the effect is only to alienate her further from him. I think this makes Claire more likely to believe that Stuart was involved in the assault and murder of the girl. If Stuart had been normal and not lashed out at her in specific situations, she would less likely want to question, but since he spoke so violently and rash it caused her to question his motives.

A common characteristic of a criminal can often be substance abuse, and Stuart fits this description. Many criminals have problems that root from an alcohol addiction or other drug problem. In the short story, Stuart is constantly drinking and smoking, even around his child. When Claire mentions she wants to go to the store, alcohol is the first thing Stuart asks her to get. When Stuart seems upset or wanting to do something, smoking or alcohol is seemingly the first thing he turns to.

Throughout "So Much Water So Close to Home" Claire is afraid that her husband has been involved in the murder of a young girl. Stuart's actions become increasingly confounding and distancing to Claire and she struggles with believing him and eventually with even being near him. Indeed, Stuart's behavior would make many people believe he is guilty. Carver convey's the way that a person's actions in the face of trauma can have a great impact on the people around them, and in Claire and Stuart's situation, can expose and widen the fractures already present in a relationship.

5.6 Revising Multimedia Projects

Although this chapter focuses on revising academic essays for your first-year composition classes, you may also be given assignments that require you to work in other media, such as wikis, blogs, videos, posters, Web pages, and speeches, among others. While many revision considerations for these projects may be similar to essay revisions—for example, attention to both global and local revisions and to your audience and purpose—you may also need to think about specific aspects of the media forms you are composing. For example, multimedia projects often involve a greater level of interactivity between the "user" (a member of the target audience) and the project, as in the case of websites where users navigate from page to page at their own discretion. While revising, you need to anticipate how your target users might interact with your project and how your design can accommodate users with a variety of abilities. Because multimedia projects encompass more than just written words, your revisions must also take into account the visual, aural, spatial, interactive, and design elements of your project during the revision process.

Your instructor will help you guide your revisions if you are working with multimedia, and you'll likely spend a good amount of class time discussing the medium in which you're working. However, to get you started, here are a few questions you might ask yourself when revising multimedia projects:

- What are the conventions and expectations of the medium I'm working in? Have I worked within these conventions and expectations? For example, if I am creating a Web page, have I considered navigation, page design, interactivity, and other elements?

- In what ways does this project differ from essay-writing? Have I been attentive to these differences in composing my text?

- What am I trying to achieve with my multimedia project? Does my purpose come across clearly? Do I use textual, visual, auditory, and spatial strategies that effectively speak to this purpose?

- Do all the multimedia components work together to convey an idea or meaning, or do they seem disconnected? If they do seem disconnected, how can I make them work together to express this idea more effectively?

- Are all the multimedia components appropriate for my intended audience? Do I use them to appeal to the audience I'm trying to reach?

- In what ways can users interact with my project and what are the potential outcomes of these interactions? Are the design and scope of my project user-friendly and are they geared toward a variety of users? Have I possibly excluded certain users or made it difficult for users with disabilities to interact with my project?

- Do I use an effective document design? Do I use design strategies that bring emphasis to key points and ideas? Does my design appear balanced? Are elements in my text aligned effectively? Do I use color and font choices that work for the audience, purpose, and medium?

As is the case when revising essays, revising multimedia projects is an ongoing, or recursive, process. You will need to make changes in the design of your project much like you would make changes to the organization and development of an analytic essay, and these choices will need to be informed by the situation in which you're working. And even if you are working in a medium other than writing, you still need to follow fair-use guidelines when using the work of others.

Whether you're composing an analytic essay or another kind of text, revision will be a crucial part of the writing process. The more time you take to review and revise your work, the more effectively you will be able to communicate your ideas.

For more on composing multimedia texts, see Chapter 12.

Works Cited

Carver, Raymond. "So Much Water So Close to Home." *Writing as Revision*. 3rd ed. Boston: Pearson, 2010. Print.

Yagoda, Ben. *About Town: The New Yorker and the World It Made*. New York: Scribner, 2000. Print.

Working with Sources: Summary, Paraphrase, and Quotation

6.1 Working with Sources: An Overview

This chapter explains how to write using sources. Specifically, it will help you:

- Name the text's author and appropriate pages that were consulted (in-text citation).

- List the text's author, title, and other relevant publication information in a bibliography at the end of your text.

- Demonstrate clear distinctions between your own ideas and the ideas of the sources you use.

- Represent the ideas of your sources fairly and accurately by using effective summary, paraphrase, and quotation.

- Incorporate peer and instructor feedback about your use of sources into the final version of your text.

Whether you are writing a poem, an engineering report, a grant, or a paper for a biology class, you will often draw upon the ideas of other writers and integrate them into your own writing. There are occasions when writers do *not* borrow from others, but most of us don't even realize the extent to which we are influenced by what we read. Especially in the context of college writing, skilled writers are also skilled readers, and the quality of their work demonstrates the depth of their knowledge. Writers make good use of the energy and ideas that they encounter in texts. In fact, it's a good bet that the coursework in your first-year writing class began with the close reading and analysis of another person's work: a story, a poem, a film, or some other text. Up until now, you may have been focusing more on your own close reading or analysis of the text itself, rather than "how to use the text" to support your own analysis. Eventually, though, you have to work on incorporating the ideas of others in your own work, especially when writing for academic audiences.

Writing documented essays would be simpler if all writers cited their sources in exactly the same way. However, different writing situations call for specific rules about how to incorporate other people's work into your own. There are three major ways that you'll borrow other writing in your work: summary, paraphrase, and quotation.

- A **summary** is an abbreviated version of a longer text—your statement of what you see to be the major points of a text *using your own words*. A summary can be one sentence long, one paragraph long, or one page long, depending on the length of the text and your purpose as a writer.

- A **paraphrase** is often confused with summary, but in a paraphrase you work much more closely with the original source. To paraphrase is to rephrase part of a source in your own language, often just a sentence or even a phrase, while retaining the general meaning of the original source. Your paraphrase may be shorter (or even slightly longer) than the original, but it must *always change the language, sentence structure, and word order* so that it is recognizably distinct from the original.

For more information on MLA in-text citation, please refer to *Rules for Writers*, pages 427–36.

- A **quotation** uses the exact words from a writer's original source, with *no changes in language or punctuation* (although some words may be omitted, which will be explained below). You may quote an entire sentence or a part of a sentence, depending on what is most useful for your writing purpose.

For more information on creating a list of works cited, please refer to *Rules for Writers*, pages 437–63.

Whether you are summarizing, paraphrasing, or quoting, one rule remains constant: **Always cite the source you are using so that your readers know where the material is coming from.** This chapter explains how to cite sources when writing for academic audiences and how to use the work of others effectively and properly.

6.2 Summary: Main Ideas

Whether you are reading a journal article, a book chapter, or a story, writing a summary can help you to put the writer's most important ideas into your own words, which in turn will help you develop a deeper understanding of the text. By condensing the most important ideas of a text, you make it easier to use the ideas later. This process also helps you to understand which aspects of a text are most interesting to you, and this is important to consider when you begin to make an argument about a text. Summarizing also helps you to point out for *your* readers the most important parts of a text you're discussing. However, summary can be more complex than it seems because it requires you to figure out ideas and arguments that may be quite difficult.

The length of a summary varies depending on the length of the text you are summarizing and your purpose for summarizing. In other words, the amount of information or details you choose to include in your summary depends on how you wish to use that information later. A summary can be as short as one or two sentences. For example, if you were to summarize Stephen Crane's "The Snake" for the purpose of defining its relationship to your other sources, your summary might focus only on the text's overarching ideas instead of all of Crane's points. Your summary might look something like this:

> In "The Snake," Stephen Crane describes a man who encounters a rattle-snake while walking with his dog. As the man and the snake face each other, both are filled with a rage and desire to kill the other that is likened to the experience of war and to instinctual violence.

You can find a full version of Stephen Crane's "The Snake" in Chapter 3.

On the other hand, if you were writing a textual analysis of "The Snake" that focused on Crane's ecological language, you might write a longer and more detailed summary of Crane's story that mentions several of the most important ecological moments in the text. This kind of summary might be longer because it spends a good deal of time thinking about specific moments in the text rather than summarizing the plot in order to compare it to another text.

Strategies for Summarizing

- **Introduce the author before or early in the summary:** A good summary needs to make sense to someone who hasn't read the original text. The above sample summary of "The Snake" shows a simple way to introduce an author early in a summary.

- **Integrate a summary smoothly into your own writing:** Summaries don't usually evaluate a source. When summarizing, you should clearly distinguish your own opinions from those of your source. However, in academic writing you can blend a summary with your own judgments and analysis of the various texts you are working with. In other words, you can integrate a summary into a larger paragraph or section of your writing in order to orient your reader, to introduce a quotation, or to initiate a discussion. Look at the sample student essays included in Chapter 14 to study how writers integrate summaries with their own ideas in their writing.

For more information about annotating texts, refer to Chapter 3.

- **Begin with section summaries:** A good way to begin a summary is to create smaller section summaries. See Chapter 3 for a discussion of how to write section summaries. A sequence of section summaries can provide a sense of the sequence of ideas in the original text. However, merely restating the main ideas of a text in their original order does not make a good summary. You also need to fill in the logical connections between the author's main ideas and you might need to reorganize them so they make more sense to someone who isn't as familiar with your source as you are. If you are summarizing an argumentative text, focus on the main claim and the most important supporting evidence so that you can capture the logic of the analysis.

For more information on summaries, refer to *Rules for Writers*, pages 417–18 and 424.

6.3 Paraphrase: Specific Ideas

A **paraphrase** is more specific than a summary but is less precise than a quotation. Writers paraphrase in order to include specific information and ideas from other writers in their own work. While a paraphrase does not have to retain all of the content from the original, the meaning and intent of the original passage should not be changed. When you paraphrase, you borrow from the writings of others, but you must use language that is different from the original source. For example, you might paraphrase Crane's "The Snake" as follows:

Paraphrase Practice

1. **Read the following passage from Edward Said's *Culture and Imperialism* and before reading further, try to put the passage into your own words while keeping to the spirit of the text's meaning.**

Appeals to the past are among the commonest strategies in interpretations of the present. What animates such appeals is not only disagreement about what happened in the past and what the past was, but uncertainty about whether the past really is past, over and concluded, or whether it continues, albeit in different forms, perhaps. This problem animates all sorts of discussions—about influence, about blame and judgment, about present actualities and future priorities (3).

A one-sentence summary of the above paragraph might read as follows: "Fights over the past are not just about 'what happened' but where the past ends and the present begins." This sentence summarizes Said's paragraph well because it captures the main idea of the paragraph. But it isn't exactly a *paraphrase* because it loses important details and context. Nothing is mentioned about "interpretation" or "blame and judgment," for example.

2. **Read the following attempt at paraphrase. Does it effectively paraphrase the passage without plagiarizing the language?**

References to the past are some of the most typical strategies used to interpret the present. These appeals are animated not just by disagreements about things that happened in the past, but also about whether the past is really over or just continuing on in a different form. This problem gives life to discussions about blame and judgment and about present realities and future priorities.

Original Text:

A man and a dog came from the laurel thickets of the valley where the white brook brawled with the rocks. They followed the deep line of the path across the ridges. The dog—a large lemon and white setter—walked, tranquilly meditative, at his master's heels.

Paraphrase:

Crane opens his story by describing a man walking through the mountains, with his dog following him closely as they pass over a stream (Crane 1).

This paraphrase retains much of the specific detail of Crane's original story, but you'll notice that it doesn't use any of Crane's original language.

There are a few paraphrase "rules" you need to keep in mind to avoid plagiarism and to paraphrase effectively:

- Always include a **signal phrase**, a few words that identify the original speaker and make it clear that you're borrowing from someone else's ideas. See 6.4 for examples of signal phrases.

- **Change the language** so that it no longer follows the original.

The above example has **serious problems**, enough that the writer could be accused of plagiarizing Said's passage. Why? Although some words are changed and some of the word order appears to be different, **too much of the original passage's language and sentence structure remains intact**—these are the hallmarks of an incorrect paraphrase. Also, notice that **the passage is not cited**, giving no indication that the material actually comes from a source.

3. Here is a more effective paraphrase:

A standard tactic used to make sense of the present is to refer to the past. As Said notes, discussions of the past are often marked by disagreements over what happened and what it means. However, another important consideration concerns whether the past has actually ended or whether what has happened before is still taking place, but carrying on in a new way. Disputes over where the past ends and the present begins lead to problems about responsibility, material realities, and what the future should look like (Said 3).

Notice that this successful **paraphrase** features very **different sentence structures and word choices**. The writer also **uses a signal phrase to name Said** at the beginning of the paraphrase and at the end **includes an in-text citation**. Paraphrasing is especially useful when there is no compelling reason to use the exact words of your source in order to further the discussion. However, when the author's language seems especially effective or unique, or you want to analyze it in more depth, you should choose the last method of working with sources: quotation.

- **Change the word order** and sentence structure so that it no longer resembles the original.

- **Cite the source** using in-text citation so that readers know where the original material comes from.

Look again at the paraphrase of "The Snake" to see if it follows all of the guidelines above:

Paraphrase:

Crane opens his story by describing a man walking through the mountains, with his dog following him closely as they pass over a stream (Crane 1).

This signal phrase clearly identifies the original author.

"Mountain" replaces Crane's original "ridge" and "stream" replaces "brook."

Crane puts the brook first and the description of the dog second; this paraphrase reverses that order.

An in-text citation clearly locates the original placement of the passage so a reader could find Crane's language easily.

6.4 Quotation: The Source's Words

Writers use quotations for a variety of reasons. Quotations can demonstrate a key point using the source's exact words; they can set up the writer's analysis or close reading of a source; they can begin or conclude an essay with a provocative, exact statement from an author; and they can honor the particular language or style of a particularly well-said phrase. Using quotations effectively can be difficult because it's sometimes hard to determine how and when you should add a quote into your own writing. You don't want to "overquote," where the voices of others take over your essay. But you also don't want to "underquote," which makes it tough to provide specific details of the text you're analyzing. Below are some guidelines for deciding when to use a quote in your writing.

When to Quote

- When the wording of the source is especially effective or unique or expresses a point so well that you cannot restate it without altering the meaning or effect.

- When the words of reliable and respected authorities, scholars, or authors support your point.

- When you wish to emphasize an author's opinion.

- When you wish to cite an author whose opinions challenge or vary greatly from those of other experts; or when you wish to disagree with a particular author.

- When you are going to discuss the author's choice of words (this is close reading!).

Integrating Quotations Successfully

Another challenge when using quotations is including them in a way that does not break up the fluidity of your own writing. There are a few strategies to follow any time you include a quotation in your writing:

- **Always cite every quote.**

  This includes adding opening and closing "quotation marks" at the start and end of the borrowed language as well as including the correct in-text citation information, such as the author name and page number, of each quote you use.

- **Always frame your quotes with signal phrases.**

  Like with paraphrases, you should always alert your reader that you're about to use somebody else's language by providing a signal phrase that names the author you're quoting before you start. Below, we've listed some commonly used signal phrases. You could replace "X" with the name of the author(s) you're quoting, or you could name the title of the story, essay, or other text in place of X.

As X writes	X explains that	X states
X argues	In the words of X	X suggests
X shows	X interrogates	According to X

It's also a good idea to **introduce** your source by explaining why he or she is worth being quoted in the first place. You might wish to note, for example, that the person you're quoting is a chemist, a professor, an author, a star basketball player, and so forth. The idea here is to introduce the author you're quoting by including relevant details that make him or her an authority figure on the topic. For example, you might try:

> *In a paper talking about the style of a specific poem:*
>
> As U.S. poet laureate W.S. Merlin writes, …

> *In a paper weighing the benefits of recycling:*
>
> Al Gore, producer and director of the environmentalist documentary *An Inconvenient Truth*, suggests that…

- **Always explain the quotation.**

There are two ways to explain a quote. The first method is just like it sounds: explain what the quote means. Even if you don't actually leave this explanation in the final draft of your paper, it's always a good idea to be *able* to explain what a quote means, just to make sure that you understand it yourself. Sometimes, though, the meaning of a quote is self-explanatory. In these cases, you should explain how the quote relates to what you're saying in your essay. You can also choose to include both types of explanation—what the quote means *and* how it relates—in your discussion of a quote.

Composition scholars Gerald Graff and Cathy Birkenstein call quotes that have no signal phrase and no explanation "**hit-and-run quotations**," because dropping a quote into a paragraph without explaining who was responsible for it is similar to bumping into a car in a parking lot and then driving away without

For more information on using and integrating quotations, please refer to *Rules for Writers*, pages 415–26.

6.4

117

leaving a note (41–2). Below is an example of a classic hit-and-run quotation:

> A standard tactic used to make sense of the present is to refer to the past, but people don't always agree about what really happened in the past. "This problem animates all sorts of discussions—about influence, about blame and judgment, about present actualities and future priorities" (Said 3).

While the above example accurately cites the quotation, it doesn't include any kind of signal phrase to explain where the quote came from *or* why the quote is important. A revision of the hit-and-run quote might look like this:

> A standard tactic used to make sense of the present is to refer to the past, but people don't always agree about what really happened in the past. As Edward Said argues, "[t]his problem animates all sorts of discussions—about influence, about blame and judgment, about present actualities and future priorities" (3). In other words, people sometimes have trouble moving forward because they're still caught in the cycle of disagreeing about the past. This kind of disagreement underscores current debates about the Mexican/American border.

In the above example, the quotation uses a clear **signal phrase**, then **explains** the meaning of the quote. It goes beyond a simple explanation of the quote's meaning, though, by **connecting the quote to the topic of the paper**, which in this case is border security. Finally, it **cites the quote** accurately using MLA style. By including all three of these elements each time you use a quotation, you'll ensure that your purpose for including the quotation is clear to your readers.

- **Consider pairing quotation with summary or paraphrase.**

Pairing quotes with summary or paraphrase is a more in-depth way of framing and explaining quotations. Summarizing or paraphrasing what an author was saying before a quote can help your readers understand the context of the quotation. Consider this example of how to use paraphrasing to lead into a quotation:

> Said concludes his argument by criticizing how the dominant legacy of imperialism has been to convince people of their differences from one another. He writes, "No one today is purely one thing. Labels like Indian, or woman, or Muslim, or American are not more than starting-points [...]. Imperialism consolidated the mixture of cultures and identities on a global scale. But its worst and most paradoxical gift was to allow people to believe that they were only, mainly, exclusively, white, or Black, or Western, or Oriental" (336).

Notice how the writer frames the quotation with a paraphrase of Said's text, followed by the full quotation. While readers may have an idea of what is meant by "to convince people of their differences from one another," the full quotation from the original source gives us a much clearer picture of the type of "differences" involved in this discussion, including race, national identity, civilization, and gender. Furthermore, offering the paraphrase before the quotation helps readers understand how the quote fits into the larger picture of Said's argument.

6.5 The Mechanics of Quoting: In-Text Citation Guide

Beyond integrating your quotes effectively, using punctuation correctly will also add to the fluidity of your writing. Below are some of the most common types of in-text citation you'll use in first-year writing. You can find a comprehensive discussion of how to properly use in-text citations in your *Rules for Writers*. Quotes can go at the beginning, middle, or end of any sentence as long as you follow some basic rules for grammar and punctuation. Always set off a quotation using quotation marks ("quote"). The parenthetical, or the part where you cite the author and page number, usually goes at the end of a sentence.

Parts of a Quotation

Quotation mark

Signal phrase/ frame for quote → Anzaldúa suggests that some people can "see in surface phenomena the meaning of deeper realities" (60).

Quoted text

End punctuation

Parenthetical

Basic in-text citation styles:

Quote without a signal phrase:

Formula: Frame for quotation, "quoted text" (Author Page#).

Example: Some people can "see in surface phenomena the meaning of deeper realities" (Anzaldúa 60).

Quote with a signal phrase:

Formula: Signal phrase "quoted text" (Page#).

Example: Anzaldúa suggests that some people can "see in surface phenomena the meaning of deeper realities" (60).

Beginning with a quote:

Formula: Set quote off with a comma and place the parenthetical at the end of sentence.

Example: "When Gregor Samsa woke up one morning from unsettling dreams he found himself changed in his bed into a monstrous vermin," begins Franz Kafka's famous story of transformation and realization, *The Metamorphosis* (3).

Ending with a quote:

Formula: Parenthetical goes directly after quote but before end punctuation mark.

Example: In *Borderlands/La Frontera*, Gloria Anzaldúa describes the experiences that lead one to develop *la facultad*, or "the capacity to see in surface phenomena the meaning of deeper realities" (60).

Quoting in the middle:

Formula: Be sure to clearly mark where the quote begins and ends. Parenthetical goes at end of sentence.

Example: Stevenson shows that Mr. Hyde's acquaintances describe him very differently, but they all perceive his "haunting sense of unexpressed deformity," which suggests that Hyde possesses an abstract yet observable abnormality (64).

Dividing with your words:

Formula: Use commas and other punctuation as the grammar of your sentence calls for. Parenthetical goes at the end of sentence.

Example: "Enlightenment's program," Horkheimer and Adorno write, "was the disenchantment of the world" (1).

In-Text Citation Troubleshooting

The following chart represents the most common types of in-text citation that you're likely to encounter in your first-year writing class. Remember that you can find a fuller guide to citation in your *Rules for Writers* starting on page 427.

Citing What?	What to Do	Example In-Text Citation
Prose (includes essays, short stories, novels, and scholarly articles)	Cite the author and the page number. Don't use the word "page" or "pg."	(Anzaldúa 122)
Poems	Use line numbers for your citation—the first time, use the word "line" or "lines"—after that just use the line number(s).	*First Use*: (Donne Line 11) *Subsequent Uses*: (Donne 12–3)
Plays	Give act, scene, and line numbers	(Shakespeare 4.2.145–7)
Websites	Cite author, title of article, or title of website. You don't need page numbers unless you're looking at an electronic document with stable page numbers, like a PDF.	(Ewing) ←Best option: if author is known. ("Euro Zone Strain") ←Second best option (*NYTimes.com*) ←Third best option
Multiple texts by same author	Include author name, part of the title of text, and page number.	*Quote from first story*: (O'Brien "Things" 19) *Quote from book by same author*: (O'Brien *Cacciato* 124)
Multiple authors	For 1–3 authors, list all authors in the same order they appear in the publication. For 4+ authors, name the first author then follow by the Latin abbreviation for "and others," et al.	*1–3 Authors*: (Bolter and Grusin 227) *4+ Authors*: (Miller et al. 116)
Quote from a source that is not its original source (source-within-a-source)	Give name of person you're quoting, then say "qtd. in" and give name of the source where you found the quote. (Note: It's always best to find the original source) **or** Provide name of person you're quoting as a signal phrase, and start citation with "qtd. in."	"All wisdom is rooted in learning to call things by the right name" (Kung-fu Tze qtd. in Hamill 548). **or** According to Kung-fu Tze, "All wisdom is rooted in learning to call things by the right name" (qtd. in Hamill 548).

6.5

Citing What?	What to Do	Example In-Text Citation
Long quotes (quotes of more than four lines of prose or more than three lines of poetry)	Use "block quote form." Set the quote off on a new line with 1" indentations on the left side. Don't use quote marks. End the quote with a period and put the citation after the period.	After all, imperialism has led us to see only how we are different from one another: No one today is purely one thing. Labels like Indian, or woman, or Muslim, or American are not more than starting-points. (Said 336)
Two quotes from different sources in one sentence	Place the parenthetical for the first quote directly after the quote, then put the parenthetical for the second quote at the end of the sentence.	Stevenson and Kafka both discuss deformity, but Stevenson's comes in the form of "unexpressed deformity" (64) while Kafka transforms his protagonist into a type of "monstrous vermin" that his family refuses to acknowledge (3). *Note that both of these quotes use signal phrases. If you don't have a signal phrase, include the author in the parenthetical citation, as well.

6.5

Changing the Quotation

- **If the quotation has an error**, copy it as-is and add the notation *sic* in brackets:

   The citizen wrote, "I felt vindicated [sic] by out [sic] actions and rules" (Archive).

- **When you omit words**, use ellipsis marks in place of the missing words. Use three dots if you're only taking out part of the sentence. Use four dots if you're taking out more than a sentence.

   Omitting less than a sentence:

   Rackin observes the "liberatory potential of Shakespeare's...cross-dressed heroines" (74).

   Omitting more than a sentence:

   Kundera writes that "the struggle of man against power is the struggle of memory against forgetting....to hide and feel guilty would be the beginning of defeat" (4).

- **To insert your own material** into a quotation, use brackets. You should only insert material to clarify or to change the tense so it makes sense within the grammar of your own work:

   "[This group] is a quasi-historical community" (Sartre 145).

   Most prisoners of Soviet gulags believed that "the struggle of man against power [was] the struggle of memory against forgetting" (Kundera 4).

6.6 Using Sources in the Writing Process

Summarizing, paraphrasing, and quoting is not in and of itself an analysis. However, in an analysis or research essay, using sources effectively will help you to support your interpretation. Focus on using your sources clearly, being sure to set off your own opinions from your summaries and paraphrases. If you focus on summarizing or paraphrasing the source clearly before responding with your own opinion, you may be able to understand the source more fully.

You should always seek to create a context for the summaries, paraphrases, and quotations that you use. Your writing will not be effective if you just list a bunch of quotes from the text—you need to show *how* the author uses the material by setting up your summary to demonstrate the context of the language you quote. For example, if you are in the middle of a paragraph and decide to list three examples of the author's racy language in order to illustrate your point, you will have to set this up by explaining *what* she is talking about when she uses this language. If you do not do this, your use of the source will be confusing to readers—even if they have read the text. Why? Because you are trying to do something specific with that quotation—you are illustrating your point. Therefore, it is up to you to explain *how* that particular quotation supports your point.

Summarizing, paraphrasing, and quoting texts may seem like trivial academic skills. However, don't forget that college writers must live up to high academic integrity standards. There are ethical issues in the way you use texts that your instructors expect you to understand. For example, when you paraphrase an author or quote directly from the text, you want to make sure that you are representing the context accurately, without twisting the text's words for the sake of your own argument. That is, if you take quotations out of context, you could make it seem that the author expresses an idea that is not actually present in that text. True, readers will interpret texts in different ways, so two people might come to a different understanding of what an author means. But there is a significant difference between reading a text in a unique way and changing its meaning altogether. Make sure that you work to give an honest representation of the text itself and the context surrounding the author's words. The guidelines in this chapter will help you cite sources honestly and enable you to work with texts in ways that are appropriate for academic audiences.

Works Cited

Anzaldúa, Gloria. *Borderlands/La Frontera: The New Mestiza*. 2nd ed. San Francisco: Aunt Lute, 1999. Print.

Crane, Stephen. "The Snake." *The Literature Network*, n.d. Web. 16 March 2008.

Graff, Gerald and Cathy Birkenstein. *They Say, I Say: The Moves that Matter in Academic Writing*. New York: Norton, 2006. Print.

Hamill, Sam. "The Necessity to Speak." *Writing as Revision*. Ed. Beth Alvarado, Barbara Cully, and Michael Robinson. Boston: Pearson, 2003. 546–53. Print.

Horkheimer, Max and Theodor W. Adorno. *Dialectic of Enlightenment: Philosophical Fragments*. Trans. Edmund Jephcott. Palo Alto: Stanford UP, 2002. Print.

Kafka, Franz. *The Metamorphosis*. New York: Bantam, 2004. Print.

Kundera, Milan. *The Book of Laughter and Forgetting*. New York: HarperCollins, 1994. 1–5. Print.

Lamberton, Ken. "Sacred Regrets." *Wilderness and Razor Wire*. San Francisco: Mercury House, 2000. 33–44. Print.

Newman, Louise M. Rev. of *Woman Suffrage and Women's Rights*, by Ellen Carol DuBois. *The Journal of American History* 88.1 (2001): 215–16. *JSTOR*. Web. 9 May 2009.

Rackin, Phyllis. *Shakespeare and Women*. New York: Oxford UP, 2005. Print.

Said, Edward. *Culture and Imperialism*. New York: Vintage, 1993. Print.

Sartre, Jean-Paul. *Anti-Semite and Jew*. New York: Schocken, 1995. Print.

The September 11 Digital Archive. Center for History and New Media and American Social History Project/Center for Media and Learning. 2007. Web. 30 June 2008.

Stevenson, Robert Louis. *Dr. Jekyll and Mr. Hyde*. New York: Signet, 2003. Print.

6.6

6.6

Research as Part of the Writing Process

7

7.1 Research: An Overview

You probably wrote a research paper at least once in your high school career, and it may seem at first that the research you do at the university will simply be more of the same kind of work. However, just as expectations for writing at the university level frequently differ from how you were taught to write in high school, research at the university will likely vary from the process you learned in high school. This chapter provides a basic introduction to the important role research plays in first-year writing at the University of Arizona. As you work through your research process, you might also work through the set of research tutorials developed by the University of Arizona libraries. These tutorials will help you learn to use your local resources more effectively. In addition, each instructor will also help you learn how to conduct research tailored specifically to his or her particular course, assignment, and your topic. You can also learn a great deal by going to the University Main Library and asking for help at the Information Commons Reference Desk. The librarians are an invaluable resource because they are specially trained to find and evaluate information. You

CHAPTER 7

Visit the UA Library in person and visit it online at <http://www.library.arizona.edu>.

can get general reference assistance and you can also consult with one of dozens of subject specialists who will be glad to help you with any of your projects throughout your college career.

You may think of research and writing as two separate activities: First, you go to the library or search online to find sources and take notes, and then you write your paper. However, as you become a more experienced writer, you will be asked to integrate research into your own writing in a more sophisticated manner. Instead of thinking of research as an isolated activity to complete before you write your paper, consider it part of the writing process. Research and writing enrich each other, and the insights and knowledge you gain by researching an idea can strengthen your arguments. As you learn more about the subjects you study, your professors will expect you to do more than simply report your findings. You will also be required to formulate your own opinions and present and support those perspectives in carefully thought-out papers. This chapter asks you to think of research in several related ways:

- Research means entering into a conversation rather than simply collecting and reporting information.

- Research is a way of becoming aware of the range of viewpoints on a given topic or in a particular discipline.

- Research is a way of helping formulate and refine your ideas.

For more information on reading critically and evaluating sources, see Chapter 3.

Research as entering into a conversation: Your research will generally reveal a wide range of differing opinions about your topic. In fact, if you're taking English 102, you'll likely write a Controversy Analysis essay in which you find and analyze the different arguments that surround your research topic. When you write an academic research essay, you should think of yourself as responding to the ideas of others. In other words, you shouldn't accept all the material you read at face value; instead, you should evaluate and assess its merits. Positioning your opinion within the context of varying claims is often referred to as "entering into a conversation" with your research sources.

Research as a way of becoming aware of a range of viewpoints: Before you have researched your topic in depth, you may think that there are only two sides—a "pro" and a "con"—and that you will be required to choose one of them. However, academic discourse frequently works outside of these kinds of "yes or no" binaries, and your job as a researcher is to understand how your sources qualify their opinions beyond pro/con positions. You will find that some sources are more extreme than others, and you may want to discuss their suitability with your instructor before deciding whether they will be appropriate for your particular project.

See Chapter 11 for more information on thinking outside pro/con positions.

Research as a way to discover your own opinion: Even if you begin your research with a firm opinion on your chosen topic, you may find that your reading will help clarify or enrich your point of view. For instance, in reading the

7.1

extreme "pro" and "con" positions, you may realize that you prefer to situate your argument in between the two ends of the spectrum. Other times, you may identify more strongly with one side of the issue and find that arguing against the other side will help you explain why you hold a certain position. After researching an issue, you may even find that your initial viewpoint has changed.

It is important to realize, however, that even for experienced writers and researchers, conducting research can lead to confusion about how to incorporate the ideas of others into their own writing. Sometimes students become confused about where their own ideas start (and where the ideas of others begin) or they feel discouraged because another writer has already expressed a similar opinion. However, all well-researched ideas build from existing ideas. Learning how to choose the appropriate sources, how to interact with them, and how to properly incorporate them into a paper will help to alleviate those concerns. With your instructor's help and with the assistance of the librarians, you can learn how to conduct research that will support rather than overpower your own ideas, which will help you to become a more confident academic writer and thinker.

For more information on conducting research, see *Rules for Writers*, pages 381–404.

7.2 Choosing a Research Topic

Sometimes discovering what you want to write about and finding an appropriate focus are the hardest parts of writing a research paper. Some students are accustomed to working with assigned topics and may find it difficult to choose one that they find sufficiently interesting to research. Others are interested in so many ideas that they find it hard to choose the "right" topic. Whether you fall into one of these groups or somewhere in between, you should carefully choose your research topic for a given assignment. You will spend a great deal of time thinking, reading, talking, and writing about your research essay, so be sure that the topic is one you are committed to exploring. If you are bored by the topic before you begin researching, you are less likely to enjoy or to learn from the research process than if you enter into the research process with a topic that genuinely interests you. Your instructor will likely help you decide if your topic is appropriate to the assignment, but you should begin by thinking of several possible research topics from which to choose.

In addition, most first-year writing classes will include assignments that ask you to find a "debatable" topic. **Debatable topics** must fulfill two criteria. First, they have to stimulate some sort of argument or disagreement, meaning they go beyond reporting the "facts." Second, debatable topics are issues that other researchers have investigated enough for you to be able to locate sufficient resources to inform your understanding of the topic.

You'll often find that the best research topics aren't chosen from thin air but rather relate to something else you're currently doing or thinking about. The following are three approaches to finding a research topic:

For more on choosing a research topic, see *Writing Public Lives*, Chapter 7.

7.2

Explore a topic introduced in one of your classes: A good place to begin exploring topics is to reflect on the discussions and readings in your classes, both in your first-year writing courses and your other courses. If you are in a history class, for example, you might explore a historical event for which there are different interpretations and decide which one seems most compelling to you based on your research and prior knowledge. Or you may simply want to explore more fully a subject that was discussed in a class because you found it intriguing or problematic. In addition, many first-year writing courses are organized around particular themes that will allow you to take a position on a debatable issue or idea within that theme.

Research an issue in your chosen major: Another effective way to decide on a topic is to explore issues in your chosen major or in a particular field you find interesting. Each academic discipline contains its own set of hot topics or controversial issues, and if you are interested in this field as a possible career, you may find it helpful to discover what topics are currently debated in that discipline. For instance, pharmacy students may want to debate the merits of current laws that require medications containing pseudoephedrine to be dispensed only from behind the counter because of the use of that substance in manufacturing methamphetamine, while future teachers may choose to explore the efficacy of current testing standards in evaluating student and teacher performances.

Investigate an extracurricular interest: Your instructor may ask you to identify your non-academic interests as a way of discovering potential issues to write about. For example, students who are passionate about sports might look into the regulations governing university athletics and suggest different approaches, while people who follow current events or environmental issues could take a position on the economy or a local environmental concern.

For more on generating ideas for the researched essay, see Chapters 4, 11, and 12. For more on posing a research question that leads to a debatable topic, see *Rules for Writers*, pages 383–85.

No matter what approach you take when choosing a topic, it is important that you maintain your authorial voice and your own point of view. Your instructor wants to learn about your opinion, so try not to lose it in the voices of your sources. One way to be sure that your voice is prominent in your research paper is to choose a topic based on your own interests, experience, knowledge, and prior opinions. The research you do can then *support* your point of view, not overtake it. It is often a tricky balancing act, but keep in mind that the research should achieve several goals: It should show that you are informed about the history of your topic, that you are aware of the complexities of the debate on which you are choosing a position, and that you have explored the various controversies, as well as the definitions and assumptions that are important in the arguments you have researched.

It is extremely important to communicate with your instructor as you consider research topics. Some instructors set limits on topics that have been overly debated or those that tend to be difficult to write about, such as capital punishment, euthanasia, the legalization of marijuana, or abortion. Other instructors may allow students to write about such "hot button" issues, depending on the student's individual approach to the topic.

7.2

When choosing a **topic**, you should also keep in mind an important distinction: a topic is *not* an argument. A topic is a general area of inquiry, the overall subject of your essay. Using the examples discussed above, a topic might be "federal laws regulating pseudoephedrine," "educational testing standards," "plans to stimulate the economy," or "climate change." Once you have identified a topic, you will have to refine its focus in order to generate an **argument** and a thesis. If you are writing a public argument for English 102, for example, your thesis should take a position or express an opinion about your topic. You might argue that the laws regulating pseudoephedrine are either beneficial or harmful to the public or to professional pharmacists, for instance, or you might present a position that acknowledges some of the benefits as well as drawbacks of these regulations. Or, you might want to argue that the federal government should implement certain specific measures to address the problem of climate change.

In each case, there is probably someone in your audience who will disagree with all or part of your argument, and you will want to consider that reader's position when you express your own. Finding a paper topic that interests you will make it easier to conduct research with an open mind and a willingness to learn more. Remember, though, that you are not a passive reader; you should read a wide variety of sources, evaluate their credibility and effectiveness within the context of your assignment, and present a well-balanced argument.

> For more on writing an effective thesis for an argument, see *Rules for Writers*, pages 23–24 and 360–62, and Chapter 4 of the Student's Guide.

7.3 Narrowing Your Research Topic

One of the most important steps in the research process happens early, at the stage of refining your research topic. Sometimes a research idea that seems like a good paper topic turns out to be so broad that sifting through all the available research can be overwhelming. It's crucial to find a topic that is large enough that other scholars have done research about it, but that is narrow enough for you to be able to identify the most important sources and arguments. Below, you'll find a few tips for narrowing your research topic.

Brainstorm sub-topics *after* you think you've found your topic: After you've found a topic that interests you, try making it even more specific by brainstorming sub-topics. It will be helpful to do some preliminary research at this point to learn what sub-topics exist. For example, the UA research librarians recommend checking out what's been written about your topic in *CQ Researcher* or another UA library database to begin narrowing your topic.

> *Broad topic:* Alternative energy sources
>
> > *Possible sub-topics found through preliminary research:* Biofuels, electric cars, solar power, environmental activism efforts in Tucson

Through your research, you might find that even a sub-topic can be narrowed further.

New topic: Solar power

> *Possible sub-topics:* solar energy high-speed trains, solar ovens, solar panels on electric cars

Pair your topic with a related issue: Sometimes pairing one topic with a second one helps to provide a more specific and defined lens for your research. As you do preliminary research on your topic, keep an eye out for an angle that you might bring to your research idea.

Research topic: Solar ovens

> *Possible pairings:* Solar ovens in disaster zones, solar ovens in developing countries, solar ovens and elementary education

Ground your research in something you know: Approaching a research topic when you already know something about it helps you to develop a personal stake in your findings. Try narrowing your topic so that instead of it being an abstract idea (such as environmentalism), it evolves into something more concrete and complex. Your topic should also be narrowed into something in which you already have an interest. Mechanical engineering majors might narrow "alternative energy sources" to solar cars, for example, whereas a sociology major might be more interested in studying environmental activism in Tucson. Ask yourself: *What do I have to say about this topic?* If you can't answer that question, you need a narrower topic.

Write a pointed research question: A clear, focused research question is one of the best ways to develop a strong research topic. Remember that if you aren't interested in learning the answer to your question, chances are good that your future readers won't be so interested in the answer, either. Always write a question you are interested in answering.

Research topic: Solar ovens

> *Research Question 1:* How have solar ovens been used in recent disaster zones, and what are the positive and negative effects of this use?

> *Research Question 2:* How do environmental factors influence the effectiveness of solar ovens, and are they better suited for some geographic places than for others?

> *Research Question 3:* What has been the most influential solar oven project, and how has it shaped the way solar ovens are used and made today?

Strong research questions share a few qualities:

- **They can be answered in the space you have available.** For example, it would be nearly impossible to answer the question about whether climate change exists in the space of a five-page paper, but it might be manageable to learn about the political reasons for and impacts of George W. Bush not signing the Kyoto Protocol in 2005.

- **They are clearly significant; they carry an answer to the "so what?" question.** For example, Research Question 2 sets the writer up for an argument about why solar ovens should only be used in certain parts of the world.

- **They have not already been answered by somebody else.** For example, asking "What is climate change?" is not an original research question, although it might be a question you have to answer in your essay to make your own researched argument.

7.4 Finding Sources

Once you have settled on a topic for research, the next step is to decide where to go for more information. The first and most appropriate places are the University of Arizona libraries. You may think of the library as one place or building, but in reality, the University maintains many different collections in various locations and an extensive online library. In addition to the Main Library, sometimes you will want to visit the Science-Engineering Library, the Fine Arts Library, the Law Library, Special Collections, or the Center for Creative Photography (CCP). You can use the UA library resources electronically or in person. Below are some tips for finding both online and print sources using the library.

Using Online Library Resources

College-level research will require you to access the more specialized resources available only in the databases to which the University libraries subscribe. These **databases** are collections of a wide variety of resources, such as newspapers, magazines, and scholarly journals that have been compiled into electronic collections that are searchable by keyword, author, title, subject, and more.

You can access the library's databases by title and subject from the library's website: <http://www.library.arizona.edu/search/articles/>.

Some are available in **"full-text,"** which means that the entire article is readable online. Others provide an abstract or summary that will allow you to decide whether you want to read the entire article. Part of your university tuition is used to pay for the information available at the library, so be sure to take advantage of this resource. There are a few ways to search for materials using the UA library database:

Go to <http://lro.library.arizona.edu/subject-guide/23-English-Compostion to use the English Composition Subject Guide.

1. **Use the library website directly.** This strategy involves going directly to the UA library website and searching for articles using the databases described above. One good way to do this is to use the library's online **English Composition Subject Guide**. The subject guide provides links to the online library catalog, many appropriate article databases, and other

131

resources that you will need to successfully complete your research. This is just one of many subject guides; there are guides for almost every discipline taught on campus.

The library databases hold many electronic articles, but sometimes you'll come across an article you'd like to use that is not immediately available in full-text. Don't worry: you can request an electronic copy of articles that the library does not have through its databases using **Express Document Delivery**. You can also request an electronic copy of a single chapter or article from a larger book that the library holds. While these services are convenient, they do take time. Allow up to a week, and sometimes longer, for electronic document delivery.

2. **Use Google Scholar**—but only after you change the Scholar Preferences to search the UA library system for full-text availability. If you've updated your Scholar Preferences to include the UA library as one of your "library links," then a link appears on the right-hand side of any article that you can get in full-text from the UA library.

3. **Never pay for an article that you find on the Web.** If you are ever asked to pay for an article, try finding it using a UA library database such as *Academic Search Complete* or *JSTOR* first. Even if our library doesn't hold a full-text version of the article, you can always request it through Express Document Delivery. If you have trouble locating the article using the UA library website, write down the citation information and get in touch with a librarian at the Information Commons Reference Desk. He or she will be able to help you find it for free.

Using Print Sources

Although online researching is becoming increasingly convenient, sometimes you also need to go to the library. Not all journals are online yet; some are still available only in hard copy. Books are still a valuable source of information for researchers. Visiting the library can also lead to the discovery of new resources that you didn't find using an online search. Library books are catalogued by topic, which means that books with similar topics are often shelved near one another. Experienced researchers know that when they find a book they think will be useful to their projects, they can often find other useful books simply by scanning the shelves around the first book. For instance, if you located a book that analyzes Shakespeare's *Hamlet* by using the library's online catalog, you might see a book near it that looks at the relationships between *Hamlet* and Shakespeare's other dramas, one that you had not found in the online catalog. Another way to use print resources is to skim the bibliographies and works cited sections of books and articles you have already found for more possible sources.

Sometimes the book you want is not available at the library, but can be requested via "**ILL**," or **Interlibrary Loan**. Libraries maintain lending policies with each other that allow you to borrow a book that is not held locally, but of

You can find more information on Express Document Delivery at <http://www.library.arizona.edu/services/docdel/index.html>.

See complete instructions for linking Google Scholar with the UA library system here: <http://lro.library.arizona.edu/subject-guide/23-English-Composition>

To find print resources using the library's online catalog, go to <http://sabio.library.arizona.edu/search/X>.

7.4

course it takes a few days to have a book mailed from another library so you have to plan ahead to use ILL.

As mentioned in Section 7.1, you should also take advantage of the librarians' specialized training in finding and evaluating information. Go to the reference desks or contact the subject specialists via e-mail and ask for tips on where to find the kinds of resources you need.

7.5 Evaluating Sources

Every day you encounter information from multiple sources: books, instructors, friends, the Internet, television, magazines, and more. When researching an essay or project, your job as a student and a critical thinker is to sift through the many conflicting claims and competing opinions and decide which are the most credible and reliable. Evaluating sources is as important a part of the research process as finding them. One of the most important questions to ask when evaluating a source is whether or not that source is **credible**. How believable is the information? To answer this question, you should be aware of a few basic academic rules of thumb. An important distinction in academic research is that made between **scholarly** and **popular** sources.

- A scholarly source is a text written for an audience with specialized knowledge about a particular subject. You might think of a scholarly source as a text written by an expert for an audience of experts in a given field.

- A popular source, by contrast, is written for a general audience rather than for an audience of experts. You may think of a popular source as a text written by a non-expert (or occasionally by an expert) for a broad audience of non-experts.

See the box below to compare the major distinctions between scholarly and popular sources.

Scholarly vs. Popular Sources: A Quick Reference Guide

Characteristic	Scholarly Source	Popular Source
What does it look like?	• Generally longer and more detailed than a popular source. • Usually includes many citations to other texts. • Front covers are often bland with few pictures.	• Generally shorter than a scholarly source. • Usually includes few to no citations to other texts. • Front covers and inside pages are often full of photographs and short snippets of text.

> Information about getting help in the library is found on the library's website at <http://www.library.arizona.edu/help/ask/index.html>.

> For more advice on determining if a source is scholarly, see *Rules for Writers*, page 401.

> Tutorials and Guides created for English writing students, including a quick lesson on the differences between scholarly and popular sources, can be found on the English Composition research guide at <http://www.library.arizona.edu/search/subjects/englishcomp/>.

7.5

Characteristic	Scholarly Source	Popular Source
What is its purpose?	• Seeks to contribute to an ongoing academic debate or discussion.	• Seeks to inform the general public about news or entertainment.
Where is it published?	• Published through a process called "peer review," which means that before being accepted for publication, the article is read by experts in the field who assess its reliability, its relevance, and the quality of its research and writing. The scholarly review process can take years. • Generally found in academic books and academic journals.	• If it is edited, editors are usually specialists at editing rather than specialists in the topic the work covers. Popular editing generally takes anywhere from a day (think of newspapers) to years (think of long fiction books). • Generally found in newspapers, magazines, and online sources such as blogs.
What kinds of sources does it cite?	• Usually quotes experts to back up claims. • Almost always includes in-text citations and a bibliography of cited texts. Citations may include quotations, paraphrases, summaries, footnotes, endnotes, and bibliographies. • Quotes serve to situate the new position the author is advancing within the existing body of knowledge and to guide readers to the other credible sources of information about the topic.	• May quote experts. • May also quote non-experts as sources to help back up claims. • Does not usually provide information on how to access those expert opinions beyond naming them. In other words, does not include in-text citations. • Quotes are generally shorter and are less frequently analyzed than in scholarly sources. They usually serve as evidence for the claim the work is seeking to make.

7.5

Characteristic	Scholarly Source	Popular Source
Who is the author?	• Authors are experts in their field writing for other students or experts in their field. • Many scholarly sources are written by professors, including the professors you take classes from at the UA.	• Authors are generally not considered experts on the topic and are writing for other non-experts. • Many popular sources are written by journalists, bloggers, and everyday people who are interested in their topic but might not be trained to do research.
Who is its intended audience?	• Intended to be read by other experts in the field. • Assumes readers already have some specialized knowledge.	• Written for a general audience. • May not assume that their readers have any specialized knowledge.
How did I find it?	• Accessible through academic databases like *JSTOR* or *Academic Search Complete*. • Often found in academic libraries such as the UA Main Library.	• Generally accessible using popular search engines such as Google or Yahoo! • Often sold at newsstands or at bookstores.
What are some examples?	• *Arizona Quarterly, Journal of Insect Science, Rhetoric Review** *All of these journals are published by the UA.	• *Time, Newsweek, The Wall Street Journal, Popular Science*

Evaluating Internet Sources

As more and more material becomes available on the Internet, it is increasingly important to know how to evaluate the credibility of online sources. In fact, one of the first discussions about research in your first-year writing courses will probably center on the differences between using a search engine such as *Google* and using a library database such as *Academic Search Complete* or *LexisNexis Academic Universe*. Generally speaking, most texts you find using library databases are either scholarly or news sources, both of which are fairly credible resources. On the other hand, sources available through popular search engines range in terms of credibility from well-researched information published by respectable organizations to incorrect assertions published by misinformed in-

For more information on rhetorical analysis, see Chapter 10.

dependent authors. Web pages are not subject to the review process of a peer-reviewed scholarly source or even that of a respected popular source such as the *New York Times* or *Time* magazine. Anyone with the technical skills and access to the Internet can publish a Web page on any topic even without expertise in the subject. For instance, an angry consumer can publish a Web page denouncing a certain product even if the consumer's dissatisfaction arises out of misuse rather than any defect of the product itself. If student researchers rely only on that consumer's Web page, the research and any conclusions drawn by the researchers would be limited at best and perhaps seriously incorrect. Therefore, it is important to employ the skills of rhetorical analysis when evaluating Internet sources. Looking critically at the audience and purpose can shed light on the credibility of the source.

The UA library also has an online tutorial you can complete to learn how to evaluate different types of Web resources. Go to < http://www.library.arizona.edu/tutorials/evaluating_web_resources/> to use this tutorial.

A commonly cited Internet resource is the online encyclopedia, which can range from *Encyclopedia Britannica*, available through the university library, to *Wikipedia*, a free online resource that can be edited by any Internet user. Your instructor may or may not allow you to use encyclopedias, but if you research using these sources, you should be aware of the distinctions between them; although *Wikipedia* may well be authoritative, its reliability is not monitored in the same way as an encyclopedia such as the *Encyclopedia Britannica* is monitored.

If your instructor allows you to use non-scholarly sources in your research papers, it's still important to verify that these non-scholarly sources are credible. Even when a Web page looks and sounds official, you should be careful to verify that it is valid and credible. Below is a list of questions to help you evaluate the credibility of online information. These are by no means the only questions possible, but they do serve as a starting point.

For more information on evaluating sources, see *Rules for Writers*, pages 397–404.

- What is the URL? Does it end with .com, .edu, .org, .gov, .biz, .name, .info, or .net? What does each of these domain names imply? Which would indicate that the source is credible?

- Can you identify an author for the information? Can you verify the author's expertise?

- Does the Web page provide information about when it was last updated? Is there any way of determining whether the material is out-of-date? What sorts of links are on the page? Where do these links lead you? Are the links still working?

- Is there any information on how to cite the source? Websites catering to academic audiences are more likely to include this information than those geared for more general audiences. When citing an online article from a library index or database, the name of the database is part of the citation.

7.5

- What is the intention of the text? Is its purpose to inform, entertain, or persuade the reader? Or is the purpose to promote a commercial product, an idea, philosophy, or way of seeing something?

- Are there graphics? If so, what do they illustrate and why?

- Is the source biased, one-sided, incomplete, or erroneous? Who profits if viewers of the website believe its information to be true? Can you verify the information with other online or print sources?

- Does the source suggest avenues for further inquiry such as possible readings, research, or links? Does it cite reputable sources or note the extent to which claims in the text are connected to recognized authorities in the field?

Evaluating websites carefully is an essential part of your research process, since the reliability of your own argument in an academic context will depend in large part upon the credibility of your citations and sources. Whenever you are in doubt about the suitability of a certain source, consult your instructor and the UA librarians.

7.6 Engaging with and Keeping Track of Sources

As you research your topic, make a conscious effort to keep track of the sources you find. Keeping track of sources is about more than organization, although staying organized while you do research will save you a lot of time in the long run. In addition to keeping track of basic information about your sources, you can begin the actual writing process as you collect your sources by taking notes in which you interact with each source. This section will address both aspects of tracking sources.

Recording Crucial Information

When you search for books and journal articles and as you copy or print articles, it is easy to forget to keep track of all the bibliographic material you will need to compile your Works Cited page at the end of your essay. It can be time-consuming and frustrating to retrace your steps later to find a publisher's name, a page number, or the database for an online article. Here are a few tips:

- **Keep track of your research in a research log.** To do this, record the databases and indexes you search and the keywords that you use in each database. Keep this log with the notes you take. This will help you keep track of where you have looked and what sources were good for your topic. Write down sources you review that are not helpful, too, so that you don't waste time by accidentally reviewing a source twice.

7.6

- **Copy materials you cannot check out of the library for an extended period** (such as journals). Print or download articles or texts that you find online. Do not assume that you will be able to find such sources again later; they may be in use or in the process of being reshelved when you look for them again. In the case of online materials, don't assume that you can find the article again easily. It will save you time to print or download the article at the time you find it.

You can learn more about RefWorks at <http://www.library.arizona.edu/search/articles/dbDetail.php?shortname=refworks>.

- **Try using RefWorks or other bibliographic software.** Another option for compiling resources is an application available through the UA libraries called RefWorks, which formats and organizes your citations and bibliographies as you work. A librarian can help you learn to use this resource.

- **Immediately write down any information that you will need** every time you copy or print materials out of a book, journal, or online database. This information will include the page numbers you read as well as all of the bibliographic information for the source. Make it a habit to write this information on the first page of anything you copy or print and record it in your research log. You can find an in-depth explanation of how to cite various types of sources in your *Rules for Writers* handbook. In the box on pages 142–143, you'll find sample citations for books, journal articles, and websites using MLA style. The first entry lists the information you'll need to write a citation; the second is a sample citation.

- **Compile an Annotated Bibliography**, in which you include all the bibliographic information (in the required format for your paper) and a brief description of each text. This will help you keep track of who said what. You can easily flip through it to remind yourself of each author's main points. See the discussion of Annotated Bibliographies in the next section of this chapter.

- **Write the citation as soon as you use a quote, summary, or paraphrase of any source, then immediately add that source to your Works Cited page.** That way you will be certain to cite all your references, and when you revise you won't have to look through all your materials to find the correct citation again.

- **Refer to "MLA Documentation" in *Rules for Writers*, starting on page 426.** Also view the UA libraries' MLA tutorial at <http://www.library.arizona.edu/help/tutorials/citation/mla/>.

Engaging with Your Sources

Engaged reading takes more than just reading through a text and underlining passages. One of the best ways to engage with your sources is to take notes as you read. Think about taking notes as having a conversation with a source and asking questions you might eventually address in your paper. Although reading takes longer when you take notes, you'll save time later because you'll already have a record of what you found interesting about the source and where you found it. Chapter 3 illustrates how to annotate a primary text as you read. When you take research notes, you can follow a similar process, only you are **responding** to each source and considering it under a particular light instead of just trying to understand what it means. If you write or type substantial notes while you study your sources, you will find it much easier to integrate ideas about those sources into your essay. Looking back over your notes, you will probably find that you have already recorded ideas, made points, and interacted with evidence that can fit nicely into your working draft.

When reading through your sources, **do not just highlight large sections of the text**. When you look at such highlighted text later, you will likely not remember why you highlighted that section, or you could be overwhelmed by the amount of text, leading you to quote too much of the source in your essay or to skip that section of the source altogether. Asking questions and making comments while you read your sources helps you to think critically through the issues as you work through the research process. Note taking can also help you see patterns among sources, which may help you identify where your voice comes into the conversation. You may also realize that you have only found one-sided sources, thereby giving you a direction for further research while you still have plenty of time left to write.

> For more information on paraphrase, summary, and quotation, see *Rules for Writers*, pages 408–10 and 415–26. Also see Chapter 6.

Sample Research Notes

On the following page, you'll find a sample entry for taking research notes. Creating two columns helps to record the ideas you have about specific parts of a text, and it can save you from having to go back and hunt down specific quotations later on in the writing process. This student-written entry was provided by UA librarian Vicki Mills. The research project explored how elementary school minority children are able, or unable, to relate to the characters in the books they read.

7.6

At the top of the page, record the bibliographic information.

In the right column, record your response to the passage on the left.

In the left column, write the page number and a quote or paraphrase that you find interesting, relevant, or even incorrect or confusing. Writing the quotation will help you consider it more fully than if you just looked at it on the page and recorded the page number.

Your notes should include questions or challenges you have for the text, as well as your possible responses to these questions.

Note other research you need to do, including new searches and looking up experts named in the source text.

Write yourself notes that will help you to construct your argument when you start drafting.

Don't worry about writing in full sentences; taking notes is like talking back to your sources. Being casual can make the process more comfortable and generative, and you can always dress up your language in your actual draft.

This kind of research note might very well become a central part of your paper. Keeping research notes helps to save these important insights you have as you engage with your sources.

Tolson, Nancy. "Making Books Available: The Role of Early Libraries, Librarians, and Booksellers in the Promotion of African American Children's Literature." *African American Review* 32.1 (1998): 9–16. *Academic Search Complete*. Web. 1 Oct. 2008.

Source Material	Notes, Questions, etc.
"African American children's books are in existence today because of the determination and dedication of African Americans who decided more than sixty years ago to remove negative depictions of servile, impoverished African Americans from library shelves. These people were able to establish criteria, petition publishers, and creatively write stories for African American children that reflected positive images at a time when few of these books could get published." (Tolson 15)	This seems to be Tolson's thesis, and I agree with it. The focus is pretty historical throughout the article though. My question would be, what is happening with the depiction of minorities in children's books now? Surely they are still problematic at times. Look for more contemporary articles on this. What did these negative depictions do to children's desire to read and to their own identity? I need to look for other articles that relate the lack of books with positive minority role models to the reading ability of minority children.
"Bontemps, being both an educator and the father of six children, knew the importance of writing books that would reflect positive African American images; this meant, among other things, freeing his African American characters from the heavy dialect that most other authors had imposed upon them." (10)	This is one way I might go with this paper—the importance of parents reading to children and the problem of minority parents finding enough appropriate books to read. Like how Tolson says that the depictions in Bontemps' books meant "*freeing*… characters from the heavy dialect." The same thing happens in the depiction of other minority characters—American Indian, Hispanic, or Asian American—they are basically trapped and limited by the language and the behavior the author assigns them (particularly if that author is not from the minority group). So minority children see in these books what they are supposed to sound like and act like, not what they actually sound or act like, which must be really confusing for them sometimes.

7.7 The Annotated Bibliography

One useful way to keep track of your research is to create an **Annotated Bibliography**. The Annotated Bibliography, which consists of alphabetical lists of topic-related sources, each with a summary paragraph, provides a useful way for researchers to share their information. Annotated Bibliographies are highly valued by scholars because they allow researchers to quickly review the best sources on a given topic. Even if you don't end up publishing your Annotated Bibliography for other researchers, it can be a useful way for you to keep track of the best sources for your research topic.

Putting together an Annotated Bibliography will help you gather and analyze information before you sit down to write. When working with many sources, it can be very helpful to have brief summaries of each article as a quick resource guide. Often, instructors will distribute Annotated Bibliographies among students in a class as a way to share ideas and sources. Since students sometimes need the same kinds of sources, another student's Annotated Bibliography can make you aware of other material that might be useful for your particular project. For these reasons, it is important to realize that your classmates as well as your instructor are your audience for this assignment. To that end, take care to write in a voice and style that appeals to this general, non-expert audience, translating technical material into your own words where you can. If you are too brief in your annotations, those summary paragraphs may not help you recall the details of the articles, and they may not give others enough information to assess the usefulness of the articles. Your Annotated Bibliography should include a short discussion of how each reference will be useful for your writing.

Following is an Annotated Bibliography that was written by UA student Stephenie Mirka. Please note that the citations are in MLA format and in alphabetical order and that, in each entry, Stephenie considers not only what the source is about, but also how it could contribute to her research.

Note that this sample Annotated Bibliography includes mostly newspaper and academic journal articles. There are many other types of texts that you should consider when you conduct research, and each type of source uses a slightly different style of citation. **Always refer closely to your *Rules for Writers* as you compile a list of Works Cited.**

Annotated Bibliography

Hardesty, Dawn Wotapka. "Long Island Landlord Group: Sex Offender Law Goes Too Far." *Long Island Business News*. The Dolan Company, 17 Nov. 2006. Web. 24 Feb. 2007.

> Hardesty claims that a bill in Long Island, regarding landlords renting to sex offenders, is ridiculous. The author utilizes many quotes from people, who agree and disagree with her claim. By including both points of view in her argument, she strengthens her essay. She also ex-

plains the disadvantages of this law, and how it victimizes sexual offenders. Her purpose is to show that some sex offender laws are too extreme. This article will provide a point of view different than mine for my persuasive essay. It will give me an example of a sexual offender law that is creating problems for landlords. Hardesty provides information from the creator of the bill, which will be useful to back up my claims. I chose this source because it gave a good example of why some laws do not work against sexual offenders.

Longo, Robert E. "Megan's Law Does Little to Increase Safety in US." *Community Care*. Reed Business Information Limited, 3 Aug. 2006. Web. 25 Feb. 2007.

Longo claims that the development of Megan's Law has not been proven to decrease the number of sexual abuse cases within the United States. The author proves this by including background information, statistics, and examples. He discusses the many implications of Megan's Law, such as cost and victimization of sexual offenders. This victimization has caused many to become offenders again because they are not able to live normal lives after their release from prison. Longo's purpose is to show his readers that the only way to put an end to sexual abuse is to stop it before it occurs. Megan's Law does not aid in this since no evidence exists to prove that it has prevented reoccurrences of sexual abuse. This article will aid in my research question of deciding whether sexual offenders should be integrated back into society. It shows examples and statistics that could be used in my paper.

Sample MLA Citations

You can find examples of how to cite almost any kind of source in your *Rules for Writers* textbook. Below are sample citations for the three most common texts you'll cite in first-year composition: a book, a scholarly article, and a Web page.

Book

Generic Citation	Sample Citation
Author's last name, Author's first name. *Title of Book*. Place of publication: Publisher name, Year of publication. Print.	Anzaldúa, Gloria. *Borderlands/ La Frontera: The New Mestiza*. San Francisco: Aunt Lute, 2007. Print.

Journal Article from an Electronic Database

Generic Citation	Sample Citation
Author's last name, Author's first name. "Title of Article." *Title of Journal* Volume number. Issue number (Month Year of Publication): Page numbers. *Title of Electronic Database*. Web. Day Month Year Accessed.	Antoniou, Maria and Jessica Moriarty. "What Can Academic Writers Learn from Creative Writers? Developing Guidance and Support for Lecturers in Higher Education." *Teaching in Higher Education* 13.2 (Apr. 2008): 157–67. *Academic Search Complete*. Web. 17 Apr. 2010.

Miller, Kathleen. "Wyoming Fears It's Luring Sex Offenders." *Chron.com*. The Houston Chronicle, 25 Feb. 2007. Web. 25 Feb. 2007.

> Miller discusses the number of sex offenders that are moving to Wyoming as a result of the harsh laws in other states. Miller uses quotes from a representative of the U.S. House of Representatives, sex offenders, a police officer, and many others. These add substance to her article, when used with background information and other facts regarding laws in Wyoming. Miller's purpose is to inform people of the lack of laws for sexual predators. She wants this to change so that more sexual predators will have to be registered, and harsher laws will be created. In my paper, this article can provide me with an opposing point of view. This will help me to draw my own conclusions about the opposing viewpoint.

Seipp, Catherine. "The Sex-Offender Lobby." *The Wall Street Journal*. Dow Jones and Company, 6 Oct. 2005. Web. 25 Feb. 2007.

> Seipp states in her editorial that laws regarding sex offenders and landlords in California do not coincide well. She proves her point by explaining Megan's Law. Also, Seipp's article contains quotes from opponents and advocates of Megan's Law. By including the views of a landlord who is unable to move a sex offender out of his mobile-home park, but still needs to inform angry residents of their presence, she makes her case far more understandable to the reader. The author's purpose is to let people know that lawmakers should not oppose Megan's Law. This applies to my research question by showing the opposing point of view. I

General Web Page

Generic Citation	Sample Citation
Author, editor, or corporation in charge of site. *Title of website*. Sponsor or publisher of site, Date of last publication or update. Web. Day Month Year Accessed.	Eidenmuller, Michael E. *American Rhetoric: The Power of Oratory in the United States*. Michael E. Eidenmuller, 2010. Web. 25 Jan. 2011.

Article from an Online Periodical (Non-scholarly)

Generic Citation	Sample Citation
Author's last name, Author's first name. "Title of Article." *Title of website*. Sponsor or publisher of site, Day Month Year Published. Web. Day Month Year Accessed.	Forney, Matthew and Arthur Kroeber. "Google's Business Reason for Leaving China." *The Wall Street Journal*. Dow Jones and Company, 6 Apr. 2010. Web. 25 Feb. 2011.*

*If you've been using MLA citation style for a while, you might notice that the newest version of MLA does not require you to include the URL for online sources in your Works Cited.

can use this in my persuasive essay to show readers what others think regarding the issue of sex offenders. Seipp includes various quotes, which could be added into my paper to expand on the opposing viewpoint.

Sullum, Jacob. "Zoned Out: Sex Offender Residency Restrictions." *Reason* 38.10 (2007): 9–12. Web. 24 Feb. 2007.

> Sullum suggests that laws restricting where sexual offenders live are unnecessary and create stress for prior sex offenders. Sullum does this by describing how the majority of the laws apply to people who committed crimes when they were teenagers. He also says that restrictions for where these offenders reside may end up making them less likely to register, which would make it impossible to track their whereabouts. The author includes some quotes from officials and statistics, as well. This article demonstrates that sexual offenders should not be segregated from the rest of the community. It will help to answer my research question by providing me with statistics that prove that laws against sex offenders should not be as harsh.

Wing, Arthur. "Housing and Sex Offenders." *Child Abuse Review* 7.6 (1998): 449–52. Web. 24 Feb. 2007.

> Wing argues that sex offenders need to live somewhere in the community, but also need to live somewhere that minimizes their risk of offending children again. He develops his claim by providing many detailed solutions to the problem. Also, he includes the advantages and disadvantages to each solution. Wing's purpose is to convince people that local authorities should be involved in the housing of registered sex offenders. He desires this change to come about while still protecting the children in the surrounding community. The author basically sums up my view of my research question. I believe that sex offenders should still have rights because they are citizens, but the safety of children should also be taken into consideration when housing these former criminals. The author discusses various acts, such as the Crime and Disorder Act 1998, which will help the authorities and health professionals to work together in finding suitable programs and housing for offenders. This will definitely provide much of the needed information that I will use to back up my claims.

7.8 Research Checklist

The following checklist can help you remember and keep track of all the stages in the research process and assess your progress as you work through the process.

☐ Brainstorm topics.

☐ Form a list of possible topics.

☐ Browse a site like *CQ Researcher*, the *Hot Topics* part of the *English Composition research guide*, or one of the subject encyclopedias on the library's website to gather ideas about topics.

☐ Narrow down list of possible topics to one or two ideas.

☐ Get more details and sources on your topic or topics using keyword searches in the Library Catalog and databases like *Academic Search Complete*. Remember you can also find other good sources from the bibliographies of the books and articles you find.

☐ Record promising sources (links to full-text articles, call numbers, etc.).

☐ Get books from the stacks. Skim for appropriateness. Check out the best sources from the library. When you find good books for your topic, browse the shelves around your book.

☐ Photocopy, print, or download articles from scholarly journals and periodicals.

☐ Formulate focused research questions.

☐ Read through your sources. Take notes and summarize your best sources.

☐ Keep track of your sources. Keep a research journal. You may also want to use a service like RefWorks or Zotero for this.

☐ Schedule an interview with an expert on the issue you're interested in. Prepare questions and talking points ahead of time.

☐ Meet with a librarian, either at a reference desk or by appointment.

☐ Double-check that you have all of the sources you need. Check also that you've written down all information needed for your own Works Cited list.

☐ Consider writing an Annotated Bibliography to help keep track of your sources and their primary arguments in relation to your paper.

☐ Begin writing your first draft!

7.8

7.8

PART III
ASSIGNMENTS

Analysis

Goals

Your Textual Analysis essay should:

- Demonstrate that you have read a text closely, carefully, and critically.

- Show a critical awareness of the author's choices and strategies.

- Develop a clear and specific thesis that invites the reader to read the text in the same way that you do.

- Analyze the strategies authors use to construct a text's effect or message.

- Integrate evidence from the text to support your thesis.

- Provide a clear and persuasive argument for your interpretation of the text.

- Develop well-organized paragraphs using standard written English.

- Provide meaningful feedback to your peers during the revision process.

- Incorporate peer and instructor feedback in the final version.

CHAPTER 8

149

8.1 Analysis: Reading with a Critical Eye

All of the assignments you will complete in your first-year writing courses require **analysis**. In fact, in much of the work you do at the university, you will be asked to analyze something and to support your own understanding of it. In your first-year writing class, that "something" might be a written text, an image, or an audience; in your art history class it might be a particular social or historical **context**, an artist's technique, or a particular medium. In your biology class, you might analyze cellular function, an ecosystem, or the life cycle of a particular organism; in your chemistry class, you might analyze the chemical properties of a compound or the results of a chemical reaction. Regardless of what "something" you are analyzing, you are essentially performing the same cognitive task: closely and carefully examining the subject in an attempt to understand it better. That is, any type of analysis asks you to examine, to read something with a critical eye. Analysis plays a significant role in any field of study, and it will likely play a significant role in your success as a college student.

In your first-year writing courses, analysis requires an ability to explain **how** and **why** a written or visual text works to make meaning using concrete examples from the text. The skills you will need for analysis in first-year composition are fairly consistent and can be applied to all types of texts, as you will see in the other sections of this chapter. But before we move into our discussion of analysis, let's take a moment to define some key terms for this chapter:

> For more information on analysis, and to see a sample student analysis, see *Rules for Writers*, pages 352–57.

- **Analysis:** The act of explaining *how* and *why* a written or visual text does something and whether or not it does it effectively. This goes a few steps beyond summary/description. Summary/description explains *what* is happening with a topic, while analysis explains *how* and *why* something is happening with the same topic. Analysis is the act of breaking a text into parts and examining how those parts create a message and affect a reader's or viewer's response. Remember that analytical statements reveal a careful consideration of the text beyond just its main point and open up a space for dialogue about the text and how it speaks to an audience.

> For a full definition of "summary" and how it differs from analysis, see Chapter 6 of the *Student's Guide*.

In your first-year writing courses, you will want to be careful not to confuse **analysis** with **summary**. Unlike analysis, summary is a statement of the facts about a text, not a critical examination of it. When you summarize a text, you are not engaging in analysis. Instead, summary functions as a way of familiarizing your reader with a given text so that she or he can understand your analysis of it. For example, if you were to write, "This short story focuses on two relationships that are falling apart," you would be summarizing because you are stating what the story is about. To make this statement more analytical, you would need to move beyond summary. For instance, you might write, "The narrator's point of view shows only one side of the arguments these couples have. Without hearing every character's thoughts, it is impossible to be sure whom to blame for the conflicts. Perhaps the author restricts the narrator's point of view like this to warn against one-sided interpretations." Notice how the analytical statements reveal a careful consideration of the text beyond just its main point and discuss the strategies the author is using to communicate a message to the reader.

- **Text**: Any "something" that you analyze—whether written or visual. In your first-year writing courses, you'll be dealing with a variety of texts. For example, a text might refer to a book, a newspaper article, a short story, a poem, a speech, a movie, a picture, a video game, a person, an event, a space, a place, and so on.

- **Strategies:** How writers, artists, architects, and other creators of texts decide to present their texts and ideas. Strategies include repetition of key terms, use of extended metaphors, arrangement of the text, choice of color and medium, and so on. For specific strategies for different kinds of texts, see sections 8.2 and 8.4–8.6.

When applying these terms to analysis, maintaining focus is essential. In other words, you should have a particular focus when doing analysis because no single essay on a particular text can pretend to say everything there is to say about that text. If you try to take on too much in your essay, you will find that the thesis will lack specificity and the paragraphs will be unfocused. Therefore, you will want to read the assigned texts for the textual analysis unit carefully, paying attention to particular choices and strategies each author uses, and you should try to group together those strategies that seem to have a similar focus or goal. Ask yourself:

- What **strategies** stand out as most interesting to you in this text?

- What **message** is the author communicating to the reader by using a particular strategy?

- Can you find other moments in the text where the author seems to communicate the same message?

In addition to focusing on a text's strategies, analytical writing must also be **persuasive** in order to be effective. In any type of analysis, you are inviting the audience to see the text in the same way that you do. However, your goal is not to uncover the one "true" meaning that the artist/writer intended. As film scholar Greg M. Smith argues, "One of the first steps that the budding critic should avoid is thinking that a film can be understood as having a single message that we either 'get' or don't get" (66). In other words, texts do not consist of a singular message; rather, they comprise **several potential messages** that the viewer or reader works to uncover in the act of analysis. Texts are complex expressions that invite many interpretations. How you interpret a text will depend on your unique interests, cultural background, experience, knowledge, and perspective. In analytical writing, you are enhancing the complexity of the text's message by inviting an audience to see the text through your perspective. Therefore, it is important to think about what you see in a text that others might not.

Once you choose a **message** that you would like to focus on in your analysis, you need to devise a strong, clear thesis that you can support with specific references to the text. Although different methods of analysis require writers to focus on different features, all methods of analysis are similar in that they provide a way to look closely at selected aspects of the text. Keep in mind that analysis always goes beyond mere observation. You should articulate the significance of your observations in a coherent argument. In an analysis essay, you should demonstrate your ability to develop a clear interpretation of a text based on **evidence** from the text itself. This evidence usually consists of examples of your strategies or quotations that demonstrate the patterns you have found.

Paragraph Structure for Textual Analysis

Once you have chosen a message to analyze in your text, identified strategies that communicate that particular message, and chosen key examples of those strategies, you will need to put all of this together into paragraphs that follow **PIE** structure. For a textual analysis essay, your paragraphs should:

- Open with a **topic sentence** that relates a strategy or pattern to the message you will focus on (**Point**).

- Present your evidence, or examples from the text, of that strategy or pattern (**Illustration**).

- Analyze these examples by clearly connecting each to the message you are emphasizing (**Explanation**).

Each paragraph in this structure does what your overall essay intends to do: answer both "how" and "why." By identifying strategies, you are addressing the "how" question, examining how the author chose to construct the text. Then, by attaching significance to those strategies, you are answering the "why" question and therefore analyzing one potential **message** of the text.

In the next section, we will look at specific strategies that are used in written texts. Section 8.4 will help you to analyze visual texts and 8.5 specifically addresses analyzing films.

8.2 Textual Analysis: Written Narratives

We mentioned earlier in the chapter that all the analysis you will do in first-year composition will involve some kind of text, and we also said that "text" in your first-year composition courses can refer to anything from a book to a photograph. However, there are significant differences in the ways you read written texts versus the ways you read visual ones. In this section, we will focus on the analysis of written narratives, although we want to emphasize that the term "textual analysis" is not specific to only written texts. When you engage in textual analysis, you could be examining something written, like a poem or short story; something visual, like a photograph, or a film; a song, or even a specific place or space you've visited.

For more information on writing an effective thesis, see Chapter, 4 and the craft boxes on pages 156 and 176, as well as *Rules for Writers*, pages 21–24. You can then organize your analysis into an essay using Chapter 4 in the *Student's Guide* and *Rules for Writers*, pages 11–16.

For examples of PIE paragraphs used for textual analysis, see Chapters 4 and 14.

The thing you want to remember about textual analysis is that it focuses primarily on the text and may not consider factors outside of the text, such as the author's or artist's background, the audience for whom the piece was intended, or the historical period in which it was created. This is the **context**. When you write a textual analysis paper in your first-year writing courses, you will likely be asked to examine the text alone, in isolation of these outside factors.

Analyzing written texts begins with **close reading**—and reading closely means reading a text actively: annotating the text, underlining key ideas and phrases, posing questions, and responding to the ideas presented in it. It also means reading the text multiple times, because each reading will grant you a new way of seeing it that you may not have considered in your previous reading. Close reading will help you to identify the strategies that the author of the text is using to communicate. As you read, ask yourself the following questions posed by composition scholars Rosenwasser and Stephen:

For more on close reading, see Chapter 3.

- Which details are significant and which aren't? Why?

- What is the significance of a particular detail? What does it mean? What else might it mean?

- How do the details fit together? What do they have in common?

- What does this pattern of details mean?

- What else might this same pattern of details mean? How else could it be explained?

- What details don't seem to fit? How might they be connected with other details to form a pattern?

- What does this new pattern mean? How might it cause me to read the meaning of individual details differently?

A "strategy" might also be referred to as a "pattern of details." If you notice that an author is beginning many of his/her sentences the same way, for example, that is a **strategy** that the author is using in the text. By asking yourself why the author chose to follow a specific pattern, you can begin to discover the **messages** that the author is communicating.

Once you've identified a pattern of details in the text you're reading, you can use a literary term to describe it. There are many different terms for strategies that describe the ways authors communicate in written texts. The strategies defined below are from *The Bedford Glossary of Critical and Literary Terms*. Consider the questions following each strategy's definition to begin connecting these strategies to a possible message that an author communicates to a reader.

List of Textual Strategies
- **Alliteration:** the repetition of sounds in a sequence of words. Alliteration generally refers to repeated consonant sounds. For example, "Peter Piper

picked a peck of pickled peppers." Assonance is the repetition of identical or similar vowel sounds, as in "fate" and "cave."

o   What is the effect of relating two words to one another through alliteration or assonance?

- Allusion: an indirect reference, often to a person, event, statement, theme, or work. Allusions enrich meaning through the connotations they carry, or the associations that they evoke in a reader's mind. For example, authors may allude to a historic event by mentioning its name or to a play by Shakespeare by using the same language in their writing. In Chapter 3, Lucretia Mott and Elizabeth Cady Stanton allude to the language of the *Declaration of Independence* in their *Declaration of Sentiments*.

o   What effect does an allusion have on the primary text you are reading? What associations does the allusion bring with it?

- Atmosphere: the general feeling created for the reader or audience by a work at a given point. While this is often referred to as tone, their meanings differ. Tone is an author's attitude toward the reader, audience, or subject matter and can be optimistic, morbid, etc. The atmosphere, or **mood**, of a text can be dreary, peaceful, etc.

o   How does the mood of a text effect how you feel about its subject matter? Why did the author choose that atmosphere for that part of the narrative?

- Cliché: an expression used so often that it has become hackneyed and has lost its original impact. For example, using "under the weather" to indicate feeling ill is a cliché.

o   How does it make you feel as a reader to see a cliché in a text? Do you think that feeling was intended by the author? Why?

- Figurative language: language that employs one or more **figures of speech**, such as metaphor, simile, synecdoche, or personification. A **simile** compares two distinct things by using words such as "like" or "as," while a **metaphor** associates two distinct things without using a connective word. "That child is like a cyclone" is a simile, while "that child is a mouse" is a metaphor. In **synecdoche**, a part of something is used to represent the whole, such as referring to a car as "wheels." Finally, **personification** involves giving human characteristics to anything nonhuman. For example, "Father Time" is a personification.

o   What sorts of things are being compared when the author uses figurative language? What is the effect of associating these things?

- Foreshadowing: the technique of introducing into a narrative material that prepares the reader for future events or revelations. Examples of foreshadowing could include mentioning a gun early in the narrative that will later shoot someone, or implying that a character is threatening through suggestive language before his actions become villainous.

o How does it feel as a reader to read these presentiments early in a text? Why do you believe the author included them?

- **Hyperbole**: employing deliberate, emphatic exaggeration, sometimes intended for **ironic** effect. Saying something is "the very best in the world" could be a hyperbolic statement. The opposite of this is **understatement**.

o What effect does exaggeration or understatement have on a reader? How does it make you feel about the subject?

- **Point of view**: the vantage point from which a narrative is told, either **first-person**, **third-person**, or, uncommonly, **second-person**. First-person narratives are told by a narrator who refers to himself or herself as "I" and is often a part of the action. Third-person narrators can either be **omniscient**, all-knowing and reliable, or **limited**, restricted to a single character at a time. Second-person narrators speak directly to the reader as "you."

o In what ways is it different to be directly addressed as opposed to reading the personal thoughts of the narrator? How does the narrator make you feel about the other characters? Why did the author choose to frame his or her text through this narrative point of view?

- **Symbolism**: the sustained use of **symbols** to represent or suggest other things or ideas. For example, you could say that an author "uses symbols of nature" to evoke certain associations for the reader.

o Look for patterns of symbols in a text. Why did the author choose to focus on these images in particular? What do the symbols used in the text have in common, and what do they reveal about the author's overall message?

By building your analysis of a text on strategies, you are providing support for your overall claim about the author's message. There are many more possibilities for strategies than those listed here. Whenever you see a pattern in a text, ask yourself why the author chose to include it. In your textual analysis essay, you will group together those strategies that seem to be communicating the same overall message.

In the following section, Beth Alvarado discusses the process of reading a written text for the purpose of textual analysis, and she models what it means to find entry points into a text, even when it disturbs or confuses us. As she explains, writing itself can be a process of discovery that has the potential to lead to new understanding.

> For examples of what an analysis essay may look like, please refer to the sample essays in Chapter 14 in the *Student's Guide*.

8.3 Writing as Inquiry

By Beth Alvarado

[W]hen students raise meaningful questions about incongruities in their own worlds, they gain genuine motivation and direction for writing, and...when students discover new understanding through writing, the writing becomes valuable to them and worth sharing with others.

—Janice Lauer, from "Writing as Inquiry: Some Questions for Teachers"

In order for writing to become a process of inquiry or discovery—rather than an act of setting down the obvious or what is already known—Lauer suggests that we start with something that disturbs us or causes us cognitive dissonance. She explains that cognitive dissonance is a term psychologists use to describe

the perception of a gap between a current set of beliefs or values and some new experience or idea that seems to violate or confound those beliefs. This clash engenders puzzlement, curiosity, a sense of enigma, sometimes of wonder, a pressure to restore equilibrium. While some people suppress such tension, the inquirer, the learner strives to resolve it by searching for new understanding, by going beyond the known. (20)

Thesis Statement Recipe for Textual Analysis

By Carie Schneider

Here's the basic "recipe" for a textual analysis thesis. It is important to remember that this recipe works well for a draft, but that it is only one option for a thesis statement and you might want to change around the word order or specific word choice as you revise to make it more unique. You also don't have to include the author and title in the thesis if you've already mentioned that elsewhere in your completed introduction. At an early stage of drafting, this thesis recipe can function as an agenda for your essay, laying out exactly what you plan to prove and how.

[Author's Name]'s [Genre], [Title], uses [techniques, elements, features] in order to express [meaning, message, interpretation].

I can fill in these blanks from my notes. I used my "Observations/Inferences" chart and the photograph from Chapter 3 to create this example draft thesis:

T.C. Reed's photograph, *No Swimming*, uses color, composition, and symbolism in order to express the decline of America's urban centers.

This thesis can be improved by adding specific details—don't just say "color," tell your reader something about the color! Don't just say "the decline," tell your reader what message or statement the text is making *about* that decline! How does the author seem to *feel* about that decline? Here's the expanded example:

T.C. Reed's photograph, *No Swimming*, uses unusual color tinting, creative composition, and symbolic objects in order to express the upsetting decline of America's urban centers.

In other words, when you are confronted with a text that is off your mental radar, when you experience that dissonance or static in your thinking, you have a starting point for an essay. Instead of ignoring or dismissing your reaction, go on and explore why you are experiencing the "puzzlement."

This approach to analysis is based on several assumptions:

- A text does not have a fixed meaning;

- Each reader, based on his/her own assumptions or experiences, will "read" a text differently; and

- Analyzing a text is like figuring out a puzzle: You have to go back and forth, from your reactions and inferences about the text to the pieces of text to figure out the puzzle for yourself.

What I'm asking you to do, then, is to trust your own reactions to a text and write those down, but then to suspend judgment about the text (or author) and see if you can locate the parts of the text that elicited the strongest responses. Then do a closer reading of those parts. You might look at any number of characteristics of the text: word choice, tone, implications, metaphors, etc. Try to figure out why you had that reaction: What in the text caused it? Also, how did your own assumptions or background influence your thinking? This tension or dialectic between your responses and the text, if explored, can help you come up with unique ideas for a paper and perhaps a new understanding of the text, one that will teach your reader something she might not have seen for herself.

Let me give you an example of how this might work. When students read Gloria Anzaldúa's essay "The Homeland, *Aztlán/El Otro Mexico*," many feel silenced by her tone; perhaps they feel unjustly accused by passages like this:

> The Gringo, locked into the fiction of white superiority, seized complete political power, stripping Indians and Mexicans of their land while their feet were still rooted in it. *Con el destierro y el exilo fuimos desuñados, destroncados, destripados*—we were jerked out by the roots, truncated, disemboweled, dispossessed, and separated from our identity and our history. (471)

Two things might bother some readers about this passage: One may be that they feel she is making sweeping generalizations about white people (or is retelling history in a biased way) and one may be that they don't understand Spanish. This gives those particular students two things to note in their re-reading of the text: where are the places they feel accused or that she's being biased? and where and how is she using Spanish? If they go back to the text and note evidence, they'll see that either reaction would give them plenty to investigate. In other words, if these are their reactions, they now have a choice of two topics for a paper.

Let's say you are the writer and you choose the use of Spanish as your topic. In the passage above, for instance, as is *not* true in other parts of the essay, Anzaldúa translates the Spanish—so that gives you two specific strategies to investigate: When does she translate the Spanish and when does she not? Then, let's say, you remember from class discussion that someone brought up the family stories, where she switched from Spanish to English, sometimes in the same sentence. Now you have at least three ways she uses Spanish or **three possible patterns to investigate—where she translates, where she doesn't, and where she switches back and forth in the same sentence**—and use as possible organizing principles for your paper. You also have a **central question to guide your inquiry**—or, as Lauer would put it, a "known unknown"—which is: Why does Anzaldúa use Spanish in the three different ways she does? Is there some kind of significance to the patterns? Is she trying to exclude readers?

This leads you to the issue of audience. In class, some people, like you, said they felt excluded, and so you might conclude that she is trying to exclude some readers—non-Spanish speakers? whites?—or, perhaps, you think, she is using the piece to recreate for her readers feelings of exclusion she has experienced. On the other hand, readers who understood Spanish said they felt included by the very strategy that others cited as alienating. In fact, there were people in class who loved the family stories because they were reminded of the way their grandparents talked. Maybe, you think, the ways Anzaldúa uses *both* languages illustrates something about her heritage and identity. Or about her conflicts? Or the border region?

Now you have a few possible **hypotheses**: "Anzaldúa uses Spanish in her essay to recreate for non-speakers the feeling of being an outsider in the hopes, perhaps, that the reader will come to understand the injustice she feels." Or: "Even though Anzaldúa risks alienating some readers by not translating from the Spanish, she is using both English and Spanish to illustrate her conflicted identity." Or: "The use of Spanish and English in the essay replicates its use in the border region." You can see how the process of inquiry can lead to different—but equally valid—positions on the same text. The next step, now that you have a tentative thesis, is to go back to the text, where you can gather and arrange your evidence, test it against your hypothesis, and begin to write a draft of your paper.

8.4 Visual Analysis

Like written texts, visual texts consist of a variety of potential interpretations and messages. But unlike written texts, messages in visual texts are made primarily through images, illustrations, and design. Because the messages are made differently in these two types of texts, they require different interpretive strategies. That is, as a reader, you will look for and notice different things about visual texts than you would about written ones. For example, in written texts, a comparison using the words "like" or "as" signals a simile. In visual texts, where words may or may not be present, such a comparison would be made through visual cues within the text—perhaps by juxtaposing two images in an unexpected way. You would have to read the visual elements of the text closely, as you would a written text, in order to pick up on such a message. As you investigate visuals, you want to look for aspects of the text that pique your interest, and then ask yourself why those particular aspects had an effect on you. You will also want to consider the ways in which the visual text works to make a message (design choices, areas of emphasis, symbolic representation, and so forth), as well as the underlying message—or messages—you see being conveyed.

The following key terms for visual analysis, based on the guidelines for analyzing a photo presented by the UA Center for Creative Photography, will help you develop the language to analyze a visual text, whether it is a painting, a photograph, or a digital image. These basic strategies can lead you to an analysis of the artist's overall message(s).

List of Visual Strategies

- **Angle**: From what vantage point was the photograph taken? Imagine the photograph taken from a higher or lower angle or view. How does the vantage point affect the photograph?

- **Framing**: Describe the edges of the view. What is included? What does the framing draw your attention to in the photograph? What do you imagine might have been visible beyond the edges of the picture?

- **Dominance**: Close your eyes. When you open them and look at the photograph, what is the first thing you notice? Why is your attention drawn there? Are there other centers of interest? How are they created? How do the focal points help move your eye throughout the photograph? Why do you think the artist made those features dominant?

- **Balance**: Is the visual weight on one side of the photograph about the same as the other—is there more to grab your attention on one side than the other? How about top to bottom or diagonally? What elements help or hinder the weight balance? How does it change the way you feel toward the subject of the image for it to be balanced or unbalanced?

- **Contrast**: Are there strong visual contrasts—lights and darks, shadows, textures, solids and voids, etc? Why would an artist choose to emphasize contrast between two parts of an image?

- **Focus**: What parts of the image are clearly in focus? Are some out of focus? Is the subject of the image in focus or not? What is the effect of having one part of the image in focus and another out of focus?

- **Scale**: Discuss the size of the objects within the work. Does the scale seem natural? How does it change the way you look at a part of the image when it seems unnaturally large or small?

As practice, take a minute to study the following pictures taken of the "Border Dynamics" sculpture located on the Southwest side of the Harvill building. Although each picture represents the same sculpture, the way in which the sculpture is represented differs from picture to picture. The pictures on the left and bottom of the page show only a partial perspective of the sculpture, while the one on the right shows the sculpture as a whole. How do these differences in perspective change the message(s) conveyed by the visual?

Now, take a moment to focus on just one of the pictures. Using the key terms introduced in this section and the questions about them, practice analyzing the picture you've chosen. Write a brief, one-paragraph response that addresses the following questions:

- What message(s) are being conveyed in the picture? What do you believe the photographer wants his/her viewers to think about after viewing this image?

- What specific strategies used by the photographer led you to this interpretation?

- What aspects of the picture did you find most interesting and why?

8.5 Analyzing Film

By Amy Parziale

Like visual analysis, we tend to interpret films without acknowledging that we are thinking critically about the images we see. When asked about a film, you might answer, "I really liked that film" or "I hated it." You may not immediately be able to articulate why you had such a reaction, but if pressed, most people will actually give a close reading: "The dialogue was stilted and unrealistic," or "The main character wasn't fully developed so I didn't care about her." These close readings are the beginning of film interpretation. In this section we will go over some basic filmic terminology and strategies in order to assist you in improving your ability to analyze film. All elements of a film are carefully chosen and constructed in accordance with the filmmakers' vision. Because they are made by people, films express those individuals' personal and cultural ideologies. By examining a film critically, you will be able to analyze the messages being expressed. As with other types of analysis, you will need to come up with a unique argument about the film and substantiate your claims by interpreting specific strategies.

Shot: what is captured during an uninterrupted period of time by one camera. An **establishing shot** is an initial shot that establishes the setting and orients the viewer to the world of the film. **Shot/reverse shot** is an editing technique often used between characters or actions. This technique is most often used during conversations in order to capture both the speaker and the reaction of the person being spoken to. Establishing shots, shot/reverse shots, **eyeline matches**, and **match on action shots** are all components of Continuity Editing (see below).

Cut: during editing, the process by which two shots are joined; in the finished film, the instantaneous transition from one shot to another. The cut is the most common technique used to transition between shots. Other transition techniques include wipes, iris open/close, dissolves, fade-in/fade-out, and fade to black or white. **Continuity editing** is the system by which most films' shots are combined. Continuity editing uses cuts and other transitions to establish the reality of the world of the film, construct a coherent sense of time and space, and tell stories efficiently and effectively. A **take** is the amount of time a particular camera rolls without stopping. In continuity editing, filmmakers tend not to use overly short or long takes. But, a filmmaker may decide to build suspense by quickly cutting between the same shot/reverse shot over and over again, or she may decide to use a **long take** in which viewers will become uncomfortable because they are not used to watching from one position for a long period of time.

Diegesis: the world of the film. The diegesis does not need to follow our understanding of reality but needs to be consistent throughout the film to create a sense of time and space, a world that the viewer can believe in during the viewing. The diegesis of a film includes things that are situated in both on-screen and off-screen space. **On-screen Space** is the space seen within the frame, what is on the screen. **Off-screen Space** is the space not seen within the frame. When a character or object is off-screen, the viewer will continue to believe in its presence.

Framing: the use of the camera's limits to determine what appears on screen and what does not. **Mobile framing** is framing in which the camera moves. Some common types of mobile framing are: **handheld shots**, **crane shots**, **dolly or tracking shots**, **panning** (in which the camera moves on a vertical axis), and **tilting** (in which the camera moves on a horizontal axis).

Shot Scale: the distance of framing in a shot or how much is captured by the camera. There are seven generally accepted shot scales. An **extreme long shot** can capture more than the human body; it may show a landscape, building, or crowd of people. A **long shot** is capable of showing the entire human body at once. A **medium long shot**, called an **American shot**, captures the human body from about the knee up. The **medium shot** will show a person from the waist up. The medium close-up shows a person from the chest up. A **close-up** can be of any object shown up close so it appears quite large and fills the majority of the screen. Many close-ups are of the human face, generally from the neck up. An **extreme close-up** shows a part of a larger object, a part of the human body, or a very small object. The object or part of an object appears very large taking up the entire screen. Shot scales vary; it is possible to have a shot that is in between a medium and a medium close-up, for example. Naming a shot's scale is not an exact science but should follow these widely accepted definitions.

Shot Angle: the angle of the camera lens relative to what it is capturing. A **high angle shot** looks down at its subject from a higher angle. A **low angle shot** looks up at the subject from below. Using different angles can create messages in the film. A character who is always shot from a high angle may seem powerless and trapped while a character who is always shot from a low angle may seem powerful and imposing. Of course, this interpretation of the angle depends upon the other elements of the film. Like all cinematic elements, shot angles do not have specific, set meanings.

Mise-en-scène: literally "put on stage" in French. In films, mise-en-scène is created by four components: **lighting**, **setting/props**, **makeup/costume**, and **figure behavior**. These are elements within the frame that the filmmaker has the power to control.

Lighting: the type of light used in a particular shot or sequence of shots. The most common lighting technique is **three-point lighting**, which consists of a backlight, key light, and fill light. By using these three points of light, the human face can be lit in such a way that there are no shadows on the face, thus allowing the viewer to see even minute changes in the actor's face. **Backlighting** is a technique used that illuminates the set from behind. **Key lighting** is the brightest light in three-point lighting and generally illuminates the face from the front. Because this bright light creates shadows, three-point lighting also uses a **fill light**, which fills in the shadows created by the key light. The fill light is generally positioned to one side of the character and near the camera in order to eliminate shadows. **High-key lighting** refers to a scene with a very bright key light causing the scene to have almost no shadows. **Low-key lighting** refers to a noticeable difference between the brightness of the key and fill lights, creating deep shadows.

Setting: the location of the film. The setting can be on-location, on a set, or created digitally. Many filmmakers attempt to create an authentic setting for their story. A film's settings can move across several spaces, even several countries, or a film can have a more restricted setting, for example one room of a house. The setting creates the mood and can affect how we interpret the plot of the film.

Props: any object in the setting that has a function within the film. "Prop" is actually short for "property" and is a term borrowed from the theater. Props can act as catalysts for action, as a motif, or as foreshadowing. A famous example of a prop used as a foreshadowing motif is the use of oranges in *The Godfather* trilogy to symbolize death and betrayal.

Costume and Makeup: how the characters are dressed and stylized. Costume and makeup also tend to be aspects in which the filmmaker wishes for authenticity within the diegesis of the film. Costume and makeup can help an actor's performance seem more believable. Choices in color palette, patterns, and contrasts have meaning and affect the overall effect of a film.

Figure Behavior: the movement and behavior of an actor or other element (animal, object, etc.). Figure behavior includes expression, movement, and posture as well as acting style and degree of realism.

Sound: There are two major types of sound in film: diegetic and non-diegetic. **Diegetic sound** is produced by something within the world of the film. **Non-diegetic sound** is produced by something outside the time and space of the film, such as voice-over narration or soundtrack. A great example of the difference between diegetic and non-diegetic sound occurs in *Blazing Saddles* when music is heard while the main character rides his horse through the desert; the audience assumes the music is non-diegetic until the character comes across the musicians playing the music out in the desert.

Film Genres: There are many different genres and subgenres of film that have particular narrative and thematic conventions. Some examples of genres are:

western, horror, musical, comedy, action, mystery, and romance. Because viewers understand the conventions of each genre, filmmakers can play with audience expectations.

Now that we've walked through some cinematic terminology, let's examine the opening sequence from *Star Wars, Episode IV: A New Hope*. When analyzing a film, it is helpful to try to write down what happens in each shot, where people and objects are placed and any themes, motifs, or patterns that emerge.

After the now infamous text crawl that sets the scene along with the **non-diegetic soundtrack**, the camera **tilts down** through space to show viewers a planet with two moons. A spaceship enters from the upper right portion of the screen to the center of the screen, capturing viewers' attention. Quickly, another spaceship enters the screen from the same direction. This ship is massive compared to the one it chases. The ships exchange fire. This **long take** sets up the central conflict: the Rebels against the Empire.

The film then cuts to a closer shot of the small ship. We see a green flash strike the ship causing a large explosion. The film finally cuts to the interior of the Rebel ship and our first two characters are introduced in a **long shot**: C-3PO and R2-D2. We see the hallway shake due to the explosion just witnessed. The **mise-en-scène** of the shot is quite stark. The hallway **setting** is all white with grey floors. The lighting is **high-key**; we can see many details and light reflects off of the robots as they move down the corridor. The shot cuts from an **American two-shot** to a **medium shot** of C-3PO, who finally speaks the first line of **dialogue**: "Did you hear that?" The conversation is made up of **shot/reverse shots**. Through dialogue we get a glimpse into the character of C-3PO, a neurotic, worry-wart robot.

The Storm Troopers then force their way into the Rebel ship. After a shoot out between the two sides, the film cuts to our first glimpse of Darth Vader, the villain. The **slightly low camera angle** causes Vader to seem even larger and more menacing. The **music** signals his entrance with loud horns and we hear his mechanical breathing. His **costume** becomes clearer as he walks toward the camera; we can see his long black robe and full helmet as well as the circuitry on his chest, signaling that he is perhaps not human. He stands over the bodies of dead Rebel soldiers with his hands on his hips; this **figure behavior** is aggressive and indicates his power. By constructing these shots in this way, the filmmaker seems to be emphasizing the inhumanity of the Empire, especially that of Vader.

These **shots** are immediately followed by a **close-up** showing an arm reaching out to R2-D2. The bare feminine arm is in stark contrast to the previous shots of Vader, thereby marking the humanity of the rebels. Without even showing whose arm it is, the contrast immediately causes viewers to see this person as the complete opposite of Vader, making her a leader for the Rebels and potentially the hero of the film. We get a quick glimpse of Princess Leia. She is crouching down, showing her vulnerability and desire to hide. Her costuming is also the exact opposite of Vader's; she is wearing a white, flowing gown. Her femininity is emphasized by the fact that she wears a long dress and her hair is tied up on each side of her head in intricate buns.

Having seen only the first few minutes of the film, it becomes quite clear who viewers are meant to root for and against. If we were to analyze the entire film, we may pay attention to the ideas touched upon during this opening sequence. For example, we may decide to trace how gender is constructed in the film: Is Princess Leia a "damsel in distress," or is she a heroine? Do characters follow traditional gender roles, or do they play with social expectations? We may also continue to trace the contrasts between the Rebels and the Empire: Is the Empire always portrayed as inhuman, or are there moments in which its humanity is made clear? Are the Rebels always portrayed as morally superior to the Empire, or are there moments in which their morals can be questioned? In order to answer these questions, you would need to watch the film several times, especially scenes that are the most important to your argument. You would most likely need to pause to take notes about the various cinematic elements that construct each scene.

By using the film terminology discussed in this section, we are better able to support our claims about the film by analyzing its construction. Film analyses that ignore the ways in which the cinematic elements are organized and constructed tend to talk around a film rather than closely reading it. Such analyses generally fall short when compared to papers that base their argument and claims on carefully analyzed details. Being aware of how films are constructed will allow you to think more deeply about film as an artistic medium.

8.6 Spatial Analysis

While much of the analysis you do in your first-year writing courses will focus on written and visual texts, your instructor may also ask you to think critically about the places and spaces you inhabit on a regular basis. In this section, you will learn about methods for place- and space-based analysis, as well as what these methods of analysis can tell you about human relationships, identity, and social constructions of class, politics, culture, race, gender, and so forth. In order to understand these methods of analysis, you will need to know the following key terms:

Place: According to social theorist Michel de Certeau, places are fixed locations that are constructed through the positioning of material things, such as people, cities, buildings, or roads. Places are informed by the way people use them and experience them in their everyday lives, as well as by the emotional attachments people form to the places through these experiences.

For instance, a house is a place. It has a physical location (a street, a city, a country), and it is made of tangible materials (wood, stucco, windows, and so on). People gather together as a family to sleep, eat, and store belongings in their houses because that is how people have used these places over time. Since each person experiences and uses a place differently, places will hold different meanings for different people.

Space: Space can be understood as the area in which social action takes place. A place becomes a space based on the way that place is used by people—a house becomes the space of "home" by the actions and social exchanges that occur within it. Any given place can offer multiple uses of space. For example, think of the UA mall, a place built to ease access between buildings on campus. Its physical intent may be to help with transportation, but think of all of the activities you see happening on the mall: Students meet friends, do homework, play Ultimate Frisbee, listen to speakers, join in protests, and participate in various "street" fairs. Each day, the UA mall can be a different kind of space based solely on how the people in that place use it. Spaces, then, can be understood as areas that exist within places where people exist, move, and interact with one another.

As you think about the distinctions between space and place, you will want to note that the concepts are closely related. UA Composition Instructor Jenna Vinson offers the following examples to show the relationship and distinctions between place and space:

> [T]he University of Arizona is a place. It is located in a specific region of Tucson, with stable buildings made of durable materials. It is a campus ordered by buildings that hold colleges, departments, and programs, each with their own organizational framework for staff, faculty, and students. These diverse elements of the university are consciously ordered and designed to assist with the functioning of the education process in *this place*....

> On any given day the University of Arizona is a space. It is composed of students learning (or sleeping, texting, giggling) in the classroom, speakers calling out to the crowds on the mall, instructors hurrying to office hours, delivery trucks moving across campus streets, etc. Though the university is designed as a *place* for education, education is not the only thing that occurs in the space of the classroom. Or sometimes, it is exactly what occurs.

But why should you be interested in space and place? Why can you learn about the way the world works by closely reading spaces and places? Many people who study space and place, including students and instructors of geography and urban planning, know that space and place affect the way we think about society, culture, and politics. Students and instructors in other disciplines, like engineering, architecture, rhetoric, women's studies, and sociology, also study space and place. For example, if you were interested in learning about the American political system, you would investigate the spaces and places where politics play out—state capitol buildings, community meetings, the office of your local senator or congressperson, and even the White House. Carefully examining how people interact and work within these spaces and places can give you insights into how political systems are formed by people.

The idea here is that social structures like class, race, and gender discrimination come into being through and within certain spaces and places. By analyzing people's interactions and experiences within these sites, we can come to understand the social structures that operate within a society.

Place plays an important role in the formation of identity and culture as well. If your instructor were to ask you to analyze a place that holds significance for you—the house where you grew up, for example—you would want to think about how you use and experience the spaces within your house, as well as the kinds of emotional attachments you have formed in relationship to it. You might also consider how home has been defined in society—what kinds of places function as houses for people and how do these houses change depending on the cultural, political, social, and economic context? What do people do in the space of home? What kinds of cultural practices happen there? Finally, you might even consider the ways in which your own identity has been shaped by your experiences in this place. What did you learn in your home that has informed who you are today?

Studying places and spaces can tell us a lot about cultural practices, social "norms," and individuals' personal connections to certain locations. When studying places and spaces, your aim is to explore the individual and collective experiences that make space "*a practiced place*" (a space that people have created and use for certain purposes) and to analyze the larger social structures working within it (De Certeau 117).

Applying Spatial Analysis

To illustrate how place- and space-based analysis might work, let's return to the pictures of "Border Dynamics" on page 160 of this chapter. These pictures represent both place and space, but the places and spaces represented in these photographs may be differently understood by different people. In your earlier examination of these photographs, you probably noticed that the figures in these photos are being separated by a large physical border. Each figure reacts to the border in a different way—some push and some stand nonchalantly. You might have also noticed that these figures appear to be without skin, all similar in color and build. Yet, what else can you glean from these photographs?

To understand these photos from a spatial perspective, you might consider the following questions:

- How are the figures interacting with one another?

- What do you understand these interactions to mean?

- How are place and space being represented visually in the photograph?

- What do the depictions of place and space tell you about the relationships between these figures?

- How are figures in the photos using this space? What are they doing and what seem to be their experiences in this space?

- Based on the figures' actions in the space, what place(s) do you think are being represented here?

- What are these figures' connections to this place? What clues in the photos tell you so?

- Finally, what can these representations of place and space tell you about larger social issues that might connect with the ideas in these photographs?

Answering these questions requires "reading" this photograph with a critical eye, applying the strategies for analysis you've been reading about in this chapter. Since close reading necessitates an interaction with the text, you might even want to annotate the photograph like you would a poem or a short story. Since our focus right now is on spatial analysis, your annotations should pay particular attention to the concepts of space and place in this photograph and how people are interacting within these spaces. For example, your annotation might end up looking like this:

"Border Dynamics" Sculpture on the UA Campus

The neutral colors give me the sense that these figures could represent anyone—and the fact that the fence looks like any other steel fence I've seen implies that it could be anywhere.

It's hard to tell from the picture, but it looks like the figure is really close to this wall, pushing with the entire weight of its body.

The border itself represents a place—borders exist between countries, but also within individuals (emotional, mental, etc.). Because it's on a border campus, this makes me think of the U.S./Mexico border and the fence that will soon go up there.

Large wall represents an obstacle, as shown by the figure to the left who is pushing against it. When I look at the height of the figure in relation to the wall, it seems like the figure is tall enough to climb over it—maybe a symbolic overcoming of the obstacle?

The buildings and trees in the background imply an urban landscape, but the sculpture itself seems to be removed from the urban—there is no landscape, only bodies and a fence.

The two figures are positioned near each other spatially, but do not seem to be interacting with each other. They have completely different responses to the wall—one is engaged, the other seems to be pretty removed from whatever's happening.

Concrete tiles again suggest an urban landscape.

Now that you have closely read and interacted with the text, you can begin analyzing and interpreting it, using the previous questions as a guide. To further investigate the use of space in this sculpture, you may even want to visit it, walk around it and through it, and experience it in its full dimensions. As you do, consider how your perceptions of space and place changed, if at all, once you had a chance to experience its spatial mass in person. Finally, remember also to think about what your interpretation might tell you about human relationships, identity, and the social structures you notice there.

Clearly, your first-year writing classes will require you to read, write about, and even compose different types of texts. You will be challenged to think beyond the surface-level message of the texts you read in class in order to uncover the more complex interpretations you can bring to them. In order to uncover the hidden intricacies of any text, you must read it closely, interact with it, locate sites of inquiry, and use your own lived experiences to guide your responses.

Works Cited

Anzaldúa, Gloria. "The Homeland, *Aztlán/El Otro Mexico*." *Writing as Revision*. Ed. Beth Alvarado, Barbara Cully, and Michael Robinson. 2nd ed. Boston: Pearson, 2003. 546–53. Print.

de Certeau, Michel. *The Practice of Everyday Life*. Trans. Steven Rendall. Los Angeles: The U of California P, 1984. Print.

Lauer, Janice. "Writing as Inquiry: Some Questions for Teachers." *Writing as Revision*. Ed. Beth Alvarado, Barbara Cully, and Michael Robinson. 2nd ed. Boston: Pearson, 2003. 19–23. Print.

Murfin, Ross and Supryia M. Ray. *The Bedford Glossary of Critical and Literary Terms*. Boston: Bedford/St. Martin's, 2009. Print.

Rosenwasser, David, and Jill Stephen. *Writing Analytically*. Fort Worth: Harcourt Brace College P, 1997. Print.

Smith, Greg. "'It's Just a Movie': A Teaching Essay for Introductory Media Classes." *Writing as Revision*. Ed. Beth Alvarado, Barbara Cully, and Michael Robinson. 2nd ed. Boston: Pearson, 2003. 64–71. Print.

Text-in-Context (Contextual Analysis)

9.1 Text-in-Context: An Overview
9.2 The Hero's Journey as a Lens *by Jen Neely*
9.3 Comparative Analysis *by Jean Goodrich*
9.4 Culture: Another Kind of Text

Goals

Your Text-in-Context essay should:

- Exhibit a careful analysis of primary and secondary texts.

- Smoothly incorporate research materials and correctly document them to support your analysis.

- Make insightful comparisons among texts.

- Support your thesis with examples from primary and secondary materials.

- Anticipate the expectations of your specific audience and address its concerns.

- Provide meaningful feedback to your peers during the revision process.

- Incorporate peer and instructor feedback in the final version.

9.1 Text-in-Context: An Overview

Text-in-context essays, also referred to as **contextual analysis** essays, build on the skills that you began to develop with the textual analysis paper. Your textual analysis assignment asked you to look at an isolated text closely and to interpret it with descriptive evidence from that text. Text-in-context adds a new layer of complexity to your analysis. In this essay, you still analyze a text, but you'll do so using additional sources to enrich your understanding. You might also hear people call this use of outside sources "building a context" or "building a framework." Because some of the terms used for this assignment are similar to one another, we have clarified the terminology that is often used when discussing text-in-context essays in the following list:

- Primary text: This is the text that you are analyzing—the main focus of your analysis. It might be a book, an article, a movie, a photograph, a painting, or even a place.

- Secondary text: These texts create the context or framework—they add to your understanding of the primary text by introducing historical, philosophical, theoretical, and biographical information that casts the primary text in a new light. Secondary texts are not necessarily about the primary text. Instead, they enrich your close reading of the primary text by adding new contextual information. The secondary text may also be called a "**lens** text" because you can look "through" it in order to discover new things about the primary text that you might not have seen otherwise. These are also not always one concrete "text" in the sense that you may be used to—they can also be a broader collection of **themes** or a **contextual frame** that you use to focus your analysis.

- Secondary source: These are sources that comment on and have a direct relationship to the primary text. Some common examples of secondary sources are an analysis of a literary text, a critique of a painting or photograph, a movie review, or an opinion about an interview. An easy way to think about primary and secondary sources is the difference between movies and movie reviews: the movie is the original work, the primary text. The movie review is critiquing and talking about the primary text, making it a secondary source to the movie.

For an extended analysis of *The Matrix* using Campbell, see Section 9.2.

Unlike secondary sources, a secondary text does not have to directly address the primary text. For example, if you wanted to analyze the film *The Matrix* as your primary text, you might use Joseph Campbell's book *The Hero with a Thousand Faces* as a secondary text. In this book, Campbell writes about hero archetypes, or common features among heroic figures. You might use Campbell's archetypes as a lens through which to consider Neo as a hero in the *The Matrix*. By comparing Neo's actions to the archetypes Campbell sets out, you might argue in your essay that Neo is not a radical hero, but rather a stereotypical one. The secondary text in this instance allows you to read the primary text in a new way, even though *The Matrix* hadn't been filmed when Campbell wrote his book.

Unlike secondary sources, which directly address a primary text, you must develop the relationship between a primary text and a secondary text. Making this relationship between primary texts and secondary texts can be thought of as creating a **contextual frame**.

Choosing a Contextual Framework

The text-in-context essay invites you to view a text from a broader framework, through a **lens**, in order to see things you wouldn't notice if you only looked at the text itself. These frameworks might derive from historical, theoretical, biographical, social, or cultural information, and they serve as contexts in which you can analyze your primary text. The ideas from the secondary texts should continue to add to your understanding of the primary text because they provide new and different information. To write your own essay effectively you'll need to read closely, analyze, perhaps do some research, argue, and, of course, revise.

The contexts you can apply to a text are various, and they can be used in different ways. The list we present here is not exhaustive, but it does offer a start for thinking about different possible contexts:

- **Historical:** What are the historical events and facts surrounding your primary text, and how does this affect how you read your text? Here, you might consider when the text was written or composed, or you can consider the time period in which a text's narrative takes place, or you might think about other factors concerning the time period of a text, such as historical objects or artifacts important to the text.

- **Biographical:** What occurred in the author's life? What were the author's beliefs, values, experiences, and so on, and how do these affect the ways that you understand the author's purpose in your primary text?

- **Social:** This context is very similar to historical context because it asks that you look at the social influences of the time. What were the social values, events, discourses, and so on, and how are these social contexts reflected in the primary text?

- **Cultural:** What kinds of culturally-specific values, beliefs, and patterns do you see in the primary text? How has the primary text been shaped by cultural influences, such as religion, nationality, family traditions, and so forth?

- **Critical:** What have other people, such as literary, film, or art critics, said about the primary text, and how can that influence or change your understanding of the text's meaning?

- **Theoretical:** This is a huge category with many possible subcategories. There are many different theories that enable writers to critically examine the features of societies and texts. Some examples of theoretical lenses include: feminist, Marxist, modernist, post-modernist, cultural studies, rhetorical, and so on. Here, you might draw on the theories of a certain scholar or movement to examine your primary text. Your instructor might suggest specific theoretical lenses to choose from, or you might ask your instructor for suggestions for possible lenses if you're interested in taking a theoretical approach to your text-in-context essay.

- **Reverse Context:** A primary text in some cases can become a secondary text, depending on how it is applied. For example, you could read Gilman's "The Yellow Wallpaper" and apply it to an analysis of Andrea Yates, the Texas woman who killed her five children in 2001. This kind of essay might take broad themes or arguments from the primary text, such as the main character's relationship to conventional women's roles, and use this framework to analyze the social context of the 2001 murder, your new primary text.

Getting Started on Your Text-in-Context Essay

The text-in-context essay is still an exercise in analysis and builds on many of the skills from your textual analysis assignments. Text-in-context essays, however, also ask you to include secondary texts to support your assertions. In order to successfully complete the text-in-context essay, you need to do the following:

For examples of how to incorporate research into your essay, see Chapter 11 and Chapter 12

- Argue a controlled thesis using contextual evidence (e.g., evidence collected from your secondary text or texts).

- Find specific evidence to support your claims from both the primary and secondary texts.

- Examine *how* the secondary texts create a new context (or contexts) in which to read a primary text.

- Explain how the primary and secondary texts relate to one another in terms of a specific theme or lens.

- Explain *why* this new context is important and/or significant to the understanding of your text.

Like analysis essays, contextual analysis essays are persuasive. How you decide to present the text and what evidence you decide to include convinces your reader to analyze the text the same way you do—it asks the reader to believe that your analysis is effective and credible. Therefore, your thesis should come from your own ideas, taking an analytical stance that invites the audience to share your understanding of the text. Use secondary texts only to bolster your points, not to structure your essay or make your arguments for you.

Paragraph Structure for Text-in-Context

Contextual analysis essays still rely on the basics of **PIE** paragraphs for structure, whether they are incorporating secondary sources or not. In this sample paragraph from student Cody Vandewerker's essay, "The Power of Perception," he demonstrates PIE structure in a contextual analysis paragraph that **does not incorporate a source**. He is analyzing Sharon Olds' poem, "On the Subway" through the contextual lens of racial discrimination. When writing a PIE paragraph that does not incorporate a source, you should:

- Open your paragraph with a topic sentence (**Point**).

- Present textual evidence that relates directly to the context (**Illustration**).

- Provide analysis by explaining the connection between this textual evidence and your context (**Explanation**).

For more information on analysis, see Chapter 8.

9.1

For example:

> This dream of a life without discrimination is juxtaposed with culture; the celebration of culture highlights racial or cultural differences and taking pride in those differences, ultimately creating social distance between races. A white woman and a black man might look at the same individual differently—this is true in the poem when the speaker, a white woman dressed in fur sees a boy and immediately sees the difference in race: "he is black / and I am white" (Olds lines 21–22). The noting of these differences implies on a basic level a color blind society does not exist, and also that she makes certain assumptions like family history or social standing based only on the first glance. This point is further illustrated when the speaker also believes that the boy on the other side of the tram is poor and believes she is "Living off his life, eating the steak / he does not eat" (18–20). The speaker does not know him, and has no merit to base her judgment upon him except her past knowledge, yet she comes to conclusion about his standing based on race and apparel.

When incorporating secondary sources, it is essential to remember the importance of analyzing your text after bringing in the context. This final step is when the analysis begins. This sample paragraph from student Ali Flath's essay "A Utopian Future" **incorporates a source** while analyzing the novel *Starship Troopers* through the context of colonization. When writing a **PIE** paragraph that **incorporates a source**, you should:

- Open your paragraph with a topic sentence (**Point**).

- Create the context by drawing on the secondary sources or quoting directly (**Illustration**).

- Apply the source's statements to the primary text (Illustration).

- Provide **analysis** by explaining the significance of your observations (**Explanation**).

For example:

> The 'frontier thesis', written by Frederick Turner in 1890 and discussed in Jamie King's essay "Bug Planet", explains how humans have, and will always have, the urge to expand into a new frontier (i.e. Manifest Destiny). As long as a piece of land is unoccupied, humans will always feel the need to own it. In *Starship Troopers*, Earth has been colonized completely by humans, leaving no room for further expansion. Any and every sort of "violent relationship with [an] indigenous other" has been experienced by the human race and has been terminated on Earth (King 1017). Now that absolute peace has been achieved, man is forced to look

9.1

outward onto a new stage, which happens to be outer space. This is the point at which the Bugs threaten the human race. The Bugs are able to take asteroids that are infested with their own kind and hurdle them towards Earth, intending to exterminate mankind and colonize in their place. Naturally, man retaliates with the same intentions of their enemy: to exterminate the "Other". At this point, both the Bugs and the humans are seeking their own "new frontier", which is the cause of the war. Ironically, each species has completely colonized their own planet and is now targeting the destruction of the opposite's planet for the sake of the proliferation of their own species. The frontier thesis, or "frontier mythology" can be applied to both the Bugs and mankind since each species is fighting for the same reason: to exterminate the other (King 1019). A feeling of detachment from the other species also creates a sense of protectionism, generating a dislike for anything that attempts to rid a race of its personal property.

> For how to introduce sources and quote from them correctly, see Chapter 6.

Instead of simply connecting the secondary source—the "frontier thesis"—to the novel and then moving on to another point, this writer analyzes the way that each species is attempting to colonize the other instead of targeting an unoccu-

---

Thesis Statement Recipe for Text-in-Context

by Carie Schneider

Just like the thesis recipes from your other assignments, this is just one possible format which can be helpful in your drafting stages. As you revise your essay, you'll probably want to also revise your thesis to make the structure more unique and less rigid. Remember that you can make these sentences less awkward while holding onto the essential pieces. Here are some examples of how to do this:

One secondary (theoretical) text, one primary text:

[Primary Text's Author]'s [genre], [primary text title], connects with the concept of ["lens" theme] as expressed in [Secondary Text's Author]'s [secondary text title] by referring to [subthemes connecting primary text and secondary text], which it accomplishes through the use of [techniques, elements, features].

Here's an example:

Ruth Kluger's biography, *Still Alive*, connects with the concept of writing as a social witness as expressed in Beth Alvarado's essay "Writing as a Social Witness" by referring to dealing with a difficult past and speaking up for the voiceless, which it accomplishes through the use of personal stories and historical references.

This is a somewhat unwieldy and repetitive sentence, so we might want to revise it like this:

Ruth Kluger's biography, *Still Alive*, connects with the concept of writing as a social witness as expressed in Beth Alvarado's essay by analyzing methods of dealing with a difficult past and speaking up for the voiceless. Kluger's biography represents these themes through the use of personal stories and historical references.

Two (or more) primary texts, one secondary (theme/theoretical) text:

pied, weaker territory. This connects the source to the context while making an original observation through analysis. While all of the steps in **PIE** paragraphs matter, it is this final step that allows you to advance your thesis.

In the next two sections, Jen Neely shows how to use the "Hero's Journey" as a secondary "theoretical" context, or lens, while Jean Goodrich offers steps and strategies on how to develop a comparative analysis between two film texts. These sections offer two types of approaches for the text-in-context essay.

> For examples of what a text-in-context essay may look like, refer to Chapter 14.

9.2 The Hero's Journey as a Lens

By Jen Neely

Viewing a text through a theoretical **lens** is much like playing with the color or filter settings on a camera: some settings will heighten certain details, like light and shadow, color and detail, while at the same time blurring or obscuring others. When applying a theoretical lens, you will be asked to analyze the ways in which the theoretical text or texts you are using accomplish the same tasks.

[Primary Text 1's Author]'s [genre], [primary text 1 title], and [Primary Text 2's Author]'s [genre], [primary text 2 title] relate to each other in their shared connection to the concept of ["lens" theme] as expressed in [Secondary Text's Author]'s [secondary text title] in their references to [subthemes connecting primary text and secondary text], which are accomplished through the use of [techniques, elements, features].

This can get completely out of hand as a single sentence, and it may be even longer if the two primary texts are using different techniques to express their shared themes—let's rework it as a two sentence thesis:

[Primary Text 1's Author]'s [genre], [primary text 1 title], and [Primary Text 2's Author]'s [genre], [primary text 2 title] relate to each other in their shared connection to the concept of ["lens" theme] as expressed in [Secondary Text's Author]'s [secondary text title]. Both [primary text 1] and [primary text 2] refer to [subthemes connecting primary text and secondary text], through the use of [text 1's elements/techniques] in [text 1] and the use of [text 2's elements/techniques] in [text 2].

Here's how it would look when revised:

Ruth Kluger's biography, *Still Alive*, and Ariel Dorfman's poem "Vocabulary" relate to each other in their shared connection to the concept of writing as a social witness as expressed in Beth Alvarado's essay. Both *Still Alive* and "Vocabulary" deal with speaking for the voiceless and the need to express difficult truths, through the use of personal stories and historical references in *Still Alive* and through word choice and poetic structure in "Vocabulary."

What is being highlighted? What is being obscured or complicated? While this may sound simple enough, it can sometimes be difficult to identify the ways in which the lens you have chosen may be coloring your primary text. This section shows how one theoretical lens can shape the way we view a primary text by highlighting the development of the hero in a story.

In order to perform a theoretical analysis, you must first understand the theory you will use as your lens. In this example, we'll use Joseph Campbell's theory of the **Hero's Journey** (also referred to as the **Monomyth**). Campbell's theory uses classical mythology as a basis for determining the stages of the hero's journey, beginning with the departure from home and ending with his/her successful return. The diagram below presents the Hero's Journey as Campbell describes it in his work, *The Hero with a Thousand Faces*.

Tests
The hero goes through a series of tests to prepare for the final battle. These can be confrontations with monsters or sorcerers, puzzles or forces of nature. They frequently occur in threes, and the hero often fails one or more along the way.

Crossing the Threshold
The hero undergoes a test or ordeal in passing from the real world into the mythical world. This other world can be referred to as the underworld, or the "belly of the whale."

Supernatural Aid
This initial guide and protective figure can take a variety of forms, from a wizard to a fairy godmother, and often bestows a weapon or protective amulet.

Helpers
In addition to the initial guide, who may or may not be a constant presence along the journey, the hero also encounters additional helpers to aid him or her in the journey through the underworld.

Call to Adventure
The hero is called to adventure by an event or person. S/he may be reluctant to accept this call, but eventually they commit to the quest.

The World of Adventure

Campbell's Monomyth Cycle

The Real World

Birth
The beginning of the hero's journey establishes the hero as a person of great potential and promise.

Climax/Final Battle
In this step the hero engages in his/her ultimate battle, which may be a confrontation with a monster, wizard or warrior. The hero often does not have to win this battle, but through it will gain the Elixir.

Home
Upon returning home, the hero is now able to use the knowledge and strength gained to make his/her own world a better place.

Flight
The hero must return to the threshold in order to pass again into the real world. If s/he has gained victory by defeating all opposing forces, this may be an easy journey. On the other hand, if there is still danger it will be a swift flight.

Return
The return to the real world can take multiple forms, from an easy passage through a forest to an awakening, rebirth or resurrection. It may also take the form of a final confrontation or battle.

Elixir
This is the knowledge or artifact that the hero has gained along the journey. This may have restorative or healing properties and also serves to solidify the hero's importance within his/her own society.

As you can see from the above diagram, the Monomyth can easily be identified with stories from classical mythology like Homer's *The Odyssey* or Old English tales like *Beowulf*. The hero begins his/her journey with the **Call to Adventure**, crosses the **Threshold** into an unknown world, must pass through a series of **Tests**, and participates in a **Final Battle** before returning home with the new knowledge gained along the journey. Modern-day tales often also fit within the Monomyth, like *Star Wars* or even comic book stories. After examining your theoretical **lens**, the next step is to identify how it may relate to your primary text. A series of careful questions will help you to begin to analyze.

- **What does the theoretical text ask me to understand or believe?**

It's easy to see that **home** is an important place within the myth. The hero both starts from and returns to a home where s/he is not only a person of importance, but also meant to contribute to the well-being of the people there, who may be the family or even a larger society. In this sense, you can say that the Monomyth values the family and home. The fact that the hero receives aid in the form of a spiritual or mystical guide and helpers once s/he has passed into the unknown world also suggests that it is **important to recognize and accept help from those around you**. In addition, that the hero must face the final battle alone places importance on the idea of **self-reliance and facing one's own challenges.** This is by no means a full reading of the Hero's Journey, but does offer an example of how to look closely at your theoretical text in order to identify what it is asking you to understand or believe.

- **Does my primary text share in or differ from that knowledge or understanding?**

One way to begin to answer this question is to make a list of the similarities and differences of the two texts, similar to the list in 9.3. As mentioned earlier in this chapter, establishing this textual relationship is a way of creating your **contextual frame**. As the Monomyth is laid out in specific steps, we will use those as a basis for comparison in looking at the film *The Matrix* (1999) and how specific steps may be related to Keanu Reeves' character Neo:

The Monomyth	The Matrix
The Call to Adventure	Neo receives a phone call from Morpheus and a warning from Trinity at the nightclub
Crossing the Threshold	Neo takes the red pill and is awakened from the Matrix
Climax/Final Battle	The final fight with Agent Smith
Elixir	Neo has learned how to manipulate the Matrix and now holds power over life and death

This chart above is just an example of how stages in the Monomyth can be seen to relate to the film and it is easy to see how the other steps in the journey may as well. If we were merely conducting a textual analysis of *The Matrix*, we might

9.2

say that Neo represents a kind of reluctant hero, and that the film re-envisions the traditional role of the hero through its use of technology (in the form of the Matrix itself) as a way of creating a new, radical vision of the hero. Instead of battling monsters or villains, Neo must confront a technology that has enslaved the human race.

However, when we apply Campbell's theory of the **hero's journey** and use our comparisons to analyze the film, we come to see that Neo's journey is much like those represented by classical mythology. He must cross a **threshold** into a world of adventure, he goes through **tests** and trials, he faces a climactic **battle** through which he gains the **elixir**, and it is assumed that he will use this new-found ability to aid in the fight against the Matrix. Nevertheless, there is a major **difference** or point of departure from the traditional journey, and that is related to the **threshold** and its opposing worlds.

- **If there are specific steps or points made in my theoretical text, are those represented in the primary text?**

An important piece of the Monomyth is the **transition** between the real world and the world of adventure. *The Matrix* begins in a world that looks similar to our everyday one. People are seen going about their daily lives in a cityscape that looks and feels familiar and as the viewers we recognize this. Looking back to the Monomyth, this is the place within the journey that represents **home**, and ultimately what the hero is fighting for. Once Neo crosses the **threshold** we are introduced to a world that seems unfamiliar and alien, a world in which human beings are grown and harvested, kept in pods filled with a pink gooey fluid, and hooked into the power grid for their energy. This would seem to match with the theory of the world of adventure. However, as the story progresses this world becomes the one associated with the idea of **home** and family. Unlike the tra-ditional journey, once Neo crosses into this world, it is the original **home**, the Matrix, that becomes the mythical world.

How might we translate this into an **analysis**? This is a key difference between our theoretical text and the film, and examining how those changes affect our understanding of what the film means will lead to a worthwhile analysis. Points of difference or conflict between your primary and secondary texts are often the place wherein you will find your **thesis**. While being able to identify and explain points of similarity is important, focusing on the **differences** will be crucial to conducting a well-developed contextual analysis.

Questions to ask as you construct your thesis include:

- On what points do the texts differ?

- Do these differences signal a change in what the text(s) value?

- How do these changes affect the text as a whole?

The Monomyth places high value and importance on the idea of **home**. The entire journey begins and ends there, and it is only once **home** that the hero uses the **elixir** and establishes him/herself as a figure of knowledge and power. Neo is left at the end of the film as master of both worlds (in his ability to control the Matrix and his establishment as "the One"), but the question is debatable as to whether or not the "real" world has become his **home**. Without a clear sense of return (note that Neo does not return across the **threshold**), we are left between the two worlds. With this change, **what can we say the film is valuing**? If it

Practice with the Hero's Journey

Practice using the **Hero's Journey** or **Monomyth** to analyze a text that you have looked at before. Fill out this chart with the corresponding scenes from a film or novel. If you were going to "chart" *The Matrix*, for example, you would simply write, "Neo takes the red pill" in the bubble that points where the threshold is crossed.

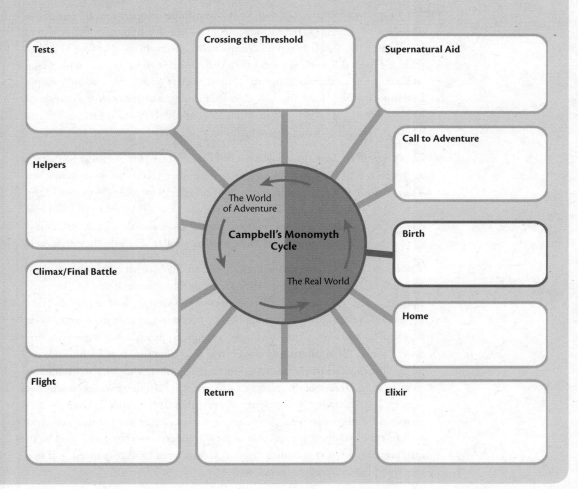

isn't home and family, what is it? Beginning with these questions and identifying how specific **strategies** such as lighting, set design, cinematography, and others are used will help you identify what the film emphasizes and values. The answers will be your thesis for this assignment.

Using a theoretical **lens** to view a primary text begins with a clear understanding of both the lens and the text. Once you have identified how your lens is shaping your view (coloring some details, heightening or obscuring others), it is then your job to conduct an analysis of how your primary text reveals those details. Just like the textual analysis you have already done, you will need to focus on specific details to help support your argument and then place it in relation to the contextual framework you have identified.

9.3 Comparative Analysis

By Jean Goodrich

The human brain seems especially skilled at making comparisons. It's one of the first skills we develop as babies: hot or cold, wet or dry, hungry or full. We may be able to judge better based on **comparative** observations: that blue is darker than this blue, this noise is louder than that. But this fact does not imply that a comparison is a naturally simplistic skill. It doesn't necessarily lead to a simple conclusion either; quite the contrary. Performing a **comparative analysis** of two complex objects can lead us to interesting observations we might not see when considering just one object by itself.

To perform a comparative analysis of two literary texts, for instance, you might approach the analysis as if the two texts were in conversation with each other. They might be in agreement; they might disagree. Consider the **genre** of the texts: are they both poems? Do they follow the same genre conventions? Or is one text a short story and the second a poem? Does one develop a certain image and the second its opposite? How are they similar? How do they disagree?

Two texts coming from a similar background are likely to have a number of characteristics in common. Perhaps they are from the same time period, the same culture, or the same author. The texts may be the same type of poem reflecting an aesthetic preference of the time, or they may develop a similar theme. They may share a common point of view or attempt to describe a common experience. Finding the **similarities** between two texts can provide you with evidence for an **interpretation** about the authors' society, their culture, their points of view, or their literary predecessors or influences. This interpretation might not be as clear or obvious when studying one text alone. Alternately, finding the **differences** between two texts that seem similar can highlight the way each text is distinctive. Studying two texts in apparent disagreement may also lead to an interpretation of how one text's original audience read and responded to it in a time and place different from our own.

Remember also that texts may be similar or different in subtle ways. Most things we see aren't clearly opposite or diametrically opposed; a comparison may show that there are gradations of difference. The atmosphere of a short story may be dark, but finding one that is darker wouldn't make the original story upbeat or happy.

To begin a comparative analysis in preparation for an essay, you can select any of the critical approaches introduced elsewhere in *A Student's Guide*: textual, literary or rhetorical analysis, visual, spatial or cultural analysis. You may select a method either with the direction of your instructor or based on a textual detail that intrigues you. Here is one way to get started:

- Make a list of two columns, one for each text to be analyzed.

- List or describe the **similarities** you find between the texts.

- List or describe the **differences**.

- Look for **patterns** or **connections**.

From these observations, you can begin by crafting a working thesis. Begin with answering **what** makes the texts similar or different, and then move gradually toward **how** or **why** they are similar or different. An essay thesis that answers **how** or **why** usually makes for a stronger and more interesting essay.

Consider the following sample analysis that does a comparative analysis of two popular films, Disney's classic *Cinderella* (1950) and the more recent *Shrek* (2001) by DreamWorks. First, make a list of the **similarities**:

Cinderella	Shrek
animated film	animated film
primary audience is children	primary audience is children
Uses fairytale conventions of:	*Uses fairytale conventions of:*
the worthy hero on a quest (Prince Charming)	the worthy hero on a quest (Shrek)
damsel to be rescued (Cinderella)	damsel to be rescued (Princess Fiona)
damsel locked in tower room	damsel locked in tower of castle
magic (the spell to send Cinderella to the ball)	magic (that turns Fiona to an ogress)
a fairy godmother provides magic	a witch casts the spell
magic ends at midnight	magic changes at sunset and sunrise
talking animals (the mice)	talking animals (Donkey)
finding "true love"	finding "true love"
happy ending	happy ending

9.3

Next, make a list of the **differences**:

Cinderella	Shrek
stepmother/sisters are antagonists	Lord Farquaad is antagonist
heroine is made a servant	heroine is under an enchantment
protagonist point of view is the damsel (Cinderella)	protagonist point of view is the monster (Shrek)
story is told straightforwardly, requiring the audience to suspend disbelief	story is told self-consciously skeptical of the unbelievable and fairytale elements
humor in the antics of the mice	humor expressed by main characters through "toilet" humor, farting, wisecracks
"true love" at first sight	"true love" is not at first sight but through interaction and getting to know the person
appearance matters: Cinderella must be dressed appropriately for the ball and is unrecognized in her daily servant clothes	appearance should not be trusted and beauty will not make you happy

Then, look for **patterns**. For instance, Cinderella's stepmother thwarts her wish to go to the ball to allow her own daughters access to the prince and the possibility of a royal marriage. She wants to use her daughters to "marry up" into wealth and privilege. Similarly, Lord Farquaad needs to marry a princess so he can be king of the perfect kingdom; otherwise, he's just a lord. For him, the title is what defines perfection. As a servant (Cinderella) and as an ogress (Fiona), both damsels are undesirable to most of society and the prince/lord they wish to marry. Both women have been raised on fairytale dreams and are looking for "true love." These are just a few of the patterns that seem to emerge from the comparison of the two films.

From this exercise, you can then start to craft a **thesis statement**. Here are a few possibilities:

Possible thesis #1: *Disney's* Cinderella *and DreamWorks'* Shrek *demonstrate that marrying for love, as opposed to marrying for power, money, or beauty, is the only way to live "happily ever after."*

To support this thesis, you could argue that the stepmother and stepsisters in *Cinderella* are unsuccessful in their scheming to marry the prince. Their conniving is not rewarded. The stepmother is depicted as mean, cruel and manipulative; the stepsisters as silly, shallow and quarrelsome. They are not worthy either of a prince or "true love." Cinderella is kind, hard-working, and full of dreams: she is worthy. In *Shrek*, we see Lord Farquaad as cruel when torturing the Gingerbread Man, in rounding up and evicting the fairytale creatures because they don't fit his image of perfect citizens, and in his final rejection of Princess Fiona in her ogress form. He values the appearance of perfection, as demonstrated by the sterility of Duloc (itself a satire of Disneyland), but not the deeper substance. He is also unsuccessful in marrying the princess, and meets an unfortunate end. Shrek does not desire money and power, preferring to live a simple life in his swamp. Fiona gives up being a princess, living in luxurious comfort, and her human beauty for love. In both tales, love is the precondition for "happily ever after."

Possible thesis #2: *Many children are raised on lessons gleaned from fairytales read to us as children, but both* Cinderella *and* Shrek *demonstrate that fairytale ideals can be misleading when it comes to living life in the real world.*

This one may seem harder to support. In the case of *Cinderella*, the story naïvely and wholeheartedly embraces the fairytale ideals and the fairytale ending. There doesn't seem to be any downside to the fairytale life. In contrast, the ogre Shrek's frequent sarcastic comments and the film's skeptical tone questions fairytale ideals. However, it ultimately upholds the basic fairytale conventions listed above with its "happily ever after" ending.

But consider the elements of both stories that support this thesis. In *Cinderella*, the heroine is impoverished and works at back-breaking labor on a daily basis doing the kind of chores that would make her hands rough and cracked, her hair disheveled, her clothes tattered. Cinderella has no friends besides the mice, birds, and dog that she encounters. There's no evidence she can read, write, or has a basic education, nor does she have access to wider society. In short, her topics for interesting conversation are quite limited. Cinderella is abused by her stepfamily, and rather than fight back or run away, she endures for years. The reward for enduring abuse is marrying the prince, whom she has only met once. He's handsome, sure, but who knows what kind of person he really is? Finally, she can only appear beautiful, and therefore socially acceptable, through magic. Since magic is usually not available to most of us in the real world, if we wait for it to happen as Cinderella did, we may find ourselves enduring an unbearable existence or outright abuse. The fairytale seems to advocate exactly this.

In *Shrek*, the town of Duloc is held up as the example of a fairytale town: no trash, no pollution, no traffic jams. But it is disturbingly homogeneous: all of the houses identical, with stacked Tudor-style facades, the streets lined with identical trees, and over all is piped-in bland "elevator music." If the film is critiquing the town as a banal example of suburbia and planned communities, we should note that the only other places people live are in swamps or in lava-moated ruined castles inhabited by man-eating reptiles. Princess Fiona has spent years locked in the highest tower waiting to be rescued, with little to do but plan out her fairytale future, practice martial arts, and breathe in toxic fumes from the molten lava. We might find ourselves asking where she got her food and water in so desolate a place, or why she didn't just get herself out. It was probably her fairytale ideals that got her there in the first place. And regardless of his civilized table manners and cultivated sense of humor, Shrek is still hunted by the local villagers, and is still likely to be hunted. Despite his (admittedly empty) courtesies, Fiona still judges Lord Farquaad for his short height. Like *Cinderella*, *Shrek* shows that even in fairytale land, nothing is ideal.

Possible thesis #3: *Animated films for children often teach us the values that our culture holds. While Disney's* Cinderella *portrays the fairytale ideal of "love at first sight,"* DreamWorks' Shrek *demonstrates that outer appearance is not a reflection of inner worth and will not guarantee happiness.*

This thesis seems more obvious and easier to prove. For Cinderella, happiness results after displaying her true beauty—perhaps inner and outer—to the prince, though it has been hidden by menial jobs, poor clothing, lack of social status, and scheming stepfamily. Cinderella's dreams of a better future, her hope and endurance have made her worthy of escaping her drudgery.

In *Shrek*, Princess Fiona faces the prospect of a loveless marriage to the "perfect" man in the "perfect kingdom." She instead chooses Shrek, despite his monstrous appearance because of his personality and his true love for her. In the end, her choice results in her own permanent transformation to ogre-form, which she has despised all along. However, if beauty is only intended and needed to find true love, she has found Shrek and therefore has found happiness. Maybe she doesn't need beauty anymore, once she's found her man? Maybe even an ogre can be beautiful in a fairytale? Or maybe the tale suggests that beauty comes from within. So while there may be people in our society who value beauty over all things, characters in these films who find happiness are rewarded for their inner values, not for their outer appearance.

The challenge in supporting this thesis is the number of details that don't seem to support the thesis. While such details don't automatically invalidate the thesis, a good essay will acknowledge or account for disagreement. For instance, the people around her may be blind to plain Cinderella in her work clothes, but it is her own worthiness rather than beauty that earns her a fairy godmother to make the magic of the ball happen. After all, Cinderella is kind, takes care of helpless animals, listens to her elders, does her chores, and above all, has hope. But what of the stepsisters, who are probably in greater need of help, given their own homeliness and being dominated by such a mother? Despite their need, they don't deserve a fairy godmother. Similarly, in *Shrek*, Lord Farquaad's appearance does in fact seem to be a reflection of his small, narrow mind. Characters who looks like witches are witches, and monsters are monsters. Though Shrek has suffered from people judging him for his appearance, he doesn't hesitate to make disparaging remarks about Farquaad's short stature. This thesis also does not address the fact that marriage does not always lead to happiness, nor does romantic bliss always mean a heterosexual relationship.

By themselves, the two films may have given us completely different messages. Generations of girls since 1950 have grown up waiting to find Prince Charming, and perhaps an equal number of boys have grown up unable to fill such unrealistic expectations. But without the stories of Cinderella, Sleeping Beauty, Snow White, the three little pigs, and the gingerbread man, Shrek would have had no fairytale conventions to re-imagine and subvert.

9.4 Culture: Another Kind of Text

Some of your instructors may assign you a different kind of text-in-context, one that asks you to incorporate notions of "culture" into your analysis. The difficulty, of course, is that there is no such thing as one single "culture." We may live inside certain cultures but feel distinctly excluded from others, which makes it difficult to discern and analyze how "culture" works. However, the text-in-context essay offers a way to make culture visible through textual analysis. This section will address how to use culture as a lens for your text-in-context essay.

Analyzing culture asks us to step outside so that you can examine and discover culture as a text. Through cultural analysis, you will become more aware of the ways a text and its reception reflect the ideologies—values, assumptions, conflicts, desires, anxieties, and so forth—of the culture that produces them. The underlying assumption of cultural analysis is that "any cultural product [...] carries, implicitly or explicitly, ideas about how the world should be seen" (Corrigan 88). In terms of your essay, the "cultural product" might be the text you're analyzing, and your job is to analyze how the text "sees" the world. This can be extremely difficult because often culture operates invisibly. The task of cultural analysis is to make visible those structures of culture. In other words, you want to take what is familiar to you and make it strange—to do so you have to work hard to perceive cultural aspects in a different light.

Cultural analysis asks you to analyze the many layers of meaning that influence the writer's construction of a text and/or the reader's interpretations of a text. Culture, in other words, becomes a context for the ways in which we understand ourselves and each other. Below is a list of terms used by cultural theorists. Your instructor may ask you to use some of these theories and not others in order to focus your research. However, if you do research or reading in the area of cultural studies, you will often see these words used (and sometimes used and defined in different ways).

- **Ideology**: underlying values, assumptions, conflicts, desires, anxieties, and so on. Ideology involves the beliefs that people hold, the prominent ideas that tell us what should be, must be, or what seems normal. Sometimes called "cultural values" when in reference to a popular or widely held belief. For example, the idea of *democracy* in the United States is an ideology—it assumes that everyone should have a voice and that everyone's voice should be equal, whether people are uneducated or college professors, politicians or people who never read the news, and so on. Other ideologies include capitalism, religion, and education.

- **Assumptions:** the beliefs that a person takes to be true/false, good/bad, valuable/unimportant, and so on, reflecting that person's worldview. For example, a member of Generation X (born in the mid-1960s through the late 1970s) might assume that constant connection to the Internet is excessive and has limited potential. Members of the "plugged in" Generation Y, which includes college students and people in their early twenties, have always been surrounded by digital technologies. Gen X and Gen Y members are likely to make assumptions about one another (Gen Y might consider Gen X members to be "technology dinosaurs"; Gen X might accuse Gen Y members of having short attention spans). Neither assumption is exactly right or exactly wrong, but both reveal something about each generation's differing worldviews. It helps to work backwards when analyzing assumptions: start by locating the assumption, then begin to question what that assumption might reveal about the person, character, or author.

- **Rhetoric:** the art, practice, or study of the persuasive functions of language. For example, when you were in high school, maybe you had to ask your parents for permission to use the car whenever you wanted to go out. To do so, you used rhetoric—you had to persuade them by assuring them you would be careful. Perhaps your arguments were based on the fact that you had not gotten into an accident, you had your own money for gas, or you would be home before they needed the car again. All of these pleas were rhetorical strategies. When you analyze culture, you need to explore how culture affects rhetorical strategies. For example, when you watch an "Old Navy" clothing commercial, you will notice that the commercials often use nostalgic music from the 50s and 60s, that the models are always thin, smiling people in that clothing line, and on top of that, the models represent different ethnicities, such as African American, Caucasian, Asian, and so on. What is persuasive or rhetorical about these choices? How are these rhetorical strategies reflecting the target culture of this commercial?

> For more discussion on rhetoric, see Chapter 10.

- **Semiotics:** the study of sign symbols; an analysis of signs to understand the ways that they convey meaning; the process of conveying meaning in human communication; the structure of language as a matter of symbols, both spoken and written. For example, consider the heart symbol ♥. This symbol does not look like a real heart, yet it represents a heart. When you see a heart symbol, you understand the cultural meanings attached to it—love, Valentine's Day, romance, and so on. Words are like this as well. Consider the word *love* for example. What does this mean when you say "I love you" to your partner, your friend, your parents, your aunt, your dog? Are any of these feelings the same as when you declare that you love a movie?

- **Power and institutional structures:** the ways in which power can only act within supporting social structures. French theorist Michel Foucault argues that power is always situated in historical movements that create institutional structures. These institutional structures create, reproduce, and maintain power. This is actually a fairly difficult theory. In order to think through this, consider sexism as an example: the idea that women are weaker than men, subordinate to men, or not as capable as men. Arguably, this form of oppression is maintained in the workplace (where women hit the "glass ceiling" faster than men), in school (where women are not always encouraged to excel in math and science), and in the media (in which women's sexuality is used to objectify them for commercial purposes). These structures work together to maintain power over women; however, Foucault argues that these power structures cannot be practiced unless there are *points of resistance*. When women and men resist these forms of power, their acts of resistance affirm that the power exists. Questions that you might want to ask are: Who is being disempowered? What institutional structures are disempowering those people/things? What forms of resistance are being offered and what is the effect of the resistance? Who, then, is being empowered?

- **Inequalities:** the structures in our society that privilege some and oppress others. This is intimately linked with the previous definition of power and institutional structures. Once power acts on a situation, whether that situation is a person or a political event, power is unequally distributed and therefore creates hierarchical relationships. Those in power then attempt to find ways to maintain and reproduce their power through different strategies such as representation, litigation, and so on. You can then look at the ways in which inequality is formed and maintained.

- **Sameness:** the ways in which people share similarities in worldviews, lifestyles, social interactions, and so on. These similarities can be constructed for certain rhetorical (persuasive) means. Think, for example, about those bumper-stickers that say "Aren't we all human?" or "Many people, one world." The rhetorical strategy here appeals to sameness. Sameness is a very strong strategy that can be misused. For example, when the Japanese attacked Pearl Harbor during WWII, America reacted by placing all Americans of Japanese ancestry into internment camps. These people were grouped in with the enemy because of their sameness, and as such, were forcefully taken from their homes and jobs. When you consider sameness, you might want to think about how it is used both positively and negatively in our society and how that affects your perceptions of certain peoples or events.

The above list is by no means comprehensive. Cultural analysis is extremely difficult because we have been living in our culture, so it has become natural to us and we no longer think about it. It is good to remember though, that culture maintains both positive and negative structures in our society. Even when we question negative structures, they do not always go away. Think about the Civil Rights movements of the 1960s, when Dr. Martin Luther King, Jr. challenged the inequities between African American and Caucasian people in America. Unfortunately, these inequities have not vanished—there are still structures within our society that support racial inequity. Arizona faces these problems, particularly with people of Latino and Native American heritage. You might want to question why the English language is privileged over Spanish, and why there is not more racial diversity in your classrooms when the city itself is incredibly diverse.

Getting Started on Your Cultural Analysis Essay

There are many similarities between cultural analysis and the other forms of analysis that you have done in your first-semester writing. There are also many similarities between cultural analysis and rhetorical analysis. Nevertheless, the tools of analysis for all of these papers are the same. You will need to do the following:

- Narrow your topic to something manageable.

- Find specific evidence to support your claims.

- Examine *how* a cultural element works or what it means in your text (mere description of a cultural element is not sufficient).

- Explain *why* the cultural element that you examined is significant.

While engaging in cultural analysis, you will be looking for ways in which texts and culture are intricately connected, the ways that culture affects audiences' readings of a text, and/or the value that is placed on cultural texts. You need to also consider whether the text you're analyzing challenges or accommodates dominant beliefs—who is being empowered/disempowered and how? Doing this form of analysis is necessarily persuasive. By making visible the structures within your cultures, you are able to convey your new understandings to other people, potentially changing their world views.

For a more in-depth discussion of writing your essay, see Chapter 4. Also, for more information on writing thesis statements and using evidence, see *Rules for Writers*, pages 21–24 and 361–64.

Works Cited

Campbell, Joseph. *The Hero with a Thousand Faces*. 3rd ed. Novato: New World Library, 2008. Print.

Cinderella. Dir. Clyde Geronimi, Hamilton Luske and Wilfred Jackson. RKO Radio Pictures, 1950. DVD.

Corrigan, Timothy. *A Short Guide to Writing about Film*. 6th ed. New York: Longman, 2006. Print.

The Matrix. Dir. Andy Wachowski and Larry Wachowski. Warner Home Video, 1999. DVD.

Shrek. Dir. Andrew Adamson and Vicky Jenson. DreamWorks Animation, 2001. DVD.

9.4

Rhetorical Analysis

Goals

Your Rhetorical Analysis should:

- Evaluate the overall effectiveness of a text to persuade an intended audience.
- Provide a clearly defined thesis and focused argument.
- Identify the relevant arguments in the text.
- Identify and analyze the rhetorical strategies the text employs.
- Effectively appeal to your chosen audience.
- Effectively incorporate peer and instructor feedback.

10.1 Rhetoric: From Analysis to Rhetorical Analysis

You've probably heard the word **rhetoric** before. In popular culture, rhetoric is often used to describe flashy, empty speech that politicians use to manipulate their audiences. While scholars sometimes think of rhetoric in this negative sense as manipulation, rhetoric is best thought of as any type of communication that seeks to *move* an audience toward a specific position, understanding, or action. Because the definitions of rhetoric are varied, you may encounter many different ways of conducting rhetorical analysis. This chapter introduces the most widely used methods of rhetorical analysis that you can apply in your first-year writing course.

In English 101, you were asked to look beyond the surface information in a text to make critical evaluations of the author and text. You may have looked at a text's theme, use of language, historical or social context, and general message as you analyzed it. **Rhetorical analysis** continues these investigations by focusing specifically on how a text works to persuade its audience toward a specific argument or to communicate a certain viewpoint to its audience. In your rhetorical analysis, you will identify and analyze the **rhetorical strategies** a text uses in order to be persuasive. This chapter will help you to understand the **rhetorical situation** of a text, to identify and analyze specific rhetorical strategies the text uses, and to consider the overall effectiveness of the text's **arguments** based on these rhetorical principles. Most arguments are complex, nuanced, and sometimes even contradictory. Your job as a rhetorical analyst is to provide your audience with a better understanding of *how* and *why* a text makes an argument for its specific audience. By rhetorically analyzing how a text builds its argument, you are making an argument about how the text ought to be read.

One resource beyond this chapter for learning more about rhetorical analysis is your *Writing Public Lives* textbook. Your writing instructor may have other suggestions for you to learn about other types of rhetorical analysis.

10.2 Foundations: Rhetorical Situations

One of the most central ideas in modern rhetorical studies is that of the **rhetorical situation**. Almost any situation in which communication occurs is a type of rhetorical situation, or a situation in which one person (the **author/speaker**) attempts to communicate some **message** to another person (the **audience**) for a specific reason (the **purpose**). Every rhetorical situation also includes the **context**, or the circumstances that affect how the author seeks to move the audience toward her or his position. One of the first steps in rhetorical analysis is identifying and analyzing each of these five elements of the rhetorical situation: the author, the audience, the message, the purpose, and the context.

The Rhetorical Situation

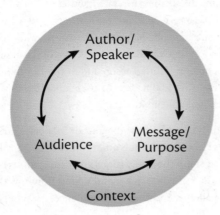

Author/Speaker

The **author/speaker** in a rhetorical situation is easily recognizable: it's the person or people seeking to communicate a specific message. In many rhetorical situations, such as in a scholarly article or a political speech, it's easy to discover who is sending the message. Some rhetorical situations have less obvious speakers, however. Consider a television advertisement for Welch's grape juice, for example. While the visible speaker might be a little girl drinking a glass of grape juice, the actual speaker in this situation is the organization behind that advertisement, such as Welch's, the company trying to sell its grape juice.

Once you've identified the author or speaker in a rhetorical situation, it's useful to make a list of things that you know and that you need to learn about that author/speaker. Ask yourself:

See Section 10.3 for more about an author's credibility and character.

- Who is the author/speaker?

- What organizations, political parties, viewpoints, or other interests does this author/speaker represent?

- How does the author/speaker portray himself or herself? What kind of character does this author/speaker establish?

Audience

The **audience** is the person or people who are reading or listening to the message of the rhetorical situation. Analyzing a rhetorical situation's audience means thinking about who, *specifically*, the author/speaker intends to reach with her or his communication. An accomplished rhetor almost never writes or speaks to a "general audience" without understanding who comprises that audience. For example, even when a United States President makes a primetime televised address that could be viewed by anybody in the world, the primary audience is comprised of a more specific audience of Americans, and even more specifically, *voting* Americans. Most writers and speakers have a much more specific

See Section 12.2 for more about audience.

audience in mind, and they make rhetorical choices based on what they know and what they assume about their intended audience. An audience can differ in education, gender, class, race, age, political beliefs, and a host of other differences. Thinking about audience helps writers choose what tone, language, and rhetorical strategies to use. Consider a Tucson mayoral candidate who wants to earn the votes of people in South Tucson and in the Foothills. What might the candidate need to consider about each of these audiences? What might be the expectations of each neighborhood?

As you examine a text, consider how the author may have adapted the message to reach a particular audience. Often an argument's success hinges on the author's ability to understand the motivations and expectations of the audience. As you analyze a rhetorical situation, it's useful to question how the author/speaker has worked to persuade her or his specific audience. Ask yourself:

- Who is the intended audience? How do I know? (What clues can I find in the text that help me determine the specific intended audience? What types of words does the text use? How do the examples in the text help me understand the audience?)

- How does the author/speaker position herself or himself in relation to the audience? Does she identify herself as a member of the group? Or does he separate himself from the audience? Look to the author's use of pronouns such as "you," "we," and "I" to help determine this.

- What is the author's/speaker's attitude toward the audience? What attitude does the author/speaker assume the audience has toward him or her? How do I know?

Because they can be reproduced, re-read, and copied, texts almost always have more than one audience, whether or not the writer or speaker intended for this to be true. In the example of the U.S. President making a televised address, the primary audience might be Americans, but any person capable of watching the broadcast on international television or on the Internet is a secondary audience member of that rhetorical situation. When you analyze texts, begin by identifying the primary audience, since it is the audience the author has in mind. Then you can focus on secondary audiences, who are not the author's target audience and for whom the effectiveness of the text may differ from the primary audience.

Message and Purpose

Wash, rinse, repeat. You've likely seen that **message** on the back of every shampoo bottle you've ever taken the time to read. The message in this case is fairly self-explanatory: it gives instructions for using the product. The **purpose** of the message is somewhat different, however. By telling consumers to "repeat" their shampooing process, shampoo companies can persuade their users to go through shampoo twice as quickly. Thus, the purpose of this message might be to sell shampoo twice as quickly than if the message simply instructed users to wash and rinse once.

10.2

It's important to identify and distinguish between the purpose and the message when you analyze a rhetorical situation. The idea here is to think about the specific goals the author/speaker has for the text and the audience. Ask yourself:

- What message does the author/speaker intend for the audience to understand?

- What response or reaction does the author/speaker intend for the audience to have as a result of understanding this message? Does the author/speaker wish the audience members to act, to react, or to think differently as a result of this message?

- Are the message and the purpose the same in this rhetorical situation, or are they different? Why might this be?

Context

As you already know from English 101, texts do not exist in a vacuum. Texts are created in the real world, and they deal with real-world issues and the people affected by them. Each text interacts with the world around it. The specific situation that surrounds and shapes a text is its context. The context of a rhetorical situation deeply shapes what a text will mean to its audience. Consider George W. Bush's address to the Joint Session of Congress and the American people shortly after 9/11. His audience members were not the same people he would have addressed on 9/10. The audience was deeply influenced by the 9/11 attacks; therefore, fully analyzing his speech requires a clear understanding of the post-9/11 context in which the speech was delivered. Whether you are analyzing a written rhetorical text or a rhetorical situation in which the message was delivered orally, visually, or spatially, the questions necessary to evaluating a rhetorical situation's context are often the same. Context can include many factors, including:

- The date of the publication

- The type of publication

- Recent events that may have shaped how people think about the topic

- Specific associations that readers of the publication may have

- Social movements that are related to the topic

- The cultural and linguistic backgrounds of the primary and secondary audiences

- The physical and material surroundings of the event or text, such as the city where a speech is delivered or the magazine in which a text is published

When a text exists in a different time or place, its meaning can change. As an example of how context changes, consider again Bush's post-9/11 speech. Although we can speculate on the meaning of the speech in the place and time it was delivered, our understanding of the meaning has changed over the years.

10.2

In its original context, this speech served as a point of national solidarity in the wake of a disaster. Looking back at the text after a decade has passed makes it impossible to understand the speech as it was understood in its original context, because the ways that we interact with terms such as *terrorists*, *Taliban*, and *freedom* have changed. In short, the context has changed and thus the meaning of the text has changed for a new audience.

10.3 Strategies for Rhetorical Analysis

Once you've identified the different elements of the rhetorical situation that you're analyzing, you'll be ready to conduct a more in-depth Rhetorical Analysis. Texts use numerous strategies to be convincing, and your task in a Rhetorical Analysis essay is to identify the rhetorical strategies in the text that are most important, most effective, or otherwise most notable. Like with textual analysis, once you've identified *what* rhetorical strategies a text uses, your next step will be to discuss *how* the text uses that strategy and *why* the strategy is or is not effective, given the text's specific rhetorical situation. Most Rhetorical Analysis essays will identify and analyze a range of rhetorical strategies that a text uses, although it is also possible to write an entire essay that centers in-depth on just one of the strategies below. It's important to remember that most texts use a combination of rhetorical strategies that are interconnected in order to be persuasive. The list of strategies below is far from complete, but it does outline some of the most useful strategies you might identify in your Rhetorical Analysis essay.

Ethos, or Appeals to Credibility and Character: *Ethos* refers to the ways that an author establishes **credibility** and **character** in a text. An author establishes credibility in a variety of ways. One ancient Greek thinker, Aristotle, urges us to look to the text itself to see how an author establishes credibility. By expressing sound logic and demonstrating knowledgeability on a subject, authors can convincingly establish credibility even if they do not have a well-known background in the subject matter. This kind of credibility can also be established visually and spatially: think of the ways that a speaker's choice of clothing, grooming, and body language makes us believe that he or she is worthy of our trust.

Ethos also refers to an author's ability to establish credibility by showing that she or he has a good **character**. To put it another way, the author establishes credibility by exhibiting the traits of a good person who cares about the well-being of the audience. This frequently appears in the style and tone of an author's writing. Writers can easily lose credibility by using an inappropriate tone. For example, a writer who seems to be addressing adult readers as if they were young children may find that s/he loses credibility. Likewise, a writer who uses jargon and terminology that will be unfamiliar to the audience may also lose credibility with readers.

When you evaluate an author/speaker's *ethos*, consider:

- How does the text itself create a sense of credibility? Does it demonstrate sound logic and knowledge of the subject at hand? Does it draw on personal experience or other types of solid, credible evidence?

- What kind of character does the author/speaker develop in this text?

- How does the author/speaker's *ethos* work to move the audience toward the author's position?

Gender Criticism: Rhetorically analyzing a text in terms of gender involves examining the ways that a text seeks to reinforce, challenge, or disrupt systems of inequality based on gender. For a longer explanation of gender-based rhetorical criticism, see Adrienne Crump's section at the end of this chapter.

Identification: Rhetorical scholar Kenneth Burke saw rhetoric not merely as a means of persuasion, but rather as a way for people to level with one another despite the fact that every person has a slightly different background and perspective on any given topic. Thus, Burke tells us that it is important to analyze the ways that an author/speaker works to **identify** with the members of an audience by pointing out the qualities, characteristics, assumptions, beliefs, and goals that they share with one another. Some authors/speakers will have many ways to identify with their audiences; for example, the speaker might identify with the audience's political beliefs, financial needs, common experiences, or common history. At a basic level, all humans can identify with one another through the fact that they share the common characteristic of having a body. However, as Burke argues, we can never *fully* identify with one another. For example, we each experience our own body very differently from one another—our unique physical traits such as race, biological sex, health, and so on make it impossible for any two people to share the exact same experience of having a body. Therefore, it's important to keep in mind that identification does not mean "sameness," and an author/speaker must define and explain the importance of any type of identification he or she draws on.

Contemporary rhetorical theorist M. Jimmie Killingsworth suggests that one of the strongest types of identification rests in appealing to common *values* that the audience shares with the author/speaker. For example, because all humans share the experience of having a body, we generally share the value of good bodily health. While the notion of "health" differs from person to person, establishing "healthiness" as a shared value is one way in which a speaker can identify with his or her audience. For example, a speaker might claim that a certain product or choice will ensure that the audience will be physically safe and healthy—and who doesn't want to be healthy? By identifying the qualities or values that he or she shares in common with the audience, an author/speaker can make a compelling case for why they might also share a common goal. When you analyze the ways that an author/speaker identifies with his or her audience, consider the common qualities that the speaker and the audience share. Ask yourself:

10.3

199

- What common characteristics, experiences, assumptions, beliefs, or goals does the author/speaker claim to have with the members of the audience?

- How does the author/speaker use language or images to show that he or she identifies with these qualities in the audience?

- What values does the author/speaker portray as having in common with the audience? How does the author/speaker use these shared values to create a sense of identification with the audience?

- How does the author/speaker use these points of identification to move the audience toward a common goal?

Ideological Criticism: You may be familiar with the term **ideology**, which refers to a set of beliefs and ideas that govern the way that people in a given group or culture behave. When we analyze ideology rhetorically, we examine the ways that an author/speaker uses language to reinforce, challenge, or modify an audience's ideological understanding of the world. For example, you might read a text in which the author argues that all houses in Arizona ought to have solar panels. This argument rests on many ideological assumptions, including the belief that the use of electrical and gas resources for power is less desirable than the use of other means of energy. There are even deeper ideological assumptions that you could look for in this text; for example, is solar power more desirable because it is a cleaner source of energy or because it keeps the U.S. from depending on foreign energy sources? All of these arguments rest on ideological assumptions about how the world should operate. By analyzing the ways the author uses language and organization to make this argument, you can begin to uncover the ideological assumptions that hold the text together. The next step in ideological criticism is to analyze how the author/speaker uses his or her specific ideological assumptions to persuade or move the audience. This analysis can help you build an argument about how the text's rhetoric reinforces, challenges, or modifies existing ideological beliefs. When you conduct a rhetorical ideological criticism, consider:

- What ideological assumptions does the author/speaker base his/her arguments on? How do you know?

- How does the author/speaker feel about these ideological assumptions? Is s/he seeking to reinforce or to change the way the audience thinks about them?

- What key words, images, or metaphors does the author use to reinforce or challenge the ideology in question? How does the author's use of language reveal his/her position about the ideology?

For more on ideological criticism, see Chapter 3 of *Writing Public Lives*.

"Inartistic" Proofs: Often called "facts," inartistic proofs refer to persuasive strategies that are "uncontestable." Data in the form of statistics and forensic evidence are examples of inartistic proofs. Imagine that you wanted to argue

10.3

for the establishment of an after-school community center for "at-risk" youth in a particular inner city. Your argument could be strengthened by statistical evidence; statistics that demonstrate a causal relationship between a youth's involvement in a community center and improvement in academic performance would be helpful to your claim. Remember, however, that even "facts" should be read and used carefully; it's easy to misinterpret or misrepresent an inartistic proof such as a statistic. Therefore, inartistic proofs should always be approached with a reasonable amount of caution. In the above example, just because a community center was helpful in one city, it doesn't necessarily mean that a center in an entirely different city will yield similar results. In general, statistics and other types of inartistic proofs are most effective when the speaker or author acknowledges their limitations. When analyzing a speaker/author's use of inartistic proofs, consider:

- Does the speaker reveal where the data comes from? If so, how reliable is the source of the data?

- What are the limitations to the data being presented? Does the speaker effectively address these limitations?

- Could the speaker have done more? In other words, are there any additional sources of data that could have made the speaker's claim even more persuasive? Can you think of any data that might contradict the data presented?

Logos, **or Logical Appeals:** *Logos* refers to the ways that a text appeals to an audience by making **logical arguments.** There are many ways to judge how a speaker uses logic to make a convincing argument, and your instructor may teach you a specific way to analyze logical arguments. This section provides an overview of the most common types of logical appeals. Keep in mind as you read this section that a logical appeal doesn't necessarily mean an author/speaker is using *good* logic; nevertheless, even faulty logical appeals can be persuasive.

The conclusions people make in their arguments generally follow one of two types of reasoning: inductive and deductive. At the most basic level, **inductive reasoning** draws from specific personal experiences or examples to make more general claims. For example, the statement, "All cacti I've touched have hurt my hand; therefore all cacti will hurt my hand" involves inductive reasoning. The persuasive strength of inductive claims relies heavily on the experience of the listener/reader and on the probability of the claim. However, not all inductive reasoning is generalizable to all audiences. Claims like, "I like chocolate ice cream; therefore all people like chocolate ice cream" fail to persuade since counterexamples are easy to imagine, if not demonstrate.

See the example of a "Hasty Generalization" on page 203 for more about the limits of inductive claims.

On the other hand, **deductive reasoning** draws conclusions about specific examples from a general premise. For example:

Premise 1: All Tucson residents like hot weather.

Premise 2: Michael is a Tucson resident.

Conclusion: Therefore, Michael likes hot weather.

If we knew that premise 1 were true, that all Tucson residents did in fact like hot weather; then the conclusion would be valid and true. But we know that it is not necessarily true (there are a lot of people who live in Tucson who simply do not like the hot weather), so we can't really know if the conclusion is true or not. Remember that just because a conclusion is true, it does not necessarily mean that the reasoning employed has been valid. For example, one may say:

Premise 1: **Some** Tucson residents like hot weather.

Premise 2: Michael is a Tucson resident.

Conclusion: Therefore, Michael likes hot weather.

In this case, imagine that Michael is your friend and you happen to know that he does in fact like hot weather: the conclusion is now "true." But the conclusion is necessarily *invalid* or *fallacious* because it is derived from the premise that "*Some* Tucson residents like hot weather." This is important to note because some speakers may, knowingly or unknowingly, use fallacious logic to effectively persuade an audience to accept claims that are not valid. In an actual speech or essay, a speaker or author will usually not spell out the inner workings of a claim for you. You would likely see something like, "Michael lives in Tucson, so he must like hot weather." This claim leaves out both premises that led to the speaker's conclusion. When a speaker leaves a premise unstated, it becomes your prerogative to determine what the premise is and to argue whether or not that premise is true.

Now, imagine that you conducted a survey of every single Tucson resident and discovered that 85% of Tucson residents like hot weather. You can now say "Most Tucson residents like hot weather." Or, if you want to be more precise, you'd say "85% of Tucson residents like hot weather." So long as we **qualify** our statements, we can present a conclusion that is both true and valid:

Premise 1: **Eighty-five percent** of Tucson residents like hot weather.

Premise 2: Michael is a Tucson resident.

Conclusion: Therefore, Michael **probably** likes hot weather.

In rhetorical analysis, you are evaluating the effectiveness of a text's arguments for a particular audience. Logic is one element of that effectiveness, one connection to the audience.

When you evaluate a text in terms of its *logos*, consider:

- How does this text build logical arguments on a global level? You may look at the text's organization and arrangement, its major assumptions, and the types of reasoning it uses to answer this question.

- How does the text build logical arguments on a local level? You might look at specific examples, specific arguments, and even the way the text uses sentences logically (or illogically) to answer this question.

- Are there parts of the text that are *not* logical? Why is this effective/ineffective for moving this audience?

Logical Fallacies: Your instructor might also teach you about logical fallacies, or the ways in which points of an argument are questionable or invalid. The following are some examples of logical fallacies:

Ad Hominem: This Latin phrase means "to the man." An *ad hominem* argument attacks an individual's character or behavior rather than focusing on the actual issue at hand. Think about the "attack ads" that frequently appear during political elections. Often, these advertisements focus on attacking the opposing candidate's character rather than addressing real voting issues.

Causal Generalizations: involve the assumption that a correlation between two events proves that one caused the other.

> Example: *"Since we've implemented the dress code, the average student's GPA has risen drastically. Therefore, the dress code must be the cause for our students' improved academic performance."*

Just because the rise in average student GPA coincides with the new dress code, it doesn't necessarily mean that the dress code was the cause for the increase, which makes this claim a causal generalization.

False Analogy: involves the use of an analogy between two apparently similar, but nonetheless very different, things.

> Example: *"In pro football, the starting quarterback plays in almost every game, but in pro baseball, a starting pitcher only plays once about every five games. Therefore, baseball pitchers have less stamina than football quarterbacks."*

Here, the speaker neglects the fact that pro football teams play once a week, whereas pro baseball teams play anywhere from five to seven times a week, which makes the comparison a faulty one.

Hasty Generalization: involves the use of a few particular examples to make a general conclusion.

> Example: *"I've met 10 people from California, and they all love going to the beach. It looks like all Californians love the beach."*

You can't draw any "real" conclusions from 10 people who just so happen to have the same opinion. Watch for how polls and surveys are collected: how many people were surveyed? What demographic groups were represented in the surveys? Hasty generalizations are made often, even in largely published statistics.

10.3

Non Sequitur: Meaning "does not follow," a **non sequitur** draws a conclusion from a premise that isn't necessarily related.

> Example: *"Marijuana should be decriminalized. My friend smokes pot every day and still gets straight As."*

In this example, it does not follow that one person performing academically well under the influence of marijuana means that the drug should be decriminalized. Watch for non sequitur arguments in speeches and advertisements, especially—they're more common than you might think.

There are many other logical fallacies besides those outlined in this list, but these are some of the most common ones you might encounter during your rhetorical analysis. Sometimes a logical fallacy can still be effective as an argument, such as when it creates an illogical argument but still moves an audience emotionally. When you evaluate a text in terms of its logical fallacies, consider:

- What are the logical fallacies used to build this argument?

- Are the logical fallacies persuasive to this particular audience? Why/why not?

Metaphor: Authors and speakers also seek to persuade their audiences through the use of metaphors. When we rhetorically analyze the metaphors in a text, our primary goals are to locate, define, interpret, and possibly reconceptualize the metaphors an author constructs. Ultimately, metaphoric criticism asks *how* an author uses metaphors in order to build an effective argument. For example, a metaphoric analysis could analyze the immigration metaphors in a popular politician's speeches. To do this, you would first identify the relevant metaphors and then make claims about the meaning and effect of using the metaphors. Let's say the politician claims, "immigrants are flooding across the border." The use of the term "flood" as a metaphor for how immigrants cross the border has interesting implications for that politician's argument. "Flood" refers to a rushing of water that is uncontrollable and often damaging. By using "flood," the politician characterizes the manner in which immigrants cross the border: too fast. We could continue the analysis by pondering the specific implications of a flood versus other fast-moving waters, like a gush or river. "Flood" has some inherently negative connotations that are not carried with gush and river, making flood imply both uncontrollable water and bad water. This characterization of immigrants, we might reason, lumps all immigrants into one giant, uncontrollable mass working in unison to cause harm to the United States. Turning our attention back to the politician, we can say that the surface arguments of the speech seem innocuous, but the subtext presented in the metaphors offers a much stronger message to the audience: "immigrants are damaging." Your task in analyzing the metaphors of the text, then, is to consider the rhetorical implications of the metaphors the text uses. When you look at metaphors in a rhetorical text, consider:

10.3

- What major metaphors does the author/speaker construct in the text?

- How does language affect the audience's explicit and implicit understanding of the metaphor?

- Is the use of metaphor consistent with the tone and message of the text?

- What are the implications of the author's use of metaphor for the text's larger argument?

Pathos, or Appeals to Emotion: *Pathos* refers to the ways that a text appeals to an audience's **emotions** in order to move the audience toward the author's position. The term *pathos* might remind you of the more familiar word "pathetic." In fact, the words *pathos* and pathetic are connected; we say something is "pathetic" when it inspires in us the emotional response of compassion or sympathy. Emotional appeals can come in the form of a story or image, individual words, or a change in the tone and pace of a speech or written text. Language can emotively direct the audience's attention in one direction rather than another. Consider these two sentences:

> *The increase of carbon emissions potentially leads to high amounts of greenhouse gases.*

> *Our cars are choking the planet to death.*

Both sentences argue for essentially the same thing, but the second sentence uses emotionally charged language to further the argument. When you evaluate a text in terms of its *pathos*, consider:

- Which emotions does the author/speaker seek to inspire in his/her audience?

- How does the text create this emotional response? Does it use moving stories, examples, or images? Does it use language that evokes a certain emotional response?

- Why are these emotions effective or ineffective for this particular audience and rhetorical situation?

10.4 Putting it Together: Writing a Rhetorical Analysis

As the previous section shows, authors/speakers draw from a variety of rhetorical strategies when addressing an audience. Your goal in a rhetorical analysis is not to make a list of all of the rhetorical strategies a text uses. Rather, as with textual analysis, you should focus on the most important, intriguing, or disturbing rhetorical strategies in your chosen text. For example, you might find that the most central rhetorical strategy used in the PETA advertisement you're analyzing is *pathos*, and your essay might center on all of the ways that the ad appeals to its audience's emotions. Or, you might find that your text uses two or three of the strategies in combination with one another. In this case, your Rhetorical Analysis essay might focus on how the particular strategies you've identified work together to create a convincing argument.

Your Rhetorical Analysis essay should connect key rhetorical strategies to the overall argument that an author/speaker is making in his/her text. It can be useful to think about an author's rhetorical strategies in terms of how the author is trying to *move* her or his audience. Does the author want the audience to be moved to take a particular action? To understand a situation differently? To react with a particular type of emotional response? In other words, *how* do the author's rhetorical strategies lead to an effective or ineffective argument for the particular rhetorical situation you're analyzing?

It's Greek to Me! Using *Ethos*, *Pathos*, and *Logos* Effectively

It can be easy to get tripped up on the specialized language of rhetorical analysis, such as the Greek terms *ethos*, *pathos*, and *logos*. Below are some tips and examples to help you effectively use the language of rhetorical analysis in your own essay.

Tips for Using Specialized Terminology

- Always provide a definition of a specialized term the first time you use it in your essay. Even if you assume that your instructor and classmates also know the terms you're using, it's good to ensure that you're sharing a common understanding of the definition with your readers.

- Alternate between using the specialized term (like "*logos*") and its translation (like "logical appeal") for variety and clarity.

- Italicize Greek terms (and other words in languages other than English) in your text.

Sample Uses of Greek Terms

Ethos Examples

Author B effectively establishes her *ethos* by drawing on personal experiences and relating to her audience's sense of morality.

The use of *ethos* in terms of credibility is the most convincing rhetorical strategy Author B develops in her essay. By highlighting her extensive knowledge of immigration laws and her personal experiences living on the Mexican/U.S. border, Author B establishes a strong sense of her authority to argue about this issue.

Pathos Examples

The advertisement uses the *pathos* strategies of humor and sarcasm to emotionally move its viewers toward an appreciation of Product Y.

The advertisement appeals to its audience's *pathos* by developing a shared joke about Product Y.

Logos Examples

Author J's explanation of this chart demonstrates his overall effective use of *logos* throughout the essay.

By using a combination of inductive reasoning and *ad hominem* claims, Author J builds a highly effective sense of *logos*, or logical appeal, for his audience of college students.

10.4

Connecting the rhetorical strategies an author uses to the type of action or reaction the author wishes an audience to have can help you to explain the "so what" in your Rhetorical Analysis. For example, a strong thesis sentence for a Rhetorical Analysis essay might read:

By using an extended flood metaphor to describe immigrants coming to the United States, Politician A develops in her American audience a sense of fear and urgency that reaffirms the idea that the U.S. is facing an "immigration crisis."

This thesis sentence uses metaphoric and ideological criticism to explain how the speaker moves the audience toward a position of fear.

The images of animals in pain in the PETA fundraising advertisement lead to an overwhelming emotional response of sadness and anger in an audience of college students who may never have been exposed to such images before. This shocking use of pathos effectively moves college students to visit the PETA website to learn how to stop the cruelty.

This thesis sentence indicates that the essay will discuss how the advertisement's images lead to the *pathos* responses of sadness and anger in a specific audience of college students. It will also explain how PETA intends to transform these emotions into audience action—becoming active in PETA.

By sharing personal experiences visiting a nuclear meltdown zone, Author M builds credibility with her first-world audience as a spokesperson for developing clean energy technology. Moreover, Author M effectively portrays clean energy as a value that all humans ought to share if they wish for life on Earth to continue.

This thesis sentence prepares for an essay that will both analyze the author's *ethos* as well as the author's strategy of identifying with "first-world" readers through the shared value of a clean environment even for people removed from the direct effects of a nuclear meltdown.

As you can see, there are many ways to successfully conduct a rhetorical analysis. Like with textual analysis, the way you approach rhetorical analysis will depend on the type of text that you read and the elements of that text that you find most interesting, intriguing, or troubling. The next sections of this chapter explain three specific types of rhetorical analysis that you might wish to use as you consider the text you are analyzing.

> You can read more about specific rhetorical analysis methods in Section 1 of *Writing Public Lives.*

10.5 Reading Visual Rhetoric

By Amy Parziale

We all interpret and analyze visual messages every day. This section's purpose is to make you more aware of visual rhetoric so that you may be more critical of the messages you see. Why is understanding visual rhetoric important? Consider the controversy over the different versions of a single photograph, O.J. Simpson's 1994 mug shot. In 1994, both *Time* and *Newsweek* ran O.J. Simpson's mug shot on the cover of the magazine after he was accused of murdering Nicole Brown Simpson and Ronald Goldman. The editors of *Time* altered the photograph, darkening Simpson's skin. Many argued this was done to stereotype Simpson as the "violent black man" in order to imply his guilt. By thinking critically about the images around us like those on magazine covers, we become more aware of the ways such images affect our perspectives.

Visual rhetoric is a form of communication in which visual elements create meanings and arguments. Advertising is the most obvious form of visual rhetoric in the contemporary world, but works of art, photographs, websites, brochures, and even bumper stickers contain and create visual rhetoric. Think about the meaning(s) and argument(s) created in a stained glass window at a local church, a political cartoon in *The New Yorker*, or the brochure sent to prospective students by the University of Arizona. Each creates a specific message that the visual elements of the piece are meant to communicate to the intended audience.

Just like textual rhetoric, the author's purpose in using visual rhetoric is to best persuade her audience to her position—whether it is which shampoo to purchase or who to vote for in an election. Thus, there are some overlaps between analyzing visual rhetoric and analyzing textual rhetoric. Like with textual rhetoric, when you analyze visual rhetoric you should consider:

- **Audience:** Who is the author's primary audience? Does she have any secondary audiences?

- **Purpose:** What is the work's purpose? What is it attempting to persuade its audience to do/think? Are there potential secondary purposes? (These can be conscious or unconscious.)

- **Strategies:** How does the work seek to identify with its audience? Does it create *ethos*, *logos*, and/or *pathos*? What other strategies does this work use to move the audience?

- **Success:** How successful is it in achieving its purpose(s)? Which elements work in harmony together? How could it be improved? Which elements are less successful? Are there elements that seem to contradict or challenge the message or purpose?

When you analyze visual rhetoric, you should also be aware of some elements worth analyzing that are not usually present in written texts. These elements include:

- The **type** of visual (text, images, clip art, photographs, etc.),

- **Color palette** (individual element's color, background, contrast, etc.),

- **Font choices** (size, color, typeface, etc.), and

- **Organization** and **arrangement** of the elements in the work (foreground, background, top, bottom, etc.).

10.5

To examine a work's visual rhetoric, start by writing down everything you see.

For more visual strategies to consider, see Section 8.4.

- **Visuals:** What elements make up the piece? How are they arranged? How are they related? What shapes, colors, texture, lighting, shadows, and types of lines are used? What is lightest? What is darkest? Do the elements complement or contrast with each other? Is a specific element repeated? Is there variety in the elements?

- **Technique:** How do you think the piece was created (photography, painting, film, computer-generated techniques, etc.)?

- **Focus:** What is in focus and what is out of focus? What size are the objects in comparison to each other? Are the objects to scale? How does your eye move around the piece? What elements draw your eye and how is that accomplished?

- **Space:** What sense of space is created? Do objects overlap? What is in the foreground, middle ground, and background? What is in each third of the piece—top, middle, bottom, left, middle, and right?

- **Point of View:** What vantage point is the piece created from? How is the piece framed? What is included? What do you think lies beyond the edges?

- **Overall Feeling:** Does the piece feel balanced? Is there a sense of unity? What feeling and mood best summarize the piece?

Next, consider how the visual text creates meaning and how well it persuades its audience with its argument.

- **Message:** What is the overall message? How persuasively is that message communicated? Do any of the elements feel as if they are in opposition to that message? What is left out of the piece?

- **Credibility:** Does the work create a sense of credibility? Does it include facts and figures? Is there a narrative or story? Does it appeal to you on a specific emotional level?

- **Audience**: Who is the intended audience? Who does the intended audience include/exclude?

- **Context:** Does the piece interact (consciously or unconsciously) with issues of culture, language, class, race, ethnicity, country of origin, gender, or sexual orientation?

- **Persuasion:** Are you persuaded by its rhetoric? Do you agree with its message?

Let's take a look at a photograph and consider some of the elements that contribute to its visual rhetoric. Here's a photograph used for marketing purposes by the University of Arizona.

Organization and Arrangement: Notice how the students are **posed**. Do you think it's more likely that the two students were just sitting there and someone took their picture, or that they were asked to sit in this particular position at this particular location? Look at their **body positions**. Why are they not facing each other? Does this suggest that they are merely posing? Look at the **expressions** on both of their faces. While they are both smiling, how comfortable do you think they look with having their picture taken? Consider all of these elements and think about whether this photo was a candid photo, or one posed for the purpose of using it in marketing.

Message and Context: After making that determination, we might want to consider the choice of **these two students**. Why two male students? Is it important to consider the fact that one of the students is of Asian heritage, especially since Asian males make up less than 4% of the UA student population, according to the 2008–2009 University of Arizona Fact Book? Why are they sitting in this **location**? What's going on in the **background**, and how does that affect our reading of the photo? What **message(s)** and **feeling(s)** do you think the University wishes to portray through this photo? Who is their intended **audience**? Does the photograph come across as **credible**? Is the image **successful** in representing the desired message?

Understanding visual rhetoric allows us to engage with the multitude of images we are bombarded with each day on a more critical level. The next time you are driving by a billboard, strolling through a museum, or flipping through a magazine, pause and consider how the image constructs its meaning through visual rhetoric.

10.6 Rhetorically Analyzing Graffiti as a Visual-Spatial Public Medium

By Marissa M. Juárez

The skills you learn in this chapter will help you rhetorically analyze print, oral, visual, and spatial texts. Some texts, like the graffiti art we deal with in this section, blur the boundaries between visual, spatial, and print forms of argument.

As a result, public art forms like graffiti encourage you to think about how arguments and meaning are made on multiple levels:

• Through a visual rendering of a message,

• Through the space or place context in which it exists, and

• Through its multiple purposes, whether as creative expression or political protest.

Graffiti is a contentious genre—some see it as a form of vandalism while others view it as a valuable artistic medium. Contextualizing graffiti historically will help us to rhetorically analyze how its meanings, uses, and purposes have changed over time.

Historic Developments of Graffiti Art

The word "graffiti" conjures the drawings, paintings, and sketches we see daily on public walls, in bathroom stalls, and on freight trains, but humans have been marking on walls and other surfaces for millennia. Long ago, indigenous populations across the Americas painted petroglyphs on rock faces and in caves, and ancient examples of graffiti remain at the Mayan site of Tikal, the Catacombs of Rome, and Pompeii ("Graffiti"). Professor of Art Education Janice Rahn notes that graffiti even had an impact on artists like Pablo Picasso and Jackson Pollock (9). However, the history of modern graffiti—the graffiti with which we are most familiar—can be attributed to Cornbread and Cool Earl, who "tagged" the city of Philadelphia in the early 1960s (Ehrlich & Ehrlich 1). By 1971, graffiti had spread into New York and other urban areas.

The art form garnered media attention when a young New Yorker who called himself "Taki 183" scrawled his name wherever he went in the city. The ubiquity of "Taki 183," combined with its elusive meaning, resulted in an exposé by the *New York Times*. The article exposed the identity of Taki 183, who by then had inspired several other youths to leave their marks in the city. As graffiti in New York became increasingly prevalent, then-mayor John Lindsay declared a city-wide "war" against the practice and worked to fight it through lawmaking. This period represents the time in which graffiti first became politicized and criminalized (Castleman 21–24).

The history of graffiti grew richer still once it became a part of hip-hop culture in the late '70s and early '80s. In its earliest days, hip-hop was what scholar Greg Dimitriadis has called a "live event," involving participation from DJs, beatboxers, breakdancers, MCs, graffiti artists, and audience members; he argues that "dance, music, and graffiti were all equally important in helping to sustain the event" (16). Hip-hop historian Tricia Rose has noted that graffiti was integral to early hip-hop: Graffiti was a stylistic marker that appeared on the clothing of hip-hop heads, it was a tool used to design marketing materials for hip-hop

10.6

events, and it was a medium in which artists could visually commemorate their favorite hip-hop artists and songs (35).

- How has the role of graffiti changed over time, and why might it have changed?

- In what ways has the politicization and criminalization of graffiti changed since the time of Mayor Lindsay's New York, and in what ways do current politics and laws surrounding graffiti remain similar to that time?

- In what ways does modern graffiti challenge our notions of ancient forms of writing and art like the ones mentioned at the beginning of this section?

Asking these questions complicates any simple definition of graffiti. Further, we believe that sharing some of graffiti's history might help you better understand how graffiti's rhetorical situation has changed, and continues to change, over time. These historical changes in graffiti's authors, audiences, and contexts lead to a wide variety of possible interpretations for contemporary graffiti art.

Spaces of Graffiti Art: Public Art or Vandalism?

Contemporary graffiti artists often use the art form to share political messages. For example, the infamous British artist known as "Banksy," whose stencil graffiti creations have appeared in China, Britain, Israel's West Bank, and the United States and on buildings, cargo ships, billboards, and shipping trucks, often shares messages of social protest in his artwork. Take, for instance, the artwork shown on the following page. The piece, which Banksy stenciled on the Israeli West Bank in 2005, features Mahatma Gandhi holding up a peace sign.

Photo source: *Wikimedia Commons*/Szater. Graffiti paintings on the Israeli West Bank barrier by Banksy near Qalandia. (July 2005)

- Considering the graffiti appears on Israel's West Bank, where conflicts between Israel and Palestine have played out for decades, how might the spatial context of this graffiti affect its argument?

- Why might Banksy have chosen to include Mahatma Gandhi, known for his path of nonviolent resistance, in a place that has been riddled with violence?

- Considering that Gandhi is holding up a peace sign, what might be Banksy's purpose(s) behind this particular graffiti art?

- Since graffiti is itself a contested art form, what might it say that this work, produced in a contested medium, appears in the contested space of Israel's West Bank?

Rhetoric and composition scholar Nicole R. Brown writes that "in general, graffiti writers inhabit space(s) between artist-citizen and vandal" (242). In other words, graffiti exists on the border between being public art and being vandalism; like vandalism, it disrupts a specific place with its unauthorized tagging, but like public art, it seeks to impart a message in a mostly visual way. While graffiti is usually unauthorized and public art is usually authorized, even commissioned, both seek expression on buildings and other public spaces that already serve a different purpose. Ethnographer Ralph Cintron notes that unlike public art, graffiti art declares "itself outside the law, [...] potentially uncontrollable in the midst of public space" (174). Graffiti—even the kind that, like the Banksy piece above, urge the public to find peace or that impart other positive messages—always challenges the ability of authorities to control public space.

Knowing that graffiti signifies a challenge to official lines of control, consider what it means to capture graffiti art through photography and thus turn it into authorized art, even going so far as to publish it in a textbook. Whereas Cintron tells us that graffiti art intends to be "uncontrollable," doesn't the reappropriation of graffiti seek to return some level of order and control over this art? Through the previous example, we can see how important space is to the power of any message. Tagged on the side of the Israeli West Bank, the unauthorized message of "Peace" conveys a different set of possibilities than it does when plastered to the pages of a composition textbook. On the wall, the image of Gandhi and his peace sign might tell the public audience to find peace in the space around them, to engage in peaceful acts around that space. In the pages of a textbook, the peace sign perhaps reads more like an imperative to students: Peace on the West Bank! Peace in the world! Or even: Peace in the classroom! Likewise, each of the photographs throughout this book, whether they be graffiti or authorized public art, has a slightly changed message or argument within the pages of the book than it has or had on the walls on which they originally appeared.

10.6

Rhetorically Analyzing Visual and Spatial Images

Below, and on the following page, you will find photographs of graffiti and public murals in Tucson. Drawing upon what this chapter teaches you about visual and spatial analysis, take some time to look at the following images.

Photos on these two pages by Hallie Bolonkin.

As you look at these images, think about the similarities and differences between graffiti, a contested art form that has legal implications, and public murals, a form of art that is more socially accepted by mainstream society. You might want to ask yourself:

- Consider the intended message of each example. How do you think the author used medium, color, size, and images to help convey these messages?

- In what city spaces and places do these two forms appear? Based on the location of the images, what inferences can you make about the target audiences for the art? What effects do the space and place have on the viewer?

- What spaces and public places do you feel are appropriate or inappropriate for murals and graffiti? What contextual factors determine whether a space is appropriate? For example, which art form is more appropriate near an elementary school?

- Unlike public art murals, graffiti usually has a negative reputation among police officers, property owners, city officials, and some citizens. What makes art on public property socially acceptable—what qualities should it have and why? How does the negative image of illegal graffiti affect its persuasive capacity?

- Some muralists receive a monetary commission when they paint a mural. How does this practice of commissioning determine whether a piece of public art is classified as a mural or as graffiti? Does the absence or presence of a commission change your conclusions about the artist's message or intentions in producing the art?

- Now, as a class, discuss your reactions to the questions above. How do your responses compare to your classmates'? Can you use your class discussion to locate some of the entry points you might explore in a rhetorical analysis of one of these images?

10.7 Conducting a Critical Feminist Rhetorical Analysis

By Adrienne Crump

Feminist rhetorical criticism draws on many of the tools of rhetorical analysis already explored in this chapter, but it is different in that it focuses specifically on understanding how language affects issues of gender, difference, and power. Rhetorical scholar Sonia Foss identifies feminist critique as working to "intervene in the ideology of domination" or, more specifically, working toward breaking down and analyzing relations of power which oppress and dominate individuals on the basis of gender, sexuality, race, ethnicity, age, and/or ability (157). In other words, feminist rhetorical criticism is a way of working toward social justice.

Feminist critique seeks to eradicate inequality for all people. It is important to understand that feminist critique presupposes that American society "not only oppresses women but everyone else who does not fit into the category of white, male, and heterosexual" (Foss 153). Although feminist critique can be used to interrogate unequal power relations involving sexuality, class, and/or race, this section specifically examines notions of gender as a lens of rhetorical analysis. While gender is the primary interpretive lens for this section, the lens can be can be interchanged or combined with additional lenses, such as sexuality, class, or race. Feminist rhetorical analysis works from a few other basic assumptions. In general, feminist rhetoricians:

- Recognize gender as distinct from biological sex. Biological sex refers to physical, embodied traits and gender refers to the ways you act out masculinity or femininity.

- View gender as constructed by society, or as Foss says, a "culture's conception of the qualities considered desirable for men and women" (157).

- Use the term **gender performance** to characterize performing masculinity and femininity in culturally appropriate ways, such as wearing a skirt and high heels to emphasize femininity.

- Assert that rhetoric is used to create and maintain social constructions of gender.

- Seek to identify how rhetoric communicates masculine and feminine gender constructs.

- Seek to identify how language serves to naturalize gender performance.

To conduct a feminist rhetorical analysis of a specific text, start by identifying the rhetoric or language in the text that reveals the text's ideological attitudes toward gender, difference, or power. To do this, you might ask the following:

- **How is gender rhetorically constructed in the text?** Foss suggests that you look for language that the text "presents as standard, normal, desirable, and appropriate behavior for women and men" (158).

- Who is the **intended audience**?

- Does identifying the intended audience influence your "reading" of the text? If so, how?

- What **overall beliefs** about gender, difference, and power can be inferred from the text?

- How does the **language** in the text communicate these beliefs about gender, difference, and power?

> For more on ideology, see 9.4 of the *Student's Guide* and Chapter 3 of *Writing Public Lives*.

10.7

Once you have identified rhetoric in the text that communicates specific ideologies for feminist critique, an equally important goal is to **make a judgment** or **form a claim** about whose interests are served by what Foss calls the "conceptions of femininity and masculinity" in the text (159). For example, you might decide that the discussion of gender in your text contributes to ideologies of domination or relations of power that oppress and dominate individuals on the basis of gender. On the other hand, you might find that your text challenges gender norms and stereotypes in some way. To make sure that your analysis addresses the "so what" of what you have uncovered regarding rhetorical constructions of gender, your essay will likely address one of the following three questions:

- How can your rhetorical analysis help others understand how domination is maintained through rhetorical strategies?

- How can language be used to disrupt, challenge, or transform systems of domination based on gender (or sexuality, race, ethnicity, age, and/or ability)?

See Sections 10.5 and 10.6 of this chapter for more discussion of visual rhetorical strategies.

- How can visual strategies be used to disrupt, challenge, or transform systems of domination based on gender (or sexuality, race, ethnicity, age, and/or ability)?

An excellent example of a feminist rhetorical analysis is Peggy Orenstein's "The Way We Live Now: Empowerment Mystique," which can be found at this URL: http://www.nytimes.com/2010/09/26/magazine/26fob-wwln-t.html?r=2. In this article, Orenstein analyzes the images of girls in several corporate ad campaigns, including Target, Verizon, and Nike.

In her article, Orenstein describes how the images equate femininity and empowerment through depictions of happy, confident, independent, goal-oriented girls. While this might be a positive representation of girls in our society, Orenstein cautions that these images of female empowerment are constructed in a manner that primarily serves the interests of corporations.

To view the Verizon "Prejudice" commercial analyzed by Orenstein, visit: http://www.adstorical.com/commercial/1254/verizon-prejudice/.

According to Orenstein, the primary purpose of these ads is to persuade viewers that by buying and using their products they are directly contributing to a girl's self-esteem and equal opportunity in life. Through contextualizing the ad campaigns in America's contemporary economic crisis, Orenstein further identifies her audience as American consumers, particularly parents, and argues that corporations are playing on the ideology that "daughters have supplanted sons as the repository of hope in tough economic times." The conclusion—the "so what"—of Orenstein's article is alarming in that she admits that even though she has demonstrated the "vacuous" content of the rhetoric in these ads, she "couldn't shake the feeling that with the right school supplies, she [her daughter] could rule the world." In other words, Orenstein successfully demonstrates how to rhetorically analyze visual rhetoric for feminist purposes and writes a compelling critique of how gender ideology (and race ideology in the Verizon campaign) can be manipulated to serve corporate profiteering interests. At the same time, Orenstein leaves her readers with something to think about—the power of persuasion.

Works Cited

Burke, Kenneth. *A Rhetoric of Motives.* Berkeley: U of California P, 1950. Print.

Brown, Nicole R. "Metaphors of Mobility: Emerging Spaces for Rhetorical Reflection and Communication." *Going Wireless: A Critical Exploration of Wireless and Mobile Technnologies for Composition Teachers and Researchers.* Ed. Amy C. Kimme Hea. New Jersey: Hampton P, 2009. 239–52. Print.

Castleman, Craig. "The Politics of Graffiti." *That's the Joing! The Hip-Hop Studies Reader.* Ed. Murray Forman and Mark Anthony Neal. New York: Routledge, 2004. Print.

Cintron, Ralph. *Angel's Town: Chero Ways, Gang Life, and the Rhetorics of the Everyday.* Boston: Beacon P, 1997. Print.

Dimitriadis, Greg. *Performing Identity, Performing Culture: Hip Hop as Text, Pedagogy, and Lived Resistance*. New York: Peter Lang, 2001. Print.

Ehrlich, Dimitri, and Gregor Ehrlich. "Graffiti in Its Own Words: Old-timers Remember the Golden Times of the Art Movement that Actually Moved." *New York Magazine*. New York Media LLC, 25 Jun. 2006. Web. 17 May 2010.

Foss, Sonja K. *Rhetorical Criticism: Exploration & Practice*. Long Grove: Waveland P, 2004. Print.

"Graffiti." *A World History of Art*. All-Art.org. 25 Nov. 2009. Web. 17 May 2010.

Killingsworth, M. Jimmie. *Appeals in Modern Rhetoric: An Ordinary-Language Approach*. Carbondale: Southern Illinois UP, 2005. Print.

Orenstein, Peggy. "The Way We Live Now: The Empowerment Mystique." *The New York Times Magazine*. The New York Times Company. 24 Sept. 2010. Web. 21 March 2011.

Rahn, Janice. *Painting without Permission: Hip-Hop Graffiti Subculture*. Westport: Bergin & Garvey, 2002. Print.

Rose, Tricia. *Black Noise: Rap Music and Black Culture in Contemporary America*. Hanover: Wesleyan UP, 1994. Print.

Szater. "Banksy, Gandhi Graffiti on Apartheid Wall." *Wikimedia Commons*. Wikimedia Foundation, 30 Dec. 2010. Web. 6 Mar. 2011.

10.7

Exploring a Controversy

11.1 Controversy Analysis: An Overview

11.2 Getting Started on Your Controversy Analysis

11.3 The Importance of Invention and Discovery

11.4 Tips on Choosing a Topic for the Controversy Analysis

11.5 The Research Proposal

Goals

Your Controversy Analysis should:

- Provide a clearly defined thesis that presents a comprehensive overview of the controversy.

- Demonstrate significant background knowledge of the controversy.

- Demonstrate that you have conducted thorough academic research.

- Incorporate research materials to explore the multiple perspectives surrounding a controversy and correctly document them.

- Employ analytical and rhetorical skills to demonstrate your understanding of key arguments surrounding a controversy.

- Effectively incorporate peer and instructor feedback in the final version.

11.1 Controversy Analysis: An Overview

There's controversy everywhere in the world. Whether you're listening to political pundits argue over health care reform or reading about historical debates on the events surrounding John F. Kennedy's assassination, you're witnessing argument, and argument is the driving force behind today's most pressing controversies. Although controversy can be generally defined as debate, contention, or dispute, you might also think of a controversy as a social issue or topic that is steeped in disagreement. With any controversy, there is something "at stake," a larger relevance that has an impact on a society or those living within it. If there were no larger relevance and nothing "at stake," then the issue probably would not be controversial. Thus, when considering a controversy, you want to ask yourself, "What's at stake for those involved?" Answering this question will help you discover a sense of why the issue is being debated—why it matters.

Most controversies are more complex than simple pro/con, for/against, and yes/no distinctions. Determining these binary distinctions is a first step in understanding a controversy, but it rarely provides a full understanding of the actual issue. When you explore a controversy, part of your goal is to ascertain the **in-between areas** that exist within the controversy—the arguments that fall in the gray area and that may not be as simple as "for" or "against." Finding and understanding these gray areas takes time and research, and the more you research a controversy, the more you are able to comprehend the arguments made on *all* sides, by *all* those involved.

For example, if you were to explore the issue of fighting in the National Hockey League (NHL), on the surface it might appear as though there were only two sides of the debate: those who are for it and those who are against it. However, once you conducted some research, you would discover that it's a far more complicated issue than just for and against fighting in the NHL. You would learn that:

- Some people are fine with keeping it, but argue for stricter penalties.

- Others are fine with keeping it as well, but argue for stricter regulation of rules by referees.

- Still others are fine with keeping it, but are primarily concerned with potential injuries to players.

- Some believe it makes the sport appear barbaric.

- Some believe that the Players' Association should make the final call.

- Others argue that the Board of Governors should make the decision.

- Some simply want to do what's best for the long-term sustainability of the league, regardless of what that means for the fate of fighting.

If you investigate even further, you'd quickly be able to add to this list. For now, keep in mind that once you research a topic, you discover nuances to arguments that you hadn't thought of, enabling you to understand a controversy on a much deeper level. Such an understanding will enable you to anticipate **counterarguments** (challenges to your position), as well as to create a more educated standpoint on the issue. Comprehending the multiplicity of viewpoints surrounding an issue will better prepare you to engage in discussions surrounding the issue, even with those who may not hold the same opinion as you.

But why explore a controversy? As part of your English 102 course, you are exploring argument by analyzing arguments, researching arguments, and making arguments. The Controversy Analysis assignment requires you to research an existing controversial argument. This research will inform your third major essay, the Public Argument, in which you will make your own argument about an issue—possibly about the same issue you research in your Controversy Analysis. Many instructors require students to use the research they gather during this paper as the basis for the Public Argument. Since you'll be spending so much time on one topic, you should select a topic that interests you.

See Chapter 7 for advice on finding an interesting research topic.

While the Controversy Analysis and the Public Argument assignments are linked, they are still separate assignments with different goals. The following images may help you to understand the primary difference between the Controversy Analysis and the Public Argument.

The Research Process

YOU

The figures in the image represent the ongoing "conversation" on a particular topic. They have already presented an "argument" on that topic, whether it was through a newspaper editorial, an article in a magazine, a documentary film they produced, or through an essay in a scholarly journal. Notice that you are sitting and merely **observing**, not participating in the conversation. During the research stage you are simply trying to determine what has already been argued on your chosen topic.

11.1

The Controversy Analysis

Now that you have conducted a considerable amount of research, you can **analyze** individual arguments that you've encountered in researching a controversy. More details on the Controversy Analysis assignment are provided elsewhere in this chapter. The point here is to notice that you're talking *about* what these individuals have said. You're not talking *to* these individuals yet, because this is what you'll do in the Public Argument assignment.

The Public Argument

Chapter 12 of this *Guide* and Chapters 11–16 of *Writing Public Lives* offer more comprehensive guidelines on the Public Argument assignment. Notice for now that it is not until this final step and in this assignment that you are "**entering the conversation**" with those who have presented their arguments on the topic—you are now presenting your own argument. Before you can do this, you must develop some sort of expertise on the topic, by conducting research and by investigating and analyzing existing arguments individually and collectively.

In this chapter, you will learn strategies for writing an analytical essay on a controversy, including locating a line of inquiry, creating a research proposal, conducting research, and annotating key sources.

11.2 Getting Started on Your Controversy Analysis

A **Controversy Analysis** is an analytical essay that incorporates research on the key arguments made by people who have a stake in an issue. More than just outlining these arguments, however, a Controversy Analysis should

- Evaluate the validity of specific claims.

- Examine the persuasive strategies employed by key stakeholders.

- Explore the similarities and distinctions between diverse viewpoints.

Remember, the purpose of a Controversy Analysis is *not* to assert a position on the issue, which is what you will be asked to do for the Public Argument assignment. Your purpose with the Controversy Analysis is to demonstrate a thorough consideration of a variety of viewpoints on a topic and to analyze the arguments made by others.

Another goal for your analysis is to demonstrate how the various texts you cite are in "conversation" with one another. By showing how these sources develop their lines of argument, comparing these lines of argument, and evaluating the effectiveness of their persuasive strategies, you are essentially developing an analysis of the range of opinions that figure in to a controversy. The difficult part of initiating this conversation, however, will be letting your own voice control your analysis. Because you will be relying heavily on your research in your Controversy Analysis, it can be easy to let these "voices of authority" dominate your essay. But a well-written Controversy Analysis should forefront your voice, stressing your analysis and evaluation of the sources—not the sources themselves. Keep this in mind when you prepare to draft your Controversy Analysis.

To write a Controversy Analysis, you must first locate a controversy and, more specifically, a line of inquiry related to the issues surrounding that controversy. For instance, let's say you are interested in exploring the topic of stem-cell research. Once you begin researching this topic, you realize just how broad the topic is. There is so much information available on the subject that you would likely have a difficult time trying to outline key arguments surrounding the issue. In order to make your topic more manageable, you need to focus on one area of stem-cell research. You decide to look at how stem cells have been used in cancer research, and you are particularly interested in whether or not stem cells have proven potential for finding cures for cancer. As you move forward in your research, you will want to consider the following questions:

- What do you want to find out? What is your purpose for exploring this controversy?

- What is at stake in the issue? What is its larger social significance?

- Who are some of the key groups or people who have a stake in the issue?

- What else do you know about this issue?

The next section will help you locate a line of inquiry (that is, a particular way of looking at a topic) and will guide you through the process of invention and discovery.

11.3 The Importance of Invention and Discovery

Sharon Crowley and Deborah Hawhee explain that the word *invention* comes from the Latin word *invenire*, which means "to find" or "to come upon" and the Greek word *heuriskein*, meaning "to find out" or to "discover" (20). As these definitions indicate, invention is an active process. The invention process involves finding existing arguments and ideas pertaining to your topic and then discovering ways in which you can contribute to the conversation. But the invention process does not end there; it also involves building, presenting, and shaping your arguments for a particular audience; it is an ongoing process. The earliest stages of invention, however, involves the research process where you seek out all sides of the argument and explore how all of those sides work (or fail to work) on their intended audiences. Whereas analysis deals with *how* and *why* questions, invention examines the *what* and *how* of arguments.

In Chapter 4 you learned various *invention* strategies to help you develop ideas. When you write about a controversy, you might already have such a strong opinion about an issue that you can be tempted to skip the invention process entirely. However, if you don't think about opposing points of view, you risk overlooking good counterarguments that might lead you to modify your position. You also set yourself up to conduct one-sided research that results in a one-sided essay. Because a Controversy Analysis should provide a comprehensive overview of key arguments surrounding an issue, being too one-sided will undermine the effectiveness of your essay. Also, when you get ready to assert your own position, readers will be more likely to agree with your argument if you acknowledge the complexity of your issue.

For more ideas for invention, see *Rules for Writers*, pages 11–17.

For example, suppose you want to write about the issue of animal rights. Your research question might be, "Is it ethical to conduct medical experiments on chimpanzees?" Going into the research process, you might strongly believe that animal-rights activists are ethical guardians or violent extremists. However, if you answer your research question without conducting online or library research, you may miss the complexities of the issue. If you hold to your initial impression, you'll be tempted to find only those sources that agree with your opinion rather than seeking a rich array of sources. If you support the use of chimpanzees in medical research, you might overlook the fact that chimps have DNA that is 99 percent human. If you oppose such research, you might overlook important advances in medicine that have resulted from the practice. Think of your initial opinions as hypotheses and then test them against the diverse evidence and arguments you encounter during your research. The more you learn about your issue, the more you'll be able to write a detailed and thoughtful Controversy Analysis and, later, to create a well-informed Public Argument.

Entering the Conversation

One way to enter into a conversation with your sources is to actively make notes in the margins, underlining or copying excerpts for future reference and writing down your reactions to the claims you encounter. The conversation becomes analytical when you then return to your notes to study both the content and underlying assumptions in what you wrote. In addition to encouraging you to look at your own perspective with a critical eye, the following questions ask you to consider the other perspectives that are present in your issue:

For more information about annotating, see Chapters 3 and 7. For specific advice about evaluating texts, see *Rules for Writers*, pages 397–404.

- What are the various viewpoints on the issue you are studying?

- Who might support these viewpoints and why? (Describe these people and then analyze what you included/excluded in your descriptions.)

- In the conversation you are studying, what are the various groups' unstated, underlying assumptions? What are yours?

- How did the issue get to be an issue? What is its history and how have the viewpoints and arguments changed over time?

- Who is affected by the issue and why? How would you characterize the viewpoint of those who are immediately affected?

- Who are the experts? What do the experts present as "facts"? What "facts" are open to interpretation?

- What new and/or slightly different positions or strategies can you imagine people creating in the future to advance or derail the argument(s) within your issue?

- What is likely to happen in the future? Will the issue have more serious effects? Will more people be affected? What will happen if we do nothing? (Different groups may forecast different scenarios, so there may be multiple answers to these questions.)

- How do the various groups present themselves and each other? Are there particular appeals that different groups rely on?

- What rhetorical strategies do those who agree with you use effectively? Can you use the same strategies to make your argument convincing?

Answering these questions during your research process will help you to understand the spectrum of arguments that form a controversy and will also help you develop your stance when you get ready to create your Public Argument. During the invention/discovery stage, your instructor may ask you to write a proposal. This document will help you plan your work, select your sources, and organize your research. Your instructor will use the proposal to help you shape the research and writing process in an organized way.

11.4 Tips on Choosing a Topic for the Controversy Analysis

The first step in making the Controversy Analysis assignment a rewarding exercise is to choose a topic that is just right for you. You will likely have several questions, such as "Should I pick something I know a lot about already?" Or "Should I pick something I know nothing about?" The following guidelines will answer some of the questions you may have, and will ultimately help you to choose a topic that will make this assignment a productive experience.

Avoiding Common Pitfalls of the Controversy Analysis

1. **Don't Argue (Yet).** The point of the Controversy Analysis is to analyze a controversy, but a common mistake is to present an argumentative essay, which is an entirely different type of essay. Remember, you'll have an opportunity for this in the next major assignment, the Public Argument. See Section 11.1 in this chapter for a refresher on the difference between the Public Argument and the Controversy Analysis. Another common mistake is to make subtle arguments, which usually happens unconsciously. See the craft box "Guidelines for Avoiding Subtle Arguments while Analyzing a Controversy" in this chapter for tips.

2. **Don't Polarize the Issue.** Another common mistake is to present issues as "black and white," as having only two perspectives that are polar opposites. Remember, just because there are extreme perspectives on an issue, it doesn't mean that there are only two. Don't

forget everyone else in between. See Section 11.1 for a refresher on how to avoid polarizing a controversy.

3. **Don't Avoid Academic Research.** A common mistake is to go to Google and type in some key words on your topic and click on the first five search results. You'll then likely end up with a Wikipedia page, an About.com overview, and a few random blog pages. Almost anyone can do that kind of Internet research, and almost no one will be able to effectively summarize or analyze a controversy from such a cursory examination of viewpoints. The point of this assignment is to learn the basics of conducting *academic* research. True, academic research isn't easy, and it might even be a bit intimidating, but learning how to conduct academic research is a central goal of your second semester first-year writing course. And don't worry, your instructor and your reference librarian are going to be more than willing to help you out with this. See Chapter 7 for more on research.

1. **Choose a topic that you can become an "expert" on.** Many first-year students are drawn to hot-button issues such as "abortion" and the "legalization of marijuana." However, even after just thirty minutes of researching one of these topics, you'll quickly discover that there is *way too much* material out there. Here is a list of topics that many instructors will **discourage**:

    *   Abortion
    *   Birth Control
    *   Capital Punishment (Death Penalty)
    *   Climate Change/Global Warming
    *   Eating Disorders
    *   Euthanasia (Assisted Suicide)
    *   Legal Drinking Age
    *   Legalization of Marijuana
    *   Gay Marriage
    *   Gun Control
    *   Illegal Immigration
    *   Stem-Cell Research
    *   Steroid Use in Sports

This list isn't meant to be comprehensive but rather to demonstrate topics you might consider avoiding. What these topics have in common is that they have been argued so much that they have been exhausted, so it becomes virtually impossible for any of us to say anything new on them—you will, in all likelihood, end up repeating something that has already been said. Instead, try to think of something smaller, maybe something local, or maybe something that nobody in your English 102 class has thought about or knows about.

While you technically don't need any prior knowledge to complete this assignment successfully, the **topic should be small enough to be manageable**. Your instructor will be able to help you determine if your topic is too large and she or he can guide you toward a more suitable topic.

With all this being said, remember that **research is crucial** to this assignment. Although each instructor will provide different guidelines on what types of sources you should consult, all instructors will expect that you do a considerable amount of research. One important point to remember is that not every source you encounter will have a place in your Controversy Analysis assignment. In other words, don't expect to be able to use the first few sources that you encounter. You will need to consider several sources so that you can selectively narrow them down to a few that will provide your reader with a somewhat comprehensive overview of the controversy. Chapter 7 provides more general guidelines to the research process.

11.4

2. **Choose a topic that will be of interest to you.** You're going to be working with this topic for several weeks, so you want to pick a topic that you are **genuinely interested in exploring and investigating**. As you research, you're expected to do a considerable amount of reading on your selected topic, so select an issue that you're curious about. In other words, you are likely to do better on these assignments and learn a lot more from them if the topic doesn't bore you.

Sometimes you'll find it's helpful to be interested in a topic if you have a **stake** in that topic. Let's just say you want to write on the regulation and enforcement of seasonal daily limits of sport and sustenance fishing of sockeye salmon in Alaska's Kenai River by the Alaskan Department of Fish and Game. Even if you've never been to Alaska, or even if you've never tried sockeye salmon, you can still have a stake in this issue. Maybe you like fishing. Maybe you like eating fish. Maybe you want to visit Alaska one day. Maybe you've thought about eventually working for a local or state department of fish and game somewhere.

Guidelines for Avoiding Subtle Arguments while Analyzing a Controversy

Sometimes it's hard to hide how we truly feel about something. When we're talking or writing about someone we disagree with, our true feelings often manifest themselves without us being aware of it. As you're composing your Controversy Analysis essay, while there is nothing wrong with disagreeing with a particular author, try your best to maintain objectivity, even if it's difficult. One purpose of this assignment is to assess your ability to "back away" from an issue, to maintain a critical distance, as you analyze it. The following chart provides examples of phrases that make a subtle argument and reveal a writer's bias, along with examples that help to maintain more of a critical distance.

Sentences that Make a Subtle Argument (What to Avoid)	Sentences that Enable Objectivity
Author X does not seem to realize that…	Author X's argument might have been strengthened had he/she addressed…
Author X loses his credibility when…	Author X's credibility might be less effective when…
Author X mistakenly believes that…	Author X argues that…
Author X fails to mention that…	Readers might find Author X's argument more convincing had he/she addressed…
Author X's argument is not convincing because…	Some readers may find Author X's argument unconvincing because…
There is an obvious logical fallacy in Author X's argument.	An analysis of Author X's argument reveals a logical fallacy.

Maybe you're worried about the larger issue of overfishing around the world. Maybe you're interested in environmental issues at large. All of these are ways in which you might see yourself as having a stake. Even if your stake is simply that you want an interesting topic, that can be enough to keep you engaged.

3. **Choose a topic that you can analyze *objectively*.** Sometimes, we're so invested in an issue that we simply do not listen to those we disagree with. So while it is advisable to pick a topic that you have a stake in, you still want to be able to **listen to and engage with viewpoints that differ from your own** in a thoughtful, critical, and respectful manner. For example, if you or someone you love were involved in an accident with a drunk driver, it would be completely understandable for you to have difficulties accepting or even considering an argument for reduced penalties for first-time DUI convictions.

There is nothing wrong with disagreeing with arguments that others make. However, if the topic you have selected for the Controversy Analysis assignment is so important to you that it renders you incapable of engaging with an argument that you disagree with or acknowledging that it is logically sound, then you might consider choosing a different topic. If you encounter an argument and find that your impulse is to reject or dismiss it, that you see no reason to try and bother analyzing it for its positive points, you will find it very difficult to complete this assignment successfully. The Controversy Analysis assignment requires that you **avoid committing to an argument**; after you've conducted a fair amount of research and explored and analyzed the intricacies of the assignment, you will present your own argument in the next major assignment: the Public Argument.

11.5 The Research Proposal

Proposals help people in various fields plan complex research and collaborative projects. Scientists write proposals for grant money, instructors for new courses, students for changes in policy, manufacturers and designers for new products, and managers for reorganization. Likewise, when freelance writers hope to sell articles, they must query magazine editors by sending in brief descriptions of the articles they would like the magazines to purchase. Even an artist might write a proposal for an installation. Writing a research proposal for a Controversy Analysis gives you practice in writing a concise projection of your intended work. Also, writing your proposal will force you to think globally about the different voices you wish to represent in your analysis. Additionally, your research proposal will enable you to receive feedback early in the process about important matters, such as the quality of your sources, the feasibility of your topic, and the overall coherence of what you plan to investigate.

Your Controversy Analysis research proposal will likely include the following components:

- The controversy that you plan to investigate.

- An awareness of the range of arguments or positions that exist.

- A discussion of which arguments you will analyze and why.

- An annotated bibliography or other accounting of the research that you have already completed.

Invention Strategy: The Rhetorical Précis

Some of your instructors may assign a "Rhetorical Précis." In French, the word "*précis*" (pronounced "pray-see") means "summary" when it is used as a noun. However, the purpose of the *rhetorical* précis is to offer a short account of an article that does more than summarize the content. The rhetorical précis, which is generally four sentences long, accounts for the author's main assertion as well as an explanation of how the author develops or supports the thesis. The précis also includes the author's purpose in writing (how she wants to change her audience), a description of the intended audience, and the relationship the author established with that audience (Woodworth 156–64). Examining issues of audience and purpose are essential to writing descriptions that analyze rather than summarize the content of a source.

Sentences of the Précis

1. Name of author, [optional: a phrase describing author], genre and title of work, date in parentheses; a rhetorically accurate verb (such as "assert," "argue," "suggest," "imply," "claim," etc.); and a THAT clause containing a major assertion (thesis statement) of the work.

2. An explanation of how the author develops and/or supports the thesis, usually in chronological order.

3. A statement of the author's apparent purpose, followed by an "in order" phrase indicating the change the author wants to effect in the audience.

4. A description of the intended audience and the relationship the author established with the audience.

For the Controversy Analysis assignment, you will be asked to provide an overview of several arguments that comprise a larger controversy, which requires you to fully understand individual arguments. The Rhetorical Précis can be helpful because it forces you to think about what an individual author is arguing and how that author develops his/her central claim(s).

Sample:

Douglas Park, in his essay "Audience" (1994), suggests that teaching audience is an essential but elusive aspect of teaching writing. Park develops this idea by exploring different definitions of audience, looking at how a text itself can delineate audience and then discussing specific strategies writers can use to create contexts for audience. His purpose is to help teachers of writing understand and teach the different aspects of audience in order that they can help students improve the sense of audience in their writing. Park establishes an informal relationship with teachers who are interested in strengthening their students' weak writing.

- A brief discussion of how you intend to analyze the sources you include in your essay.

- Questions that you have about your project for your peers and instructor.

Even after you write your research proposal, you might find that your understanding of the controversy changes as you learn more about it. Once your proposal has been approved, you can start organizing your research and closely analyzing your sources. You may also be asked to write an annotated bibliography, which is explained in Section 7.7.

Works Cited

Crowley, Sharon, and Debra Hawhee. *Ancient Rhetorics for Contemporary Students.* 3rd ed. New York: Pearson, 2004. Print.

Woodworth, Margaret K. "The Rhetorical Précis." *Rhetoric Review* 7.1 (1998): 156–64. Print.

11.5

Writing Public Arguments

12

Goals

Your Public Argument should:

- Articulate a clear position within the controversy you previously researched.

- Effectively appeal to your chosen audience.

- Show a critical awareness of the rhetorical situation for your argument.

- Provide a clear, persuasive thesis and focused argument.

- Exhibit an understanding of the genre in which you make your argument.

- Incorporate research from the Controversy Analysis to support your points.

- Demonstrate an understanding of argumentative writing conventions.

CHAPTER 12

12.1 Public Argument: An Overview

In your Controversy Analysis, you learned to locate and analyze the arguments that other people have made about a controversial subject. For the Public Argument assignment, you'll craft your own argument, likely in response to the discoveries you made while conducting research for the Controversy Analysis. You may have noticed that the most successful authors carefully consider their audiences before making their arguments; you will also need to be savvy about analyzing your audience as you begin to develop your argument for a public audience.

Before you can begin writing your *Public* Argument, you should start by learning about the foundations of argument. Argument styles can vary widely across contexts. For example, imagine you are having an "argument" among your close friends about who is the better baseball player; Ichiro Suzuki or Albert Pujols. In this context, either claim could be based solely on opinion and that would be fine. If, however, an ESPN sportscaster were engaged in the same debate with colleagues, he/she would have to provide evidence as to why: batting averages, fielding percentages, number of awards, etc.

What about "academic arguments," the written arguments you produce for your courses? What are the key features of these types of argument? Academic arguments generally involve a suitable subject matter, the use of reliable evidence, and a tone and style appropriate for an academic audience. That is to say, the tone and style will probably be unlike what you would find in an e-mail or text message to a close friend. Academic arguments often involve a fair amount of research as well.

Academic arguments can make a significant impact, but as a student, you may not always realize this because you understand that usually your ultimate objective is to submit your arguments to your instructor in hopes of earning a certain grade. This chapter will help you understand and produce ***public* arguments**: arguments that are created for reasons beyond completing an assignment for a class, arguments that are specifically created in order to have an impact on a real public audience. These arguments cannot be contained within the walls of the classroom.

What does it mean to write a *public argument*? The term "public" derives from the Latin term *publicus*, which meant "belonging to the people" ("public"). Of course, when the term was first used, "the people" referred to a small population, and even that population was limited to voters, which excluded women and slaves ("People"). In other words, even in its beginnings the term "public" referred to a specific group of people rather than all people. Likewise, the Public Argument unit challenges you to address a specific sector of "the public". You might write an argument for a very different public audience than the audiences your classmates choose, but the one thing that your arguments will have

See Section 3 of *Writing Public Lives* for a detailed description of how "publics" are defined.

in common is that you will all seek to be persuasive outside the private discourse community of your English class. There are three major steps you'll take in preparing for this assignment:

- Choose a position to argue.

- Choose and rhetorically analyze your target public audience.

- Decide on the genre and/or medium that will be most persuasive to your audience and most fitting for your argument.

You might have noticed that so far this chapter hasn't mentioned the word "essay" at all. That's because it is entirely possible that your chosen audience might find a different genre more convincing than an English essay. This chapter will offer advice on how to choose a public audience and how to choose the best genre and/or medium for that audience. Before you can start crafting your own argument, though, it's important to understand the difference between academic and public arguments, and the following section will help you make this distinction.

12.2 Understanding Public Arguments

Developing the Elements of an Argument

Even though not all public arguments follow the conventions of academic argument, most arguments do share a few common elements. These elements include an **issue** around which the argument revolves, a **claim** you make about that issue, a **thesis** that argues your claim, and **supporting evidence**. Once you have determined where you stand on the issue, it is time to develop claims to support your argument.

> For more on public argument strategies, see *Writing Public Lives,* Chapter 12.

Issues

An issue is a point of concern or controversy within a topic, usually something that is debated in society or a scholarly field. It's possible that you have already defined your topic by writing your Controversy Analysis. As you begin building your stance, it may be helpful to create a question about that topic to frame the topic as an issue. You might start with a yes-or-no question that has two sides. An example of a yes-or-no question would be something like this:

Topic	Indian mascots for sports teams; e.g., Cleveland Indians, Washington Redskins, Florida Seminoles
Issue Question	Should the governing bodies of sports organizations (the National Football League, the NCAA, Major League Baseball, etc.) ban the use of Indian mascots?

Once you've located a clear question at issue, then you can begin building your claim. With a "yes-or-no" question, it's easy to write a claim that answers your issue question:

Claim For	Yes, professional and collegiate sports organizations should ban the use of Indian mascots.
Claim Against	No, these institutions should not ban the use of Indian mascots.

As you discovered in your Controversy Analysis, though, there are always more than two "sides" to an issue because no complex problem offers only two possible ways to approach it. Thus, a more advanced claim will combine some "yes" elements and some "no" elements.

Combination Claim	The governing institutions of sports teams should establish strict ethical guidelines for mascots (not quite a ban, but could be used to get teams to dialogue about effects of this social practice).

Some of the topics you are interested in may not appear to be suited for argument-making. They may seem inappropriate because they lack two obvious and opposing sides. For example, "people with disabilities" is a topic or descriptive category, but framed as such it is not a "problem" that would lead people to disagree about anything. However, there are topics related to disability that are considered controversial issues.

Topic	People with disabilities and the law
Issue Question	Should drug use, alcohol use, and other addictive behaviors be considered disabilities, conferring certain legal rights and services to those who are diagnosed with them?

As this example shows, by refining the general topic of "people with disabilities and the law," you can arrive at a controversial issue. One of the most important features of your Public Argument will be that it speaks to some kind of controversial issue, so take care with this first step.

Claims

The second step when developing an argument is to make a claim. When you make a claim, you are declaring that an issue does or does not exist and that a solution is or is not needed. The claims you make in your argument will be for one side of your issue or another—or a reasonable compromise. In the previous example of the mascot controversy, you could make several possible claims, two of which include:

Claim 1	Using names such as "Indians," "Savages," or "Seminoles" as mascots demonstrates an ignorance of the historical realities experienced by the indigenous peoples of North America.

Claim 2   "Indian" mascots freeze representations of Native Americans in time; they are always "braves," "savages," and "warriors," not people experiencing everyday life.

When making a claim, it's always important to also consider the **counterclaims** that might arise against your own arguments. For example, if you argued that Native American mascots are harmful, you would also have to show that the cost of changing the mascots (both monetary costs and the change in public opinion) will be worth the time and trouble because it addresses a subtle racism that is harmful to society.

Thesis

Although arguments tend to have more than one claim, the thesis of an argument is its primary claim. Like a claim, a thesis must be arguable. It should not just be based on opinion but should indicate a clear position on the issue.

Thesis   Using "Indian" mascots demonstrates that contemporary U.S. society has an **inadequate understanding** of both the history of Native Americans and their continued presence as active members in local and national communities; therefore, **these "mascots" should not only be challenged**, but the **communities in which they exist should have open forums** in which the histories and current lived experiences of the many Native American tribes are openly discussed for everyone's education.

> For more information on thesis statements, see Chapter 4 and *Rules for Writers*, pages 21–25 and 361–62.

The preceding example shows that the thesis of the paper often includes a series of claims that must be developed in the paper (the three primary claims are highlighted in bold). Especially in a public argument, your thesis might not be stated outright the way it is in an academic essay. However, you should ensure that your audience will walk away from your argument with a clear understanding of—and hopefully an agreement with—your thesis.

Evidence

Generally, a thesis has little credibility without evidence to support it. Depending on your audience, the evidence you use to support a claim may be comprised of facts, including statistics or references to the law, or your evidence can take the shape of personal or anecdotal experience. In addition to the techniques you summon, it is important to include evidence from credible outside sources, and it's likely that you'll have encountered many of these sources through your research for the Controversy Analysis. Not all types of evidence are appropriate in academic essays. In academic essays, you typically incorporate evidence through quotations, summary and paraphrase. Evidence in public arguments, on the other hand, can take on a variety of forms. Following are some ways you might bring in evidence, but keep in mind that the following list is not exhaustive, and not every strategy will work for every genre or medium of public argument:

> For more information on rhetorically persuasive evidence, see Chapter 10.

- **Bulleted lists of information:** Bulleted lists provide quickly accessible facts, statistics, and examples to bolster a claim.

- **Facts or statistics presented in charts, graphs, and tables:** Like bulleted lists, graphical representations of information allow audiences to quickly see a great deal of information. Graphs and charts can also show relationships between different types of information in order to compare or contrast that information.

- **A public opinion poll or survey:** You can find reliable public opinion polls or you can conduct your own. Polls and surveys can offer an "on the ground" style of evidence to your argument, and they often work best when paired with other types of evidence on this list. When offering findings from a poll or survey, be sure to acknowledge the limitations of your findings. Interviewing 100 UA students may seem like a lot, but not when we remember that our campus has almost 40,000 students. Also, be sure that the population you are sampling is appropriate to the claim you are making.

- **Quotations:** You can use quotes to establish your own credibility, to add to the emotional appeal of your argument, or to draw on an authority voice in the matter at hand. The best time to use a quotation is when the source says something uniquely and more precisely than you could say it in your

Developing Thesis Statements for Public Arguments

By Kenneth Walker

As you produce your Public Argument, remember that there are already a significant number of existing arguments that you will be engaging with. You might even say that an ongoing conversation on the topic already exists. Listed are three models that may help you argue a position within this ongoing conversation and for an audience with multiple perspectives. Try to enter your claims into the models to see which works best for your particular Public Argument. We've included a sample thesis using the debate about sports mascots mentioned previously.

1. **A thesis can *correct false impressions*:**

   Model: Although many believe X and Y, a careful examination suggests Q and Z.

   Sample: Although many people believe "Indian" mascots are harmless representations of Native Americans, evidence suggests that these mascots promote mythical stereotypes, and conceal the marginal position of Native American people.

   If you believe the topic you are arguing on has somehow been misrepresented or misconstrued, these types of thesis statements can be useful.

2. **A thesis can also *fill the gap*:**

   Model: Although many people talk about X and Y, many people miss the importance of Z.

own words. Quotes should usually be contextualized by your own writing or argument, but in arguments that are primarily visual, it can be effective to list a quote by itself.

- **Stories or anecdotes from individuals affected by the issue at hand:** Stories and anecdotes can add a personal quality to arguments that are otherwise steeped in facts and statistics. It's especially helpful to include stories from individuals affected by the issue at hand. Think of how often politicians will bring in an "Average Joe" to show how a specific policy might influence people's lives.

- **References to commonly recognized cultural sources:** Referencing a commonly recognized source, such as a film or television show that your audience will be familiar with, is a great way to establish a rapport with your audience. Think of this like sharing an inside joke, but be careful; like inside jokes, it's easy to exclude people who might not be familiar with what you're referencing. Other types of cultural sources include poetry, lyrics, and idioms.

- **Images:** Images can inspire a quick emotional response in audience members, but they can also help to illustrate points that have been made textually or verbally. In multimedia presentations, images can be paired with most of the other types of evidence on this list.

Sample: Although the argument over "Indian" mascots tends to revolve around subtle versions of racism and harmful stereotypes, people forget Pirates, Raiders, Vikings, and Rangers are living, historic cultures too, and any proposed regulation about sports mascots should also take these cultures into consideration.

If you believe that certain information or perspectives have been neglected from the topic you are arguing on, these thesis statements are particularly effective.

3. **A thesis can *argue through extension*:**

Model: I agree with people who argue X and Z, but it is also important to extend/refine/limit their ideas with Z.[1]

Sample: Although I agree "Indian mascots" are racist, it's important to refine this argument since these mascots represent a complicated, confused, and often paradoxical relationship of love and theft.

This thesis often takes a qualified position toward the conversation by invoking the arguments of others while demonstrating the writer has something new or important to say that will bring the conversation to a different level.

Once you've found a model you think will work for your purpose and the multiple perspectives of your audience, edit your thesis for clarity and style.

[1] Adapted from Stuart Greene and April Lidinsky's "Developing a Working Thesis: Three Models" in *From Inquiry to Academic Writing: A Practical Guide*.

- **Color choices, font typeface, style, and size:** All of these can help make a document more visually appealing, but they can also invoke emotional responses from audiences. For example, consider what you might think if you saw the word "Earth" written in large green letters versus what you might think if you saw it in large red letters. In addition, you can use font typeface choices to help establish your credibility. Think of how different a font like **Comic Sans**, which is playful and found frequently in comic strips, can be from **Times New Roman**, which is formal and found most often in newspapers.

- **Sounds and music:** Sounds can draw an audience into a presentation by being soothing, exciting, imparting danger or fear, and so forth. To get an idea of how important sound can be in audience response, try watching a scene from your favorite scary movie with the sound turned off. Is it as suspenseful without the music promising impending doom? For more on sound, see Angel Miller's section later in this chapter.

- **Spaces and places:** *Where* you choose to make your argument is just as important as *how* you convey it. The kind of space you choose for your argument will determine your range of audience and, often, how your argument will be contextualized overall. For more discussion on how important space and place is to arguments, see "Analyzing Graffiti as Visual-Spatial Public Medium" in Chapter 10, which discusses the way that choices of space help determine whether or not graffiti is considered art.

As you choose and organize your evidence, it is important to forefront your argument and not to let somebody else's words take over. A balanced argument features strong claims that are supported by compelling evidence. Of course, when constructing a strong, balanced argument you must always keep the audience in mind.

Analyzing Your Audience

Some questions you might brainstorm as you begin to analyze your audience include:

- How many viewers/readers/listeners might I have?

- What do I know about my audience? Do I know their age, locations, educational level, race, gender, political tendencies, etc.?

- What might my audience members already know about this topic? What do I need to tell them?

- What do I know about how my audience already feels about the topic? For example, which of my points will likely draw the most contention?

- What specific values or beliefs does my audience hold that I might draw upon?

- What genres or forms of argument is my audience most familiar with? What kinds of arguments are they most likely to be interested in and responsive to?

Choosing a Public Audience

Think of how, in ordinary conversations, you can express the same opinion differently when talking with a friend as opposed to talking to your professor or your parents. In order to simplify the issue of audience, it might be tempting to write for a "general public," but that general reader might not be the person who can or will help you achieve your purpose. For example, say you are writing as a physiology major with the goal of becoming a physical therapist, and your purpose is to convince insurance companies to extend their clients better coverage, particularly for physical therapy. You should write your Public Argument to people who can make this happen—people who have undergone physical therapy and are willing to argue for better insurance coverage, or people who could persuade the insurance industry to change (patients' rights groups, for example), or to the insurance companies themselves. No matter who you choose, you will need to have a medium in mind—that is, a way of reaching that audience, whether via a letter to the editor of a magazine, a direct letter to the audience, or an article on a Web page. From the beginning, your target audience helps shape your argument's goals and intentions, the tone you adopt, the persuasive strategies you choose, and the level of sophistication you bring to the conversation.

To read more about choosing a specific audience within the "general public," see *Writing Public Lives*, Chapter 11.

While it might appear that most of the essays you have come across in your research are directed to a "general audience," the fact is that most journals, newspapers, and magazines cater to different populations within the "general public." The people who commonly read *Time* are different from the people who commonly read *The Wall Street Journal*, who in turn are different from the people who commonly read *People*. While on the surface the writing may appear to reach the same audience, the authors have made choices about the types of topics they will explore, the relative depth of their analyses, the examples that will be most appropriate, and so on. If you were to conduct a comparative analysis of these articles, you would uncover many ways that the authors have shaped their work for the magazines' or newspapers' reader-profiles.

Even if you were to write for the "general public," who would that be? The U.S. is made up of so many diverse groups—we come from different racial, ethnic, sexual orientation, religious, language, and socioeconomic backgrounds, just to name a few—so as you know, you can't count on "the general public" to think like you or even to understand where you're coming from. Stretch yourself to think about views that are drastically different from your own. For example, if you identify as a conservative Republican, how might you reach an audience of liberal Democrats? What beliefs would you want to tap into? What information do you need to have to figure out how your beliefs differ? Just as in everyday interactions with people who have backgrounds other than your own, when you're creating an argument for a particular audience, it's important not to assume that they will have the same views as you. That doesn't mean you can't address your public argument to these different publics—you just have to spend time reflecting and discovering where and, more importantly, *why* your views on a particular issue might diverge from another person's views.

12.3 Getting Started on Your Public Argument

As you move from the Controversy Analysis unit to the Public Argument unit, your first concern should be to decide upon your position in the controversial issue you've been researching. As the previous section explains, taking a position does not necessarily mean that you have to choose between two sides. In fact, some of the most sophisticated arguments draw from both or many sides of a controversy, creating a new stance that benefits from the strengths of what's already been argued about an issue. As you decide on a position, think about angles that haven't already been brought up in the sources you've researched. And, just like every source in your Controversy Analysis essay had a stake in their argument, some writers will find that they are most motivated when they hold some kind of stake in an issue, although this is not always the case. Your position will also depend on the choices you make regarding your specific public audience, the purpose of your argument, the medium or genre you choose for your argument, and the persona and tone you choose for your argument. All of these elements work together in building a strong public argument. The following section makes suggestions for how to start thinking about each of these elements.

> To read more about stakeholder relationships, see *Writing Public Lives*, Chapters 11 and 12.

Narrow and Analyze Your Audience: There are many different publics that you might target for your Public Argument. Some English 102 instructors will team up, making another section of English 102 your default public audience. Or, your instructor might ask you to create a Public Argument specifically tailored to the First-Year Writing Showcase, an annual event in which first-year writing students present their original public arguments. If this isn't the case in your class, you might think about addressing an issue you feel strongly about in a discourse community you belong to, like presenting a speech to a UA club or team or submitting an opinion piece in the *Daily Wildcat*. You could envision a narrow audience with a wide capacity for public change, such as a member of Congress, a special interest group, or non-profit agency in Tucson. Or you could look to wider, less controlled public venues, such as writing on a blog, creating a Web page, or even performing your argument on the UA mall. Regardless of what audience you choose, the Public Argument assignment will require that you think critically about the means of persuasion that will best suit your argument and your audience.

Before you can make any choices about *how* to construct your argument, it is essential to decide *to whom* your argument will be directed. When you write a Public Argument you should always keep in mind the nature of the specific "public" that you are targeting. The most important step in writing a Public Argument is identifying your audience and analyzing it rhetorically to understand its members' needs and expectations. Keep in mind that you can't always know or control the members who make up your specific audience—that's precisely what makes it public. What you can do is devise a strategy for how to appeal to most of your readers or listeners based on what you can know about your target audience.

After you have a handle on your audience, there are several **rhetorical** factors you should consider as you develop your Public Argument. Following, you'll find the steps you might take and the types of questions you might ask as you decide how to make your argument persuasive to your chosen public.

Determine Your Purpose: The purpose of an argument is usually to move an audience, whether you're moving them to act or simply to react to what you're saying. Most essays you'll write in college share at least one purpose—to earn a certain grade. But public arguments have diverse purposes. For example, if you are making an argument about water conservation laws to a group of Tucson voters, your purpose would be to persuade your audience to vote a certain way on election day. Other public arguments, such as developing a public service announcement, might have less clear-cut purposes. It's important that you take the time to answer these crucial questions about the reason you're making your argument in the first place. You should be able to articulate what that purpose is to anybody who asks. Ask yourself:

- Am I moving my audience to *act*, to *react*, to *know*, or to *feel*, or all of the above?

- What do I want my audience to *do* in response to my position?

- Am I making it clear *how* my listeners or readers can take the action I want them to take?

Medium: Besides words on paper, there are many modes of argument that might appeal to your audience, such as a speech or performance, a compilation of images accompanied by text, a digital argument that uses hypertext, and so on. While academic audiences and some other public audiences might expect to read a twenty-page research paper, many audiences are more likely to pay attention to other types of communication. For example, an audience of college students rushing to class would be unlikely to listen to a ten-minute speech about animal rights, but they might glance at an installation of large photographs with shorter, "bite-sized" portions of written text. Your medium should complement your purpose—if you hope to evoke your audience's sympathy about animal rights, for example, photographs would be helpful to gain an emotional response. By considering the purpose and location of your argument you should be well-prepared to decide the best medium for your claims. This doesn't mean that writing is out of the picture, of course—many public arguments are written, and even visual and spatial texts rely on a great deal of prewriting before they take on non-written forms. As you consider your medium, ask yourself:

- How much time will my audience have to "read" my argument?

- What kind of format is most likely to serve the purpose of my argument?

- What kind of media are most familiar to my audience members? Will they know how to interact with my chosen medium, or will I have to teach them how to read it?

Ultimately, the choice of medium is also a choice of genre: what genres will be most effective for your chosen audience? You can read more about choosing a genre for your argument in Ashley Holmes's section later in this chapter.

Persona: The term **persona** refers to the ability to present yourself differently according to different situations. For instance, imagine yourself in the following scenarios:

- At a late-night fast food restaurant with your closest friends on a Saturday night.

- At brunch with your grandparents on a Sunday morning.

Even if you haven't been in these situations recently or at all, you should realize that these two scenarios might determine how you dress, how you talk, and what topics of conversation are appropriate or not. True, for some people the persona they present to their closest friends or to their grandparents will be similar. The point is that everyone will encounter different situations in which a particular persona is more appropriate than others.

Developing a persona is similar to developing tone and voice in an academic essay. Unlike in an academic essay, though, you are often present in real time for a public argument and you are often arguing to an audience who has no idea who you are. To develop a persona, you must think carefully about the tone you wish to take toward your subject and your audience, about the type of voice you wish to develop to characterize yourself, and about how well you can embody these choices if you are making an in-person argument. Some politicians are noted for being able to change their personas based on their audience; when giving a speech in Texas, for example, they might don a cowboy hat and develop a light drawl, but when speaking to accountants in New York, they'll wear a formal suit and employ a more formal speaking style. All of these choices work toward the development of a persona. Your persona isn't a matter of misrepresenting who *you* are. Rather, you have the opportunity to emphasize certain parts of your personality to develop a persuasive persona. This persona could be one of neutrality, such as in a brochure that seeks to present unbiased facts. Or, your persona might be humorous, compassionate, angry, or energized. The subject matter, medium, and **context** of your Public Argument will help you decide on the most persuasive persona to embody. Below are some questions to help you decide what kind of persona will be most persuasive for your argument.

- What is my relationship to the issue? Do I have experience that makes me an authority on the subject, or am I relying mostly on outside research?

- Will I be making the argument in person, or will a text make the argument for me?

- What is my relationship to the audience? Do they already know who I am? How will I explain my stake in the issue?

- What kind of persona best matches the subject matter and purpose of my argument?

- How will I convey my persona—through my tone, my words, my designs?

Language: The level of knowledge and expertise of the public you're targeting will ultimately determine your choice of language. For example, if you are seeking to convince your local hospital to buy an MRI machine, you'd likely use technical language about the medical benefits of magnetic resonance imaging to a group of doctors and nurses, but that same language might frustrate a more general audience of patients. Both of these audiences might be "public," but they demand very different uses of language. The medium also plays a role in your choice of language—if you're making a documentary, you wouldn't use a plethora of fancy words that your viewer might have to look up in a dictionary, even if such jargon would be perfectly appropriate for a written essay.

- What kind of language will my audience be most comfortable with? Specialized terms/jargon that allow for more precision? Generalized language that is more understandable but less exact?

- How will my language reflect my chosen persona?

- How will my medium affect my language choices?

As you can see, writing for a public audience builds on the skills you've been developing so far in your first-year writing courses. Not only will you need to use your skills doing solid research and incorporating sources, you'll also need to perform rhetorical analysis in order to learn how to be as persuasive as possible to your chosen audience. The next section explores the many types of genre, written and non-written, that you might consider for your Public Argument.

12.4 Considering Genre When Planning a Public Argument

By Ashley J. Holmes

Can an obituary convey an argument? What about a map? According to the authors of *Everything's an Argument*, yes, they certainly can: "From the clothes you wear to the foods you choose to eat to the groups you decide to join—all of these everyday activities make nuanced, sometimes implicit, arguments about who you are and what you value. Thus an argument can be any text—whether written, spoken, or visual—that expresses a point of view" (4). While the primary purpose of an obituary may be informational (e.g., providing details on the funeral arrangements), writers of obituaries, like all writers, make choices—in this case, choices about what parts of the person's life to highlight and what parts to leave out. Though not all obituaries make arguments, an obituary—and nearly any text—has the potential to make explicit or implicit arguments. Similarly, visual texts, such as maps, also reveal the choices of a mapmaker. For instance, a map showing only wheelchair accessible buildings on the University of Arizona's campus (and leaving out buildings that are inaccessible) might be making an implicit argument about the extent to which our campus community makes accessibility a priority.

As you prepare to form your argument(s), you may find it helpful to think about the form or genre that would be most fitting and persuasive for the purpose of your message and the audience you would like to reach. A **genre** is a category or type of something that shares similar characteristics. For instance, we are all familiar with typical music genres such as heavy metal, rap, classical, rhythm & blues, country, jazz, rock, etc. Each one of these music genres can be distinguished from the others because it shares certain unique characteristics, and, as listeners, we have certain expectations for a piece of music when it carries a particular genre label. This is true for writing genres as well. Different genres of writing conform to different conventions in terms of style, format, tone, structure, and mode of delivery. On the next page, you will find a list of different types of writing genres divided and subdivided by different categories, such as public or personal, spoken or read. As you will notice, some genres overlap with other categories. For instance, a website is listed as a public, technological genre, but it most certainly shares characteristics with the visual/design genres. Also know that this list of textual genres is by no means exhaustive.

For more on genres, see Chapter 2.

Investigating Genres

Choose one of the genres from the box on the next page. Then, find three realistic examples of that genre. For instance, walk through the student union and collect three brochures, or stop by a telephone pole and collect three flyers, or go online and find three websites, or grab a newspaper and find three obituaries. Examine your examples, and use them to help you answer the following questions:

1. What purpose(s) does this genre usually have?

2. Where, how, or in what context do readers usually find this genre?

3. Who typically reads or who is the typical audience for this genre?

4. What are some of the key features or characteristics that are unique to this genre, distinguishing it from other texts?

5. Based on your answers to the questions above, come up with a definition in your own words for this genre.

6. Finally, type the name of your genre into the search box at http://wikipedia.org. (Don't cheat by doing this first!) Read what Wikipedia has to say about your genre. What else, if anything, have you learned about your genre?

Public Genre Types			
Professional or Business • business card • business letter • application • memo • brochure • résumé • flyer • proposal	*Publications (Newspaper or Magazine)* • editorial • article • letter to the editor • obituary • advice column • tabloid article • advertisement • book or movie review • interview (Q & A) • biographical profile	*Technology* • e-mail • IM conversa-tion • text message • phone conver-sation • blog • Facebook page • wiki • website	*Spoken* • eulogy • speech • dialogue *Lists* • pro/con list • top ten list • to do list • directions

Academic Genre Types	Personal Genre Types
• report • abstract • essay • syllabus • tutorial • diagram • summary • call for entries or proposals • outline	• personal letter • personal narrative • scrapbook page • diary/journal entry • memoir • blogs

Visual/Design Genre		Miscellaneous Genres
• cartoon • photograph • travel poster • award certifi-cate • comic strip • collage • illustration • movie • map • timeline	• graph • certificate • poster • concept map or web • calendar • greeting card • invitation • postcard	• petition • poem • ransom note • recipe • song • bumper sticker • wanted poster • restaurant menu

You may find this list of genres of writing helpful as you consider the form in which you would like to convey your argument. When selecting a genre, you should consider how it serves the rhetorical needs of your message and how it helps you reach your desired audience. For instance, if you were making an argument opposing tuition increases, you could choose to write a letter to the editor of the *Arizona Daily Wildcat* or a business letter to the President of the University of Arizona. However, *how* you make that argument—what you say, how you say it, and what action you call for—will certainly vary for these different rhetorical situations and audiences. Therefore, choosing a genre in which to write should coincide with your choices about audience, purpose, and rhetorical/persuasive strategies.

Once you've chosen a genre, you should spend a little time researching that genre. You may think you know what a brochure looks like, but have you ever taken the time to examine its unique features—the characteristics that distinguish it from a flyer or an advertisement? There are certain conventions that you should consider when writing a brochure, such as choosing a tri-fold design, writing in bulleted points instead of large paragraphs of dense text, and using pictures to help convey your claims. Analyzing a genre, breaking it down to see how the parts work, will help you understand how to compose that genre successfully. Try the "Investigating Genres" activity on page 248 to hone your genre analysis skills and to prepare for making your argument.

As the list of possible genres shows, the amount of text-based writing in a public argument depends largely on the genre you've chosen. The following section, "Multimedia Public Arguments" by Angel Miller, will help you plan your multimedia public argument. Although the section focuses on arguing through video, the rhetorical strategies can be applied to most multimedia forms of argument.

Analyzing Rhetorical Persuasion on the Internet

By Angel Miller

One of the best places to find multimedia public arguments is on the Internet. We all spend a large amount of our time surfing the Web (probably too much!), and most of the time we are there, we are being bombarded by public arguments of some form. Go to almost any Web page and you'll see ads along the top and sides that use color, images, and even sound to grab your attention.

Even websites themselves are carefully constructed public arguments, created by Web designers with very clear ideas and reasons for the appearance and placement of everything you see. Today, websites often include a variety of texts, both written and visual. Many websites incorporate not only words and photos, but also videos, podcasts, and interactive discussion boards aimed at persuading visitors to the site to purchase a product or take some specific action. The multimedia environment of the Internet has provided us with a whole new way to think about rhetoric and persuasion.

One good example of how text, images, and sound can work together to convey a single public argument is a website all University of Arizona students may be familiar with—the university web-

12.5 Multimedia Public Arguments: Persuading with Video

By Angel Miller

When we think of public arguments, especially for an English class, it's easy to think only in terms of written texts such as opinion pieces, speeches, and other forms of argument that rely on words to convey their meaning. But if you look around you, you'll see that Public Arguments are nearly everywhere you look—and often, those arguments rely on elements of persuasion in addition to the written word, including photos, video, and graphics. Arguments such as these use images, music, color, fonts, and artwork alongside written text to convey their message in a coherent and unified way.

Video can provide a great means of communication with your audience when developing your Public Argument. Like websites, video can incorporate **text**, **audio**, and **visual elements**, all working together to create a more persuasive piece. Just as a website works to gain the audience's interest using **photos**, **colors**, **graphics**, and **motion**, a video gains and keeps audience interest through visuals, audio, and possibly text. But unlike websites, video is self-contained, meaning that you as the rhetor have greater control over how your audience receives your argument.

Think about it—with a website, even when certain elements are placed more prominently and draw more attention, visitors can click around from one page to the next, creating their own experience as they go. But with a video, most

> For more on writing visual arguments, see *Writing Public Lives*, Chapter 13.

site itself. Type in the URL (www.arizona.edu) and think about the following questions:

- What is the first thing you see when you load the page? The image near the top? The colors? Or something else?

- Where is the second place you feel your eyes drawn to? Why do you think this is?

- What is the overall "feel" of the page? Professional? Fun? Stuffy? Clean? Try to determine what makes you feel this way.

- How does the site establish the university's credibility? Pay close attention to the use of color, graphics, and text used on the front page.

- What is the largest element on the page? An image? A word or name? What is the smallest? Why do you think this might be?

- Click on some of the most prominent links. Where do they lead you? Why do you think those links were placed on the front page of the website?

- Now go to a website that you visit frequently. How are the answers to the questions above different? How do the differences between the sites reveal the rhetorical purposes of each?

viewers will watch your argument unfold from beginning to end, meaning that you can guide your audience through the argument in exactly the way you want.

You're probably familiar with YouTube, a site set up for people to share videos. When you watch videos on YouTube, what draws you in? What makes you keep watching a video? On the other hand, what makes you lose interest and move on to another video or something else entirely? All of this is integral to understanding rhetoric—because in order to convey a persuasive message, we have to gain and keep our audience's interest.

Creating a video means thinking not only about what images portray your meaning, but also what **music** or **sounds** convey that message. With video, we are striving to engage as many of the viewer's senses as possible. Commercials are great at this trick. How many times have you seen a commercial for a restaurant that makes you so hungry you can almost smell or even taste the food in the commercial? This is because commercials depict the food close up, similar to how it would appear if you were eating it, but also because they include sounds we associate with that food in the audio: the sizzling of steak, the crunch of lettuce, the fizz of opening a soda.

Think about commercials when you are creating your own video—you want to use every aspect of this medium to draw in your audience as much as possible. You want the images to be meaningful to the viewer, so think about how the viewer might see the situation in real life. The images can come from a variety of sources: filmed interviews or scenarios, clips of stock footage, or even a slide show of still photography. Similarly, your audio might include elements such as music, dialogue, or environmental sounds that contribute to the meaning in some way.

Video Public Argument—An Example

For an example of what an English 102 video public argument might look like, take the following example. After researching the controversy of whether or not it is appropriate to assist undocumented immigrants crossing the U.S./Mexico border, an English 102 student created the video "Suffering in the Desert" to express her viewpoint. This viewpoint was the result of extensive interviews with people involved in the controversy from multiple sides, including members of No More Deaths (No Más Muertes), who work to provide humanitarian aid to undocumented immigrants crossing the border through the Southern Arizona desert, and the Minutemen, a vigilante group that patrols the border in efforts to stop undocumented immigration. After the student created her video, she decided to make it truly public by placing it on YouTube. In the following days, several area non-profit organizations, including No More Deaths, provided links to the URL, earning the video praise and recognition.

View the video at http://www.youtube.com/watch?v=-dVuTiOK2Vg and respond to the following questions. If the URL does not work, you can go to www.youtube.com and do a search for "Suffering in the Desert."

- What is the overall **tone** of the argument? What do the text, visuals, and audio contribute to create this tone? How would this tone change if any of the elements were different?

- What elements of **logic** and **emotion** can you see in the video? Does the video rely more heavily on one element than the other? Why do you think this is?

- How does the video establish **credibility**?

- How is the argument **structured**? How is this similar to or different from the structure of written arguments?

- Can you see a **storyline** in the order in which the images are presented? What does this story say? How does this storyline work with the facts presented in the text?

- Is there a **call to action**? How is it presented? How do the images add to the sense of urgency?

- How would *you* present this argument using video? In other words, what would you do **differently**?

Creating Your Own Video Public Argument

Before you begin creating your own video, you'll want to think carefully about your topic and the best way to frame it.

1. Who is the specific **audience** you are trying to target? Just saying "the general public" probably isn't enough. Think harder. What about social class, gender, age, education, or profession? These all make a difference in how you will frame your argument.

2. What is your target audience's **prior experience** with this topic? Is this something they encounter or think about on a daily basis, or is this likely to be a new concept?

3. What kind of **emotions** do you want your topic to raise in your audience? Sadness? Joy? Anger? How can you tie these emotions to your audience's lives?

4. What **text** is needed in the video, and where should it be incorporated? How should that text add to the meaning being conveyed by the images and audio?

Now Break it All Down

1. What different **visual elements** are required to create your argument? Video? Interviews? A series of photos?

2. What **auditory** (sound) elements do you need? Music? Taped conversation or environmental sounds?

3. Whom do you need to **consult** (talk to or meet with) to make this happen? Make a list of everyone you would like to appear in or be involved with the creation of your video.

4. Where do you need to go to get the **resources** (video, photos, or sounds) you want? What do you need to do in advance to prepare?

5. What **software** and **hardware** do you need to gather the pieces you need? Cameras? Tripods? Tape recorders? Video editing software? Where can you access this? (Hint: the Office of Student Computing Resources' Gear-to-Go center has nearly all the hardware you will need.)

> For information on using UA resources for video editing, see Appendix C.

Helpful Tips

Make sure that what you have planned is feasible to complete in the time that you have. Don't expect, for example, that you are going to be able to take a weekend filming state representatives in Phoenix unless you know that you can work it into your schedule.

- Try to make sure that the people you want to talk to are actually going to be available to meet with you—and don't get discouraged if they aren't. Many times, if the person you want to speak with is unavailable, a spokesperson, representative, or assistant will be able to meet with you. Be flexible and willing to adapt.

- Arrange your interviews or photo shoots well in advance of the deadline. You never know when someone may cancel or a rainstorm may ruin your shot.

- Conduct your interviews and audio recordings in a place where you won't have unwanted noise in the background. You might be surprised how distracting even small sounds can be on tape.

- Reserve equipment through Gear-to-Go up to two weeks before you'll need it, so you'll know it's available when you're ready to use it.

The Public Argument assignment requires you to make your own argument concerning a controversy. Instead of merely reporting about the controversy, as in the Controversy Analysis, you will enter the conversation and align yourself with a specific position within the controversy. You may convince someone to change his or her mind about the controversy, and even act on that position. Thus, your argument in this assignment has consequences. Do you make a strong argument? What about a strong call to action? Often we can't know what our readers do in response to our writing, but we can still write with an understanding that our research, our arguments, and our actions matter. Especially as you begin to plan your project, think about ways that you can make a real difference with your Public Argument assignment. Depending on the audience you choose, from YouTube viewers to *Daily Wildcat* readers to University of Arizona President Robert Shelton, it's possible that your Public Argument might inspire real-world change.

Works Cited

Greene, Stuart and April Lidinsky. "Developing a Working Thesis: Three Models." From *Inquiry to Academic Writing: A Practical Guide*. Boston: Bedford/St. Martin's, 2008. 85–87. Print.

Lunsford, Andrea A., John J. Ruszkiewicz, and Keith Walters. *Everything's an Argument, with Readings*. 4th ed. Boston: Bedford/St. Martin's, 2007. Print.

"People, *n*." *Oxford English Dictionary Online*. Oxford UP, 2011. Web. 11 Mar. 2011.

"Public, *adj*. and *n*." *Oxford English Dictionary Online*. Oxford UP, 2011. Web. 11 Mar. 2011.

12.5

Personal and Reflective Writing

13

Goals

Your reflection should:

- Demonstrate your ability to think about your writing and about yourself as a writer.

- Include an in-depth reflection regarding your process of revision.

- Provide evidence to demonstrate your development as a writer.

- Illustrate your ability to collaborate in peer groups to revise your writing.

Your literacy analysis should:

- Show how a personal experience has influenced the ways you think, read, write, and live in the world.

- Provide a detailed, sensory description of your experience(s), using vivid details and specific language.

- Convey a central purpose or idea in a structure or format that demonstrates audience awareness.

- Incorporate peer and instructor feedback in the final version.

13.1 Reflective Writing: An Overview

Whether writing a reflective essay, a freewriting assignment, or a personal essay, you are likely to produce reflective writing in your first-year composition courses. Some instructors will ask you to do idea-generating exercises, freewriting, or journaling as a way to brainstorm or dig deeper into your writing processes. Or, your instructor might assign a literacy narrative in which you connect a personal experience to the ways you approach reading and writing. Reflective writing, in which you analyze the ways you've changed as a writer, is a key component of your first-year writing courses. Reflecting on your own challenges, strengths, and improvements as a writer will help you to understand better how to improve your writing further. All of these examples are forms of personal writing. In this chapter, you will learn more about the process and the complexities of personal writing.

Personal writing gives you the opportunity to grow individually and intellectually. As you write about your life, your beliefs and values, and the choices that you make, you'll likely learn something about yourself or make connections between yourself and others. Although self-discovery is an important element of personal writing, it is often important to have an external audience in mind, too. Personal writing requires more than simply creating an inventory or timeline of events; rather, it is a genre in which you can inform, involve, and enlighten your readers through strategic, thoughtful uses of personal experience. Through personal and reflective writing, you can combine the skills and practices of analysis with writing that explores your own life, ideas, and experiences.

> For advice on free-writing or keeping a journal, see *Rules for Writers*, pages 14–16.

13.2 Reflecting on Your Writing

The aim of reflection is to create meaning, much like another process discussed extensively in first-year writing courses: analysis. Try to remember that reflective essays are really just another form of analysis. In Chapter 8 we defined analysis as "the ability to explain how and why a text does something and whether the choices made are effective." When you write a reflective essay on your writing experiences, you analyze your writing process and yourself as a writer. Analysis in reflective essays asks you to explain *how* and *why* you made certain choices when writing and whether the choices you made were effective. You can even go a step further, explaining what you chose to do, whether the choices were effective, and what you would do the same or differently in the future. Whatever form your reflection takes, your reflective writing needs to convey more than your memories of an event—it requires you to arrive at a new understanding of a past experience.

Writing about Writing

Discussing your own writing can be difficult because many of the strategies that you used during the semester might have been compulsory (your instructor required you to do something) or unconscious (you just did something because you always have). The reflective process asks you to think critically about what you did and why you did it. Why did your instructor ask you to do something in the writing process, and was it useful to you? Why or why not? Did you talk with your friend about the paper before you started writing it? Why? Once you consider choices that you made and how those choices affected the final product, you are ready to begin writing your reflective essay. The following paragraph, taken from student Andrew Mora's reflective essay, illustrates one way that you might reflect on challenges you faced during first-year writing:

> Even with this new understanding of peer revision, I am still aware of the fact that much help can come from other people. Another set of eyes can see something completely different than mine do. One problem with my writing that has been noticed by both my professors and my peers includes the way I start sentences. I tend to have generalized statements that do not make the paper sound as strong as it could be. These local revisions, which are within sentence revisions, were found on almost every page of my papers. For example, in one of my earlier drafts of the persuasive paper about globalization and the effect it is having on youth, I wrote, "It is estimated that 17 million people would have died if this war had taken place." After discussing my paper with my professor, we noticed that I often started sentences with "It is," "There was," "They are," etc. Openers like these typically do not make strong points. This statement later became "In June of 2002, the U.S. Defense Intelligence Agency estimated that as many as 17 million people would be killed during the first few weeks." Though I can see how this error changed, I still feel I might not be able to catch myself using these words as I write in the future. It is one of the many areas that I will need to continue to work on.

Mora's topic sentence suggests that the paragraph will discuss a specific problem with his writing.

Here, Mora discusses his experiences with local revision, specifically word choices made at the beginning of sentences.

Mora adds a specific example from his writing to illustrate his point about word choice.

In this paragraph, Mora uses PIE structure by moving from the **point** that his peers help him notice problems in his writing to the **illustration** of how he starts sentences and backing that up with an **example** of a specific sentence beginning with "it is."

This sentence shows what Mora did to change his word choice habits after he became aware of them.

Phrases like "I feel," "I tend," or "I think" all show that Mora is actively *reflecting* on how his writing has changed.

Here, Mora acknowledges that this is a challenge that he will continue to face, acknowledging his responsibility to use the strategies learned in this class in his future writing.

Getting Started on Your English 101 or English 102 Reflective Essay

Your first-year composition instructor will likely ask you to write a reflective essay at the end of the semester. When writing a reflective essay, it is important to remember that the analysis should focus on process—the writing process, the process of becoming a writer, the peer-review process, and so on. Textual analysis focuses on the text (your finished essay); reflective analysis of your writing focuses on the writing process, a topic on which only you can provide special insight.

Although it might not seem like it at first, you'll soon realize that there are many possible topics you can choose for your end-of-semester reflective essay. You might choose to focus only on the writing process in the classroom, or you might talk about your writing experiences throughout your life and how those experiences shaped your writing in first-year composition. Below are some parts of the writing process you might consider as you start reflecting on your writing:

- The ways that prewriting did/didn't help.

- The peer-review process, what you gave and what you received.

- Conferences with instructors.

- Global revision choices.

- Local revision choices.

- The discussions you had about your paper with people not in your class.

- How you approached revision for each paper.

- The different style/word choices that you made.

- Your understanding of different writing options.

- What you would change if you knew then what you know now about writing.

- How college writing fits into your life.

Once you have generated some topic ideas, you might want to think about what was effective/useful or ineffective/not useful about certain choices, events, or experiences. The following questions might help you develop a thesis argument for your reflective essay:

- What did you learn (from a specific writing assignment, from a specific experience, or from the semester as a whole)?

- Did the choices you made, or writing experiences you had, reinforce something you already knew about yourself or about writing?

- If you did not gain as much from a particular project as you hoped to gain, what are the possible reasons for this, and what might you do the next time around?

- Think about the course objectives listed on your course syllabus as you consider your success as a writer. What course objectives did you meet? What objectives are you still working on?

In other words, this is an excellent time for you to analyze yourself in the process, noting your own responsibilities within the larger scope of the writing project, the course, or your ongoing development as a writer. It is as important to address any disappointments or even failures in your experience as it is to discuss the successes and achievements. Most writing processes include a combination of good and bad reactions and effects. Exploring the complex relationships between these reactions and effects can be the most interesting and useful part of writing a reflective essay.

Whatever choices you make in your reflective essay, you will want to consider the following guidelines:

- **Analyze the process** of writing the paper or papers (not just the final drafts), or analyze the process of becoming a writer.

- **Give concrete examples** from your own writing (either quotes from your writing or rich descriptions of specifics in your writing process).

- **Explain why certain choices were made** (not just "my instructor told me to") and whether those choices were effective.

- **Use the language of writing.** For example, if you explain that you revised something, name what sort of revision it was (local, global, stylistic, and so on).

In the end, reflection is a practice that helps you to take responsibility for your own development as a writer. After you have completed your required writing courses, you will often have to write for new situations, audiences, and purposes. Only by reflecting upon your writing will you be able to continue to learn how to improve your writing in courses in your major, on the job after you graduate, and in your life outside the classroom.

While you'll almost certainly write end-of-semester reflective essays in first-year writing, your writing instructor might also ask you to write essays that incorporate a different kind of reflection: personal writing. Personal writing challenges you to reflect on your past experiences and to make meaning of those experiences. In the following section, Kelly Myers explains how you might approach personal writing in first-year composition.

13.3 The Personal Writing Process

By Kelly Myers

Composition scholar David Bartholomae refers to personal writing as "a corrupt, if extraordinarily tempting genre" and he's got good reason for concern (71). Basically, he's worried about people like me. I'm a shameless snoop. I'm the kind of person who used to hold a glass up to the wall so that I could listen in on my brother's slumber parties. One summer I read letters from my boyfriend's ex-girlfriend while he was away on a family vacation. I used to spend long hours sitting in my closet with a flashlight reading my sister's diary. I long to both hear and confess juicy secrets—and, if I'm being totally honest with myself, that's why I was drawn to personal writing. But the truth is, even though it is extraordinarily tempting, personal writing is not about confessing secrets or snooping around in people's personal lives.

Personal writing exercises can help to complicate our stories, uncover our motivations, and access our assumptions about the world, all of which can lead to more complex personal writing that moves beyond the realm of confession or therapy. When you approach personal writing assignments, it is important to work toward creating a space between the person (yourself) and the personal (your stories or experiences) so that you can examine the choices you make in recreating your experiences. Since you can never recapture an experience exactly as it unfolded, personal and experience-based writing always involves making choices (consciously or unconsciously) about what to include and exclude. In stepping back and taking the time to examine these choices, you can begin to see the complicated layers that make up your identity and life experience.

Personal Writing and/as Rhetoric

The process of stepping back to examine personal writing involves establishing an awareness of your audience and purpose. In other words, the personal writing process is intricately linked to the rhetorical analysis skills discussed in Chapter 10. Therefore, once you have a central purpose and primary audience in mind for your personal writing, you need to shape your experience(s) and the overall structure of your writing accordingly. For example, as a writer you get to shape the voice or voices that emerge in your writing. Having a "voice" in writing does not mean that you strive to transfer your speaking voice onto the page. Instead, your goal is to construct the voice(s) in your writing to create an *ethos* that suits the overall purpose. Just as credible sources are of primary importance in a research essay, the voice and *ethos* that you create are fundamental to the success of your personal essay. When you create a specific voice, you are establishing a relationship with your audience, working to earn their attention and trust.

> Your instructor may or may not use the term *ethos*, but you will definitely be asked to think about the ways writers establish credibility with their audiences. For more information on *ethos*, rhetorical analysis, and types of appeals, see Chapter 10.

For example, in his essay "This Is Emo," Chuck Klosterman argues that the actor John Cusack has forever ruined romantic love. *Ethos* plays an important role in making such an argument, as the author could easily come across as simply embittered or pathetic. In the following passage, look at the specific details, tone of voice, and sentence construction that Klosterman uses to create his *ethos* (to do a more in-depth study of this passage, refer to the workshop questions in the next section):

> I once loved a girl who almost loved me, but not as much as she loved John Cusack. Under certain circumstances, this would have been fine; Cusack is relatively good-looking, he seems like a pretty cool guy (he likes the Clash and the Who, at least), and he undoubtedly has millions of bones in the bank. If Cusack and I were competing for the same woman, I could easily accept losing. However, I don't feel like John and I were "competing" for the girl I'm referring to, inasmuch as her relationship to Cusack was confined to watching him as a two-dimensional projection, pretending to be characters who don't actually exist. Now, there was a time when I would have thought that detachment would have given me

a huge advantage over Johnny C., inasmuch as my relationship with this woman included things like "talking on the phone" and "nuzzling under umbrellas," and "eating pancakes." However, I have come to realize that I perceived this competition completely backward; it was definitely an unfair battle, but not in my favor. It was unfair in Cusack's favor. I never had a chance. (2)

In addition to creating voice in personal writing, there is also the role of emotion to consider. As was discussed earlier, personal writing is not simply a venting of emotion; however, just like voice, the audience's emotional experience is a central element of the essay's persuasive power. Maintaining a high level of emotional engagement, such as sustained anger or grief, can be exhausting for a reader and can blur the overall purpose of the essay. Such prolonged emotional commitment can be used as a rhetorical strategy depending on your purpose; however, more often you will need to zoom into and out of emotionally-intense moments. Oftentimes, a large part of structuring a personal essay involves designing the audience's emotional experience in a way that serves the greater goals of the essay.

Along with its role in persuasion, emotion can play an invaluable role in your writing process. The most powerful writing frequently comes from issues or experiences that have had a profound emotional effect on you. Analyzing your emotional connections, as well as your sources of apathy, can provide important in-roads into the personal/analytical writing process, which is essential in assignments such as the literacy narrative.

You can read more about using emotional appeals in your writing in Chapter 10.

Finally, in addition to voice and emotion, personal writing is often strengthened by research. It may seem strange to think of personal writing and research papers together, but just as facts and statistics work to strengthen an argument, concrete details and information about people, places, issues, and so forth, make personal writing more compelling and believable. Logical connections and progressions are important for the overall purpose of the essay and the credibility of the author. As so much of personal writing revolves around the author, rhetorical appeals play a central role in building trust between the reader and the writer.

Revising Personal Writing

Once you have selected the topic or angle for your personal writing, the next step is to dig into the experiences and shape the rhetorical strategies. But how do you move between the personal and the analytical in your writing? One important approach is the involvement of other people in your personal writing process. As we have discussed, audience plays a crucial role in personal writing; therefore, it is important to actively engage an audience throughout your drafting process. Composition scholar Barbara Kamler suggests the following workshop questions as a way to begin the personal-analytical revision process:

- What is powerful in the writing? Identify an image, line, metaphor, or representation of a person that is powerful.

- What is omitted? Who/what is absent and/or hinted at or over-generalized?

- What clichés are used to gloss over experience, facts, feelings?

- What doesn't fit? What contradictions, if any, emerge?

- What aspects/issues of [fill in blank] are concealed?

- What common issues, experiences, storylines do the texts [in your workshop group] have in common? (62)

Turning Memory into Meaning

By Mary Woo

Remember a time when you told your friends about an incident, let's say a time you went to the mall? You described who was there, what you bought, what you ate. Essentially you summarized your experience for them. But did you reflect on it? Probably not, because it was a casual conversation that didn't require reflection. However, in personal essays, you are not looking to summarize an experience for your reader. You are trying to create meaning out of your experiences. In order to create meaning, you must put your experiences into a context. For instance, let's say you went to the mall and ran into an old boyfriend/girlfriend. This wouldn't mean anything to your listener unless you explained who the old friend was and what he or she meant to your life.

One of the most difficult parts of personal writing is having the distance to look back on your experiences and understand what they mean in the context of your life. That is also part of the process of writing—the attempt to understand. The following exercise may be helpful in distinguishing the real difference between summary and analysis. It will also suggest ways to transform a simple description into a reflective narrative about your transition into college.

1. First, think about your dorm room or apartment. Describe the setting, using all five of your senses. Some guiding questions might be: What is on your wall? What does the room smell like? What furniture was provided by the school? What did you have to buy? What is on your desk? How messy is the desk? What kind of pictures do you have? How is the space divided?

Your writing should be purely descriptive, simply detailing the facts of your living space. For instance, "There is a poster above my bed, and on my desk I have several textbooks, a laptop, potpourri," etc.

2. Read your descriptions aloud to your classmates. Make note of the descriptive nature of the writing and the common observations you shared.

Asking focused questions about what is both present and absent in the writing helps to reveal the ways in which the experience was constructed, as well as the assumptions at work in that construction. Also, looking at moments of specific detail, as well as moments where the writing becomes clichéd or overly general, can reveal levels of comfort and discomfort within the situation. Instead of trying to resolve contradictions in the writing, such tensions are often generative spaces to explore. Finally, it can be helpful to look at your writing within the context of other student writing to identify commonalities and differences in your experiences.

Of course, analyzing a personal experience in order to create thoughtful, rhetorically-savvy writing is difficult work. On an emotional level there is struggle, even grief, involved in confronting and unraveling the roots of our experiences. There is also pain in the revision process when we have to cut out parts of our

3. Then, focus in on one aspect of the room that you mentioned. It can be a picture, the loud music coming from the neighbors, the scent of old food. Whatever it is, just pick one object.

4. Now, try to move towards a more rhetorical approach to this object. More than just the *what* of the object, ask *why* and *how*? How does the object in some way encompass your college experience? Why is it worthy of your attention?

Let's take one example. You have a can of Clorox wipes sitting on your desk. It is the first cleaning item you have ever bought. Before coming to college, your parents always cleaned up after you at home. You would identify yourself as a "messy" person at home. However, in college you were placed with two roommates who were even messier than you, thus causing you to be the "clean" one.

The descriptive sentence would sound like this: *There are Clorox wipes sitting on my desk.*

5. Now, begin to ask some rhetorical questions of it: How do the Clorox wipes represent something of your identity? How has coming to college changed your identity in some respects? How is your identity different at home than here? Why did you choose to buy Clorox wipes, as opposed to paper towels and cleaning spray? How have your roommates made your identity more distinct? Notice the "how" and "why" in all the questions. Just as analysis asks *how* and *why* of a text, so does personal writing ask these same questions of your memories.

Perhaps you have discovered that your identity shifts depending on your surroundings. Perhaps coming to college has brought you a new sense of independence and maturity. Either way, in asking these questions, you have begun to move from summary to analysis and to create meaning out of your experience.

The analysis of personal objects and personal experiences can be used in many forms of personal writing. You might do this type of analysis when writing a literacy narrative, which is one personal writing genre you may work with in your first-year composition classes.

stories that are really important to us personally but not relevant to the greater purpose of the essay. However, although such revisions are difficult, they mark a crucial step in moving personal writing away from confession or self-indulgence. Since revision is so important, you will need to be sure to select your personal writing topics very carefully. Most importantly, you will need to be sure that you are ready to return to the experience(s) again and again to constantly revise and reflect on the writing.

In the end, personal writing, like any academic writing, is a *process*—one that calls on your skills in rhetoric, research, and reflection. When engaging in personal writing, it is important to understand that experiences and identities are always in motion, always developing and changing within the context of the moment. Instead of approaching your personal writing as a stagnant text that is beyond critique, this chapter invites you to approach your experiences as an opportunity to better understand the ways in which identities are shaped on both personal and cultural levels.

13.4 Analyzing a Literacy Experience

The term **reflect** has several different meanings. Earlier in this chapter, we discussed how you might reflect on your own writing process. But to reflect also means to contemplate what you were thinking and feeling when a pivotal experience took place in order to better understand what that experience has meant for you and possibly for others. This kind of reflection is often called a **literacy narrative**, in which you reflect on a specific moment that has influenced you as a writer. How did you change through the experience? How did it affect your relationships, identity, or worldview? What did it help you understand about your culture or the culture of others? In the following section, Laurie Morrison explains how you can use reflection as a tool to help shape your literacy narrative. Notice that story and memory, which were important components of the previous sections, also play a part in identifying and analyzing a literacy experience.

Analyzing a Literacy Experience

By Laurie Morrison

The literacy narrative assignment includes two main tasks: as you write your essay, you'll narrate the story of an experience you've had with language, and you'll also use that experience to make a clear point about how language works or how it has affected you. Consequently, you'll employ narrative strategies such as dialogue, pacing, and sensory detail to tell your story in a compelling way, but you won't stop there. You'll also analyze your experience to figure out what it can tell you, your instructor, and your classmates about literacy.

Sometimes, these two aspects of the literacy narrative—telling a good story and conveying a central point about language—can be difficult to bring together. But in an excellent literacy narrative, the writer thoughtfully examines an experience to come up with an insight about language and also constructs a narrative essay that builds to that insight. You don't need to finish analyzing your experience before you begin writing; you might go back and forth between drafting the story of your experience and examining its significance. You also have space to be creative with style and organization. You can experiment with storytelling techniques, and you might play around with starting in the middle of the action or holding off on stating your central point until the last paragraph. While you have some flexibility in crafting your essay, you'll want to make sure that you ultimately bring your storytelling and your analysis together. Try to avoid narrating your experience and then tacking on a moral at the end. Your essay will be much more cohesive if you have a carefully thought-out main point and if all of your narrative details advance it.

The trick to developing an insightful central point and creating a unified literacy narrative is to slow down and really commit to the process of identifying and analyzing the experience you'll write about. Wendy Bishop, a respected scholar and instructor of writing, emphasizes the importance of analyzing a language experience. She explains that students have plenty of material for writing literacy narratives because we all have complicated experiences with language. After all, we are bombarded by words that come at us from parents, instructors, friends, advertisements, songs, and TV shows, and we use language to connect to some people and to distance ourselves from others. But as Bishop points out, language affects us in such subtle ways that we need to stop and reflect on our experiences in order to understand how language shapes our identities and interactions. Therefore, slowing down and asking yourself questions can help you to understand the role language plays in your life and to reach a strong central point for your essay.

The following questions can help you to identify and analyze a rich literacy experience and, ultimately, to write an insightful, unified literacy narrative. Keep in mind that you can return to these questions at any point in your drafting process.

Questions to consider as you identify a literacy experience to analyze:

- Can you think of a significant event that helped or hurt your progress toward becoming a reader or writer? If you think of a generalized event, such as your parents forcing you to read for an hour every day when you were in middle school, push yourself to think of a particular moment within that larger event. Identifying a specific, one-time experience will help you to focus your storytelling and analysis.

- Can you think of an influential person in your life who has helped or hurt your progress toward becoming a reader or writer? Again, go for specifics: can you identify a particular instance in which that person influenced you?

- Can you think of a moment that somehow changed your views about language?

- Can you think of a time when you judged someone for the way he or she spoke or wrote? Can you think of a time when you felt judged for the way you speak or write?

- Can you think of a time when you had to switch back and forth between different ways of speaking or writing?

- Can you think of a time when you had to "learn the lingo" to be accepted into a certain group?

- Can you think of something you said, wrote, read, or heard that really *worked*—that had exactly the effect it was supposed to have on the people who heard or read it?

- Can you think of a time when you felt unable to communicate your ideas or feelings?

Questions to consider as you analyze your experience:

- Why does this experience stand out in your memory?

- What lessons can you, your classmates, and your instructor learn from this experience?

- What could a wider audience, such as parents, college students, children, instructors, or aspiring writers learn from this experience?

- How is the current "you" different from the "you" who is a character in the experience? What can you see about the experience now that you couldn't then? How would the current "you" handle the same situation?

- How has your experience affected your attitudes toward reading, writing, and communicating? What are the implications of your attitudes toward reading and writing? In what ways might your attitudes serve you well in college? In what ways might they get in your way?

- How do you think your life experiences, cultural affiliations, race, gender, and/or religion have influenced this experience and your attitudes toward reading and writing?

- In what ways is your experience comparable to the experiences that your classmates are writing about? In what ways is it different? Why do you think those similarities and/or differences exist?

- In what ways is your experience similar to or different from the experiences of the published authors whose stories you've read in class? Again, why do you think those similarities and/or differences exist?

Students often protest that they don't have anything to write about because they haven't had any significant experiences with language. But you don't need to have had a particularly juicy, hilarious, or traumatic experience to write an interesting literacy narrative. Don't worry if you haven't worked to overcome the limits of a disability like Helen Keller, or if you didn't teach yourself to read while you were locked up in jail like Jimmy Santiago Baca or Malcolm X. You just need to identify a specific experience that involved reading, writing, or communicating and that seems worth reflecting on. You might have some inkling about what the experience means, or you might just feel like it buzzes with potential meaning. Either way, the experience doesn't need to be objectively significant: Your interpretation of the experience will make it significant to you and to your readers.

13.5 Blogging as Personal Writing

Blogging is one form of reflective writing that you might already do on a regular basis. While you might not think about the blog as being a helpful practice for your writing in first-year composition, Autumn Witt explains in this section how you might use blogging in your class as a form of personal writing.

Vivid Description

In *On Writing*, Stephen King describes writing as a form of telepathy, a "meeting of the minds" in which an image is transmitted from one person to another. After providing an elaborate description of a strangely painted rabbit in a cage, King writes, "[W]e all see it. I didn't tell you. You didn't ask me. I never opened my mouth and you never opened yours. We're not even in the same *year* together, let alone the same room... except we *are* together. We're close" (106). Vivid description and concrete details can bring people closer, creating a moment of telepathy in which an image or a moment travels from one mind to another. Or, as is the case in Dave Eggers' writing, description can carry personality, fostering a connection between author and audience. For example, when looking at San Francisco through Dave Eggers' eyes, the traffic over the Bay Bridge becomes "a string of Christmas lights being pulled slowly, steadily" and foggy mornings in Berkeley are "filmstrip white" (51). His unique descriptions allow readers to experience the city in a new way.

Description becomes especially vivid when an author uses sensory detail to breathe life into places and personalities. For example, in *East of Eden*, John Steinbeck does not simply tell readers that the Salinas Valley in Northern California is a beautiful place in the springtime. Instead, he pulls his audience directly into the landscape where the "splashes" of California poppies "are a burning color—not orange, not gold, but if pure gold were liquid and could raise a cream, that golden cream might be like the color of poppies" (4). Through his word choice, Steinbeck paints a picture that can be seen, felt, even tasted. Concrete and sensory details create living moments on the page, moving a reader to see, feel, or experience something differently.

Of course, it is important to keep in mind that there is a fine line between effective detail and description abuse. Unless the description is strategic and purposeful, it can easily clutter your writing. Figurative language (e.g., metaphors and similes) can enliven writing; however, if overdone, the details become roadblocks that interrupt the flow of the writing.

Blogging for the Writing Classroom

By Autumn Witt

Blogging has become quite common in the past ten years. In fact, it is probably a safe bet that you either have a personal blog or you can name blogs that you read regularly. Depending on your interests, you may read sports or tech blogs, food or fashion blogs, celebrity or political blogs. A blog might have been your first and perhaps only outlet for self-publication—the first venue that you may have taken to share your written words with a wider public audience.

Part of the appeal of blogs is the way they blend the private and public spheres of writing. Whereas in the past, diarists may have written at length about their day, and their private wishes or concerns, blogging creates a public outlet to share those same thoughts, but with a wider audience. Blogging acknowledges the twin desires we have to tell others what we are thinking and to eavesdrop on what others are saying.

Unlike in a private diary, which might contain facts interesting only to the writer, in a public blog issues are discussed because of their potential interest-factor to a reader, as well as to the writer. Topics, tone, vocabulary choice, depth of description, background information, supplementary visual or video evidence, and design are all affected simply by the knowledge that a public audience will be reading the post. For example, writing a blog for your family to follow your semester studying abroad would be different from a blog about the dance club scene in your college town or a hobby blog that you hope to use to attract potential employers or customers. Each of these examples shows how blogging blends personal and public writing.

You may be used to the kind of writing assignment in which you wrote an essay on an assigned topic, and then that essay was read only by your instructor. In your first-year writing courses, you've already learned to extend your reading audience to your classmates for peer review. Writing a blog extends that audience even further—to a public, perhaps even an unknown, audience.

Your instructor may assign blogging for many different purposes:

- **Prewriting**, or identifying the personal body of knowledge about an issue that you bring to a topic from the outset. You may use blogging to brainstorm your past experiences, your pre-established opinions, and your attitudes toward other points of view on a particular issue.

- **Synthesis**, or bringing together what various avenues of research are telling you. It can be helpful to use blogging as a public listing of the issues that are brought up in class, and of the outside research that you find. Synthesis might also refer to a **wiki** style of blogging, in which class members can work collaboratively to build a research list.

- **Peer review**, or getting audience input on portions of your final product. Is your introduction interesting? Are your main points convincing? Well-ordered? Did you leave something out that people want to know more about? Having portions of your assignment available for the public to view and comment on should encourage you to genuinely write for an audience, and not just for your instructor, or for a grade.

Most blogs hold certain codes of conduct that bloggers must follow when writing for that blogging community. When you blog for a class assignment, there are some additional standards you should consider:

- **Politeness:** While most blogs have public standards such as no hate speech, no cursing, or no anonymous commenting, the level of politeness appropriate for a class blog might be even more stringent. You should ask your instructor what level of Web-etiquette is expected for your class before you begin blogging.

- **Commenting quality:** Many public blogs restrict blog comments that are simply the commenter's self-promotion, links to ads, or tangential ranting. The point of commenting should be to increase information, so agree to post only substantive feedback on a class blog. Everyone knows that simply saying "good job" at the end of a paper doesn't actually help you improve.

As some scholars and other parts of this chapter have noted, storytelling, dialogue, and literacy are foundational elements of learning (Huffaker 96). By using blogs in your personal life, as well as in your classes, you are developing communication skills that will help you develop critical thinking, audience awareness, and rhetorical persuasion strategies that will be beneficial in your future personal, academic, and professional endeavors.

Choosing a Blog Platform

There are many blogging platforms available online, and they vary in terms of their cost and their complexity. If your instructor uses Desire 2 Learn for your course, blogging is available through D2L. Below is a list of other free blogging platforms you might find useful as you plan your blog:

Blog.com (http://blog.com/)

Blogger* (http://www.blogger.com)

Desire 2 Learn (D2L) (http://d2l.arizona.edu)

Typepad (http://www.typepad.com/)

WordPress (http://wordpress.com/)

*Note that because the University of Arizona uses Google mail, you can "sync" your Catmail with a Blogger account. In other words, logging in to your Catmail account will give you access to your Blogger blog, as well. This might simplify your blogging experience.

Works Cited

Bartholomae, David. "Writing With Teachers: A Conversation with Peter Elbow." *CCC* 46.1 (1995): 62–71. Print.

Bishop, Wendy. *On Writing: A Process Reader*. New York: McGraw-Hill, 2004. Print.

Eggers, Dave. *A Heartbreaking Work of Staggering Genius*. New York: Vintage, 2001. Print.

Huffaker, David. "The Educated Blogger: Using Weblogs to Promote Literacy in the Classroom." *Association for the Advancement of Computing in Education Journal* 13.2 (2005): 91–98. Web. 25 Apr. 2010.

Kamler, Barbara. *Relocating the Personal: A Critical Writing Pedagogy*. Albany: State U of New York P, 2001. Print.

King, Stephen. *On Writing: A Memoir of the Craft*. New York: Scribner, 2000. Print.

Klosterman, Chuck. *Sex, Drugs, and Cocoa Puffs*. New York: Scribner, 2003. Print.

Steinbeck, John. *East of Eden*. New York: Penguin, 1992. Print.

PART IV
STUDENT ESSAYS

Sample Essays

14.1 Sample Essays: An Overview

This chapter includes essays written by first-year writing students at the University of Arizona. You can approach the student essays included in this chapter in a number of different ways. Like most writing, they contain features to emulate and learn from, as well as areas that could be improved upon with further revision. Consider them, then, as samples rather than models—they are not perfect. What we mean by this distinction is this: A "model" can be dangerously close to a static form, something that provides you with a formula to follow (write exactly like "this" and you'll get an "A"); by contrast, seeing the student essays as "samples" encourages you to identify what works well and what could work better—to take selectively from them according to the occasion or context. We have not corrected any spelling and grammar errors in the student essays, nor made changes to larger global concerns. This choice was deliberate; we believe that these essays provide a great opportunity to look at what worked and what can be revised. In other words, you can critically engage with the essays in a way that will help you think through writing choices, revision strategies, and different genres.

Because students from first-year writing classes at the same institution wrote these essays, the essays featured in this chapter adhere to shared assumptions and course guidelines; however, the writing represents the type of work produced in a program in which individual instructors tailor the assignments with slightly different visions or emphases. For example, some instructors may ask students to work with films and focus on visual analysis, others focus specifically on written textual analysis, while some might ask for autobiographical writing as a way to analyze identity or culture. Given this set of considerations, each student in each section will have an individualized response to that group assignment. As these selected writers have done, you will need to be aware of your own particular situation as you set out to produce writing appropriate for your class context. The point to emphasize here is that one size doesn't fit all—suit the form to the content, not the content to the form.

Specifically, how can you benefit from reading these essays? Aside from their value as a way to see what your peers are thinking and writing about, they may also prove useful as you produce your own writing. As you read the sample essays, examine the choices each author has made and consider what you might do differently or what you might try to emulate in your essays. Below is a list of questions that you may want to ask yourself as you examine each of the sample student essays:

- How does the author introduce the topic of the essay? Is it broad or specific? How does that lead into the thesis/point? Try to pinpoint examples.

- Is the thesis explicitly stated ("This paper argues…") or implied (the claim of the paper becomes clear but is not directly spelled out at the beginning)? Where is the main idea of the essay identified and how is it communicated to the reader?

- How do language and style work in the essay? Are sentence lengths and word choices effective? Are there any places where language and style break down or distract from the essay's purpose/meaning? How would you revise those sections?

- As you are reading, do you notice how the author has made transitions between paragraphs/sentences? How does the author link ideas? Are there any places that the transition is abrupt or does not exist? How might you revise the paper so that the connections between ideas are clearer?

- How does the author use quotations? How are they introduced and worked into the paper? Do you find the quotations useful in furthering your understanding of the topic?

- Does the conclusion of the essay simply restate the introduction or does it suggest any larger implications that open up as a result of the research/writing? How would you revise the conclusion? Do you think that a personal aspect might be useful for a conclusion/paper that is predominantly academic? Do you think that a statistical conclusion with suggestions for action would be helpful for a conclusion/paper that is predominantly personal?

These questions are designed to help you think through your reading/interaction with the student essays. Your instructor may want you to look at how an essay fits (or doesn't fit) a particular assignment. You may also notice strengths or weaknesses in a paper that we do not prompt you to notice, which is great! Bring this up in classroom conversations; show your peers and instructors what you noticed so that you can start to think through how you can use what you garner from a text in your own writing. This is what the student essays are about: helping you to become a stronger writer by looking at what others have done and adapting it to suit your own writing strategies for particular situations. Many of the essays included here were winners of the 2011 *Student's Guide* Essay Contest. This contest is offered every year and is open to all students in first-year writing classes. That means that you can enter the contest this year. A list of the winning authors and their essays can be found online at <http://english.arizona.edu/index_site.php?id=588&preview=1>.

The following chart identifies some of the characteristics of each essay. It is not intended to be all-inclusive, but if you are working on PIE paragraphs, for example, you might refer to any of the essays that are marked as "Models the PIE paragraph." This is not to say that every paragraph in those essays is a PIE paragraph, but there should be some different examples of PIE paragraphs in all the essays with this designation. Likewise, an essay that is marked "Incorporates rhetorical analysis" will address the rhetorical situation or the strategies that an author uses. We hope that this chart will be useful to you as you begin reading the work of other first-year writing students.

14.1

	14.2 From Line 1 to Death	14.3 Progress	14.4 Culpability	14.5 Becoming "Agent Orange"	14.6 Bringing Light to Problems Ignored	14.7 The Furthest Distance in the World	14.8 Within the Tendrils of Smoke	14.9 George Patton: A "Real Man?"	14.10 A Much Needed Unity	14.11 The Battle over Senate Bill 1309	14.12 How to Survive in Our Inflated Economy	14.13 Letter to President Obama	14.14 A Catalyzed Reaction
Incorporates textual analysis	✓	✓	✓	✓	✓	✓	✓						✓
Incorporates visual analysis			✓				✓						
Incorporates film analysis				✓		✓							
Incorporates contextual analysis				✓	✓	✓	✓						
Incorporates comparative analysis				✓									
Incorporates rhetorical analysis								✓	✓	✓			
Uses research		✓					✓	✓		✓	✓	✓	
Addresses a controversy										✓	✓	✓	
Addresses a public audience											✓	✓	
Incorporates reflection						✓							✓
Includes/analyzes a literacy narrative													✓
Models the PIE paragraph	✓	✓		✓	✓		✓	✓	✓	✓	✓	✓	✓
Demonstrates ESL skills						✓					✓		
Uses *Writing as Revision*		✓		✓									

14.2 From Line 1 to Death: Exploring the Difference Between "Youth" and "Deep-Sunken Eyes" in Shakespeare's Sonnet II

Textual Analysis by Jennie Elizabeth Piccarreta

Sonnet II by Shakespeare

When forty winters shall beseige thy brow,
And dig deep trenches in thy beauty's field,
Thy youth's proud livery, so gazed on now,
Will be a tatter'd weed, of small worth held:
Then being ask'd where all thy beauty lies,
Where all the treasure of thy lusty days,
To say, within thine own deep-sunken eyes,
Were an all-eating shame and thriftless praise.
How much more praise deserved thy beauty's use,
If thou couldst answer 'This fair child of mine
Shall sum my count and make my old excuse,'
Proving his beauty by succession thine!
This were to be new made when thou art old,
And see thy blood warm when thou feel'st it cold.

Sonnet II can be interpreted in many different ways but one of the basic messages is, make something of your life, because it passes by quickly. To illustrate this theme, Shakespeare brings attention to four different stages of life: the present, youth, old age, and death. However, he does not put equal weight on each stage; rather, he emphasizes the less desirable stages, old age and death, and deemphasizes the other stages. Shakespeare's methodology is reflected in the organization and diction of the poem. By applying this method, the chronology of the human life is represented through the language and structure of Sonnet II.

Mirroring the organization of the sonnet with the life cycle allows the reader to view an example of life's chronology within the sonnet. The first few lines focus on the present and youth, the next four lines, on old age; and the last line on death. If the order of the arguments didn't reflect the chronology of life, the disorganization would interfere not only with the flow of the poem, but the overall purpose as well. Since the message is not wasting your life, it is important for the speaker to not waste their audience's time by bouncing from one part of life to another in no particular order. For example, this essay would be difficult to follow if I had the conclusion before the introduction, or the body paragraphs after the conclusion. In this model, the introduction would be youth; body paragraphs, old age; and conclusion, death. The same idea applies: in life, death does not come before youth; therefore if the material were in that order in Sonnet II, they would be out of order according to a life.

True, in saying, "When forty winters shall besiege thy brow" (1), old age is implied, but the main focus is on the present, in other words: the "now" of her youth. The first word in this sentence is when, meaning at this moment the audience is still young. We know this because the word when means "in reference to a future time (whether in the present or the past)" (Oxford English Dictionary, II, 4.b). In this context, "when" cannot be referencing the past because the word shall indicates old age has not come yet. The first line is a warning the "forty winters" will pass and youth will be gone soon.

The next step in the life cycle after the "present" is youth. Note that youth is the beginning of a lifetime, just as youth is brought up in the beginning of the sonnet. The speaker argues youth is not going to last long. He reflects this point in the text when the topic of youth doesn't last long either: one line to be exact. "Thy youth's proud livery, so gazed on now" (3) is the only reference to youth in the whole sonnet. Rather than use descriptive words to create a picture of her age, he simply says "thy youth." Shakespeare spends minimal time on youth because it feels like life spends minimal time on that age as well.

In line 3, Shakespeare describes "thy youth" as having "proud livery." According to the Oxford English Dictionary, livery is "something assumed or bestowed as a distinguishing feature" (OED n.I.1). Therefore, in the beginning of life (beginning of the poem), youth is the most distinguishing feature. Next, when the "ry," is omitted from livery (livery) the word "live" is left. In the beginning of the poem, the focus is on youth, a time where you have the whole rest of your life to live. Later, when the poem is focused on old age and death, the word "live" is not used.

Next in the order of life comes old age; thus, it is next in the sonnet. Shakespeare shows this through formidable imagery when, in line 7, the speaker says "within thine own deep-sunken eyes" (7). In the previous lines, the references to age were either interpreted ("when") or just simply stated ("youth"), but in this line, the word "old" is not explicit but the imagery that takes its place is much more compelling. In the case where the poem is directed at a woman, the phrase invites her to picture her youthful, beautiful face as an old woman with saggy, wrinkly skin. She can see ahead through those "deep-sunken eyes" into what her life will be like after "forty winters"(1) have passed. For someone whose youth is their distinguishing feature ("proud livery"), aging would be a dreadful event.

The term is vivid and disturbing so the woman realizes old age is quickly approaching, and it would be foolish to let the time pass without accomplishing anything; in this context, by not having children. The statement is very persuasive because in mentioning old age, the speaker is graphic, showing her how different she will look. While previous lines are used as a warning, line 7 is used in a more manipulative way: to scare her. Making her picture "deep-sunken eyes" scares her into realizing old age is inevitable. Imagine if "deep-sunken eyes" was replaced with "old," and the term was simply "within thine old age." Although they express the same point, being explicit is not adequate because it allows the reader to interpret whether or not aging is positive or negative situation.

In previous examples, when the focus is youth, the speaker finds no need to emphasize how youthful she looks. Evidently there is a need for flattery (he is courting her), but there are no vivid descriptions of her beauty or her youth because she is already aware. For example, the word "beauty" is used in lines 3 and 5, but that is all. The speaker doesn't spend any more time describing how beautiful she is because the time is better spent scaring her with old age and death.

Later in the Sonnet, in line 13, old age is mentioned again. This time, however, there is no macabre image for the woman to picture. The line simply says "old." My previous point was that the speaker needed to emphasize old age by using powerful words to scare her. In this line, the intention isn't to scare her with age; in fact, it is more peaceful. "This were to be new made" (13) is referring to the children she will have if she listens to the speaker. "When thou art old" (13) is referring to the reader's old age. Shakespeare counteracts the image of death with a peaceful image of having a child. In contrast to previous allusions of old age, this acknowledgment is amicable because Shakespeare assumes the reader took his advice and had children. He ends the sonnet by declaring if she has children, she will age happily; if not, she will age with "deep-sunken" eyes.

As a poem comes to an end, life must come to an end, which is why the last chapter of life in the sonnet is death. The final line is "And see thy blood warm when thou feel'st cold" (14). This sentence is not meant to be eerie or disturbing, it is meant to finalize the argument. Similar to line 7, the final line focuses on vivid images to invite the audience to picture themselves after death, but with a part of themselves continuing to live on. The sonnet concludes by giving one last reason for having children: rebirth. When the speaker says the woman will "see thy blood warm," (14) he is saying she will have a child to live on for her. She wont be forgotten after death because she will continue to live through her progeny. Stating that the reader will see her blood run warm again gives a sense of immortality, as if the cycle starts all over again.

The point of this essay is not to argue that the sonnet mentions every aspect of the human life cycle, because it doesn't. Sonnet II focuses on the four parts of the life cycle that are most relevant in this context: the present, youth, old age, and death. Shakespeare emphasizes these points through imagery, lack of imagery, and the organization of the sonnet. He illustrates the difference between using a specific word ("youth") and a description of the word ("deep-sunken eyes"). With this balance Shakespeare is able to stress the brevity of life, and the importance of not wasting it.

Works Cited

"livery, *n*." *Oxford English Dictionary Online*. Oxford UP, 2011. Web. 11 Mar. 2011.

Shakespeare, William. *The Sonnets*. Ed. Stephen Orgel. New York: Penguin, 2001. Print.

14.2

14.3 Progress

Textual Analysis by Amanda Grace McRae

Too often people let a single characteristic define someone. These labels get in the way of discovering someone's true self. In Michael Lassell's poem, "How to Watch Your Brother Die," the speaker demonstrates how this phenomenon plays into his perception of his homosexual brother. As a heterosexual male, the speaker finds it difficult to understand love between two men. Pushing a relationship with his brother away led to feelings of regret. The speaker eventually puts himself in another's shoes to broaden and ultimately improve his view of his brother. Overall, the paradigm shift of the speaker is positive because the label that divided the siblings became less important. Literary devices help shape the meaning of the poem. The poem uses point of view, tone, symbolism, and diction to stress the speaker's struggle to elevate his regard for his brother. This suggests that the transformation is admirable because getting over our differences improves our relationships and promotes understanding with others.

The speaker's point of view reveals he felt distant from his brother. Many lines or sentences begin with a verb, with no explicit person identified doing the action. It is implied that the speaker is experiencing what is described. The lack of "I" being used shows distance, like he detached himself from the situation. The second stanza has lines that begin with, "Listen to the doctor…/Sign the necessary forms. /Tell the doctor…/ Wonder why doctors…" (Lassell 10-13). These lines lack the speaker's direct interaction with the events that play out, as if he has trouble connecting to them. Despite how Lassell removes the speaker from his actions, the speaker attempts to understand his brother's relationship to the lover. The speaker's actions display an effort to develop a relationship with his brother. He states to the lover shortly after meeting him, "I'm sorry, I don't know what it means to be/ the lover of another man" (32-33). This shows personal growth and an effort to appreciate love that seems different when compared to his own. This is because he actually considers his brother's way of life at his own level and not necessarily as separate or insufficient.

The speaker's perspective also emphasizes his metamorphosis from start to finish. The end of the poem implies the speaker halted further communication with his brother when he discovered he was gay. This is illustrated when the lover tells the speaker, "Forgive yourself for not wanting to know him/ after he told you" (88-89). The death of his brother seemed to bring the absurdity of his close-mindedness into perspective. The change in attitude prompted the speaker to put himself in the shoes of the lover and brother. He compares their love to his own with his wife. This shows him comparing, what had been for him, the foreign concept of homosexual love to something he was familiar with. True recognition of the brother's lifestyle is expressed when the speaker feels hate in response to the funeral director's refusal to properly take care of his brother's body. Earlier in the poem, the speaker and lover met a guard at the border of

14.3

Mexico. The speaker pointed out, "See in the guard's eye/ how much a man can hate another man" (47-48). Later, however, he expresses to the funeral director, "Let him see in your eyes/ how much a man can hate another man" (72-73). This parallels the disgust the border guard had for the lover. The speaker's point of view went from an observer of hate to a victim of hate. In that moment, the speaker stood up for his brother. This demonstrated not only acceptance of the brother, but also empathy for the brother and lover's struggles with a society that does not approve. By enhancing his understanding of their feelings, he recognized how unfair it was for him to shun his brother.

Tone reveals insight into the speaker's conflicting emotions. His skepticism becomes apparent when he describes, "Drive to Mexico for unproven drugs that might/ help him live longer" (40-41). The statement itself is discouraging; he was unsure if the trip is worth the trouble. He should want to do whatever it takes to save his brother's life, but their distance suppressed those kinds of convictions. As the story developed, grief for his brother's condition also developed. When the brother died, the speaker expressed, "Curse God, but do not/ abandon Him" (67-68). These words came from his intense feelings of loss in a brother and in a relationship. The negative, yet uplifting tone highlighted how death became a hardship to accept. The outburst is quickly suppressed with the recognition that he must understand that his search for answers to unanswerable feelings should not bring him down. It represents a more conventional reaction towards death that the speaker at the beginning of the poem may not have recognized. He admits, "When he slips into an irrevocable coma.../ Wonder how much longer/ you will be able to be strong" (59-62). This further endorses the idea of the speaker's sense of loss. The discouraged tone contrasts with the distanced speaker of the beginning of the poem. The death is not only overwhelming, but the confrontation of his brother's sexuality was also on his mind. It reveals how the apprehensiveness of seeing his dying brother turned into appreciation of the lives of those around him for whom they are. The new appreciation makes the speaker a better person.

Symbolism is used to represent longing and the speaker's effort to reconnect with the life of his brother. The scar on the speaker's eyebrow stood for, "All that's left of him" (32). The association he makes between the scar and his brother shows he still had thoughts he wanted to share with his brother. The physicality of the scar helped the speaker express these feelings because the subject matter was difficult to bring out of himself to begin with. It seemed there were more serious issues to be addressed, but the scar reminded him of his memories with his brother. The scar was a comforting childhood memory. It was used to reach out from a place of confusion to the reality of his brother's death. This visual reminder of the past made it difficult for him to ignore. The speaker also reached out for comfort in the lover. He hugged and held hands with the lover to connect with his brother, even though he was unsure how to react. This symbolized his growing comfort with his own and the lover's sexuality. The death was a humbling experience that got rid of his ideas that homosexuality should separate people. His willingness to interact with the lover in that manner shows the progress he made to break down his own insecurities.

Diction develops the emotions the speaker expressed in response to his brother's death. Several words stand out in the first and second stanza. The speaker describes his brother's body as a "cadaver" (5). This illustrates his distance and lack of tenderness for his brother. The word evokes a very cold, emotionless reaction, as if the speaker is referring to a stranger. The speaker also describes himself listening to the doctor with a "steel" face (10). The speaker seems to intentionally mask his reaction, or experiences no significant emotion when he hears about the imminent death of his brother. Either reason for having the "steel" face shows the lack of connection to a family member that should exist. The speaker's conversation with the doctor makes him wonders why doctors are so "remote" (13). This observation reflects his own uncertainties. The remoteness he feels is actually his initial detachment with the whole situation. By the end of the poem this distance turns into understanding. He states, "Know that your brother's life/ was not what you imagined," to acknowledge his ability to break down his preconceived notions of homosexuality (78-79). It is especially powerful because he does not only see or hear something involving his brother's life, but experiences it to "know" what his brother was like. The deeper level of understanding allowed him to get over his negative feelings of having a homosexual brother. The use of the word "imagined" to describe his initial feelings, hints at his own acknowledgement that there was no reason to be intolerant. The word choice emphasizes the feelings he had in reaction to the life changing events.

Lassell's use of these elements of writing enhance how the poem explains the title statement, "How to Watch You Brother Die." The speaker's transformation is apparent by the comparison of the speaker before and after his confrontation with the unfamiliar. The effects of the elements strengthen the argument that the change in the speaker is progressive. They reveal he was not quite sure how to react, but he ultimately modified his mindset about his brother's life. Together, these devices develop the meaning of the text. They highlight the internal and external conflicts experienced by the speaker to accept his brother as more than a homosexual man. The speaker learned his brother's life was not what he expected. His ignorance really prevented him from knowing his brother. A person's sexuality should not define a person because people are more than what they are attracted to. Accepting people for who they are will help us create deeper relationships with others and understanding.

Works Cited

Lassell, Michael. "How to Watch Your Brother Die." *Writing as Revision*. 3rd ed. Ed. Beth Alvarado and Barbara Cully. Boston: Pearson, 2010. 479–81. Print.

14.4 Culpability

Textual Analysis by Nisha Priyanka Talanki

Take a moment. Look around. What do you see? A wooden table, a plastic chair. A carton of milk. Glance out the window. Cars lining up languorously in the scorching heat. Towering masses of concrete and plaster and glass and brick, immovable as the mountains. Now shut your eyes. When you open them again, are you sure that everything will look the same? Although you might be tempted to say yes, you must take into account the environmental costs of living as we currently do, with all the material objects you saw and took for granted. Poet William Wordsworth and photographer Charles Lindsay, visionaries of different eras, peered into the future and saw a world drastically different from the one they lived in. Neither liked what they saw. How can we prevent their vision from coming true? Lindsay and Wordsworth demonstrate that if each of us does not take responsibility in protecting our planet, its destruction is inevitable.

Before we can fully comprehend the macroscopic consequences of our actions, we must first analyze the world on a nanoscale. Carbon. A fairly small, simple element. But the basis of all life on Earth. Lindsay pays homage to this life-giving atom by utilizing it to create and develop the photographs in his series, Carbon. Although most photographers use a silver emulsion for this purpose, Lindsay eschews the metallic element, a symbol of greed and materialism, in favor of carbon (Charlie's Experiment). Wordsworth also displays his disgust for materialism in the first few lines of his poem "The world is too much with us; late and soon, / Getting and spending, we lay waste our powers; / Little we see in Nature that is ours" (Wordsworth). The poet describes mankind's relationship with the Earth as if it were one of unequal trade. In this case, we borrow in excess from the earth to feed our lavish desires. Nature, the loser of this transaction, receives nothing from us in return. Wordsworth continues, saying, "We have given our hearts away, a sordid boon!" (Wordsworth). The only thing we have given up to participate in this unfair operation is our conscience. He further states, "For this, for everything, we are out of tune; / It moves us not" (Wordsworth). The single drop gratitude we might muster up for our Mother Earth is overwhelmed by the torrents of our greed.

Wordsworth tries to remind us of our simple beginnings by alluding to the idyllic past. In his poem "The World is Too Much with Us" Wordsworth states that he would "...rather be/ A Pagan suckled in a creed outworn" than live in a developed, technologically advanced world. William Wordsworth lived through a major turning point in British history - the Industrial Revolution. Wordsworth saw factories rising up, huge smokestacks in steel mills, steam engines, large scale coal mines, and the advent of mass manufacturing. The whole nation chanted a single mantra - "progress" (Mahoney 16-17). However, Wordsworth refused to see this whirlwind of change as creative destruction. His naturalistic viewpoint is evident from his stated desire to live in a "backwards" manner and celebrate the natural world instead of material advancement. Wordsworth continues with his pagan motif by alluding to the Greek deities: "So might I, standing on this pleasant lea, / Have glimpses that would make me less forlorn; / Have sight of Proteus rising from the sea; / Or hear old Triton blow his wreathed horn" (Wordsworth). Wordsworth, by referring to these ancient Greek deities, conjures up an image of human oneness with nature. Proteus and Triton both represent the natural world, in the form of the oceans and seas (Bulfinch 478, 488). By referencing these gods, Wordsworth gives his appreciation for nature religious intensity – he idolizes the powers of nature instead of the power of man. In addition, the mythological allusions hearken back to ancient times, before the steam engine or textile mills. Wordsworth's tone is sentimental in these final lines of his poem. He laments the loss of these natural divinities, and therefore the loss of mankind's appreciation for the Earth.

Unlike William Wordsworth, Charles Lindsay uses his visualization of the future to demonstrate his distaste for the planet's destruction. Lindsay says of his photographic series, *Carbon*, "*Carbon* is a creation of fictitious worlds, drawing on my interest in the aesthetics of space exploration, microscopic discovery and abstract symbols. I am intrigued by the idea that so much of our expanding scientific knowledge is based on images from beyond our body's normal scope of vision" (Charlie's Experiment). Lindsay views scientific discovery not as a means of achieving dominion over nature, but as a means of comprehending and celebrating it. Through this lens, Lindsay's depictions of the future world are particularly devastating.

A dry, seemingly lunar landscape. Our Earth, thousands of years in the future. Dust settles, piling slowly and gradually until everything—the ground, the mountains, and all former life forms—are suffocated and erased from existence. We lay fallen at the bottom of the hole we dug ourselves into, the layers and layers of sediment stretching upwards around us. The layers spiral infinitely higher; we are engulfed in the disastrous cycle of technological advancement. We have sucked dry the fertile lands we once had in the name of progress, and nothing is left. The world is quiet. All the hustle and bustle of urban life has slowed to a standstill. The only proof that life ever existed on earth is the brittle remains of an insect. Lindsay focuses close on the carcass with the hopeful desperation that its vitality may be sparked again. But the insect stares blankly into the distance, its inert features made gaunt by the rotting of a thousand years (Lindsay). There is no hope.

Who is guilty of this murder? Who is to blame for the destruction of our home? Lindsay and Wordsworth attempt to address these questions in their works. Wordsworth prefaces his poem by naming its audience in the title, "The World is Too Much with us". Through his usage of the word "us", he makes sure not to exclude himself from any blame. It is especially significant that he makes use of the first person plural. If Wordsworth had distanced himself from the problem by using "you" and the second person, his tone would have seemed more accusatory. This accusatory tone in turn may have offended his readers, preventing them from taking his message to heart. Wordsworth continues with his use of "us" and "we" until the middle of the 9th line of the poem. At this point, Wordsworth takes a more reflective tone and switches to the first person singular. By using himself as the subject, Wordsworth takes personal accountability, and sets a goal for himself to be "...a Pagan suckled in a creed outworn" (Wordsworth). Although his description hearkens to the past, his eyes are set on the future, as he calls for a return to the days of yore. His intent is to gently persuade the readers of the poem to follow in his footsteps.

Lindsay takes a totally different approach. He uses the tactic of guilt to shock his audience into taking action. The dead insect stares head on at the viewer of the photograph, as if to blame the viewer for its demise. Its vacant, cold expression demonstrates the insect's clear hatred for its murderer. As if this were not enough, the viewer is seemingly pelted with the small meteorite-like objects that erupt from the picture's foreground (Lindsay). This might be considered Lindsay's suggestion for the castigation deserved by viewer for destroying the Earth. Photographs are static; once they are developed the image is lasting. The insect cannot turn its gaze away from anyone whose eyes meet it. If Charles Lindsay himself were to look at his work head on, even he would be assailed by the insect's pointed stare. In this manner, Lindsay blames himself just as much as any other man or woman for the ruination of the planet Earth. Although Lindsay's forceful method is drastically different from Wordsworth's use of gentle goading, it is just as effective.

We have seen the rejection of materialism and our ingratitude for the Earth's blessings. We have seen the remembrance of the idealized past, and the frightening future in store for us. But what can be gained from this knowledge? In Wordsworth's poem, "the world" is the subject, what is being acted upon, and the damaging element (Wordsworth). Mankind is both equated with and held in opposition to the bountiful planet, and its tendency toward worldliness is the poison that instigates the degradation. By this logic, the solution to our problem is painfully simple—by worldliness and greed we are fallen, and by taking personal responsibility for our own selfish sentiments, we can be saved.

As I learned from both Wordsworth's "The World is Too Much with us" and Lindsay's *Carbon*, it is not enough for me to make a general suggestion to humanity and call my work done—I must fulfill my own duty to the planet that sustains me. Unless I accomplish this, I am nothing but an accessory to murder. Earlier in this essay, I asked you to take a look around you and imagine the future. I now do the same. I see a wooden table, a plastic chair, and a carton of milk. I too see cars and roads and buildings. But when I shut my eyes and imagine the world years from now, I will see something better.

14.4

Works Cited

Bulfinch, Thomas. *Bulfinch's Mythology: The Age of Fable*. Philadelphia: Running, 1987. Print.

Lindsay, Charles. "Carbon III." *Charlie's Experiment*. Charles Lindsay. 2008. Web. 01 Nov. 2010.

Lindsay, Charles. *Untitled*. 2008. Photograph. Center for Creative Photography, Tucson.

Mahoney, John L. *William Wordsworth: A Poetic Life*. New York: Fordham UP, 1996. Print.

Wordsworth, William. "The World Is Too Much With Us." *Connections: Literature for Composition*. Ed. Quentin Miller and Julie Nash. Boston: Houghton Mifflin, 2008. 1331. Print.

14.5 Becoming "Agent Orange": An Investigation of the Relationship Between Colors and the Unconscious

Contextual Analysis by Michelle Moraila

Though it may be hard to believe, entertainment is not the sole purpose of movies. They are an escape for the audience, a world that strays from reality because of the creative ambience the director has created. However, this strategically stylized atmosphere is not generated for mere attractiveness, but rather to provide the specific effect the director wants the audience to feel while observing the characters. An excellent way to comprehend this is to take Sigmund Freud's psychoanalytical theories of the id, ego, and the superego when watching a movie and asking why the protagonists look or behave in a certain way. Michel Gondry's 2004 film, *Eternal Sunshine of the Spotless Mind*, speaks to this type of analysis because of the way Gondry presents the protagonists, Joel and Clementine. The movie explores their falling in and out of love and their decision to erase each other from their memories after the relationship ends. The storyline is visually guided by Clementine's appearance and the different dyes she applies to her hair throughout the telling of their quirky love story. Gondry utilizes Clementine's dynamic hair colors and their respective names to reflect the presence of the repressed id in her unconscious mind, subsequently representing the phases of Joel and Clementine's relationship.

Overall, Clementine is an extremely spontaneous person. In Freudian terms, her personality appeals to the id more than the two concepts of the ego and the superego because Freud describes the id as "the source of all our aggressions and desires" and goes on to say that it wants "to satisfy its impulses for pleasure" (Guerrin 205). Acting on urges pleases the id because the person in question is doing what he or she wants without taking the consequences into consideration.

Even other people notice this trait in Clementine. When Joel asks his friends Carrie and Rob why Clementine would suddenly decide to erase him from her memory, Carrie responds, "You know Clementine, she's impulsive" (Gondry). No one saw this coming because she has a tendency to surprise people with her actions. This is the kind of behavior that prompts her to constantly change the color of her hair.

Her hair becomes a main focus during the film because it is so distinct. One's attention is first drawn to it in the scene where she and Joel are conversing in the train after going to Montauk and she mentions that Joel might not remember her because her hair color changes often. When one analyzes this scene closely, one realizes that she names all the colors that are applied to her head throughout the movie: "It's called 'Blue Ruin.' Snappy name, huh? Anyway, this company makes a whole line of colors with equally snappy names. 'Red Menace,' 'Yellow Fever,' 'Green Revolution...' 'Agent Orange.' I came up with that one" (Gondry). Though she is not conscious of it, she flaunted the majority of these colors in her hair while she dated Joel. Yet she still mentions them to him and even associates her hair with Joel's lack of remembering her. This is the repressed id attempting to resurface. Freud observed that through repression, which constitutes as attempting to forget "unresolved conflicts, unadmitted desires, or traumatic past events, so that they are forced out of conscious aware " (Barry 97), there is still a "strong *tendency* towards the pleasure principle" (Freud 6). Those memories that have been symbolically erased become the repressed id because she cannot retrieve pleasure from them since they are no longer there. It is her brain trying to master those past events but being unable to return to them.

Nevertheless, her unconscious connects the names of the colors with recollections from past events because of the presence of the id in her mind. Clementine says that she applies "her personality in a paste" (Gondry) alluding to the idea that she bases her choice of color according to her spontaneity, which is why it changes so often. Her id is evident because she is acting upon impulse every time she dyes her hair. Each hair dye is, thus, named specifically to represent what was happening in Joel and Clementine's relationship due to the fact that she applied them herself. Though Clementine may not have generated their names, she still dyed her hair color in a certain way that reflected what was happening in her relationship with Joel.

When Clementine converses with Joel in the train, her hair is tinted the color called "Green Revolution." The name simply correlates to their relationship because their meeting altered their lives. However, one must also take into consideration the association of the color green. Though it is commonly linked to jealousy, envy, or greed, green also represents nature. Freud's concepts propose that the id is *natural* in all humans. Thus, the name "Green Revolution" alludes to the idea that Clementine was in a natural state (an id state) because children have "certain uncontrolled impulses toward pleasure" (Guerrin et al.

205) and her life was consequently *revolutionized* the day she met Joel. During the beginning of her relationship with him, Clementine constantly appeals to the id just like a child does. She pushes him to break into a deserted beach house (an impulsive act lacking the concept of the superego) and even goes as far as describing herself as "ruthless," which is ironic because it is means the complete opposite of her name (though she only uses it as a pun). She completely succumbs to the id because she does not know how to control her urges.

With this in mind, the "Green Revolution" is defined as a transformation in Joel and Clementine's lives. This was a point in their relationship where the id was not yet repressed, but when the memories are removed, Clementine's unconscious mind still correlates the dye to Joel because she mentions the color. She could have left it completely out of the list of hair dyes in the scene where they are on the train, but her unconscious ties it to something that was once important in her life. The repressed id is trying to recover those memories because the pleasure they brought about to Clementine remains in her unconscious. The unconscious is said to have a "strong influence upon our actions" (Barry 97) and when memories are stored in this part of the mind they are known as repressed. This does not mean that they are deleted completely and is the reason Clementine still feels the need to say "Green Revolution." The unconscious is influencing what she talks about in her conversation with Joel on the train.

Following the couple's "revolution", they begin a relationship and fall in love. During this period of time, Clementine spontaneously changes her hair to a color named "Red Menace" to fit her enamored life, a quality that is commonly associated with the color red. The id, "the reservoir of libido" (Guerrin et al. 205), incessantly seeks to satisfy sexual pleasure, a concept that is commonly associated with love. Clementine is full of passion and life during this stage of the relationship. She speaks fondly to Joel and urges him to "calm down" and "enjoy the scenery" (Gondry) during a memory in which they are playing in the woods. It is a time where the pleasure principle is being completely satisfied.

In spite of this, there exists such a thing as too much of a good thing. The latter part of the name contains the word "menace" which is connected to threats and destruction. It is evident that the id is present during this phase but it is necessary to take into consideration that the id lacks morals and is very hard to restrain: "unchecked it would lead us to any lengths –to destruction and even self-destruction—to satisfy its impulses for pleasure" (Guerrin et al 205). It has been observed that Clementine is incredibly impulsive and that during this period of time the id was being fully satisfied. However, this has a negative effect on the relationship because the id has no control to the point that the individual cannot survive in society. In this case, it is the relationship that cannot survive. Clementine represses these urges when she decides to have her memory erased because they would be the most painful to ponder. Yet she still mentions the "Red Menace" in the train scene because the id is constantly seeking to turn unpleasing memories to pleasurable ones. The repressed memories are trying to make themselves known.

This complete dedication to satisfy the id has negative consequences on Joel and Clementine. She taints her hair using orange dye, a color often connected to discord and mayhem. During this stage of their relationship, one can see in Joel's memories how they constantly bickered and there was little communication. These factors strained their relationship to the point that Joel goes as far as questioning whether they have become "the dining dead" (Gondry). It is as though the "red" in their relationship suddenly faded and turned to orange. The id has sought too much pleasure to the point that it is destroying the relationship. Clementine is constantly acting on impulse during the time that her hair is colored orange, such as when she suddenly leaves after Joel insults her, resulting in the end of the relationship. The id acted upon impulse and did not notice this consequence. Her decision to remove Joel from her memory is also a result of the id taking over and acting irrationally. All of these events are penalties of the pleasure principle's desire to go to extreme lengths to find pleasure.

It is important to note that Clementine names the dye "Agent Orange" and that this is the only color that she names by herself in the train ride. "Agent Orange" is actually the name of a poisonous gas used during the Vietnam War. There is a direct correlation between the name of the poisonous gas and how the id has "poisoned" Joel and Clementine's relationship. The repressed id is speaking through this name because her mind connects it to a period in her past where there were fatal events, in this case, the end of the relationship. She does not consciously know it, but during the time that her hair was dyed this way there was a lot of poison in her life, so much that she decided that she wanted to get rid of anything that could possibly be linked to those painful memories. Her unconscious mind associates the color orange with these unfortunate experiences.

After Clementine and Joel break up, Clementine decides to dye her hair using "Blue Ruin." The color blue is known to be an emotional color associated with sadness. The name is exactly how she feels: sad and defeated. She dyes her hair after she has erased Joel from her memory, which means that she did not do it because she consciously knew that her relationship has just ended. Her unconscious mind influenced her actions completely because the repressed id was attempting to forget a "traumatic past event" (Barry 97). She is impulsive and she knows it, which is why she does not necessarily ask herself as to *why* she chose to dye her hair color with "Blue Ruin." Yet she still dyes it that specific color because it is the repressed id in her unconscious trying to master those painful memories.

Joel and Clementine's relationship in the film *Eternal Sunshine of the Spotless Mind* is without a doubt a colorful one. Clementine's constant desire to change her hair color using "snappy" names reflect the presence of the repressed id in her unconscious mind and help the audience differentiate between the various stages the relationship undergoes. The appearance of the characters that Michel Gondry created to portray Sigmund Freud's theories on the id and the unconscious provide a deeper understanding of the character itself, consequently displaying the director's intentions of the film. Michel Gondry has proven that sometimes a hair dye is more than just a hair dye.

Works Cited

Barry, Peter. *Beginning Theory: An Introduction to Literary and Cultural Theory*. New York: Manchester UP, 1995. Print.

Eternal Sunshine of the Spotless Mind. Dir. Michel Gondry. Perf. Jim Carrey, Kate Winslet, and Tom Wilkinson. Focus Features, 2004. DVD.

Freud, Sigmund. *Beyond the Pleasure Principle*. New York: Bantam, 1959. Print.

Guerin, Wilfred L., Earle Labor, Lee Morgan, Jeanne C. Reesman, and John R. Willingham, eds. *A Handbook of Critical Approaches to Literature*. New York: Oxford UP, 1992. Print.

14.6 Bringing Light to Problems Ignored

Contextual Analysis by Christopher R. Ching

Throughout American history there have been many instances of social injustices and it is only through the power of words that these gruesome acts against humanity have been exposed during those dark times. However, those times are not yet over, as recently as 30 years ago a woman was lynched for her attempt to start a NAACP chapter in California. In response to the lynching, Joy Harjo wrote a poem as a way to bring light to the horrific event. The importance of her writing is of great significance as it is a true example of writing as social witness. Writing as social witness goes beyond solely documenting social injustices, but extends to exposing every aspect of it including the pain and suffering felt by those who are victims. Sam Hamill states in his essay "The Necessity to Speak," that "Writing is a form of human communication expressing ideas regarding the human condition" (346). This means that writing is essential to show what is really occurring throughout the course of human history. The definition of writing as social witness can be simply stated as revealing the problems of society and how it affects certain individuals. Joy Harjo's poem, "Strange Fruit", connects with the concept of writing as a social witness as expressed Sam Hamill's essay "The Necessity to Speak" in its references to speak up against violence and racism, which it accomplishes through the use of personal experiences and other literary devices.

Joy Harjo uses her own personal experience to give further insight to the unjust lynching in her poem. She states, "Down the roads through the trees I see the kitchen light on and my lover fixing supper, the baby fussing for her milk, waiting for me to come home. The moon hangs from the sky like a swollen fruit" (Harjo). As horrific as lynchings may be, it is clear that life goes on even when such an atrocious act against humanity occurs as seen in the text. The kitchen light, the lover, and the baby fussing for milk create a very casual and normal image in the reader's mind as if nothing wicked has occurred, yet the reader knows the opposite to be true. Harjo purposely paints this image to help the reader see the normality of the situation and this only goes to show that lynchings must happen often or at least frequently enough for most people not to notice and/or care. These are the kinds of social injustices which writing as social witness are meant to expose; the types which people have grown accustomed to, ones where people have given up on any hope for a solution, and the ones where things could be done to end the injustice yet little is done. It is obvious that her lover accepts the injustice in the late 20th century of American society and the fact that no one else takes action or is even mentioned in the poem shows that the rest of America is also complacent. Through the normal tone and of the lines referring to her lover making supper, it is clear that nothing is being done about the lynching. A key part of writing as social witness is to shake members of society from their complacency of how things are, which is also one of the major themes in Hamill's essay. By using her own personal experiences, Harjo is able to show complacency when it comes to dealing with societal problems.

Another method which Harjo is able to paint a better picture of the injustice of the world is through the use of repetition. Harjo uses the phrase "I did not…" (547) or "I have not…" (546) several times (six times to be exact) throughout the short poem to emphasize the point that there was no way to justify the lynching. Doing so eliminates any potential thought that perhaps the woman deserved the lynching and reinforces the fact that an innocent woman was murdered for no good reason. The high rate at which she uses those phrases within such a short block of texts also creates a very fast paced reading for the reader which also accurately depicts the rapid thought process which Harjo must have gone through as she was thinking about the lynching. A particularly interesting usage of that phrase occurs in the last paragraph when Joy Harjo states, "I did not… tell you how to live or die" (547). Irony can be seen through this quote as for as long as African Americans have been in the U.S., the white man has been telling black man how to live his life, yet it is still the African Americans who are subject to violence. This quote also shows the confusion which Harjo undergoes as it makes absolutely no sense for one to hate against on another especially if the one who is hated on has done nothing except belong to a different racial group. Once again, Hamill's reoccurring theme of unnecessary violence against a particular group of people who are not of the majority can be seen through the text. When Harjo uses the phrase "I did not…" (547), it shows her rapid thought process of trying to understand why anyone would commit such an atrocious act against an innocent human being and further helps the reader understand what is really going on.

Harjo also uses imagery to induce the same type of emotions in the reader as she is feeling. The imagery used is very important as it further communicates the emotions felt by the victims of social injustice. When the Harjo uses imagery, she is also able to provide context of what is happening through the images being painted in the reader's mind. She writes, " I was out in the early evening taking a walk in the fields…, or walking to the store for a pack of cigarettes, a pound of bacon… then saw the hooded sheets ride up in the not yet darkness, in the dusk carrying the moon, in the dust behind my tracks. Last night there were crosses burning in my dreams, and the day before a black cat stood in the middle of the road with a ghost riding its back" (Harjo). In the beginning of this quote, it seems as if it is just another regular day until she realizes what has happened the night before. She begins by creating a seemingly calming scene as she takes a casual walk in the fields only to be interrupted by the evilness of the KKK. With the first few lines, Harjo communicates to the reader that within her society, the evil of social injustice contaminates the rituals of daily life. Once more, it is seen that society does not care to fight against the perpetrators as Harjo states that she sees the "hooded sheets ride up in the not yet darkness". What allows the reader to know that nothing is being done about this hate and racism is the fact that the hooded figures (members of the KKK) are going out before it is completely dark outside; if even the local police or other types of law enforcement cared about what was really going on, then the KKK would not be able to commit their acts of hate without complete darkness. The hooded figures and the not yet darkness also create a dark image as Harjo was very specific to refer to the members of the KKK not as people, but simply as "hooded sheets" to further implant a frightening depiction in the reader's mind. References to crosses burning in her dreams definitely create intense scenes within the reader's mind and seems to be an exaggeration of the situation, but is in fact historically accurate which further goes to show the extent of the racial problems during the time the poem was written. A black cat with a ghost riding its back is used as a way to create a dark and wicked image and foreshadows the fact that evil will occur in the head of the reader. These lines provide context for what happens and gives the reader insight to the background setting for the rest of the poem while simultaneously painting a vivid and emotional scene of what is going on to fulfill Hamill's belief that writing should create emotion in the audience (347).

"Strange Fruit" is an excellent example of writing as social witness as it connects with the key ideas mentioned by Hamill in his essay "The Necessity to Speak". Joy Harjo speaks out against complacency and is able to connect with her audience at a deep level to bring light to topic which has been largely covered in darkness. She does this through the use of bringing up personal experiences to give the reader a firsthand view of what she goes through. Harjo also uses literary devices such as repetition and imagery to evoke emotions and to further help her audience understand the gravity of the injustice within her society. The poem which Harjo writes records not only the lynching, but also reveals the pain, suffering, and thoughts (or lack of) of those who are victimized by it. As Hamill points out, "It begins with the end of lies and silence about violence" (353), so Harjo speaks up and breaks the silence of the violence committed against those who are innocent.

Works Cited

Hamill, Sam. "The Necessity to Speak." *Writing as Revision.* 3rd ed. Ed. Beth Alvarado and Barbara Cully. Boston: Pearson, 2010. 346–53. Print.

Harjo, Joy. "Strange Fruit." *Writing as Revision.* Ed. Beth Alvarado and Barbara Cully. Needham: Simon & Schuster, 1996. 546–47. Print.

14.7 The Furthest Distance in the World

Contextual Analysis by Yaqi Rong

The famous Indian writer Tagore once stated, "The furthest distance in the world is the love between the fish and the birds, because the former is swimming in the deep sea while the latter is flying in the sky." In Zhang Xiaoxian's novel, "Single Bed in Small Bag," the author claims that the furthest distance in the world at that point where I stand in front of you, yet you do not know that I love you. But actually, the furthest distance in the world is from one heart to another heart, not only in romantic love, but also in the love between friends, families, and even affection in humankind. That is to say, as long as long as love exists in our minds and hearts, no distance—no matter how great—is a problem.

Many texts which we have read this semester and my own personal experiences demonstrate that the greatness of the distance depends upon people's hearts. For example, even though the father and son in "Visitation" met every week, both still acted like they were strangers. The woman and the crabby man in William Trevor's story "The Woman in the House," were together every day; however, neither of them truly cared about each other. In my personal experience, my best friend was treated like a stranger by her aunt, even though they lived together. All of these examples mirror the fact that close physical distance does not necessarily correspond to close love in the heart.

In contrast, in "Sheep May Safely Graze," although the daughter walks into heaven alone and departs from her father far away, the father's love for his daughter showed no signs of waning. In the classic, Dracula shows love for his dead wife even becomes a vampire. Furthermore, because of my father's deep love for his grandmother, there seems to be an invisible connection between him and his grandmother, as if he could speak with her after her death. Also, in Home for the Holidays, Claudia and Tommy are very close, connected by the heart, but separated by the miles of the land that force them apart in two different cities. I am faced with the same dilemma: as an international student, I am separated from my family across the Pacific Ocean, but the love between my family and me will never be reduced. Physical distance is never a valid excuse for a lack of love. The question is the distance between people's hearts.

If there is a long distance between two hearts, even if two people see and interact with each other every day, they will still be strangers. Sometimes, close space will not warm the cold heart. This principle can be seen in "Visitation", written by Brad Watson; the son treats his father quite coldly while his father meets with him every month. The father in this story is very poor because his son does not like to communicate with him. Although they sit close to each other, the distance between their hearts will remain more than a billion light-years away. After the divorce with his wife, in his mind, his son and keeping the concept of family real are extremely important. "He had been painfully aware of his own despair for most of his life," (Watson 139). The father is afraid that the distance between them will destroy his relationship with his son, so "he sought distractions from his ineptitude as a father" (Watson 140). However, he goes to visit his son every month anyway, hoping that the physical closeness could somehow reconstruct the bridge between their hearts. Unfortunately, his naïve hope and ignorance causes him to forget the great distance between his and his son's heart, and is thus unable to drive to his son's heart.

The father's habit of drinking all the day and his negative attitude on life deteriorates a boy's expectation that one's father has always been the son's superhero. When the father picked him up, he "trudged after Loomis," but did not forget to say "Bye, Uncle Bob" (Watson 141). In the boy's little heart, even an uncle who is almost a stranger gets a better greeting than the one that he did not give his father. The ideal created by a father figure is that he should be a big, old, wise tree that protects his family; however, his father hurts those who could have been protected. As a result, the far distance of hearts has been created between the father and son. His son has already lost confidence in his father. Nothing can or will change their past together, even if they live together.

The story of "The Woman of the House" exposes a similar situation. The only relatives to each other left in the world live together. Unfortunately, their different perspectives on life lead them to lie to each other. Communications between them are scarce, as demonstrated by their physical tension "while she stood behind him, not wanting to look at him" (Trevor 168). Usually, when people live in the same house, the concept of distance does not reach past the expanse of four walls and a ceiling; therefore, two people should be close and dependent upon each other. However, these two people both have their own thoughts. They do not believe in each other. This problem is exacerbated by their lies to each other. In order to save more money, the woman—"particular about how she looked and dressed"—seduced the grocers (Trevor 164). She does almost everything she can, including lie to the man. Compared with money, the man in her life is much less important. Their relationship is built upon money. There is no doubt that a great distance of hearts and minds separate them. However, there are no other choices offered to the woman but to live with the man. They just take what they need from each other, acting nothing like relatives. Ultimately, the woman even despicably covers up the man's death in order to ask for more money from the government. At the man's death, she coldly and cruelly exclaims that "no one will miss the crippled man." (Trevor 173). What an awful relationship! Feelings of care, trust, respect, and kindness between two strangers is closer than those of these two relatives who live together.

Similarly, a difficult circumstance greeted Ma, my best friend. She always felt sad because she felt as if she did not belong to any home. Her mother died of cancer when she was just 6 years old. In her memory, her mother had been ill since her birth, while her father fell in love with another woman when she just 4 years old. After her mother's death, her father moved to another city far away from their hometown to live with his mistress. So, my friend was asked to live with her aunt. From that point onwards, her nightmare had begun. My friend's younger brother, or her aunt's son, was very jealous of her appearance into her aunt's house because Ma seemed to rob the attention that had originally only belonged to him. Before she came, the boy ate the entire cabinet of snacks, hogged the television screen, and played with all of the toys; however, with the arrival of Ma, he now had to learn the "obscene," new concept of sharing. He was annoyed by his new sister, so he would tell his mother many shameful and disobedient things that Ma had never done. Naturally, her aunt resented her for doing these fake actions. So, for the entirety of the rest of their time together, Ma's aunt never believed a word she said. The tension between them was great, even though they lived under the same roof. The lack of belief hurt her deeply, and divided her from her aunt's family by a long distance of hearts and minds.

To Ma, living with this family meant nothing because the term "family" had already been destroyed in her mind. She bore this kind of life for 6 years. During those 6 years, she even moved to my home because their rude attitude interrupted her studies. During this time, we both discovered that, ironically, sometimes living in a friend's house feels more like home than living in one's own family's house. Expect during meals, Ma stayed at her own room all the time when she lived with aunt. She always talked about it with me: "the distance between my aunt's family and me is quite further than that between mother and me." All of her aunt's concentration was focused on her son, so she forgets that sometimes her little niece yearns for familial love as well. The clod attitude made her feels like an extra in the family, as if no one needed her anymore. That is the furthest distance in the world, when relatives do not have any trust in each other, and one heart is too far away from another heart no matter how close they lived together.

Conversely to the previous example in which two people lived together but still acted like strangers, a father's love never waned even after his daughter's death. The strength of love will make the real physical distance between two people shorter and shorter. I believe that the father could never fathom his suffering at the death of this daughter. Jess Row's story of "Sheep May Safely Graze," describes a father who may have lost his adorable daughter forever, but nevertheless, never loses the memory of his daughter's love for one moment. "It was a tiny leak, no more than a pinprick, and a few eyedroppers' full of gas that killed my youngest daughter, Jolie" (Row, 93). The impact and damage that one seemingly insignificant item can have is magnified. He sought a lot of revenge on society in order to express his pain at his daughter's death and his longing to be with her again. Most people may comment that there is no further distance than that between life and death. However, this father's deep and passionate love makes that great distance seem shorter. For the person one loves, love can beat the distance created by space and time.

Unfortunately, the father's revenge has very bad effect on society; however, it all just demonstrates how much he loved his daughter. From the beginning, the father is characterized as a mediocre person who seems as if he will never do any harm. This observation is cemented by his own confession that "I can offer only commonplaces" (Row, 94). But after his daughter's death, he is so disappointed and depressed that he is unable to even sleep for quite a long period of time. He can't bear the impenetrable distance between his daughter and him. So he chose an extreme method to display his love for his daughter, as if compiling this list of revenge will bring his daughter closer to him. He hates the distance, he despises the person who hurt his daughter, and he is repulsed by the darkness of an uncaring society. In the night, he may hope to communicate with his girl in the faraway heaven. The distance cannot cut down the memory and love of their father-daughter relationship.

Dracula's commits a blood-less act to humans in revenge of his wife's death as well. He lost his wife when he was a man, and life without her extended the distance and the love between them. His hate caused him to want to break up that life, so he became the vampire. While he still loved his wife, all of the things he did to humans were done in order to mirror his hate of his lost wife. Some people thought vampires are blood-less and brutal animals, but in Dracula's mind, his wife has been alive the whole time. Due to this strong love, he lost his senses. He refused to acknowledge that the furthest distance in the world is between life and death. So he thought the distance could be broken by him, and then he could feel his wife's presence even though she died. He lived with another style to shorten the distance.

My father's love for his grandmother is much like the father in the previous story by Row. My father grew up with his grandmother. During his childhood, all of his beautiful memories consisted more or less about his time with his grandmother. She made bags and slingshots for him. She would leave candies or other foods she thought were delicacies for him, even when my father was 30 years of age. Usually, the food went bad, but my father had not yet tasted them yet. In my father's heart, his grandmother was the warmth that kept his heart beating. So, predictably, the news of grandmother's death knocked him sideways. He hurried back that same night, sat beside the dead body the whole day, and talked to his grandmother with tears streaming down his cheeks. However, I cannot feel that kind of deep sadness since I was exposed little to my father's grandmother. After her death, thought, I felt her presence in another side of the sky. Every festival, my father would leave the most delicious food for grandmother as if she is always there and never leaves his side.

In my father's dreams, a nice old woman always appeared. And father burnt something for her every year. He said he knows what she needs. All of the things he does for her are done as if she is still alive. Father has never felt as if there is a long distance between grandmother and him. He just keeps demonstrating that he is dutiful to his grandmother. I can hear him communicate to her when we were in front of grandmother's grave. In my father's mind, the love that they once shared and that they still have can break any distance. He can feel grandmother no matter where she is.

If we have love for others, even though we may physically be thousands of miles apart or be in different existences, that love will outlast eternity in any universe. Distance means little if that connection is a true, raw, and pure love. That love will make all of the problems that real distances bring disappear. In the movie Home for the Holidays, Claudia felt quite disappointed after conquering a sort of troubles. On the plane, she called her brother Tommy. She wanted Tommy to meet her at the airport and she told him she had many things to tell him. Their relationship is so close that they stay together almost every day. In reality, however, these siblings live in very different cities. Their relationship has been built from when they were born. They spent their childhood together and know each other very well.

No matter how long they have not seen each other, Tommy can always break into the bath room while Claudia is taking a shower. No matter how much he does not want to go back home, Tommy goes back for Claudia. The actual distance is not as important as that which will destroy their relationship. Although Claudia communicates with Tommy very little each month, when something wrong happens the first thought in her mind is of Tommy. They need each other; it is not about the space between them or how much distance separates them. They may not meet with each other frequently, but the distance of hearts between them is practically zero because they love each other. They grew up together. They know each other very well, and they share all of their happiness and troubles together. Their deep-rooted love mimics the fact that there is no distance between them.

In my personal life, I have felt the impact of the strength of love regardless of distance. My parents and I are so far apart, separated by mountains and oceans; in my mind, this distance is no less far apart than the distance between the moon and the Earth. However, our sentiment have not changed pale due to the distance. We have spent 20 years together already. In this world, my parents are the most important people in my life. We speak and see each other on the computer screen every day, and we talk about everything that is happening around me and around them back in China. And no matter how far apart I am from them, I worry about their well-being every day, just as do about mine. We would do anything to across the Pacific Ocean in a heartbeat. While this distance is thousands of miles long, the distance between our hearts will always remain zero. Our relationship will hold together, even though we may be together all of the time. Distance means nothing to us. In fact, if it has any effect, it has only made us closer.

From these examples, it can be seen that the physical distance between any great relationships may actually become a catalyst of their feelings. It is very common that people will become tired of seeing the same people every day. As a result, a bit of distance may bring forth beauty and produce beauty sometimes. Small matters could be amplified if we always stick together. Could we imagine what would happen if Claudia lived with her parents every day? She would become crazy without any space from her mother. Most teenagers cannot bear to live with a nagging mother for 365 days of the year. Obviously, Claudia's mother always blamed her sister. One of the reasons, maybe the sister lives so close to the parents. Also, another example is that couples always quarrel about small specific issues in their daily lives. All of the problems and disadvantages will emerge at last if there is zero distance between two people in a relationship.

Nowadays, young and modern people in China usually would like to work and study in another city—far away from their parents. Now, from my new perspective, I noticed how much I love and miss my parents after I board the plane destined for America. After I finished my application to the university, I had nothing to do except idly stay at home. Then, troubles start emerging as mother cannot bear the fact that I am not studying for anything like I usually am. She blamed and nagged me every moment she saw me. "What a terrible waste of time!" she would exclaim. And I would even tell her "how I wish I could live alone." During high school, I lived at home, and everyday my parents would focus on nothing but my studying. They especially restricted my free time to meet with boys because they were afraid that "puppy love" would have a bad influence on my standardized test scores. The thoughts and feelings expressed in those few months were expressed quite differently. We even had a three-weeks-long cold war.

Teenagers think they need freedom. We live with parents ever since we were born, and we are used to listening to everything our parents say and do, or we would suffer the consequences of their anger at our rebellious sides. The generation gap between children and parents cannot be ignored. Our elders may want to guide our lives in their own way, but most of the younger children have their own ideas. So World War Three often breaks out in families. And usually, there is very little probability of an agreement to be reached between the two generations of enemies. Thus, in order to avoid the increasing quarrels, young people may choose to live outside of their household. Of course, they will come back home frequently to check up on their parents and their elders, to finish some laundry, to get some money, and to, most importantly, spend time with their families. In this situation, distance gives both parents and the younger generation space to get along well.

What is the furthest distance in the world? The answer is not the distance between either ends of the earth or the universe. It is not the distance from heaven to our world. The answer is the distance from heart to heart. Space cannot prevent from the close heart. But if there are just short miles between two hearts, it means that two people can be thousands of miles apart in heart and mind. All of the themes in the stories and my personal experiments reveal that the furthest distance is that in our hearts. The truest love will not be destroyed by distance. For those people who are in love, the distance that separates their time together, their words, and their embraces is just a number and nothing else. Conversely, those people who are suspicious of each other, always living together and distrustful of each other, will only bring about increasing emotional coldness and remoteness. The distance between two hearts and minds all depends upon the people's hearts' distance and the love and care that they share with each other. Therefore, the human soul has the greatest prospect as well as the furthest distance in the world.

Works Cited

Home for the Holidays. Dir. Jodie Foster. Perf. Holly Hunter, Anne Bancroft, Robert Downey Jr., Charles Durning, and Claire Danes. Paramount, 1995. DVD.

Row, Jess. "Sheep May Safety Graze" *The PEN/O. Henry Prize Stories*. Ed. Laura Furman. New York: Anchor, 2010. 93–114. Print.

Stoker, Bram. *Dracula*. *Literature.org*. Knowledge Matters Ltd., n.d. Web. 20 Nov. 2010.

Trevor, William. "The Woman of the House." *The PEN/O. Henry Prize Stories*. Ed. Laura Fuman. New York: Anchor, 2010. 158–73. Print.

Watson, Brad. "Visitation." *The PEN/O. Henry Prize Stories*. Ed. Laura Fuman. New York: Anchor, 2010. 139–57. Print.

14.8 Within the Tendrils of Smoke

Contextual Analysis by Rae Anne Marie Martinez

As a swirl of warm hues, intricate designs of Persian rugs, tile mosaics, iconic reliefs, and the exotic sounds of lyrical sitars, Persian culture is inherently rich. The swirling smoke that weaves salient throughout the images of Persian society is more than just the hazy, mysterious background of this opulent culture. The tobacco smoke fills the intimate rooms of social gatherings and mosques; wafting through the streets is tobacco's profound, culturally important, and powerful force.

Tobacco, in less than sixty years after its introduction into the Middle East in the late 1590s became a central aspect of Persian culture. Tobacco defined a way of life for Iranians: all traditions and rituals where contingent upon the presence of it's wispy smoke. It was so intertwined with the roots of Persian social grace that the article "The art of smoking in Iran and other uses of tobacco" by William Floor asserts that "without the unavoidable [tobacco pipe] there cannot be hospitality, no commercial or other important activity, no marriage and gaiety, no food, tea, present or reward, no labor and no good travel." According to Smoke: a Global History of Smoking, by Sander L. Gilman and Zhou Xun, tobacco further developed into an indicator of social status and proper etiquette. Iranian class distinctions were shown, not through which of the various forms of tobacco were used, as was the case in many Western European countries, but through "the degree of refinement, decoration of the paraphernalia used, and the elaborateness of the surrounding ritual" (Gilman and Xun). The "qalyandar" was a symbol of wealth as only those of the highest socio-economic classes could afford the luxury of a servant exclusively for carrying their employer's smoking tools, cleaning them, and lighting them upon demand (Gilman and Xun). Both men and women were able to have qulyandars, as there were no gender barriers in regards to smoking in Persia. Public social places such as bathhouses, coffeehouse, and teahouses came to accommodate the equally addicted men and women of the lower socio-economic classes (Floor).

Eventually, tobacco's cultural influence and power surpassed that of religious authority, becoming an entity more powerful than the shah himself. Tobacco was initially opposed by Iran's religious leaders, particularly Shah Abbas I (r.1584-1629), who was the reigning shah at the time of tobacco's introduction to Iran. Shah Abbas I banned tobacco's implementation on "the pain of death and loss of property," setting a precedent for following shahs (Floor). However, the populace would not heed the words of religious leaders and refused to give up tobacco. For the Iranian people, the loss of tobacco symbolized the demise of rituals, social etiquette, and a branch of artistry in the creation of intricate smoking paraphernalia. On a more basic level, however, tobacco was an addictive drug that enjoyed widespread use for pleasure as well. "Iranians of all classes found so much pleasure in tobacco that they smoked it everywhere, even inside mosques" (Gilman and Xun). The fact that Iranian people smoked for pleasure inside mosques, places of religious sanctity, shows their direct defiance for religious law and speaks to tobacco's immense power. As shahs realized that tobacco could not be driven out of Iran, the "evil weed tobacco" eventually became a divine and accepted herb (Floor).

In the 400 years that the Middle East has known tobacco as a potent cultural force, its use has transcended being a purely cultural tradition and ritual to a broad coping mechanism for the people of Iran under emotional or psychological duress. However, smoking is so culturally acceptable in Iran that the use of it as not only a cultural symbol, but as a physical manifestation of the psychological problems of the people, a great lasting freedom, and a source of rebellion, goes unnoticed. The autobiographical graphic novel Persepolis is diary style account of the author, Marjane Satrapi's, childhood, coming of age, and early adult life throughout the Islamic Revolution of Iran from 1979 to 1994. Satrapi's novel gives an intimate look into the private lives of the Persian people in order to dispel the concept that all Iranians are religious extremists, bringing a light to life during this difficult era. By doing so, Persepolis is a demonstration and acknowledgement of tobacco's cultural power and the shift in tobacco's use, from only a cultural force to a coping mechanism.

Tobacco evolved from being a social-cultural tradition to a coping mechanism by becoming one of the few surviving forms of rebellion and freedom that women retained under the rise of restrictive extremist regime. During Satrapi's childhood in Iran, the regime of Ayatollah Khomeini, the leader of the Islamic revolution of Iran and the acclaimed Shi'a Iman, dramatically restricted women's rights. Women were no longer allowed to wear makeup, sunglasses, jewelry, or appear in public with out a "hijab," head covering. In 1980, it became mandatory for Satrapi and her female classmates to wear the veil at school (Persepolis 3). Being in violation of the dress code created by the government made women subject to public verbal and physical harassment. Satrapi recalls an instance where her mother is insulted publically for not wearing the veil by "two fundamentalist bastards... They said that women like [Satrapi's mother] should be pushed against the wall and fucked. And then thrown in the garbage... That incident made [her] sick for several days" (Persepolis 74). As a personal revolt, Satrapi begins using tobacco with a huff of a stolen cigarette around age 14. She describes this first act as a "rebellion against [her] mother's dictatorship," proclaiming that "with this first cigarette, I kissed childhood goodbye" (Persepolis 117). Yet, Satrapi parallels this act of rebellion against her mother to that of the rebellion of the Iranian people against the regime, demonstrating to the reader that the root cause of this action is a rebellion against the war and the regime's abuses, not her mother. In a broader sense, while women were limited in many social ways, the commanding regime could not limit women's smoking. Smoking was so ingrained in Persian culture that it could not be challenged, allowing women to utilize it as a form of rebellion. In a very conservative country, Satrapi is able to act in a very modern way by sitting, smoking, and conversing about divorce in a coffeehouse with her friend, Farnaz (Persepolis 332). As the regime attempted to silence and hide women's presence in public life as much as possible, smoking in settings such as bathhouses, teahouses, and coffeehouses, permitted women to continue to congregate in the very public and social manner that the government was trying to prevent.

Tobacco further transcended its purely cultural applications by becoming a physical manifestation of the Iranian people's psychological problems. Persepolis, simply by being the personal narrative of Satrapi's life, illustrates the tremendous amount of emotional and psychological stress in the lives of Iranian people caused by the Islamic Revolution and the war with Iraq. Throughout these times of high emotional and psychological duress, the characters are shown smoking. In one case, after the dismantling of the Shah's regime during the political transitional period, many of Satrapi's parents' friends have fled the country and religious extremists, who call themselves the "delivers of divine justice," have targeted and killed several others (Persepolis 66). While discussing the fate of these loved ones, her parents are depicted sitting around a table with heavy, downtrodden expressions smeared across their faces with lit cigarettes in hand (Persepolis 66). Satrapi's parents, while under emotional stress from losing loved ones and lost in great worry for their own safety, are not utilizing smoking for the reasons of social enjoyment or tradition, but as a coping behavior for their psychological anxiety. Satrapi's mother even smokes in the basement during the bombings of Tehran. Satrapi's father remarks to her "Put your cigarette out. They say that the glow of a cigarette in the easiest thing to see from the sky" (Persepolis 103). This statement indicates that not only is smoking quite common throughout Tehran, but, more importantly, that it is also quite common during bombings. It is doubtful that Satrapi's mother would choose to smoke knowing it was a risk to their safety, unless the bombings induce such an overwhelming amount of tension that she is driven to physically manifest it through the smoking of cigarettes. As Satrapi's father's remark is hearsay, it implies that many more individuals than Satrapi's mother turn to smoking as a coping behavior during the bombings and possibly other situations of intense stress.

The psychological study, "Prevalence of Cigarette Smoking in Iran," looks at various parameters in the smoking history of a population of randomly selected Iranian people. The results found that the most prevalent reason for beginning and continuing to smoke is a "release of tension." The mean age of these smokers is 21.3 years, ranging from 10 to 60 years old. This low mean age indicates that Iranians, like Satrapi, are starting to smoke younger. As tobacco is a very available drug due to it being culturally acceptable, it is easier for people to turn to it at a younger age as method for dealing with stressors.

Contemporary Western and American culture revolves around the absence of smoking and thus notices its presence, while Iranian culture lives in the presence of smoking and notices its absence. It is the strength of tobacco's cultural power over the Iranian people that masks their usage of smoking as a coping mechanism. As it is so accepted in Iranian society to smoke, it neither seems strange for children and young teens to begin smoking nor for Satrapi to smoke throughout her life. However, Satrapi fully recognizes her use of smoking as a method of dealing with the psychological stress her sense of "shame" is causing. "[She] preferred to put [herself] in serious danger [by smoking] rather than confront [her] shame. [The] shame at not having become someone, the shame of not having made [her] parents proud after all the sacrifices they had made for [her]. The shame of having become a mediocre nihilist" (Persepolis 244). Since Marjane Satrapi is both the author an illustrator of Persepolis, it was her executive decision to include the images of her family, herself, and all who surrounded her in life, smoking. By omitting these images, Satrapi would have erased an integral part of her culture; but, because Satrapi understands the deep role tobacco plays in her personal life, she chooses to emphasize its presence by including it in the images of the graphic novel and discussing her personal use of the drug.

14.8

As much as tobacco and its weaving tendrils of smoke add to the rich beauty of Iranian culture, tobacco is sinister and ugly. Tobacco is a force that has consumed a culture both socially and artistically; but now it consumes a people psychologically as well. This drug controls the lives of Iranian people to great extents, and yet it goes unnoticed, it is found ordinary to daily life, commonplace. Marjane Satrapi may be hinting at, through Persepolis, the lurking danger in tobacco or something with this immense power that is only noticed in its absence, but never in its presence. What may happen then when tobacco's role in Iranian culture evolves once again, this time for a much darker purpose?

Works Cited

Ahmadi, Jamshid, Hosein Khalili, Reza Jooybar, Nooreddin Namazi, and Pedram Mohammadagaei. "Prevalence of Cigarette Smoking in Iran." *Psychological Reports* 89.2 (2001): 339–41. Print.

Floor, Willem. "The Art of Smoking in Iran and Other Uses of Tobacco." *Iranian Studies* 35.1–3 (2002): 47–85. Print.

Gilman, Sander L. and Zhou Xun. *Smoke: A Global History of Smoking*. London: Reaktion, 2004. Print.

Satrapi, Marjane. *The Complete Persepolis*. New York: Pantheon, 2007. Print.

14.9 George Patton: A "Real Man"?

Rhetorical Analysis by Wendell Richards

George Patton was a General for the United States Army during World War II. Considered as one of the greatest generals in the history of the United States Army, Patton was both praised and vilified for his unrelenting and unapologetic battle tactics and opinions (Murphy). On June 5, 1944, Patton addressed his troops before the Normandy invasion. During this speech, Patton reinforced and redefined the traditional American gender assumptions and he used these gender assumptions as a way to motivate his men and prepare them for the D-Day invasion, the largest invasion in U.S. history.

Patton understood the gravity of the situation and his stature and how it would affect his audience. Patton had just finished commanding the U.S. Third Army in North Africa, where he defeated famed German General Erwin Rommel. This victory made Patton widely popular to the Americans and the Allied Nations, and infamous to Nazi Germany. This made Patton a celebrity to his men, and gave Patton instant credibility. Patton's audience was the troops of the U.S. Third Army. We know this because Patton addresses the audience as "men" and tells them to "be seated" prior to beginning his speech. This is typical of how a commanding officer would speak to the troops under his command. Patton's purpose was to motivate these men for this historic battle. Patton's men knew that this was the largest invasion in U.S. Military history, and they were both nervous and anxious. By speaking to his men when they needed leadership the most, Patton knew he would have their full attention. For these reasons, this was a kairotic moment for Patton. If he had given this speech two weeks prior to the invasion, any inspiration or motivation given by his speech would be diminished or altogether forgotten.

Patton began his speech by using traditional gender assumptions to appeal the audience's sense of pride and responsibility. Patton opened by stating the men were there for three reasons. "You are here to defend your homes and loved ones...for your own self respect, because you would not want to be anywhere else...because you are real men and all real men like to fight" (Patton). This statement plays powerfully on the gender assumptions that it is the man's job to protect his home and family, and that any self-respecting man would fight for what he believes in. If Patton did not think that his men had these assumptions, his efforts to appeal to the men at the beginning of his speech would have failed. The last part of the statement, "all real men like to fight" is the most powerful. This statement works in two ways. By addressing them as "real men," Patton is appealing to their pride. "Real men" could easily be replaced by masculine. Patton is also saying that those who do not like to fight are not "real men" or masculine. This works towards Patton's purpose of motivation because he assumes that all man would want to be thought of as masculine, therefore they will fight.

Patton further plays on the assumption that men want to be masculine when he states: "When you were kids you all admired the toughest boxer...the All American football players" (Patton). Here he is playing on the assumption that all boys admired these figures as children. He is assuming that these examples are admired because of the masculinity they exude. By admiring these figures you are associating yourself with them, therefore you're a "real man" like them.

Later in his address Patton appeals to another traditional American assumption about masculinity. Patton states: "Americans love a winner. Americans will not tolerate a loser. Americans despise cowards" (Patton). As American men, they are brought up to believe you have to win, no matter what. Masculinity is not synonymous with losing and being cowardly. Patton further appeals to the connection with winning and masculinity when he states, "I wouldn't give a hoot in hell for a man who lost and laughed...the very idea of losing is hateful to an American" (Patton). This also appeals to the assumptions men have of their fathers and authority figures. As children, boys are brought up to look up to and idolize their fathers. No man wanted to disappoint his father by not winning the race or getting beat up in a schoolyard fight. To these men, Patton is an authority figure, he is their leader. He plays on this by letting his men know what he thinks of losers. Another way Patton uses the American assumption of masculinity is by his use of profane language in his speech. It is masculine to speak in way that would be frowned upon by someone's mother, instead of being polite and using proper grammar. This allows his men to view him as masculine and rough, rather than polite and perhaps soft.

14.9

Patton also appeals to his men by queering the audience's assumption of masculinity. In his speech Patton states: "Yes, every man is scared in his first battle. If he says he's not, he's a liar" (Patton). This is a direct anti-assumption of masculinity in America. Masculine men are supposed to be fearless, no matter what they face. This is effective for Patton in persuading his audience because he is letting his men know they are no less masculine for being fearful. The traditional assumption of a soldier is a man who fights in all conditions, against all odds. This ideal soldier is oblivious of all dangers and gets the job done. With Patton's reputation as a winner and great commanding officer, it appeals to the men to have someone of Patton's stature tell them it is ok for them to be afraid.

Patton also queers people's masculine assumptions of heroes. Patton states:

> All of the real heroes are not storybook combat fighters, either. Every single man in this army plays a vital role…The ordnance men are needed to supply the guns and machinery of war to keep us rolling. The Quartermaster is needed to bring up food and clothes because where we are going there isn't a hell of a lot to steal. (Patton)

This is the direct opposite of the common assumption of a hero. Most people would envision a hero as a soldier pulling his wounded comrade to safety in a hail of gunfire, or one man holding off a hundred enemies by himself to protect an objective. Patton's description of a hero is far less masculine than this. His definition actually includes duties which many would consider to be feminine in nature. By queering this assumption of a hero, Patton is able to let his men know that he understands how his audience is feeling, and to motivate his men to do their job, regardless of how insignificant that man might think he is.

By using common gender assumptions Patton is able persuade his audience and accomplish his purpose of motivation. By queering the ideals of masculinity, Patton is able to reach his men by letting them know he understands what they are feeling and making them feel important. Had Patton not believed that his men had these assumptions his speech would not have had the effect that he was looking for. This adds up to Patton being successful in motivating his men for one of the biggest battles in American military history. A battle they won, perhaps in large part because of the common assumptions of gender people have.

Works Cited

Patton, George S. "Speech to the United States Third Army." England. 5 June 1944. Address.

Osborn, Jim. "US General George Patton." *Suite 101*. Suite 101 Media Inc., 9 Sep. 2008. Web. 13 Sep. 2010.

14.10 A Much Needed Unity

Rhetorical Analysis by Laura Paul

Thomas Carlyle once said, "Men's hearts ought not be set against one another, but all set with one another, and all against evil only". This quote epitomizes how President Obama successfully persuaded the country to reflect on the shooting that occurred in Tucson on January 8th, 2011. The speech was called "Together We Thrive", and was meant to serve as a memorial service at the Mckale Center at the University of Arizona to remember all those who were lost in the Safeway shooting. In the aftermath of the tragedy, President Obama encouraged citizens of the United States with his speech to unite and practice more bipartisanship than has been practiced in the past. Instead of turning on one another and placing blame for this act of violence on anyone but the shooter himself, it is important that everyone comes together and makes sure the six people who died did not die in vain. "Together We Thrive" was not by any means intended to boost Obama's own credibility and use ethos to win Americans over. Rather, President Obama was successful in persuading the citizens of our country to unite and embrace each other now more than ever, as well as create a non-combative political atmosphere in his "Together We Thrive" memorial speech. He was successful at doing this through the use of pathos and logos throughout the speech. The success Obama had in the speech of persuading us of both these things is very important for all the citizens of the United States, as everyone was shaken up by Jared Loughner's act of violence towards innocent members of the Tucson community.

The primary audience of the speech is the family members of those who were wounded or lost, or anyone who has been directly affected by the situation. The secondary audience of the speech seems to be college students, both on the University of Arizona campus and on other campuses across the country. College students represent the future of politics, which is why he chose to speak on a college campus versus a venue like Tucson Electric Park, for example. He was bound to come to Tucson to speak regardless, but the college campus atmosphere is very different than that of an off-campus venue with not as much charisma. The third audience is the rest of America, Republicans and Democrats alike. In times like this when the President's speaking about a tragedy that everyone is aware of, members of different parties are more open-minded and willing to listen with the same perspective. Just hearing all of the energy in the McKale Center was uplifting in itself, even to those who watched the event on the television.

The goal of his speech was to persuade Americans to become more united and bipartisan as a country. Obama says this explicitly, versus his implicit goal of the need the country has of toning down the political environment. This is a lesson many walked away from the situation with. Politics isn't worth getting extremely riled up about or hateful towards regardless of political affiliation. Some took this opportunity to say, "I told you so", but that isn't the right thing to do in any situation, especially one of this magnitude. The President did a great job convincing the citizens of the country to be calm for a minute and think about what happened only a few days prior. Since the shootings took place the Saturday before the speech was given, the community was still experiencing the after-shock. Everyone was still watching the news for updates on Giffords and the other victims at University Medical Center, and other hospitals across Tucson. Some people across the country began to place blame on those whom it was easiest to do so. As a politician himself, Obama telling the country to leave politics out of the situation is surprising and refreshing.

A key rhetorical strategy used in his speech is pathos. During the speech Obama states, "I want our democracy to be as good as Christina imagined it. I want America to be as good as she imagined it" (Obama speech). Out of the sadness Americans are feeling for her passing comes a new kind of motivation for the citizens of the United States to do what he says and live up to what Christina's expectations were before she was murdered. It's an awful thing when any innocent member of a community is murdered, but it is especially awful to think of a nine year old girl who was just becoming interested in politics being shot and killed. Helping the audience to see through Christina's eyes is very powerful and it was very persuasive element used by President Obama. He remembers each of the six victims who were killed, as well as the thirteen who managed to live through the horrific attack. In remembering those who passed, he gives specific details about their lives and, in two cases, describes the bravery two men showed (one of which who died) in shielding their wives from bullets. It is incredible to hear true acts of bravery like this, especially when one thinks about what great people they must have been. It's nice to remember those people for their incredible acts of bravery, not just as names on the list of those who were killed. Obama brought closure to the families as well as the rest of America by giving the audience details to understand those people's personalities and who they actually were. This enables Americans to relate to those who were killed. There was also a built-in feeling of unity among all the watchers and listeners of the speech, since everyone was watching it at the same time and felt the same kind of peace all at once during the ceremony.

He also inspired hope in the speech, being the one to announce Gabrielle Giffords had opened her eyes for the first time earlier that day. Hearing this amidst all of the sadness the citizens of the country had been experiencing was an amazing thing. That bit of positive news represented the country moving forward after the tragedy and into a positive light. Most people were watching the news for days prior to the speech, looking for any information that hadn't yet been released. Not much advancement in recovery had been announced; rather negative consequences of the shooting were being revisited over and over again. In order to move on as a country from the shooting, everyone needed to get out of that rut of negativity. Nobody was one hundred percent healed after

14.10

the speech, but it felt as if the whole country was moving forward together as Obama spoke in the McKale Center. This contributed to his overall persuasiveness, as this was a new feeling altogether for Americans.

Logos is another key rhetorical strategy used in the speech to persuade the audience. Obama said it's not intelligent to blame others for what has happened, or for anything on the same level of this awful event. Yes Republicans do want the right to bear arms more so than Democrats, but it's not fair to pin an awful situation like this on members of the any party. Even though Sarah Palin may have had crosshairs over Giffords' county on a map of the United States, it's not appropriate to say she is the reason behind the gruesome shooting. No Republicans who have spoken against Giffords in the past actually wanted her to be killed. Jared Loughner is a mad man and nobody will really understand what was going through his head when he walked into that Safeway. As the president said, "None of us can know exactly what triggered this vicious attack. None of us can know with any certainty what might have stopped these shots from being fired, or what thoughts lurked in the inner recesses of a violent man's mind" (Obama speech). In saying this, he is persuading the people of the country to accept what has happened and move on in a positive way, instead of holding onto all the anger some may feel and directing it at a specific group of people, no matter who that group may be.

Ethos can easily be applied to many parts of the speech, however it doesn't seem to be a primary goal of President Obama's in this specific salutation. It seems as though pathos and logos are much more important in the construction of the speech, and also contributed more to his persuasiveness in general. He certainly wants the country to listen to him and respect what he has to say but he didn't go into the speech looking for another opportunity to gain credibility. The speech was a memorial service, it was not by any means meant to win over any more supporters for him. He's already established himself as the President and since this wasn't a time for politics, as he said, most Republicans were listening just as intently as Democrats. Republicans, or any non-supporters of Obama, didn't need a reason to respect what he was saying. All anyone needed was closure for what had happened. Along with closure everyone needed hope, which as was previously mentioned, came also. In this case, hope is just as necessary in moving forward as closure is.

Through his usage of pathos and logos in his speech, President Obama has convinced Americans to come together as one and create a more peaceful political atmosphere in memory of those who were killed on January 8, 2011 in the violent Safeway shooting. Not many speakers are successful in persuading their audience of anything as well as Obama did in his memorial speech, but this was a time when the country needed it the most. Nobody expected to be completely healed from the tragedy by Obama, but he did an excellent job of giving the audience a sense of peace both while watching the memorial service, and as a lasting effect afterwards all without bringing politics into it. Dirty politics only harm the country and it's citizens, as well as politicians themselves. Everyone needs to think a little bit more about what they're actually saying when politically bashing or debating with others, and we all need to realize that some things are greater than politics.

Works Cited

Obama, Barack. "Together We Thrive: Tucson and America". The University of Arizona, McKale Center, Tucson. 12 Jan. 2011. Address.

14.11 The Battle over Senate Bill 1309

Controversy Analysis by Sarah Klopatek

Sex education has been a highly controversial issue for decades, but a recent bill has once again brought sex education to the spotlight. Senate Bill 1309 "requires school districts that offer sex education curricula to establish policies that prohibit a school from providing sex education instruction to a pupil unless the pupil's parent provides written permission for the child to participate in the sex education curricula" (Senate Bill 1309). This greatly controversial bill has polarized Arizona citizens. Generally speaking, the supporters of this bill are Republican State representatives, conservative parental rights groups, and right wing political scholars. These citizens hold the belief that an adolescent's education and medical treatments should be approved by the parent without exception, especially when it pertains to matters of a sexual nature. The opposition, including medical officials and liberal nonprofit organizations, believe that all adolescents should have knowledge of sexual education and be able to confidentially seek medical testing without parental consent. While proponents believe this bill helps families control what their children learn and helps deter young people from sexual activity, opponents of the bill believe it strips the young public of the knowledge they need to protect themselves from an inescapable sexual environment.

Senate Bill 1309 was signed into Arizona law by Governor Jan Brewer on May 10, 2010. There are several specific sections of the bill that have drawn a great deal of attention and are the origins for the controversies. The first major controversy that needs to be addressed is section two of the bill. This section mandates that an individual under the age of 18 must have parental consent before participating in any sexual education course (Senate Bill 1309). The second major controversial part of the bill is section three and states that adolescents can no longer seek medical treatment from any medical professional without the consent of a parent or guardian (Senate Bill 1309). This section of the bill is so controversial because it takes away a lot of medical privacy away from young adults, including confidential sexually transmitted infection testing. Although this bill has been passed into law, it is still highly debated. One such group that shows continuous support for the bill, now law, is the Center for Arizona Policy.

The Center for Arizona Policy is a research group who propositions to protect and preserve family rights. The organization views the Senate Bill 1309 as a piece of, "Critical legislation that protects and guarantees parental rights" (Arizona Policy). The bill grants far more power to parents then has even been instituted before by allowing parents, and not school administration, to control their children's education. For example, if a parent wishes to only teach their child abstinent and a school system has an all-inclusive sexual education program, then a parent can now void their child from going to this class. Deborah Sheasby a speaker on behalf of the Center for Arizona Policy says, "Parents have a constitutional right to direct the education and upbringing of their children" (Sheasby qtd. in Innes). This statement reveals Deborah's and the organization's belief that a parent is the most important educator and mentor in a child's life who's teachings will deter their child from any wrong doing. This is why this organization fought vigorously for this bill to become a law, because they saw an opportunity and need to strengthen the family unit. But not all parents believe this bill has positive impact on Arizona teens. Members of the Arizona Parent Teacher Organization voted against the bill because they believe it created unnecessary government regulations that burdened parents and violates student's rights to privacy (Fehr-Snyder 2). This polarization between parents shows how controversial this bill really is.

However, parents are not the only ones debating this issue: many others including scholars who focus in the fields of sexual health have debated this topic. In the book *Sexual Ethics*, Robert Michels addresses the issues of sexual education in the public school system by assuming the position that sex is a serious and sensitive topic that should be restrained to the home environment. Michels believes that sex education should not be taught by teachers or even doctors in the classroom. He believes that if educators other than parents teach students about sex then children, upon learning about the subject, would want to explore and engage in sexual acts. Michels metaphorically equated this desire for sex to children in a pastry shop. One cannot teach a child where the pastry shop is and what they sell, and not expect them to wander into the shop and buy something. Michels declares that in order to prevent kids from entering the pastry shop, or having sex, they must never know it exists (18). Therefore, parents can only keep their children safe from the pastry shop or sexual education when the subject is out of hands of the teachers. But not all scholars agree with Micheals. Lisa Frick, editor of *Teen Pregnancy and Parenting*, compiles numerous amounts of documents that address the issues associated with preventing adolescents from sex education. She states in her forward that ignorance is not a state of bliss when it comes to sexual education, and children need to know the truth (Frick 5). She strengthens this argument by providing research that showed how a child's rate of contracting an STI and or becoming pregnant was greatly reduced if he or she was educated about sex before initial intercourse.

Organizations that have found similar findings to the research in Frick's book include the Arizona Academy of Family Physicians, Planned Parenthood of Arizona, and Arizona Medical Association. These groups are unanimously against SB 1309. Planned Parenthood of Arizona reveals that SB 1309 only seeks to limit a minor's access to preventive health care and information that was previously available to them. They argue that even though a child should discuss medical choices with parents and or guardians, there shouldn't be a law that mandates parent child communications. Planned Parenthood of Arizona in detail describes how this bill puts teenagers in jeopardy. "This bill would make Arizona the only state in the nation to prevent minors under the age of 18 from confidentially accessing STI testing and treatment" (Planned Parenthood). Since, this bill has been signed into law teenagers can no longer screen or obtain a cure for STI's confidentially, greatly worrying Planned Parenthood. Statistics show that in the year 2009 Arizona had the third highest teen pregnancy rate in the nation and 25% of Arizona's sexual active teenagers currently have an STI (Planned Parenthood). With this already startling statistic Planned Parenthood and many other organizations believe that with the new bill in effect, these rates will only rise. This is because they assume that teenagers will be less willing to seek medical help due to the needed parental consent. Overall the opposition argues that Senate Bill 1309 gives parents more rights, but consequently puts teenagers at risk.

Members of Planned Parenthood are not the only ones concerned about the medical risks concerned with this bill, Dr. Michelle McDonald, the chief medical officer for the Pima County Health Department worries that sexual education classes will dwindle now that a parental signature is required. In an interview with the Arizona Daily Star she states, "Children lose the notes, and they never make it home or the parents are busy, and they forget to sign the notes on time. Even if they meant to give permission, half of them are not going to get it in on time" (McDonald qtd. in Kerry). Like Planned Parenthood, McDonald worries that the already high teen pregnancy rates and STI rates, including congenital s syphilis, will rise. Dr. McDonald and many other health care providers believe that education is among the most potent tools for fighting these grim diseases. She believes that SB 1309 goes in exactly the wrong direction. Although she agrees that establishing communication between parents and children is crucial, the bill doesn't accomplish this efficiently or properly (Kerry). Although Dr. McDonald does not stand alone on her opposition for the bill there are obvious politicians that viewed this bill as a way to control birthrates and STI's in Arizona. These politicians feel that by keeping enticing information about sex away from children then the likelihood of these children becoming pregnant or contracting an STI will be very small. Republican Chuck Barry, the Senate Majority Leader for the State of Arizona propositioned the bill and Governor Jan Brewer signed it. They worked together on this bill because they believe it was the right and safe thing to do for Arizona pupils. They believed that by creating a parental bill of rights they would strengthen families and keep young people out of harms way.

14.11

The controversial Senate Bill 1309 mandates that all health issues, including sexual health, must be approved by the parents before their children may come into contact with this information, leaving Arizona citizens polarized. One question that needs to be asked is should parents or school systems dictate issues involving sexual health? Do parents always have their children's best intentions of minds? Many parents are not involved with their child's education, and if this is so, then why should they be allowed to be dictating their child's sexual education courses? Another concern that needs to be addressed is whether the rates of STI's will decrease or increase with this new law? All of these questions are what drives the debate of sexual education and sexual health in the state of Arizona. Although the bill has been signed into law, the controversies surrounding it have yet to be extinguished and the battle over sexual education will live on.

Works Cited

Center for Arizona Policy. Center for Arizona Policy, 2010. Web. 15 Oct. 2010.

Fehr-Snyder, Kerry. "Sex Education in Arizona Varies Widely by District." az-central.com. *The Arizona Republic*, 11 Apr. 2010. Web. 15 Oct. 2010.

Frick, Lisa, ed. *Teenage Pregnancy and Parenting*. Detroit: Greenhaven, 2007. Print.

Innes, Stephanie. "Schools Must Get Permission from Parents to Teach Sex Education." *Arizona Daily Star*. Arizona Daily Star, 27 Jul. 2010. Web. 15 Oct. 2010.

Michels, Robert. *Sexual Ethics: A Study of Borderland Questions*. New Brunswick: Transaction, 2002. Print.

"SB 1309/SCR 1048–Minors' Privacy Fact Sheet." *Planned Parenthood Advocates of Arizona*. Planned Parenthood Advocates of Arizona, 2010. Web. 15, Oct. 2010.

Arizona State Senate. "SB 1309: Arizona Citizenship." *Arizona State Legislature*. Arizona State Legislature, 2010. Web. 15, Oct. 2010.

14.12 How to Survive in Our Inflated Economy

Public Argument by Ruiwen Yang

The rapid growth of the Chinese economy for three decades has become an unbeatable legend, and it continues, making more and more new records. After the financial crisis in 2008, the whole world, especially the West, has been suffering with the pain of a slow and long economic recovery. However, China, which still keeps its high speed growth at the rate the Chinese government plans, is expected to be the main engine of the world economy. Shall we take great pride in these magic achievements and even eulogize Chinese socialism? The Great Wall is definitely a great miracle of human accomplishment, but was only achieved through the sacrifice of millions of lives and countless stores of national revenue. The Chinese government has been constructing the Great Wall of Economy for decades to protect Chinese corporations, mainly state-owned, and aims to maintain its rapid development. The complexity of the economy determines that no one can guarantee protectionism is beneficial to the future of China, but it surely sacrifices more than one billion Chinese citizens. Although economic protectionism may seem to be helpful in maintaining the stability and competitiveness of the Chinese economy, the appreciation of its currency yuan will benefit most Chinese families eventually, because it will change the current situation in which money flows from families to corporations and will prevent more serious inflation and assets bubbles.

While the Consumer Price Index (CPI) given by the National Bureau of Statistics is around the standard line, the current Chinese economy is seriously inflated. Ordinary people probably don't care what CPI, PPI, M0 or M2 mean, but they do care how many goods they can get with their salaries. Whether the Chinese economy is seriously inflated does not depend on the numbers given by some government officers, but on the actual feelings of Chinese families. An old woman talked about the feeling of inflation when asked by a journalist, "I become so nervous every time when I hear the word 'CPI' on TV, because groceries will be more expensive after that." According to the Chinese ministry of Commerce, the prices of vegetables have raised by 64.2% compared with the same period last year. We all know the government wouldn't allow the number to be higher. Cotton is crazier. On September 1st 2010, the price of standard cotton per ton was 18002 yuan, and it reached 31281 yuan in November 2010. That is a total 73.8% increase in only two months. What about the income of Chinese families? The annual income of urban citizens had only increased by about 10% in 2009. If counted by the current price of the Red Fuji, one kind of Chinese favorite apples, the average monthly income can only afford 200 apples. It is hard to imagine the lives of people who are below the average. Serious inflation, products becoming more and more expensive, is the current situation of the Chinese economy. Why does the money in our pockets become cheaper and cheaper? It is due to the over issued money, also known as economic protectionism.

Over issued yuan not only pushes up the prices of goods but also widens the gap between the rich and the poor. Cheap yuan makes Made-in-China products more competitive in the international trade market, because undervalued yuan lowers the prices of Chinese goods. In addition, cheaper yuan makes imported products more expensive in the domestic market. Overall, Chinese corporations, mainly state-owned, are protected by the undervalued currency. In order to keep the yuan undervalued, the Central Bank of China has been over issuing massive amounts of money, which causes the inflation of Chinese economy. The reason is that the money does not equally spread out to everyone's hands, but rather through loans, which only benefit the corporations and the rich again.

Once the over issued money goes to businessmen's hands, they will only invest it in places where they can maximize their profits without considering any social consequences. The common way of Chinese businessmen is to purchase huge amounts of a certain product to push up its price, and then sell them for large profits. It is very dangerous when they manipulate the prices of groceries. Consequently, normal families need to pay more for the same products, and the extra money flows to the pockets of the rich. So, rich people become richer and the poor become poorer.

Protecting corporations is not the whole reason why the Chinese government over issues money. Everyone is for himself, including the Chinese officers. When the government needs to spend money, they use taxes, bonds and the money gained from loaning and selling lands. If the government wants to spend more money than what they have, they will just print cash, which is simple and effective. The government officers are also richer and richer. That is why China, as a developing country, has become the second largest market of luxuries. Under the current institution, it is very difficult for the government to control itself. Now, Chinese families fight with economic inflation on their own by purchasing products with potential value as houses, gold, etc. to prevent their money becoming paper. However, what people are doing is just pushing up the prices again, and the inflation becomes more serious. When the economic bubble cannot inflate any more and bursts, people's assets will melt like ice cream. What else can people do to maintain the value of their money?

The solution to this issue is to raise the value of the yuan and promote domestic consumption. Since the current economic inflation is due to the over issued and undervalued yuan, appreciation could mend the current crisis. Increasing the value of yuan will make Chinese goods less competitive abroad but promote the domestic consumption. Fewer profits will force export-oriented companies to focus more on the domestic market, and more products lower the prices for Chinese families. In addition, fewer foreign currencies flowing to China will slow down the speed of issuing yuan because of the Chinese currency policy. Nouriel Roubini, chairman of Roubini Global Economics and also professor of economics at New York University, argued about the risks of Chines model of growth, saying that it has "to be changed into more reliance on domestic consumption". The model he mentioned is that the current growth of Chinese economy is mostly relying upon exports. In fact, the Chinese government has been realizing the seriousness of the issue and shifting its economy from an export-oriented to a consumption-driven growth pattern. The value of yuan has been appreciated for a total of 1.8% in recent months. As a result, the Chinese economy grew 9.6 percent in the third quarter of this year according to the National Bureau of Statistics, "the growth has been largely spurred by domestic consumption instead of foreign markets," said by Lan Xinzhen in the article "Changing the Economic Course".

Back to the question, "how to survive in our inflated economy", no one can accomplish this demanding task if he is on his own or pinning his hopes on the government. We need to gather our strength to fight againt the inflated economy. The primary thing we need to prevent is helping blow up the economic balloons, by stopping throwing money to so-called potential investment as real estate, gold, etc. The economic bubble will hurt the last group of people who are blowing it when it bursts, and no one knows when it is going to reach its limitation. In addition, we need to try our best to push the Chinese government to raise the value of yuan and cut taxes. Tax reduction not only helps increase the income of Chinese families, but also forces the government to reduce its unnecessary fiscal spending.

Works Cited

"328 Index of Cotton Prices in China." *Ifeng.com*. Phoenix, 2010. Web. 25 Nov. 2010

China Department of Commerce. "National Trends for the Retail Price of Rice: Yuan/Kilogram." *Commercial Information Forecast*. Chinese Department of Commerce, 2010. Web. 28 Nov. 2010.

Li, Yanping. "China Should Increase Currency Flexibility, Zhou Qiren Says." Ed. Jim McDonald. *Bloomberg*. Bloomberg. 25 Apr. 2010. Web. 18 Oct. 2010.

Lan, Xinzhen. "Changing the Economic Course." *Beijing Review* 53.43 (2010): 29. *Academic Search Complete*. Web. 18 Oct. 2010.

Mankiw, Gregory N. "It's No Time for Protectionism." *New York Times*. New York Times, 8 Feb. 2009. Web. 18 Oct. 2010.

Morrision, Wayne M. and Marc Labonte. "China's Currency: An Analysis of the Economic Issues." *Congressional Research Service*. John D. Dingell. 13 Jul. 2010. Web. 14 Oct. 2010.

Oprita, Antonia. "Roubini: Asset Bubble Is Beginning Now." *CNBC*. CNBC LLC., 27 Jan. 2010. Web. 19 Oct. 2010.

Roach, Stephen S. "Cultivating the Chinese Consumer." *New York Times*. New York Times, 29 Sep. 2010. Web. 18 Oct. 2010.

Stein, Peter. "Yuan Revaluation for China's Own Sake." *wsj.com*. The Wall Street Journal, 2 Oct. 2010. Web. 17 Oct. 2010.

14.13 Letter to President Obama

Public Argument by Laken Shay Anway

Dear President Obama:

My name is Laken Shay Anway and I'm writing about an issue that is very important to me: the right of gay couples to get married. I know you're a very busy man, so I will try to make this as brief as possible. I have been researching all the aspects on this controversy and found that our country has a contradictory problem: it offers equality, yet it doesn't allow every couple to get married. I understand the many different reasons people oppose such a union and I also know there can be a solution with a little help from a trustworthy authority figure. I've found that some of the major reasons people oppose same-sex marriage are: their feelings of discomfort, the effects it would have on the already stressful economy, their personal religion or beliefs, and the loss of a traditional family. While I understand where each of these groups of people are coming from, I think you and I both know that with every problem, there's a possible solution. Throughout this letter, I will propose to you my various ideas for solutions on this topic. I know, with these and many other solutions, we can finally achieve true equality in these United States.

It has come to my attention that some people feel uncomfortable about gay couples having the to get married because it's something different from what they're used to. Like San Francisco's mayor, Gavin Newsom, so rightly pointed out in a 2009 article in NPR: gay marriage right now is similar "…to the fight for equality for African-Americans." People opposed African-American equality because it was something they weren't used to yet and that frightened them. Eventually these people realized that the difference in skin color didn't matter by slowly getting used to the idea and listening to a very powerful, persuasive speaker. I think that's exactly what we need to do for gay couples. People are uncomfortable with this new idea now because many advocates just try to shove their views into others' lives. If we could slowly get them used to the idea through powerful speeches, they will develop a comfort for it. Once these people develop a comfort for it, the amount of people who vote "yes" to legalize gay marriage will rise tremendously.

Other people in our country feel that it may have even more of a negative affect on our struggling economy. In 2009 CNN article titled, "Economy Enters Same-sex Marriage Debate," a member of the conservative Minnesota Family Council, Tom Pritchard, shows his opinion on allowing gay couples to get married and how it would "…dilute the currency—the value of marriage…" His feelings are that allowing more marriages would call for more divorces. However, what Pritchard fails to think about, is that maybe allowing these marriages would in fact boost our economy. In a study done by the Williams Institute, also known as UCLA's School of Law, researchers found that "extending marriage to same sex couples in Vermont would boost its economy by over

$30 million in three years." By allowing something as simple as same-sex marriage, they would increase the amount of people that would want to come to their state, even if it was just to visit.

Also, with the amount of weddings parading into all their churches, many jobs and money opportunities will start to open up again. These couples are going to spend tons of money and use tons of services to be united to the one they love. All this money they're spending can only help the economy, not hurt it. Introducing our country to statistics such as the one above would help assure them that same-sex marriage will only help our economy. I feel that if the people could be shown these facts by someone they trust as an intelligent, powerful authority figure, such as you, they would feel differently about same-sex marriage and our economy. Again it all comes back to easing the difficult idea in slowly by a powerful, persuasive speaker. I know our country can achieve true equality with a little push, and showing statistics of the good in gay marriage definitely helps.

A very common reason citizens don't want to see gay couples get married is because of their religion or personal beliefs. The vice president for public policy and research at the Ethics and Religious Liberty Commission, Dr. Barrett Duke tells *Newsweek* in a late 2008 article that "…the Bible is unequivocal in its teaching that homosexual behavior is sinful." However, it does not specifically state anywhere in the bible that same-sex marriage is sinful. The Bible discusses marriage in the beginning of time between a man and a woman to reproduce to create more human life. In our country today, there is an overwhelming amount of children who don't even have homes or a family to go home to. So, while reproduction is still important, not everybody has to reproduce when they find love. The group of religious people who say gay marriage goes against the bible need to be reminded that the bible is very obvious in its teaching that nobody should ever be discriminated against.

I understand that it's not easy to believe in something that's been preached as sinful for so long, but it's the only way to achieve true equality. People believed that African Americans should not have freedom because they were brought up to believe that it just wasn't right. In that same way, it was thought to be wrong for women to be equal to men. What everyone realized was that even though it's what they were brought up to believe in, that doesn't always make it right. Imagine where our country would be right now if we never granted equality to any minority group. It wouldn't be the same place in any way. If people were reminded of how ridiculous it sounds that these groups of people didn't have equal rights at one time, they might start to realize that gay couples deserve equal rights too.

Many other citizens in our country are afraid to give gay couples the right to get married because they don't want to lose the idea of a traditional family. In a 2009 *Newsweek* article titled "Less Shouting, More Talking," President at Fuller Theological Seminary, Richard Mouw shows that he "…subscribe[s] to

14.13

the 'traditional' definition of a marriage, and [he] do[es] not want to see the definition changed," but what is the true definition of marriage? According to the Wikipedia article entitiled "Marriage" the definition of marriage is a social, religious, spiritual, or legal union of individuals. Nowhere in the definition of marriage does it say that it has to be between a man and woman. For those people who complain about losing a "traditional" family, we need to remind them that the families they are talking about never used to be considered a "traditional" family at all.

As many people remember, there was a time when a "traditional" family was considered to be when a man goes to work and a woman stays home, cleans everything, and cooks the meals. Before, it was a white man who went out to work and a white woman that stayed home to cook and clean. Eventually, people realized that any race could have a "traditional" family and later that women could go to college and get a job while the man stayed at home. With home many times the definition of a traditional family has been changed throughout the years, why does it matter if it's changed once more, again for the sake of equality. Everyone should have equal rights, even if this includes allowing something that may be uncomfortable at first. Our country has come so far since the civil rights movement and the women's rights movement, but we still haven't achieved true equality. I believe that convincing these people that this change will be good can help us achieve that equality.

Our country has done many amazing things to provide the best possible life for its citizens and I think it's time we added one more to the list. All the people who care about this country will take the time to listen to a powerful speaker if they are just given the chance. They need to hear the facts that I have pointed out from someone they trust and every single speech you give makes a huge difference to these people. I know you care about this country and what comes of it and I know that this could be the action that our country needs to gain a little bit of faith again. Gay couples should be allowed the same rights to marry as everyone else and that's never going to change I hope you really take the time to consider my possible solutions as they are very important to me and to the future of our country. Thank you so much for your time and for reading this letter.

Sincerely,
Laken Shay Anway

14.14 A Catalyzed Reaction

Reflective Essay by Jessica Annette Stier

In terms of biology, an enzyme is a molecule known to catalyze a reaction, to initiate a starting point and lead a chain of reactions for the purpose of achieving its main goal: creating both a functional and beneficial end product. Having Biology set as my major, I suppose that I approach the task of thinking through the lens of science. While selecting my courses during Freshmen Orientation, it was obvious to me that I would be required to take classes such as Biology and Microbiology, to Chemistry and Organic Chemistry, throughout my years in university. Although, what was not very clear was the reason why I was also obligated to take other courses, such as philosophy, statistics, English, and unusual classes that went by the names of "INDVs" and "TRADs." At the time, these courses seemed irrelevant to both my major *and* my future as an individual. If I was going to become a nutritionist someday, then why did I need to learn about different cultures and societies that existed centuries ago? Why was it necessary for me to take an English class if I already knew how to write an essay? But, what was not very apparent to me a few months ago, is now in plain sight—in order for us to develop into distinctive, well-rounded individuals, we need a sturdy foundation point from which we can move forward.

In "biology lingo," an enzyme's ability to phosphorylate, or, "add a phosphate to," means they are capable of a transformation change, and in addition to the enzyme's new shape, comes a new function. In the few months of attending this seminar, I have learned a considerable amount. In the studio session Droodle activity and my grammar presentation, I have been made conscious of my writing techniques. With my receptiveness for constructive criticism, in both my peer reviews and graded essays, I have finally found what works well, and does not work well for me in my writing. This class has transformed me into a genuine university student, and avid writer.

Throughout the essays assigned in this course, I have been particularly goal-minded in writing professionally through the use of a stronger and more effective diction. I aimed, and still aim, to write as a college student, rather than how I would have previously as a high school student. The essay assignments inspired me to learn new words so that I could apply them in my essays and daily speech. I have always been determined to broaden my vocabulary, but what encouraged it especially this semester was the fact that I was now writing for a more professional audience. In my first essay, *Like an Instruction Manual*, I found myself continually on the lookout for any mundane verbiage that I could replace for a more complex and ornate phrasing. I sought to stand out—I was not a fan of large lecture halls and the monotony that seemed to pair with it. The small number of students in this class allowed for me to demonstrate my individuality among them.

In the beginning of the semester, I was made aware of the impact of making a strong argument. If the thesis, or, what you are arguing for, is the basis behind the essay, then your beliefs need to be made clear. It is necessary to elucidate your reader, and explain any source of confusion. In the studio session droodle activity, we were told to specify every aspect of the image we chose. I had chosen the envelope. It was an envelope (opposed to a house) because of the line descending from the top of the square, and the triangle formation above it. The line was the natural paper fold of an envelope, and the triangle was the cover flap. In specifying every characteristic presented in the image, you proved to the class that the object was what you said it was to be. In addressing the possible questions beforehand, you erase any doubt within the reader. This activity was helpful when outlining my essays, because I knew to explain any of the potential causes for confusion in my audience, prior to writing the essay. This improved my capability of creating and defending effective theses.

I am certainly proud of the grades I achieved in this course, and I am pleased to mention the positive effect it had on other classes. In the MCB181 lab, we are required to formulate hypotheses and state how we came to our assumptions. Because the nature of science is to question an experiment and disprove the results, it is crucial to point out every feature entailed in the experimentation. After taking part in the droodle activity, writing up an experiment's conclusion came easy to me. My professor no longer drew triple question marks over my labs because I had discussed every detail in my experiments, from listing the materials used to mentioning what my expectations were.

In result of this course, I can affably say that I have mastered one specific skill: the proper use of contractions. My grammar presentation on formality and contractions has showed me the importance of formality in writing, especially university-level writing. In my TRAD103 course, we were assigned to write an eight-page paper on a novel we read. Although I was handed back a score of ninety-two percent with the words, "excellent!" and "very professional" on the cover page, I was disappointed to see circles surrounding my contractions. My excessive use of apostrophes exhibited my inexperience with college-level writing, although my essay as a whole displayed proficiency in other elements. When I looked over the graded and reviewed drafts for this course, I realized that Mrs. Burstrem had also circled my contractions. Although, when I was handed back my rough drafts, I never understood why. I never saw the importance of splitting a, "didn't" into a "did not." In my second essay, *Risky First Impressions*, I finally wrote an essay devoid of contractions.

What troubles me now, is the questioning of what my essay scores *could* have been without my use of contractions. Could my ninety-two percent possibly have been raised higher if it were not clouded with noticeable contractions? Could the A- on my second essay have been bumped up to an A? If only I had been assigned to present my Powerpoint in the very beginning of the semester! If only I had known the significance of formality in writing through the proper use of contractions. But, thankfully, my grammar presentation was just in time for my second paper in the TRAD103 course, a paper that I am proud to say, was submitted contraction-free. This already proves the usefulness of the project and research behind it. If I could repeat this semester, I would surely remove this irritating attribute of my writing. But, now I know, for the future, my writing will require the usage of less apostrophes. Formality holds a special place in writing, from university essays, to job applications, to even an e-mail with a professor. Formal writing proves to others of the knowledge and expertise a person holds, and as a student attending the University of Arizona, this is something I strive for.

14.14

In the few months between August and December, I have learned a great deal from taking this course. In attending the lectures and studio sessions, writing these essays, and progressing as a writer, this course was indeed, the strong foundation and starting point to my growth as a university student—it is the enzyme that catalyzed a reaction in me, and the reason behind my transformation into a dynamic, ambitious human being.

14.14

Writing Tutors

The University of Arizona offers many resources where students can receive extra help with their writing. Some are open to all students and are free of charge; others are restricted and charge a fee. The following descriptions will help you find the center that is right for you.

The Writing Center at the Think Tank

All writers benefit from extra readers. You can find such readers in the Think Tank's Writing Center, which is administered by instructors who teach in the Writing Program. It is open to all University of Arizona students at no cost. The Writing Center is neither a remedial writing program nor an editing service. It is a place to talk about ideas and get feedback and guidance from peers. Specially trained peer consultants who are experienced writers with majors from across the curriculum can help you at any stage of your writing process: confronting your recurrent fear of a blank screen, interpreting an assignment, brainstorming ideas, organizing notes to write a first draft, explicating your instructor's comments, generating a revision plan, or editing a final draft. They can also help with writing tasks, such as lab reports, applications, and personal writing.

You can sign up for half-hour appointments by calling (520) 626-0530. You can also drop in without an appointment, although this kind of tutoring comes on a first-come, first-serve basis and can get busy during peak times of the school year. Think Tank tutoring is available from 1:00 p.m. to 9:00 p.m. Monday through Thursday, from 1:00 p.m. to 5:00 p.m. on Fridays, and from 5:00 p.m. to 9:00 p.m. on Sundays. The Think Tank is located in the Robert L. Nugent Building, as well as two other locations in the Park Student Union and the Student Recreation Center. Open hours may vary depending on the location, so check the website before you go. Read more about the Writing Center and get information about online tutoring at <http://thinktank.arizona.edu/programs/thinktank/services/writing>. Speak to your instructor or call 626-0530 for details about exact consultation times and the specific location.

Writing Skills Improvement Program (WSIP)

The Writing Skills Improvement Program was established over twenty years ago to assist minority and economically-disadvantaged students to improve their writing skills and achieve academic success at the University of Arizona. Eligible students can register directly at the WSIP office at 1201 E. Helen Street. A personal tutor will work with each student for the entire semester as needed at no cost. The WSIP also serves the academic community at large by offering a free series of Weekly Writing, General Education Writing, and Graduate Writing Workshops. The Weekly Writing Workshop is especially valuable to all students taking composition classes and covers many aspects of academic writing. The program offers a number of services to their target population, as well as to any student who desires to improve his/her writing skills on a space-available basis (preferably referred by a writing instructor). For more information visit the WSIP at 1201 East Helen Street, access their website at <http://web.arizona.edu/~wsip/>, or call (520) 621-5849.

Strategic Alternative Learning Techniques (SALT) Center

The Strategic Alternative Learning Techniques (SALT) Center offers enhanced services for students with learning disabilities and attention deficit disorders. One of the only programs of its type in the nation, it provides students who qualify with individualized academic support, learning and career workshops, tutoring in writing and a variety of other subjects, and a computer lab. Students must apply to the program through a separate application. A limited number of scholarships are available. For more information about fees and scholarships, contact SALT at (520) 621-1242 or visit their website at <http://www.salt.arizona.edu/>. The SALT center is located at 1010 N. Highland Ave.

Campus Resources and Internet Addresses

Campus Resources			
Arizona State Museum	1013 E. University Blvd.	621-6302	http://www.statemuseum.arizona.edu
Campus Health Service	1224 E. Lowell Street	621-6490	http://www.health.arizona.edu
Center for Creative Photography	1030 N. Olive Road	621-7968	http://www.creativephotography.org
Center for Exploratory Students	Old Main, 2nd Floor	621-7763	https://admissions.arizona.edu/colleges/center_for_exploratory_students/
Dean of Students	Old Main 203	621-7057	http://deanofstudents.arizona.edu
Disability Resource Center	1224 E. Lowell Street	621-3268 (V/TTY)	http://drc.arizona.edu
English Department	Modern Languages 445	621-1836	http://english.arizona.edu/
Multicultural Affairs and Student Success	Old Main, Level One	621-1094	http://mass.arizona.edu/
Museum of Art	1031 N. Olive Road	621-7567	http://artmuseum.arizona.edu
Oasis Program for Sexual Assault and Relationship Violence	Highland Commons 1224 E. Lowell St.	626-2051	http://www.health.arizona.edu/webfiles/hpps_oasis_program_about_us.htm
Office for International Student Programs and Services	915 N. Tyndall Ave.	621-4627	http://internationalstudents.arizona.edu/

Campus Resources (continued)

Strategic Alternative Learning Techniques (SALT)	1010 N. Highland Ave.	621-1242	http://www.salt.arizona.edu
The Think Tank at the Student Academic Learning Center	Robert L. Nugent Building & Park Student Union	626-0530	http://thinktank.arizona.edu/
University of Arizona Main Library Information Desk	1510 E. University Blvd.	621-6406	http://www.library.arizona.edu
University of Arizona Poetry Center	1508 E. Helen St.	626-3765	http://poetry.arizona.edu
Veterans' Affairs	Modern Languages 347	621-9501	http://registrar.arizona.edu/vets/
Writing Center (part of the Think Tank)	Robert L. Nugent Building & Park Student Union	626-0530	http://thinktank.arizona.edu/ services/writing
Writing Program	Modern Languages 380	621-3553	http://english.arizona.edu/index_ site.php?id=36
Writing Skills Improvement Program	1201 E. Helen St.	621-5849	http://web.arizona.edu/~wsip

Important Internet Addresses for First-Year Writing

Computer Centers on Campus	http://www.oscr.arizona.edu/labs/instructional/index. html
Purdue University Online Writing Lab (OWL)	http://owl.english.purdue.edu
University of North Carolina at Chapel Hill Writing Center Handouts	http://www.unc.edu/depts/wcweb/handouts
University of Arizona Home Page	http://www.arizona.edu
UA Student Policies and Codes includes: Code of Academic Integrity Code of Conduct Disciplinary Procedures	http://deanofstudents.arizona.edu/policiesandcodes
UA Libraries	http://www.library.arizona.edu

Computing Centers and Resources on Campus

There are multiple free computer labs available for students to use across campus. All of these computer labs are free, are open to University of Arizona students, and provide access to PC and Mac computers. The following labs have open access to all students. Take your university ID and a storage device (disks, flash drives, and so on) to store your information. Call the labs for hours or check the schedule at <http://www.oscr.arizona.edu/locations/hours>.

Open Access Computer Labs on Campus	
Campus Rec	621-6727
Electrical and Computer Engineering (ECE) Room 229	621-8534
Engineering 318	621-6206
Fine Arts Library Information Commons Music Building, Room 233	621-6441
Information Commons (ILC) Main Library, 1st Floor	621-6441
La Paz Residence Hall S107	626-2434
Nugent 15b	621-6727
Science Engineering Library Information Commons Science Engineering Library, 2nd Floor	621-6441

Other computer labs across campus must be reserved in advance or are open only to students in certain majors. For the most up-to-date listing of computer centers and services on campus, see the Office of Student Computing Resources (OSCR) website at <http://www.uits.arizona.edu/departments/oscr>.

Finding Computer Support on Campus

The Office of Student Computing Resources offers free assistance to students with computer problems, including support using software and help fixing a crashed computer. If you need computer support:

- Call or visit the **24/7 help desk** in the Martin Luther King, Jr. Student Center, Room 207, at (520) 626-TECH (8324).

- 24/7 technical support using **online chat** is also available from the OSCR website.

Other Computer Resources for Students

Gear-to-Go: Multimedia equipment such as digital cameras, video cameras, lighting kits, microphones, and other multimedia gear are available for free checkout through the OSCR Gear-to-Go Center. The Gear-to-Go office is located on the ground floor of the Computer Center, 1077 N. Highland, Room 214C. Call the office at (520) 621-0GTG (0484) or visit the website at <http://www.uits.arizona.edu/departments/oscr/locations/gc>.

Laptop and Projector Loan Services: You can check out laptops and projectors from the UA libraries free of charge. Depending on the equipment, laptops and projectors are available for 4–72 hour lending periods. Checkout locations exist at any of the three main libraries: Main Library (621-6442), Fine Arts Library (621-7009), and Science Engineering Library (621-6384). See < http://www.library.arizona.edu/services/borrowing/Laptops.html> for policies and for more information on checking out a laptop and projector.

ESL Resources

While college-level writing is a new experience for all student writers, writers whose first language is not English face a different set of challenges. Writing an essay in a different language and within a new culture is challenging. Knowing how to use the resources available to you will help you make the most of your experiences in your writing courses, in the U.S. academic community, and even in U.S. society. As an ESL student, you should utilize the help offered by your instructor and the resources noted in Appendices A, B, C, and D. In the sections below you will find advice from ESL instructors, tips from former students, resources available at the university, and some online resources.

Tips from ESL Instructors

"Get to know the people in your class; you will have the opportunity to form friendships with people from all over the world. Take advantage of this because it is a rare and wonderful opportunity."

—Selena Mahoney

"It is important that you pay close attention to the comments your instructor writes on draft(s) of your paper, but remember that instructors normally focus on the large elements of a paper (e.g., the thesis statement, paragraph structure, etc.). It is your responsibility to go beyond those comments, which are only a starting point for revision."

—Estela Ene

"Celebrate your linguistic and cultural diversity by weighing in on classroom discussions and writing about your linguistic and cultural experiences. You bring to the classroom an understanding of the world through at least two distinct perspectives. Share that insight with others and allow it to drive your writing. You will make grammar errors and misuse an idiom or metaphor, but don't let the small errors stop your writing."

–Jacob Witt

Tips from ESL Students

" Read more. Write more. Ask more. "

–Wing See Ng

" Always ask questions. "

–Olubusola Olatoregun

" Discuss with friends what you want to write about. They may provide you with ideas or points you never thought of to use in your essay. "

–Wenyang Tan

" I think that the most important thing for an ESL student to be successful is understanding the requirement of each writing assignment since each country may have different standards for its college students. So to understand what is required in colleges in the U.S. is a key that affects our performance in these writing courses. "

–Yuzhen Huang

Resources for ESL Students

On-Campus Resources

University of Arizona's Global Engagement website:

<http://www.arizona.edu/global-engagement>

The Global Engagement website is a gateway to more detailed information about the University of Arizona's global interactions, including a resources page for international students working at the University of Arizona.

University of Arizona's International Affairs website:

<http://international.arizona.edu/home>

This office serves as the representative and advocate for international students here at the University of Arizona. They can provide information ranging from visas to international programming.

The Center for English as a Second Language (CESL):

<http://www.cesl.arizona.edu>

CESL has served the ESL and international community at the University of Arizona for over thirty years. They offer both Intensive English Programs and programs focused on specific skills like reading, writing, speaking, and listening. While these courses are not offered for UA credit, many students have found CESL courses useful in sharpening their academic English skills.

The Writing Skills Improvement Center:

<http://wsip.web.arizona.edu/>

The Writing Skills Improvement Program was established over twenty years ago to assist minority and economically-disadvantaged students to improve their writing skills and achieve academic success at the University of Arizona. Eligible students can register directly at the WSIP office at 1201 E. Helen Street. A personal tutor will work with each student for the entire semester as needed at no cost. The WSIP also serves the academic community at large by offering a free series of Weekly Writing, General Education Writing, and Graduate Writing Workshops. The Weekly Writing Workshop is especially valuable to all students taking composition classes and covers many aspects of academic writing. The program offers a number of services to their target population, as well as to any student who desires to improve his/her writing skills on a space-available basis (preferably referred by a writing instructor).

The Writing Center at the Think Tank:

<http://thinktank.arizona.edu/services/writing>

All writers benefit from extra readers. You can find such readers in the Think Tank's Writing Center, which is administered by Writing Program instructors. It is open to all University of Arizona students at no cost. The Writing Center is neither a remedial writing program nor an editing service. It is a place to talk about ideas and get feedback and guidance from peers. Specially trained peer consultants who are experienced writers with majors from across the curriculum can help you at any stage of your writing process: confronting your recurrent fear of a blank screen, interpreting an assignment, brainstorming ideas, organizing notes to write a first draft, explicating your instructor's comments, generating a revision plan, or editing a final draft. They can also help with writing tasks, such as lab reports, applications, and personal writing.

Online Resources

Writing:

Purdue Online Writing Lab (OWL):	<http://owl.english.purdue.edu>
U. Wisconsin Writer's Handbook:	<http://writing.wisc.edu/Handbook/>
U. of Kansas Writing Guides:	<http://www.writing.ku.edu/~writing/guides/>
Hacker's Guide Online Resources:	<http://bcs.bedfordstmartins.com/rules6e/Player/pages/Main.aspx>

Grammar:

Internet Grammar of English	<http://www.ucl.ac.uk/internet-grammar>
Dr. Grammar	<http://www.drgrammar.org/frequently-asked-questions>

These sources can help you with writing in general. Remember that you also have the rest of the *Student's Guide*, *Rules for Writers*, your instructor's office hours, and your fellow students as excellent resources to help improve your writing. The writing program at the UA is centered on the process of writing, which includes a lot of peer editing for each paper. Take advantage of these sessions to improve your writing and help your classmates with their writing.

The Essay and Cover Design Contests

For the past 30 years, the Writing Program has held an essay contest for students enrolled in the first-year writing courses. Not only does the contest give instructors the chance to read the year's best essays and students the chance to share their best work, but also prize-winning essays often become samples for future students (as you can see in Part IV of this *Guide*). Even if your essay doesn't win a prize, the editors might ask your permission to print it in the next edition of the *Guide* or on the online *Guide*.

This year's essay contest winners were selected from more than 70 entries. We have reprinted some of the winning students' essays in this edition of the *Guide*, and you can find a list of all the winning essays online at <http://english.arizona.edu/index_site.php?id=588&preview=1>. The *Guide* editors separated the essays by type and then distributed all the essays to the judges to rate the top essay in each category. The judges included experienced writers and instructors familiar with the first-year writing courses.

Entering the contest is easy. Go to the Essay Contest Instructions online at <http://english.arizona.edu/index_site.php?id=585&preview=1> and follow the directions described there to submit your essay via e-mail to the *Guide* Editors. We accept essays year-round and judging happens around the middle of each Spring semester. (This year's deadline is listed online with the instructions.)

Winner of the Annual Cover Design Contest

In addition to the essay contest, the Writing Program also holds an annual cover design contest, and the winning entry is chosen as the cover of this *Guide*. The winner of the contest also creates art for the headings of each chapter and section. We invite students from across the university to participate in the cover art contest, and we allow everyone in the English department to have a vote in selecting the cover. The editors thank all contestants and those who voted in the contest. **This year's winner is Christopher Cassius Kellogg**. Christopher would like to thank David Scott Allen for his help. Our second-place winner is Michelle Wenz.

The Annual Jan Lipartito Historical Remembrance Writing Contest

The Jan Lipartito Historical Remembrance Essay Contest was established in 1998 to honor Jan Lipartito's contributions to the Writing Program and to encourage students to integrate historical research and reflection into their writing. Jan worked as adjunct lecturer and Teaching Advisor in the Writing Program for many years before retiring in 1999. She researched the "public and private" records of World War II and integrated her concern for remembering the Holocaust into her teaching and service work. Each year, the Historical Remembrance Essay Contest award is given to a noteworthy essay that includes historical reflection, personal memoir, or formal historical research. **This year's winner is Rae Anne Marie Martinez, who wrote the essay "Within the Tendrils of Smoke" for Debra Gregerman's course.**

The Hayden-McNeil Difference and Inequality Student Essay Award

The Hayden-McNeil Difference and Inequality Award was established by the University of Arizona Writing Program's Difference and Inequality Committee in 2008. This award recognizes student writing that either explicitly or implicitly brings readers' attention to issues of difference and inequality in the classroom, the individual's experience, the campus, or the world at-large. A candidate's essay should demonstrate an awareness of the D&I Committee's main objectives (described at <http://english.arizona.edu/index_site.php?id=472&preview=1>), even though the essay may not have been written with those objectives specifically in mind. **This year's winner is Christopher R. Ching, who wrote the essay "Bringing Light to Problems Ignored" for Carie Schneider's course.**

Students in all first-year writing courses may enter these contests. Entry forms are online at <http://english.arizona.edu/index_site.php? id=585&preview=1>. Deadlines and entry procedures for the contest are the same as those for the *Student's Guide to First-Year Writing* Essay Contest mentioned previously. All essays are judged on the clarity and originality of the thesis, the persuasiveness with which the thesis is defended, the effectiveness of the organization, and the clarity of expression.

Winners of the Annual First-Year Writing Essay Contest

We also want to thank the talented judges who helped with this year's contest:

Daniel Altenburg, Allison Betts, Natalie Cunningham, Adrienne Crump, Michelle Denham, Tom Do, Pete Figler, Juan Gallegos, Heidi Giles, Janel Goodman, Deb Gregerman, Laura Gronewald, Amy Hickman, Antonnet Johnson, Marissa Juarez, Matthew Kundert, Jessica Lee, Ron Lorette, Emily Lyons, Daylanne Markwardt, Krista Maxwell, Stephanie Merz, Jenna Pack, Jennifer Powlette, Renee Reynolds, Safari Natalie Ross, Marisa Sandoval, Michael Sayle, Jessica Shumake, Carie Schneider, Gina Szabady, Lily Tolhurst, Jenna Vinson, Christine Walsh, Ashley Warren, and Doug Wykstra.

Textual Analysis

First Prize: **Jennie Elizabeth Piccarretta**, "From Line 1 to Death: Exploring the Difference between 'Youth' and 'Deep-Sunken Eyes' in Shakespeare's Sonnet II." Instructor, David Buchalter.

First Prize (Honors): **Nisha Priyanka Talanki**, "Culpability." Instructor, Patrick Baliani.

Contextual Analysis

First Prize: **Michelle Moraila**, "Becoming 'Agent Orange': An Investigation of the Relationship between Colors and the Unconscious." Instructor, Daniel Altenburg.

First Prize (Honors): **Brenton Robert Woodward**, "Joy and Pain: 'Ark' and Spring Storm." Instructor, Patrick Baliani.

Rhetorical Analysis

First Prize: **Wendell Richards**, "George Patton: A 'Real Man'?". Instructor, Jenna Vinson.

Controversy Analysis

First Prize: **Sarah Klopatek**, "The Battle over Senate Bill 1309." Instructor, Jenna Vinson.

Public Argument

First Prize (Honors): **Ruiwen Yang**, "How to Survive in Our Inflated Economy." Instructor, Amy Sams.

Reflective Essay

First Prize: **Jessica Annette Stier**, "A Catalyzed Reaction." Instructor, Jessica Burstrem.

First Prize (Honors): **Hania Alexandra Grosz**, "Independent Identification." Instructor, Patrick Baliani.

Glossary

Academic Writing: Writing that follows discipline-specific style guidelines and genre conventions and incorporates credible research to support arguments and/or observations.

Ad hominem: A logical fallacy meaning "to the man." An *ad hominem* argument attacks an individual's character or behavior rather than focusing on the actual issue at hand.

Adjective: A word that describes a noun. Adjectives include words like studious, critical, helpful, thoughtful, and academic.

Alliteration: The repetition of consonant sounds in a sequence of words. For example, "Peter Piper picked a peck of pickled peppers."

Allusion: An indirect reference, often to a person, event, statement, theme, or work. Allusions enrich meaning through the connotations they carry, or the associations that they evoke in a reader's mind. For example, authors may allude to a historic event by mentioning its name or to a play by Shakespeare by using similar language in their writing.

Analysis: The act of explaining how and why a written or visual text does something and whether or not it does it effectively. Analysis goes a few steps beyond summary/description; as summary/description explains what is happening with a topic, while analysis explains how and why something is happening with the same topic. Analysis is the act of breaking a text into parts and examining how those parts create a message and affect a reader's or viewer's response. Analytical statements reveal a careful consideration of the text beyond just its main point and open up a space for dialogue.

Angle: In visual analysis, the vantage point from which the viewer is seeing into the image. An angle can be high or low and can be exaggerated for a pronounced effect.

Annotation: The process of writing notes and comments about a text. These notes can include first impressions, questions, summaries, associations, strategies used, analysis, and more.

Argument: The overall claim that your essay makes. An essay's argument should be summarized in its thesis statement. Arguments must be debatable, meaning that they must make a claim against which some readers could object.

Assonance: The repetition of identical or similar vowel sounds in a sequence of words, as in "fate" and "cave.".

Atmosphere: The general feeling created for the reader or audience by a work at a given point. Also referred to as mood. The atmosphere of a text can be dreary, peaceful, etc. This is differentiated from tone.

Audience: The person or people who are reading, listening to, or viewing a text. An author targets an intended audience by using strategies that will be particularly effective for that person or people. An audience might be a primary audience (the person for whom the text is generated) or a secondary audience (the person who has an interest in the topic because that person is connected to/ interested in the speaker, the primary audience, or the topic).

Author/Speaker: In a rhetorical situation, the author/speaker is the person or people seeking to communicate a specific message.

Balance: In visual analysis, the "visual weight" of crowded or attention-grabbing items in the image. For example, an image with most of its important focal points on one side of the image could be described as off-balance and weighted to the left.

Blogging: Compiled from the two terms "web" and "logging," blogging refers to personal or reflective writing that is published online. Blogs can have very limited or very broad audiences, and they can cover virtually any area of interest, from sports, fashion, personal experiences, political views, or celebrity gossip.

Causal generalizations: A logical fallacy involving the assumption that a correlation between two events proves that one caused the other.

Cliché: An expression used so often that it has become hackneyed and has lost its original impact. For example, writing "since the beginning of time," and "throughout history" are both clichés.

Close reading: Focusing attention on the aspects of the text that seem most important. Close reading involves first scanning a text to get a basic sense of the text and its purpose. Then you should read more closely for content and meaning, considering how the text is constructed. In addition, you should consider your reactions to the text. How does it affect you emotionally and intellectually? Finally, you should review the text and your responses to form some general conclusions.

Connotations: The associations evoked by a word beyond its literal meaning. For example, the word "water" might commonly evoke thoughts or images of an ocean, a fountain, thirst, or even a water balloon. Connotations can also be unique to a particular individual. For instance, a victim of near-drowning may associate water with terror.

Context: The circumstances surrounding the creation and reception of a text. For example, the personal associations of readers, the biographical backgrounds of writers, related historical events, and political purposes. The best contexts to study are those that illuminate the meanings and uses of the text. The context of a rhetorical situation deeply shapes what a text will mean to its audience.

Contextual analysis: Focuses on a text and its relationship to a larger context, such as the author's biography, the historical or cultural situation surrounding the text, a particular theoretical approach such as feminism or psychoanalysis, the literary tradition to which the work belongs, or a related set of texts.

Contrast: Strong juxtapositions of opposites, such as light and dark, depressing and cheerful, rigid and soft, frantic and calm, etc.

Controversy: A contentious social issue that has a larger relevance for a society of those living within it.

Controversy Analysis: An analytical essay that incorporates research to trace the key arguments made by people who have a stake in an issue. Controversy analyses evaluate the validity of key claims, examine the persuasive strategies employed by key groups or people, and explore the similarities and distinctions between diverse viewpoints.

Counterclaim: An argument will likely be presented in opposition to the argument you are making. When making a claim, it's important to consider the counterclaims that might arise against your own arguments. This reveals to your reader that you have acknowledged several viewpoints on an issue, not simply those that will be in agreement with your own.

Database: An electronic collection of a wide variety of resources, such as newspapers, magazines, and scholarly journals that have been compiled electronically and are searchable by keyword, author, title, subject, and more. Examples of databases include Academic Search Complete, JSTOR, and ProQuest.

Debatable topics: Appropriate topics for a researched argument. Debatable topics must fulfill two criteria. First, they have to stimulate some sort of argument or disagreement, meaning they go beyond reporting the "facts." Second, debatable topics are issues that other researchers have investigated enough for you to be able to locate sufficient resources to inform your understanding of the topic.

Discourse Community: A group of people who share a discipline-specific set of writing and speaking practices, as well as specialized vocabulary that is understood by members of the group.

Dominance: In visual analysis, the first thing that your eye is drawn to in an image is the dominant part of that image.

Ethos: A rhetorical strategy in which an author/speaker appeals to the credibility and character in a text.

False Analogy: A logical fallacy that involves the use of an analogy between two apparently similar, but nonetheless very different, things.

Figurative language: Language that employs one or more figures of speech, such as metaphor, simile, synecdoche, or personification.

Focus: In visual analysis, refers to whether a section of the image is clear (or in focus) or blurry (out of focus).

Foreshadowing: The technique of introducing into a narrative material that prepares the reader for future events or revelations. Examples of foreshadowing could include mentioning a gun early in the narrative that will later shoot someone, or implying that a character is threatening through suggestive language before his actions become villainous.

Form: The patterns and structure associated with a specific genre. For example, poetry is a genre. Poetic patterns such as rhythm, rhyme, meter, repeated words and images, line breaks, stanza breaks, spatial organization on the page, and more create the form of a poem.

Framing: In visual analysis, what is included in the field of the image and what is not included. For example, an artist can frame his or her image to only show part of an item and therefore call attention to it.

Freewriting: A prewriting technique designed to help a writer develop ideas. Freewriting involves designating a set amount of time (e.g., fifteen minutes), and writing whatever comes to your mind, without pausing or rereading until the set amount of time has expired.

Gender criticism: Rhetorically analyzing a text in terms of gender involves examining the ways that a text seeks to reinforce, challenge, or disrupt systems of inequality based on gender.

Gender performance: Behavior that performs femininity or masculinity in culturally appropriate ways, such as wearing a skirt and high heels to emphasize femininity.

Genre: A category of certain types of literary works based on their content, form, and techniques. Fiction, nonfiction, poetry, and drama are types of literary genres. Within these genres, comedy, tragedy and romance are subgenres. In film, common genres include action, romantic comedy, sci-fi, and horror.

Global revisions: The large-level changes you make to an essay's argument, organization, or style. These changes will have a greater impact on your essay as a whole.

Hasty generalization: A logical fallacy involving the use of a few particular examples to make a general conclusion.

Hyperbole: Employing deliberate, emphatic exaggeration, sometimes intended for ironic effect. Saying something is "the very *best* in the world" could be a hyperbolic statement. The opposite of this is understatement.

Idea mapping: As a method of organizing analysis, a visual representation of how the ideas in a text are related to both the main point(s) and each other. An idea map emphasizes the interconnectedness of ideas. This is also called "webbing" or "clustering."

Identification: A rhetorical strategy in which an author/speaker works to identify with the members of an audience by pointing out the qualities, characteristics, assumptions, beliefs, and goals that they share with one another. It's important to keep in mind that identification does not mean "sameness," and an author/speaker must define and explain the importance of any type of identification he or she establishes with the audience.

Ideology: Underlying values, assumptions, conflicts, desires, anxieties, and so on. Idealogy involves the beliefs that people hold, the prominent ideas that tell us what should be, must be, or what seems normal. Sometimes called "cultural values" when in reference to a popular or widely held belief. For example, the idea of *democracy* in the United States is an ideology—it assumes that everyone should have a voice and that everyone's voice should be equal, whether people are uneducated or college professors, politicians or people who never read the news, and so on. Other ideologies include capitalism, religion, and education.

Ideological criticism: A strategy for rhetorical analysis that examines the ways that an author/speaker uses language to reinforce, challenge, or modify an audience's ideological understanding of the world.

Inartistic proofs: Often called "facts," inartistic proofs refer to persuasive strategies that are "uncontestable." Data in the form of statistics and forensic evidence are examples of inartistic proofs.

Inquiry: A line of investigation into an issue, topic, or problem. This narrows your scope of analysis to focus on certain aspects of your subject.

Irony (ironic): A contradiction or incongruity between appearance or expectation and reality. This could be the difference between what someone says and what s/he actually means, between what appears to be true and what actually is true, or between what someone expects to happen and what actually happens. This is often subtly comic or tongue-in-cheek.

Literacy: Generally refers to the ability to understand a system of language. Literacy usually refers to the competent understanding and use of written language, including abilities in reading and writing. However, literacy can also refer to one's level of knowledge of a particular culture (cultural literacy).

Literacy narrative: A personal narrative that focuses on an event or events in the author's acquisition of literacy. Literacy narratives can explore a specific, significant experience with writing, reading, and/or language, or they can discuss how writing, reading, and/or language have played a role in the author's past experience.

Local revisions: Small-level changes that occur at the sentence and paragraph level. Local revisions include revising for grammar mistakes, typos, misspelled words, and awkward sentences.

Logical fallacies: Arguments in a text that are questionable or invalid because they rest on faulty logic. Logical fallacies may be persuasive even if they are not logically valid. Some examples of logical fallacies include *ad hominem*, causal generalizations, false analogy, hasty generalization, and non sequitur.

***Logos*:** A rhetorical strategy in which a text appeals to an audience by making logical arguments. The most basic analysis of *logos* considers whether claims are developed using inductive or deductive reasoning. Analyzing the logical fallacies in an argument is another way to consider a text's *logos*.

Metaphor: Associates two distinct things without using a connective word such as "like" or "as." "That child is a mouse" is a metaphor. When analyzing metaphors rhetorically, our primary goals are to locate, define, interpret, and possibly reconceptualize the metaphors an author constructs. Ultimately, metaphoric criticism asks *how* an author uses metaphors in order to build an effective argument.

Narrative: Can refer to any story that describes events or experiences, whether fictional or factual. Thus newspaper articles that describe recent events or novels that describe a character's journey follow a narrative structure. When you are telling a group of friends about your most recent camping trip, you are telling a narrative as well.

Non sequitur: Meaning "does not follow," a non sequitur is a logical fallacy that draws a conclusion from a premise that isn't necessarily related.

Noun: A person, place, or thing. It can be a concrete thing, like a pencil, or an abstract thing, like philosophy.

Paraphrase: A rephrasing of a text or a part of a text that is more specific than summary but is less precise than a quotation. Writers paraphrase in order to include specific information and ideas from other writers in their own work. While a paraphrase does not have to retain all of the content from the original, the meaning and intent of the original passage should not be changed. You should cite page numbers for the sections of text you are paraphrasing.

Pathos: A rhetorical strategy in which a text appeals to an audience's emotions in order to move the audience toward the author's position.

Persona: Refers to the ability to present yourself differently according to different situations.

Personification: Involves giving human characteristics to anything nonhuman. For example, "Father Time" is a personification.

PIE: An acronym for Point, Illustration, and Explanation. PIE is a helpful way to think about paragraph development, especially for analysis essays and persuasive arguments. Remember, however, that PIE is just one of several ways to develop a paragraph.

Point of view: The vantage point from which a narrative is told, either first-person, third-person, or, uncommonly, second-person. First-person narratives are told by a narrator who refers to himself or herself as "I" and is often a part of the action. Third-person narrators can either be omniscient, all-knowing and reliable, or limited, restricted to a single character at a time. Second-person narrators speak directly to the reader as "you."

Popular source: A text written for a general audience rather than for an audience of experts. You may think of a popular source as a text written by a non-expert (or occasionally by an expert) for a broad audience of non-experts.

Primary source: See "Primary text."

Primary text: The text that you are analyzing or the primary source of your information—the main focus of your analysis. It might be a book, an article, a movie, a photograph, a painting, or even a place.

Purpose: Refers to the reason and objective for writing. As a writer, your purpose, usually determined before you begin writing, can be as varied as persuading an audience to change his/her opinion on an issue, to do something, or to feel a certain way. Your purpose can also be to report facts and information, to entertain a reader, or to simply express your feelings, as you would in a diary. Much writing has more than just one purpose.

Quotation: Uses the exact words from a writer's original source, with no changes in language or punctuation. You may quote an entire sentence or a part of a sentence, depending on what is most useful for your writing purpose. Quotations must always be cited.

Reflective writing: An essay that analyzes the ways you've changed as a writer over the course of time, such as a semester or an academic year. Reflecting on your own challenges, strengths, and improvements as a writer will help you to better understand how to further improve your writing.

Rhetor: Refers to any person who is using rhetoric.

Rhetoric (rhetorical): Any type of communication that seeks to move an audience toward a specific position, understanding, or action.

Rhetorical analysis: An analysis of how writers and speakers use language in particular situations to achieve predetermined goals. Rhetorical analysis involves evaluating the effectiveness of a speaker/author's rhetorical strategies.

Rhetorical situation: A communication event in which one person (the author/speaker) attempts to communicate some message to another person (the audience) for a specific reason (the purpose) and within a specific situation (the context).

Rhetorical strategies: The rhetorical methods an author chooses to construct a text, develop ideas, and write persuasively. Examples of rhetorical strategies include *ethos*, identification, *logos*, metaphor, and *pathos*.

Rubric: A tool that your instructor may use to grade essays. It often resembles a chart with rows for categories of writing criteria and columns that describe achievement levels. These columns usually progress from the highest level of achievement on the left to the lowest level on the right.

Scale: In visual analysis, the size of objects within an image. If all objects seem to be of a normal size, then the scale of the image is natural. If some seem larger or smaller than normal, the scale of the image could be exaggerated.

Scholarly Source: A text written for an audience with specialized knowledge about a particular subject. You might think of a scholarly source as a text written by an expert for an audience of experts in a given field.

Secondary source: See "Secondary text."

Secondary text: Sources that comment on and have a direct relationship to the primary text. Some common examples of secondary sources are an analysis of a literary text, a critique of a painting or photograph, a movie review, or an opinion about an interview.

Signal phrase: Words that identify the original speaker your text is borrowing from. Signal phrases make it clear that you're borrowing from someone else's ideas. Example signal phrases include "As Author L writes," "According to Author L," and "Author L argues."

Simile: Compares two distinct things by using words such as "like" or "as." "That child is like a cyclone" is a simile.

Style: Refers to specific traits in a written work, including elements such as word choice, sentence/paragraph structure, sentence/paragraph ordering, or genre conventions. When instructors grade an essay for "style," they are often looking for a combination of the conventions of academic writing and comfortable, readable diction/sentence structure.

Summary: An abbreviated version of a longer text—your statement of what you see to be the major points of a text *using your own words*. A summary can be one sentence long, one paragraph long, or one page long, depending on the length of the text and your purpose as a writer.

Symbolism: The sustained use of symbols to represent or suggest other things or ideas. For example, you could say that an author "uses symbols of nature" to evoke certain associations for the reader.

Synecdoche: A part of something used to represent the whole, such as referring to a car as "wheels."

Text: In analysis, any artifact or object that you analyze—whether written or visual. In your first-year writing courses, you'll be dealing with a variety of texts. For example, a text might refer to a book, a newspaper article, a short story, a poem, a speech, a movie, a picture, a video game, a person, an event, a space, a place, and so on.

Text-in-context: See "Contextual analysis."

Textual analysis: An argument for how and why a written or visual text works to make meaning using concrete examples from the text with an emphasis on strategies. Textual analysis emphasizes close reading and usually means looking at a text in isolation of outside factors such as context.

Thesis: A one (sometimes two) sentence declaration of the central point of an essay, facilitating the task of the reader. The thesis helps to inform the reader of what to expect, and therefore usually comes toward the beginning of an essay. Some writers like to think of the thesis statement as a sort of "contract" with the reader; as a writer, you're making a promise to readers that the paper they're about to read is about what the thesis says the paper is about.

Tone: As a textual strategy, this is an author's attitude toward the reader, audience, or subject matter. An author's tone can be optimistic, morbid, humorous, excited, etc. This is different than a text's atmosphere, or mood. As a writing strategy, tone refers to the attitude that you, the writer, develop toward your own audience.

Topic: In a researched essay, a topic is a general area of inquiry, the overall subject of your essay. A topic is not an argument; rather, it's the more general subject about which your essay argues.

Topic Sentence: One sentence that states the main point of the paragraph. Sometimes, the topic sentence is the first sentence of your paragraph. Regardless of where it is placed, every paragraph should include a topic sentence, while every other sentence in the paragraph develops, illustrates, or defines the idea in that topic sentence.

Verb: A word that conveys action. When we talk, we use verbs to show that some kind of action is taking place.

Visual rhetoric: A form of communication in which visual elements create meanings and arguments.

Index

About the Editors

Caitlin Rose Rodriguez (left) is an MA student in English Literature at the University of Arizona. While her emphasis in the program is in British Romanticism, her previous work in both composition pedagogy and creative writing continue to influence her studies and her teaching of first-year composition. She hopes to continue to cultivate academic scholarship in each of these fields. Her current work analyzes the Romantic response to points of conflict between dualistic spheres of experience, particularly in the ways major Romantic poets draw on romance traditions. She is also an avid dancer and performer and can often be found either on a trapeze, hula-hooping, or practicing bellydance.

Jennifer Haley-Brown (right) is a Doctoral Candidate in Rhetoric, Composition, and the Teaching of English at the University of Arizona, where she has taught classes in first-year composition, business writing, and new media studies. Jennifer's research centers on public memory and digital rhetoric, and her dissertation explores the ways that recent tragedies in the U.S. have been memorialized physically and digitally across the world. When she's not teaching or studying, Jen enjoys hiking, eating spicy food, and spending time with her family, including her two cats, her three-legged dog, Pico de Gallo, and her new daughter, Zoe Marie Haley Brown.

Jerry W. Lee (center) is a PhD student in the Department of English at the University of Arizona. At the UA, he has taught First-Year Writing (ENGL 101, 102), and Business Writing (ENGL 307), and Technical Writing (ENGL 308). A native of California, he earned his MA in English at California State University, Long Beach, where he also taught for two years. Committed to programs and organizations that facilitate access to higher education, Jerry has been involved with the *Jackie Robinson Foundation* in Los Angeles and is a mentor for the *Arizona Assurance Scholars* program. His heroes include Bruce Lee, Stan Lee, Spike Lee, and Cliff Lee.